Liberal Leviathan

PRINCETON STUDIES IN INTERNATIONAL HISTORY AND POLITICS

SERIES EDITORS G. John Ikenberry, Thomas J. Christensen, and Marc Trachtenberg

G. JOHN IKENBERRY

Liberal Leviathan ≡

The Origins, Crisis, and Transformation

of the American World Order

PRINCETON UNIVERSITY PRESS

Princeton and Oxford

Published by Princeton University Press, 41 William Street, Princeton,
New Jersey 08540
In the United Kingdom: Princeton University Press, 6 Oxford Street, Woodstock,
Oxfordshire OX20 1TW
press.princeton.edu

Third printing, and first paperback printing, 2012
Paperback ISBN 978-0-691-15617-0

The Library of Congress has cataloged the cloth edition of this book as follows
Ikenberry, G. John.

   Liberal leviathan : the origins, crisis, and transformation of the American world order / G. John
Ikenberry.
       p. cm. — (Princeton studies in international history and politics)
   Includes index.
   ISBN 978-0-691-12558-9 (hardcover : alk. paper)   1. United States—Foreign relations—
21st century.   2. Hegemony,   3. Unipolarity (International relations)   I. Title.
   E895.I44   2011
   327.73009'05—dc22

                                         2011001740

British Library Cataloging-in-Publication Data is available
This book has been composed in Garamond Premier Pro
Printed on acid-free paper. ∞
Printed in the United States of America
10 9 8

"Sed quis custodiet ipsos custodes?"

["But who watches the watchers?"]

—Juvenal, *Satires*, VI, 347

"What I fear more than the strategies of my enemies
is our own mistakes."

—Pericles in his funeral oration as recorded by Thucydides

"He that is taken and put into prison or chains is not conquered,
though overcome; for he is still an enemy."

—Hobbes, *Leviathan*, conclusion

For my wife Lidia Reiko and our son Jackson Kan

Contents

Preface

This book is an inquiry into the logic and changing character of liberal international order. Over the last two hundred years, Western democratic states have made repeated efforts to build international order around open and rule-based relations among states—that is, they have engaged in liberal order building. This "liberal project" has unfolded amidst other great forces and events that have shaped the modern world—imperialism, revolution, world war, economic boom and bust, nation-building, and globalization. In the second half of the twentieth century, the United States engaged in the most ambitious and far-reaching liberal order building the world had yet seen. The result was a particular type of liberal international order—a liberal hegemonic order. The United States took on the duties of building and running an international order, organizing it around multilateral institutions, alliances, special relationships, and client states. It was a hierarchical political order with liberal characteristics. Defined in terms of the provision of security, wealth creation, and social advancement, this liberal hegemonic order has been, arguably at least, the most successful order in world history. This book offers an account of the origins and inner workings of this far-flung political order.

But in the last decade, this American-led hegemonic order has been troubled. The most obvious crisis in this order occurred during the recent George W. Bush administration as it generated worldwide opposition to its unilateralist tendencies, "war on terror" grand strategy, and invasion of Iraq. Some observers argue that under Bush's watch, the United States turned itself into an empire. The United States coerced more than it led. For those who trace this imperial turn to the Bush administration, the crisis may now be over. But for those who see imperial tendencies in the unipolar distribution of power that stands behind American foreign policy, the crisis continues. Other observers argue that the problems with the American-led order run deeper. We are witnessing a passing of the American era, a return to multipolarity, and the rise of rival non-liberal order-building projects. In the view of some commentators, it is liberal internationalism itself that is passing away.

This book engages this debate. I argue that the crisis that besets America-led liberal world order is a crisis of authority. A political struggle or contest has been ignited over the distribution of roles, rights, and authority within liberal international order. The hegemonic aspect of liberal order—that is, America's role and the old hegemonic bargains that surround it—is under pressure. But the deeper logic of open and loosely rule-based international order remains widely embraced. Problems and dilemmas about the organization and operation of liberal international order have mounted in recent years. But the solutions to these problems and dilemmas lead toward the renewal and reorganization of liberal order—not its overturning.

To get to this argument, I make some distinctions between levels—or layers—of international order. It is useful to think of these levels as geological strata. At the deepest level, you have the bedrock of the modern international order: the Westphalian system of sovereign states organized around a group of leading states arrayed in a rough power equilibrium. On this foundation, various sorts of international orders have been—and can be—organized. As I have noted, liberal international order is order that is open and at least loosely rule-based, and as such, it can be contrasted with order that is organized into rival blocs or exclusive regional spheres. But liberal international order itself can be organized in different ways. And in the past decade, its organization through the leadership of a dominant state—the American-led hegemonic order—has reached a crisis.

The crisis runs deeper than the controversies generated by recent American foreign policy. Transformations in the Westphalian system—the rise of unipolarity, eroded norms of state sovereignty, the shifting sources of violence, and the intensification of security interdependence—all make the management of liberal hegemony more difficult and problematic. But these dilemmas and problems that have made the U.S.-led liberal hegemonic order contested and unstable are not destroying liberal international order, but pushing and pulling states toward a new kind of liberal international order—more inclusive, less hierarchical, and infused with more complex forms of cooperation.

This book can be read as a sequel to my earlier book, *After Victory: Institutions, Strategic Restraint, and the Rebuilding of Order after Major Wars.* That book was published on the eve of the Bush administration and September 11. In the light of my argument in *After Victory,* the Bush administration presented an extraordinary puzzle. The strong version of my claim was that the United States had so bound itself to the larger Western and global system through layers of multilateral institutions and alliances that it would not be possible for the United States to unbind itself. But this is what the Bush administration attempted to do. The weaker version of my argument was that a president could attempt to uproot America from the liberal multilateral system it built over a half century, but it wouldn't want to—and if it did, it would be punished for doing so.

The Bush administration may well have paid a price for its policies. It certainly retreated from them in its last years. But the puzzle of the Bush administration led me to look more deeply at the underlying shifts in the global system that created pressures and opportunities for the Bush revolution. It is this puzzle that has led to my focus on the shifts in the Westphalian underpinnings of liberal order—the rise of unipolarity, the erosion of sovereignty, and the transformation of security interdependence. But the story is even more complicated than this. Yes, the Westphalian foundations of liberal order have shifted, and this has triggered problems and dilemmas that make American-led hegemonic order unstable. But these underlying shifts themselves have, for the most part, emerged out of the great postwar success story of liberal internationalism. The global liberal system has outgrown its American-led, hegemonic foundation. This is a problem—but it is a problem of success rather than failure of the liberal project.

At the end of the book, I offer arguments about how the United States might seek to pursue liberal order building in the coming era. I argue that the United States should "lead through rules" and look for ways to renegotiate hegemonic bargains with other states. I also argue that the United States needs to recapture the public philosophy of liberal internationalism—a blend of liberal and realist thinking—that served it so well in the postwar decades. It combined the liberal spirit of the United Nations and the realist spirit of NATO and the American-alliance system in East Asia. I have always thought that Harry Truman and Dean Acheson together reflected this dual vision. Truman embodied the liberal spirit. As a disciple of Woodrow Wilson, he carried in his billfold the poem "Locksley Hall," Tennyson's famous ode to the world's common humanity and the dream of universal peace. Truman really did believe that a global peace organization could be built that could tame the violence of nations. Acheson, Truman's secretary of state, was a realist. He was famously skeptical of the United Nations. In one speech, he noted: "In the Arab proverb, the ass that went to Mecca remained an ass, and a policy has little added to it by its place of utterance." Yet while these visions seemingly clashed, they ended up working in tandem. One vision inspired the building of institutions and the search for universal principles of order. The other vision built alliances and aggregated power in pursuit of safety and freedom. As I argued in *After Victory*, and as I argue again in this book, power and rules are not enemies; they can be friends, and they are both necessary in the production of liberal order.

It is perhaps no coincidence that one of my favorite Western movies is John Ford's *The Man Who Shot Liberty Valance*, which stars Jimmy Stewart and John Wayne. It is a classic morality tale. The movie takes place in a small Western town being terrorized by a gang of outlaws. Into this town rides Ransom Stoddard, played by Jimmy Stewart, a newly minted lawyer from the east. He sets up his office in town and immediately encounters the fearsome outlaw, Liberty Valance, played by Lee Marvin. Stoddard is appalled that the townspeople are not resisting the outlaw and his gang. But when he confronts Valance he is slapped down, and the gang prepares to make quick work of him. In the background stands Tom Doniphon, played by John Wayne, a tough rancher able to stand up to Valance. He tells Stoddard to get out of town before he is killed. The young lawyer's appeal to laws and what is right is useless without the ability to back it up with force—one "needs a gun in these parts." Stoddard refuses to leave ("Nobody fights my battles') and instead organizes a school to teach townspeople about the virtues of democracy and the rule of law enshrined in the American Constitution. In the inevitable gunfight with Liberty Valance, Stoddard is hopelessly outmatched. But standing secretly in the shadows, Doniphon takes his rifle and dispatches the outlaw, and the gang is run out of town. Both of these figures—the lawyer and the man with the rifle—were necessary for the story to end as it did.

The point is made over and over again across the historical eras: power is most durable and legitimate when exercised in a system of rules. Rules are most durable and legitimate when they emerge through a consensual process of rule making and are backed up by the right configuration of power. The United States has been one of the most successful order-building states in world history because it has combined the exercise of its power with the championing of rule-based order. The challenge for the United States in the coming decades is to hold on to this logic of order building even as the deeper foundations of liberal international order shift.

To reach these conclusions, the chapters that follow explore and offer arguments about:

- the logic and ideal-type relations between leading states and the international system
- the nature of hierarchical international orders
- the incentives and constraints that powerful states face supporting and operating within rule-based international relations

- the character and logic of the postwar American-led liberal international order
- the nature of the crisis confronting the American-led liberal international order
- the sources and dimensions of the transformation of the Westphalian system
- the impact of unipolarity on patterns of international dominance and cooperation
- the Bush post-Westphalian grand strategy and why it failed
- the intellectual dilemmas, contradictions, and ambiguities confronting liberal internationalism
- a liberal grand strategy for unipolar America

31 December 2010
Princeton, N.J.

Acknowledgments

The ideas in this book have taken shape over many years, and along the way I have accumulated many personal and professional debts to friends and colleagues. I am grateful to Atul Kohli, my friend and colleague at Princeton, with whom I have periodically teamed up to co-teach a graduate seminar on Empire and Imperialism. I have benefited immensely from these intellectual encounters and his incisive critiques of my work. I am also grateful to Daniel Deudney, my old friend and coauthor, who has been a continuous source of stimulation and learning. Our two decades of collaborations are woven into this manuscript in many ways. I am also grateful to Anne-Marie Slaughter, who has supported my work in untold ways and remained a great source of intellectual inspiration. Our work together on the Princeton Project on National Security, culminating in the report *Forging a World of Liberty under Law*, crystalized my thinking about liberal grand strategy. Later, we worked together again on the ideas and legacy of Woodrow Wilson, which culminated in a book with our friends Tony Smith and Thomas Knock.

I have also benefited from the kindness and generosity of many friends and colleagues who have offered comments on parts or the whole of the book manuscript, including Jeremy Adelman, Barry Buzan, Mick Cox, Christina Davis, Mary Finnemore, Andy Hurrell, Melvyn Leffler, Jeff Legro, Andy Moravcsik, Daniel Nexon, and Tom Wright. I appreciate detailed comments on the manuscript from Peter Katzenstein, Charles Kupchan, Mike Mastanduno, Bill Wohlforth, John Owen, and the reviewers for Princeton University Press. Mike Mastanduno and Bill Wohlforth generously hosted a manuscript workshop at Dartmouth, funded by the Dickey Center for International Understanding. I appreciate the comments and advice given to me by my hosts and other participants, including Steve Brooks, Ben Valentino, Barry Posen, Jennifer Erickson, Bridgett Coggins, Jennifer Lind, Tom Walker, Albert Lee, and Brent Strathman.

I am grateful to Joe Barnes and Daniel Kurtz-Phelan, who provided expert editorial comments on the manuscript. I have also benefited from excellent research assistance from several Princeton graduate students, including Michael McKoy, Alex Lanoszka, and Darren Lim. I also owe a special thanks to Chuck Myers, my friend and editor at Princeton University Press, who has patiently guided the manuscript to completion.

I thank Inwon Choue, President of Kyung Hee University, for his support and inspiration and to friends and colleagues at Kyung Hee for stimulating encounters over the years.

I first began work on the manuscript during a sabbatical leave at the Institute for Advanced Study in 2007–2008 as an NEH Fellow. I am grateful to the institute for support and to my colleagues who made the year so stimulating.

Finally, and most importantly, I express my love and gratitude to my wife, Lidia Reiko Usami, and our son, Jackson Kan Ikenberry, to whom I dedicate this book.

Liberal Leviathan

One
Crisis of the Old Order

One of the great dramas of world politics over the last two hundred years has been the rise of liberal democratic states to global dominance. This liberal ascendancy has involved the extraordinary growth of the Western democracies—from weakness and minority status in the late eighteenth century to wealth and predominance in the late twentieth century. This rise occurred in fits and starts over the course of the modern era. In the nineteenth century, Great Britain was the vanguard of the liberal ascendancy, becoming the leading industrial and naval power of its day. In the twentieth century, the United States was transformed from inwardness and isolation into the dominant world power. During these decades, world wars and geopolitical struggles pitted the liberal democracies against rival autocratic, fascist, and totalitarian great powers. The Cold War was a grand struggle between alternative ideologies of rule and pathways to modern development. With the sudden collapse of the Soviet Union and the end of the Cold War, the liberal ascendancy reached a worldwide crescendo. The United States and a far-flung alliance of liberal democracies stood at the center of world politics—rich, powerful, and dominant.

The Western democracies did not just grow powerful and rich. They also made repeated efforts to build liberal international order—that is, order that is relatively open, rule-based, and progressive. Led by Great Britain and the United States, they championed free trade and took steps to create multilateral rules and institutions of various sorts. Open markets, international institutions, cooperative security, democratic community, progressive change, collective problem solving, shared sovereignty, the rule of law—all are aspects of the liberal vision that have made appearances in various combinations and changing ways over the decades and centuries.

In the decades after World War II, the United States engaged in the most ambitious and far-reaching liberal order building the world had yet seen. It was a distinctive type of liberal international order—a liberal hegemonic order. The United States did not just encourage open and rule-based order. It became the hegemonic organizer and manager of that order. The American political system—and its alliances, technology, currency, and markets—became fused to the wider liberal order. In the shadow of the Cold War, the United States became the "owner and operator" of the liberal capitalist political system—supporting the rules and institutions of liberal internationalism but also enjoying special rights and privileges. It organized and led an extended political system built around multilateral institutions, alliances, strategic partners, and client states. This order is built on strategic understandings and hegemonic bargains. The United States provided "services" to other states through the provision of security and its commitment to stability and open markets.

In the fifty years following World War II, this American-led liberal hegemonic order has been remarkably successful. It provided a stable foundation for decades of Western and global growth and advancement. The United States and its partners negotiated agreements and built mechanisms that reopened the world economy, ushering in a golden era of economic growth. West Germany and Japan were transformed from enemies into strategic partners, ultimately becoming the second- and third-largest economies in the world. The Western powers also bound themselves together in pacts of mutual restraint and commitment, finding a solution to the centuries-old problem of how Germany, France, and the rest of Europe could exist in peace—the great "quiet revolution" of the twentieth century. In later decades, non-Western countries made transitions to democracy and market economy and integrated into this expanding liberal hegemonic system. The Cold War ended peacefully and on terms favorable to the West. The Western allies were able to both outperform the Soviet system and find ways to signal restraint and accommodation as Soviet leaders made difficult choices to end hostilities with old rivals. By the 1990s, this American-led order was at a zenith. Ideological and geopolitical rivals to American leadership had disappeared. The United States stood at the center of it all as the unipolar power. Its dynamic bundle of oversized capacities, interests, and ideals constituted a remarkable achievement in the unfolding drama of the liberal international project.

In this book, I explore the logic and character of this American liberal hegemonic order. What are its inner workings and moving parts? How can we identify and understand the specific organizational logic of this liberal hegemonic order in the context of earlier efforts to build liberal international order and the wider varieties of global and regional orders? How is it different—if it is—from imperial forms of order? If it is a hierarchical order with liberal characteristics, how do we make sense of its distinctive blend of command and reciprocity, coercion and consent?

Today, the American-led liberal hegemonic order is troubled. Conflicts and controversies have unsettled it. The most obvious crisis of this order unfolded during the George W. Bush administration. Its controversial "war on terror," invasion of Iraq, and skepticism about multilateral rules and agreements triggered a global outpouring of criticism. Anti-Americanism spread and gained strength. Even old and close allies started to question the merits of living in a world dominated by a unipolar America. This sentiment was expressed in a particularly pointed fashion by the then French president Jacques Chirac, who argued that the world must be turned back into a multipolar one because "any community with only one dominant power is always a dangerous one and provokes reactions."[1]

If the crisis of the old American-led order is reducible to the Bush administration's policies, the crisis may now have passed. The Obama administration has made the restoration of American liberal hegemonic leadership—or what Secretary of State Clinton has called a "multipartner world"—the centerpiece of its foreign policy agenda.[2] But if the crisis was generated by the inherent tensions and insecurities that flow from a unipolar distribution of power, the crisis will surely persist. It may be that a hierarchical order with liberal characteristics is simply not sustainable in a unipolar world—either because others will inevitably resist it or because the hegemon will inevitably become increasingly imperialistic.

Other observers argue that the problems with the American-led order run in a different direction. The crisis of the old is not about American unipolarity; it is about the passing of the American era of dominance. The conflicts and controversies are a struggle by states to shape what comes next, after unipolarity. This great shift is being triggered by a return to multipolarity and the rise of rival global powers with their own order-building agendas.[3] In this view, the 2008 financial crisis and subsequent world economic downturn—the most severe since the Great Depression—was an especially stark demonstration of the pressures on the American-led liberal system. Unlike past postwar economic

---

[1] See interviews with Chirac by James Graff and Bruce Crumley, "France is not a pacifist country," *Time*, 24 February 2003, 32–33; and James Hoagland, "Chirac's 'Multipolar World.'" *Washington Post*, 4 February 2004, A23.

[2] Signaling a return to America's postwar liberal-oriented leadership, the Obama administration's *National Security Strategy*, asserts that the United States "must pursue a rules-based international system that can advance our own interests by serving mutual interests." Office of the President, *National Security Strategy* (Washington, DC: White House, May 2010).

[3] On anticipations of a return to multipolarity and the end of American dominance, see Charles Kupchan, *The End of the American Era: U.S. Foreign Policy and the Geopolitics of the Twenty-First Century* (New York: Knopf, 2003); Parag Khanna, *The Second World: Empires and Influence in the New Global Age* (New York: Random House, 2008); Paul Starobin, *After America: Narratives for the New Global Age* (New York: Penguin Group, 2009); Kishore Mahbubani, *The New Asian Hemisphere: The Irresistible Shift in Global Power to the East* (New York: Public Affairs, 2009); and Fareed Zakaria, *The Post-American World* (New York: Norton, 2009).

crises, this one had its origins in the United States, and it has served to tarnish the American model of liberal capitalism and raised new doubts about the capacities of the United States to act as the global leader in the provision of economic stability and advancement.[4] With the decline of American unipolarity, we are witnessing the beginning of a struggle over leadership and dominance.

Still other observers accept this view of declining American power and go on to argue that it is liberal international order itself that is ending. The rise of new power centers will come with new agendas for organizing the basic logic and principles of international order. China is the obvious protagonist in this emerging grand drama. Rather than becoming a stakeholder in the existing order, China will use its growing power to push world politics in an illiberal direction.[5] It is the underlying openness and rule-based character of international order that is in transition.

These various claims prompt basic questions about the nature of the troubles that beset the American-led postwar order. Did the Bush administration simply mishandle or mismanage the leadership of the American liberal hegemonic order? Or is the struggle deeper than this, rooted in disagreements over the virtues and liabilities of the American hegemonic organization of liberal international order? Or is it even deeper still, rooted in a breakdown of consensus among leading states—old

---

[4] For arguments about the impact of the world economic crisis on the American neoliberal model and Washington's leadership capacities, see Joseph Stiglitz, *America, Free Markets, and the Sinking of the World Economy* (New York: Norton, 2010), and J. Bradford Lelong and Stephen S. Cohen, *The End of Influence: What Happens when Other Countries Have the Money* (New York: Basic, 2010). On the growing economic limits on American grand strategy, see Michael Mandelbaum, *The Frugal Superpower: America's Global Leadership in a Cash-Strapped Era* (New York: Public Affairs, 2010); and David P. Calleo, *Follies of Power: America's Unipolar Fantasy* (New York: Cambridge University Press, 2010). On how the financial crisis and world recession have accelerated the rise in influence of China and other non-Western countries, see Mathew J. Burrows and Jennifer Harris, "Revisiting the Future: Geopolitical Effects of the Financial Crisis," *Washington Quarterly* 32, no. 2 (April 2009), 27–38.

[5] See Martin Jacques, *When China Rules the World: The End of the Western World and the Birth of a New Global Order* (New York: Penguin, 2009). On the rise of ideological competition in world politics, see Steven Weber and Bruce W. Jentleson, *The End of Arrogance: America in the Global Competition of Ideas* (Cambridge: Cambridge University Press, 2010).

Western states and rising non-Western states—in the virtues of liberal internationalism as a way of organizing international relations?

In this book, I argue that the crisis of the old order transcends controversies generated by recent American foreign policy or even the ongoing economic crisis. It is a crisis of authority *within* the old hegemonic organization of liberal order, *not* a crisis in the deep principles of the order itself. It is a crisis of governance.

This crisis stems from the fact that the underlying foundations of the old order have been transformed. Changes include shifts in power, contested norms of sovereignty, threats related to nonstate actors, and the scope of participating states. America's hegemonic leadership of the liberal international order was made acceptable to other states during the postwar decades because it provided security and other "system services" to a wide range of states. That authority is now less securely established. This does not mean the inevitable end of liberal order. But it does raise a basic challenge for that order: establishing legitimate authority for concerted international action on behalf of the global community, doing so at a time when old relations of authority are eroding.

Although the old American-led hegemonic system is troubled, what is striking about liberal internationalism is its durability. The last decade has brought remarkable upheavals in the global system—the emergence of new powers, financial crises, a global recession, and bitter disputes among allies over American unipolar ambitions. Despite these upheavals, liberal international order as an organizational logic of world politics has proven resilient. It is still in demand. Appealing alternatives to an open and rule-based order simply have not crystallized. On the contrary, the rise of non-Western powers and the growth of economic and security interdependence are creating new constituencies and pressures for liberal international order.

Ironically, the old order has, in some ways, been the victim of its own success. It successfully defeated the threat—Communist expansionism—that, in part, drove its creation. It succeeded in creating a relatively open and robust system of trade and investment. The demise of the Soviet Union has reduced the importance of American military guarantees in Western Europe and East Asia. Economic growth in countries like China and India has created new centers of global power. These and other developments have led to profound questions about the American-centered nature of the old order. That has led not to a rejection per se of liberal order but to a call to renegotiate authority among the United States and other key stakeholders. In short, we need a new bargain, not a new system. And if this constitutes a crisis of authority, it is worth remembering that liberal international order has encountered crises in the past and evolved as a result. I believe it will again.

There are four central claims in this book. First, a distinctive type of international order was constructed after World War II. At its core, it was a hierarchical order with liberal characteristics. America played the leading role in the provision of rule and stability in that order. It was a hierarchical system that was built on both American power dominance and liberal principles of governance. The United States was the dominant state, but its power advantages were muted and mediated by an array of postwar rules, institutions, and reciprocal political processes—backed up by shared strategic interests and political bargains. Weaker and secondary states were given institutionalized access to the exercise of American power. The United States provided public goods and operated within a loose system of multilateral rules and institutions. American hegemonic power and liberal international order were fused—indeed they each were dependent on the other. But the strategic bargains and institutional foundations of this liberal hegemonic order have eroded, and as a result, the authority with which the United States has wielded power in this system has also diminished.

Second, there are deep sources for this authority crisis, rooted in the transformation of the Westphalian organization of the state system. The rise of American unipolarity and the erosion of norms of state sovereignty—along with other deep shifts in the global system—have eroded the foundations of the old order and thrown the basic terms of order and rule of world politics into dispute. In a bipolar or multipolar system, powerful states "rule" in the process of leading a coalition of states to balance against other states. When the system shifts to unipolarity, this logic of rule disappears. Rule is no longer based on leadership of a balancing coalition or on the resulting equilibrium of power but on the predominance of one state. This is new and different—and potentially threatening to weaker and secondary states. As a result, the power of the leading state is thrown into the full light of day.

The end of the Cold War ushered in a world system characterized by unipolarity and globalization. Relations between poles and peripheries shifted. During the Cold War, the liberal order was built primarily within the Western advanced industrial world. It existed within one half of the larger bipolar global system. With the collapse of the Soviet Union and the end of bipolarity, the "inside" Western system became the "outside" order. This large-scale expansion of the liberal order set new players and issues into motion. More recently, the rise of new security threats has brought into question the logic of alliance and security partnerships. After September 11, 2001, America showed itself to be not the satisfied protector of the old order but a threatened and insecure power that resisted the bargains and restraints of its own postwar order. As a result, in the decades of the new century, the character of rule in world politics has been thrown into question.

Third, to understand the nature of this crisis and the future of liberal international order, we need to understand the types of international order—and the sources of rule and authority, power, and legitimacy within them. In the first instance, this means identifying the various logics of liberal order and the ways in which sovereignty, rules, and hierarchy can be arrayed. Our most invoked theories of world politics begin with the assumption that the global system is anarchical—organized around the diffusion and decentralization of power among competing sovereign states. In other words, our theories tend to focus on the "logic of anarchy." But in a global system in which one state is so powerful and a balancing or equilibrium of power does not obtain, it is necessary to understand the logic of relations between superordinate and subordinate states. We need, in effect, to illuminate the "logic of hierarchy" that operates within the system.

I offer a basic distinction between imperial and liberal hegemonic forms of hierarchy. After this, I explore the ways in which shifts from bipolarity to unipolarity alter the incentives and forms in which leading states make institutional bargains and agree to operate within rule-based order. The rise of unipolarity has altered—and to some extent diminished—the incentives that the United States has to bind itself to global rules and institutions. But it has not negated those incentives. To the extent that the United States sees that its unipolar position of power is or will wane, the incentives to renegotiate postwar hegemonic bargains actually increase.

Fourth, the liberal ascendancy is not over. It is evolving and there are multiple pathways of change. There are pressures for the reallocation of authority and leadership within the system. But there are also constituencies that support a continued—if renegotiated—American hegemonic role. Various features of the contemporary global system reinforce the continuity of liberal international order. The disappearance of great-power war removes a classic mechanism for the overturning of order. The growth and sheer geopolitical heft of the world's liberal democracies creates a certain stability to the existing order. Moreover, liberal international order—hegemonic or otherwise—tends to be unusually integrative. It is an order that is easy to join and hard to overturn. Countries such as China and Russia are not fully embedded in the liberal international order, but they nonetheless profit from its existence. These states may not soon or ever fully transform into liberal states, but the expansive and integrative logic of liberal international order creates incentives for them to do so—and it forecloses opportunities to create alternative global orders.

In the end, it is the United States itself that will be critical in shaping the evolving character of liberal internationalism. If the United States wants to remain the leading purveyor of global order, it will need to rediscover and adapt its old strategy of liberal order building.[6] The United

---

[6] This book does not offer a general theory of the domestic sources of American grand strategy. The argument is cast in terms of government choices about the organization of international order in the context of perceived interests, opportunities, incentives, and constraints. A variety of doctrines, ideologies, and strategic visions compete for influence among foreign policy elites. The influence of these competing doctrines, ideologies, and visions is determined—at least, over the long term—by their responsiveness to these interests, opportunities, incentives, and constraints. National political identity and traditions and considerations of

States will need to renegotiate its relationship with the rest of the world and this will inevitably mean giving up some of the rights and privileges that it has had in the earlier hegemonic era. In the twentieth century, the United States became a "liberal Leviathan." Indeed, American global authority was built on Hobbesian grounds—that is, other countries, particularly in Western Europe and later in East Asia, handed the reigns of power to Washington, just as Hobbes's individuals in the state of nature voluntarily construct and hand over power to the Leviathan. Today, amidst long-term transformations in power and interdependence, there is a widespread view that no one elected the United States to its position of privilege—or at least that only the Europeans and Japanese did, and other states that are now rising in power did not. The reestablishment of the United States as a liberal Leviathan involves the voluntary granting of that status by other states. For this to happen, the United States again needs to search for and champion practical and consensual functioning global rules and institutions. In the twenty-first century, this will involve sharing authority among a wider coalition of liberal democratic states, advanced and developing, rising and declining, Western and non-Western. It is this liberal complex of states that is the ultimate guardian of the rules, institutions, and progressive purposes of the liberal order.

In this chapter, I introduce the questions and debates that are explored in this book. I first look at the enduring problem of international order. Next, I look at the rise and transformation of liberal international order. After this, I look at the logic of hierarchical political order and its imperial and liberal variants. I then follow with a road map for the chapters that follow.

---

political legitimacy are aspects of this decision environment. In this sense, elites respond both to the logic of consequences and the logic of appropriateness. For discussions of the complementarity of these logics, see Elinor Ostrom, "Rational Choice Theory and Institutional Analysis: Toward Complementarity," *American Political Science Review* 85, no. 1 (March 1991), 237–43; Martha Finnemore and Kathryn Sikkink, "International Norm Dynamics and Political Change," *International Organization* 52, no. 4 (Autumn 1998), 887–917; and Thomas Risse, "Constructivism and International Institutions: Toward Conversations across Paradigms," in Helen Milner and Ira Katznelson, eds., *Political Science: The State of the Discipline* (New York: Norton, 2002), 597–623.

The Rise and Fall of International Order

Over the centuries, world politics has been marked by repeated historical dramas of order creation and destruction. International order has risen and fallen, come and gone. At periodic moments, leading states have found themselves seeking to create and maintain rules and institutions of order. The most basic questions about world politics are on the table: who commands and who benefits? The struggle over order has tended to be, first and foremost, a struggle over how leading states can best provide security for themselves. It is a search for a stable peace. But states engaged in order building have also gone beyond this and attempted to establish a wider array of political and economic rules and principles of order. They have sought to create a congenial environment in which to pursue their interests. Along the way, the rights, roles, and authority relations that define the system are established. In all these ways, struggles over international order are moments when states grapple over the terms by which the global system will be governed, if it is to be governed at all.

We can look more closely at these underlying questions about international order. What is international order? How has it been created and destroyed? And how has it varied in terms of its logic and character?

In every era, great powers have risen up to build rules and institutions of relations between states, only to see those ordering arrangements eventually break down or transform. In the past, the restructuring of the international system has tended to occur after major wars. "At the end of every war since the end of the eighteenth century," as F. H. Hinsley notes, "the leading states made a concerted effort, each one more radical than the last, to reconstruct the system on lines that would enable them, or so they believed, to avoid a further war."[7] The violence of great-power war tears apart the old order. The war itself strips the rules and arrangements of the prewar system of its last shreds of legitimacy. Indeed, great-power war is perhaps the ultimate sign that an international order has

[7] F. H. Hinsley, "The Rise and Fall of the Modern International System," *Review of International Studies* (January 1982), 4.

failed. Revisionist states seek to overturn it through aggression, while status quo states cannot defend it short of war. And in the aftermath of war, victors are empowered to organize a new system with rules and arrangements that accord with their interests. Armistice agreements and peace conferences provide opportunities to lay down new rules and principles of international order.[8]

In this way, the settlements of great-power conflicts have become ordering moments when the rules and institutions of the international order are on the table for negotiation and change. The major powers are forced to grapple with and come to agreement on the general principles and arrangements of international order. These ordering moments not only ratify the outcome of the war, they also lay out common understandings, rules and expectations, and procedures for conflict resolution. They play a sort of constitutional function, providing a framework in which the subsequent flow of international relations takes place.[9]

International order is manifest in the settled rules and arrangements between states that define and guide their interaction.[10] War and upheaval

[8] On the politics and ideas of order building after major wars, see G. John Ikenberry, *After Victory: Institutions, Strategic Restraint, and the Rebuilding of Order after Major War* (Princeton, NJ: Princeton University Press, 2001); Kalevi J. Holsti, *Peace and War: Armed Conflicts and International Orders, 1648–1989* (New York: Cambridge University Press, 1991); Andreas Osiander, *The States System of Europe, 1640–1990: Peacemaking and the Conditions of International Stability* (London: Oxford University Press, 1994); and Jeff Legro, *Rethinking the World: Great Power Strategies and International Order* (Ithaca, NY: Cornell University Press, 2007).

[9] On the notion of postwar settlements as "constitutional" moments of order building, see Ikenberry, "Constitutional Politics in International Relations, *European Journal of International Relations* 4, no. 2 (June 1998), 147–77; and Daniel Philpott, *Revolutions in Sovereignty: How Ideas Shaped Modern International Relations* (Princeton, NJ: Princeton University Press, 2001). More generally, international legal scholars have explored the constitution-like features of the post-1945 international system of rights, laws, and institutions. See Jeffrey L. Dunoff and Joel P. Trachtman, eds., *Ruling the World? Constitutionalism, International Law, and Global Governance* (New York: Cambridge University Press, 2009).

[10] In his classic study, Hedley Bull distinguished between world order and international order. World order is composed of all peoples and the totality of relations between them, and international order is composed of the rules and settled expectations between states. See Bull, *The Anarchical Society: A Study of Order in World Politics* (London: Macmillan, 1977). For extensions and refinements of these ideas, see Barry Buzan, *From International to World Society: English School Theory and the Social Structure of Globalization* (Cambridge: Cambridge University Press, 2004); and Andrew Hurrell, *On Global Order: Power, Values, and the Constitution of International Society* (New York: Oxford University Press, 2007).

between states—that is, disorder—is turned into order when stable rules and arrangements are established by agreement, imposition, or otherwise. Order exists in the patterned relations between states. States operate according to a set of organizational principles that define roles and the terms of their interaction.[11] International order breaks down or enters into crisis when the settled rules and arrangements are thrown into dispute or when the forces that perpetuate order no longer operate.

International orders can be distinguished and compared in many ways. Some international orders are regional, others global. Some are highly institutionalized, others not. Some are hierarchical. The distribution of power in international orders can also vary. Power can be centralized or decentralized. Order can be organized around various "poles" of power—multipolar, bipolar, or unipolar.[12] The challenge for scholars is to use these various features or dimensions to capture the alternative logics and characteristics of international order.

At the outset, it is useful to characterize and compare types of international order in terms of the ways in which stable order is maintained. Generally speaking, international order can be established and rendered stable in one of three ways: through balance, command, or consent. Each involves a different mechanism—or logic—for the establishment and maintenance of order.[13] In different times and places, international

---

[11] International order in this sense involved shared and stable expectations among states about how they will interact with each other, or as Janice Mattern suggests, it is a "relationship among specific states that produces and reinforces shared understandings of expectations and behaviors with respect to each other." Mattern, *Ordering International Politics: Identity, Crisis, and Representational Force* (New York: Routledge, 2005), 30.

[12] In the chapters to follow, I will be referring to each of these ways of characterizing and comparing international orders. On regional and global systems of order, see Barry Buzan and Ole Waever, *Regions and Power: The Structure of International Security* (New York: Cambridge University Press, 2003); and Peter Katzenstein, *A World of Regions: Asia and Europe in the American Imperium* (Ithaca, NY: Cornell University Press, 2005). On variations in the institutionalization of international order, see Stephen Krasner, ed., *International Regimes* (Ithaca, NY: Cornell University Press, 1982). On variations in hierarchy, see David Lake, *Hierarchy in International Relations* (Ithaca, NY: Cornell University Press, 2009). On variations in polarity and the distribution of power, see Edward D. Mansfield, "Concentration, Polarity, and the Distribution of Power," *International Studies Quarterly* 37, no. 1 (March 1993), 105–28; and Barry Buzan, *The United States and the Great Powers* (London: Polity, 2004), chap. 3.

[13] See Ikenberry, *After Victory*, chap. 2.

order has been organized around each of these mechanisms or by a combination of these mechanisms. As we shall see, the American-led liberal hegemonic order has relied in important ways on all three.

In an international order based on balance, order is maintained through an equilibrium of power among the major states. No one state dominates or controls the system. Order emerges from a power stalemate. States amass power, build alliances, and maneuver to prevent a strong and threatening state from establishing dominance. The specific ways in which balance can be achieved can vary widely.[14] Through this ongoing balancing process, international order is rendered stable. Order based on a balance of power was manifest in Europe in the eighteenth century, and as a concert of powers in Europe after 1815; during the Cold War, international order took the shape of a bipolar balance-of-power system. But in each of these historical eras, order was established through the presence of an equilibrium of power among major states. Leading states or coalitions of states formed counterbalancing poles that checked and restrained each other.

In an order based on command, a powerful state organizes and enforces order. Order is hierarchical and maintained through the dominance of the leading state. States are integrated vertically in superordinate and subordinate positions. Command-based order can vary widely in terms of the degree to which the hierarchical terms of order are enforced through coercion or are also moderated by elements of autonomy, bargaining, and reciprocity. The great empires of the ancient and modern world were hierarchical orders, manifesting various strategies of rule and "repertories of imperial power."[15] The British and American-led

[14] A rich literature exists on the theory and practice of the balance of power. For surveys, see Richard Little, *The Balance of Power in International Relations: Metaphors, Myths and Models* (Cambridge: Cambridge University Press, 2007); Stuart J. Kaufman, Richard Little, and William C. Wohlforth, eds., *The Balance of Power in World History* (New York: Palgrave, 2007); Jonathan Haslam, *No Virtue Like Necessity: Realist Thought in International Relations since Machiavelli* (New Haven, CT: Yale University Press, 2002), chap. 2; and Daniel H. Nexon, "The Balance of Power in the Balance," *World Politics* 61, no. 2 (April 2009), 330–59.

[15] Jane Burbank and Frederick Cooper, *Empires in World History: Power and the Politics of Difference* (Princeton, NJ: Princeton University Press, 2010), chap. 1.

international orders were also hierarchical—each, as we shall see, with a distinct mix of imperial and liberal characteristics.

Finally, order based on consent is organized around agreed-upon rules and institutions that allocate rights and limits on the exercise of power. Frameworks of rules and arrangements are constructed that provide authoritative arrangements for international relations. State power is not extinguished in a consent-based order, but it is circumscribed by agreed-upon rules and institutions. Disparities of power between states may still matter in the structuring of consensual, rule-based order, but the rules and institutions nonetheless reflect reciprocal and negotiated agreements between states. The British and American-led liberal orders have been built in critical respects around consent. The contemporary European Union is also a political order of this sort.

In these various ways, states have grappled with the fundamental problem of creating order in a world of sovereign and interdependent states. The resulting international orders have differed in terms of the ways in which power, authority, and institutions have been arrayed. In some cases, international order has been maintained in the most minimalist of terms, through a decentralized balance of power. In other cases, a dominant state has created order through coercive domination of weaker states and peoples. In still other instances, leading states have sought to build ambitious systems of institutionalized political and economic cooperation. It is in this general historical-theoretical context that we can situate and explore the character and logic of liberal international order.

Liberal International Order

Over the last two hundred years, international order has been profoundly influenced by the rise of liberal democratic states. This liberal ascendancy has been manifest in the rise in the power, influence, and global reach of liberal great powers—and in the international order that they have built. Through the Victorian era and into the twentieth

century, the fortunes of liberal democratic states flourished—and with
the growth and expansion of this liberal core of states and its organizing principles, world politics increasingly took a liberal internationalist
cast. This liberal ascendancy took a dramatic jump forward in the hands
of the United States after World War II, when the United States built
postwar order within the Western world—and extending outward—on
liberal ideas and principles.[16]

The liberal ascendancy has moved through two great historical eras
dominated, respectively, by Great Britain and the United States. Each
emerged as the leading power of its day and pushed and pulled other states
in a liberal direction, looking after the overall stability and openness of the
system. In the nineteenth century, Great Britain led in giving shape to an
international order marked by great power, imperial, and liberal arrangements. In the decades following the Napoleonic war, the major states of
Europe agreed on a set of rules and expectations that guided great-power
relations. Great Britain and the other major states also pursued empire
in Africa, Asia, and other parts of the world. At the same time, Great
Britain—beginning with its famous repeal of the Corn Laws in 1846—
oversaw the expansion of a global system of commerce organized around
open trade, the gold standard, and freedom of the seas.[17]

[16] In depicting the liberal ascendancy, Daniel Deudney writes: "For most of history, republics were confined to small city-states where they were insecure and vulnerable to conquest
and internal usurpation, but over the last two centuries they have expanded to continental size
through federal union and emerged victorious from the violent total conflicts of the twentieth
century." Deudney, *Bounding Power: Republican Security Theory from the Polis to the Global
Village* (Princeton, NJ: Princeton University Press, 2007), 2. William McNeill observes that
the rise of the modern liberal West was propelled by twin revolutions beginning in the late
eighteenth century: the industrial and democratic revolutions. "Taken together, the result
was to raise the power and wealth of the Western style of life so far above those familiar to
other civilizations as to make resistance to Western encroachment no longer possible." William H. McNeill, *A World History* (New York: Oxford University Press, 1967), 411.

[17] It is important not to exaggerate nineteenth-century British liberal internationalism. The
British orientation toward international order was both liberal and illiberal. It was liberal in
its support for global free trade, although even this commitment coexisted with imperial preferences. The British empire—which encompassed almost half the world—was decidedly illiberal, being composed of colonies and other dependencies, none of which were democracies or
run liberally. As Gary Bass observes, there was a "monstrous disconnect between the growing
liberalism in Britain and the brute authoritarianism in the British Empire." Nonetheless, in

In the twentieth century, liberal order building became more explicit and ambitious. At different moments over these decades, the United States made efforts to create or expand the architecture of an open and rule-based order. Woodrow Wilson brought a vision of a liberal world order to the post-World War I settlement, anchored in the proposal for a League of Nations, although it failed to take hold. When the United States found itself again in a position to build international order in the 1940s, Franklin Roosevelt and Harry Truman extended and ultimately reinvented the liberal international project. During the postwar decades, this order itself evolved as the United States and the other Western liberal states waged the Cold War, modernized their societies, and rebuilt and expanded economic and security relations across the democratic capitalist world. After the Cold War, America's international liberal project evolved yet again. The bipolar world order gave way to a global system dominated by the Western capitalist states. If liberal order was built after World War II primarily within the West, the end of the Cold War turned that order into a sprawling global system. States in all the regions of the world made democratic transitions and pursued market strategies of economic development. Trade and investment expanded across the international system.[18]

This spread of liberal democracy and adaptation and extension of liberal international order took place amidst war and economic upheaval. At each turn, nonliberal states offered alternative models of

---

his study of British and European nineteenth-century humanitarian interventions, Bass does find liberal impulses behind British military operations to stop atrocities in troubled areas such as Greece, Syria, and Bulgaria. Bass, *Freedom's Battle: The Origins of Humanitarian Intervention* (New York: Random House, 2008), quote at 343–44.

[18] For explorations of the rise and spread of Anglo-American liberal internationalism, see Mark R. Brawley, *Liberal Leadership: Great Powers and Their Challengers in Peace and War* (Ithaca, NY: Cornell University Press, 1993); Tony Smith, *America's Mission: The United States and the Worldwide Struggle for Democracy in the Twentieth Century* (Princeton, NJ: Princeton University Press, 1994); Michael Mandelbaum, *The Ideas that Conquered the World: Peace, Democracy, and Free Markets in the Twenty-first Century* (New York: Public Affairs, 2002); Walter Russell Mead, *God and Gold: Britain, America, and the Making of the Modern World* (New York: Knopf, 2007); and David Ekbladh, *The Great American Mission: Modernization and the Construction of an American World Order* (Princeton, NJ: Princeton University Press, 2010).

socioeconomic development and rival ways of ordering international politics. In the 1930s and into the Cold War era, geopolitics was not just a struggle for power but a contest between alternative pathways to modernity. Imperial Japan and Nazi Germany embodied the authoritarian capitalist alternative. The Soviet Union embodied the state socialist pathway. World politics was, in a profound sense, a competition between these alternatives. Success was defined in terms of the ability to generate power and wealth, build coalitions and alliances, and overcome geopolitical challengers. With the defeat of the Axis states in World War II, the "great contest" shifted to a struggle between communism (or state socialism) and liberal capitalism.[19]

Following from this, it is possible to make several general observations about the rise of liberal states and liberal order building.

First, liberal international order can be seen as a distinctive type of international order. As noted earlier, liberal international order is defined as order that is open and loosely rule-based. Openness is manifest when states trade and exchange on the basis of mutual gain. Rules and institutions operate as mechanisms of governance—and they are at least partially autonomous from the exercise of state power. In its ideal form, liberal international order creates a foundation in which states can engage in reciprocity and institutionalized cooperation. As such, liberal international order can be contrasted with closed and non-rule-based relations—whether geopolitical blocs, exclusive regional spheres, or closed imperial systems.[20]

In ideal form, liberal international order is sustained through consent rather than balance or command. States voluntarily join the order and operate within it according to mutually agreed-upon rules and arrangements. The rule of law, rather than crude power politics, is the framework

---

[19] For a depiction of this "great contest" that emphasizes the contingent character of the Western liberal triumph, see Azar Gat, *Victorious and Vulnerable: Why Democracy Won in the 20th Century and How It Is Still Imperiled* (New York: Rowman & Littlefield, 2010).

[20] For a survey of types of international orders, including nonliberal varieties, see essays in Greg Fry and Jocinta O'Hagan, eds., *Contending Images of World Politics* (New York: St. Martin's/Macmillan, 2000).

of interstate relations. But of course, the real-world liberal international political formations have been more complex orders where power balance and hierarchy intervene in various ways to shape and constrain relations.

Second, the more specific features of liberal international order vary widely. The liberal vision is wide ranging, and the ideas associated with liberal internationalism have evolved over the last two centuries. In the nineteenth century, liberal international order was understood primarily as a commitment to open trade, the gold standard, and great power accommodation. In the twentieth century, it has been understood to entail more elaborate forms of rules and institutional cooperation. Notions of cooperative security, democratic community, collective problem solving, universal rights, and shared sovereignty have also evolved over the last century to inform the agenda of liberal order building.

Generally speaking, liberal international order in the twentieth century has traveled through two phases—marked by the two world wars. After World War I, Woodrow Wilson and other liberals pushed for an international order organized around a global collective security body in which sovereign states would act together to uphold a system of territorial peace. Open trade, national self-determination, and a belief in progressive global change also undergirded the Wilsonian worldview—a "one world" vision of nation-states that trade and interact in a multilateral system of laws creating an orderly international community. "What we seek," Wilson declared at Mount Vernon on July 4, 1918, "is the reign of law, based on the consent of the governed and sustained by the organized opinion of mankind." Despite its great ambition, the Wilsonian plan for liberal international order entailed very little in the way of institutional machinery or formal great-power management of the system. It was a "thin" liberal order in which states would primarily act cooperatively through the shared embrace of liberal ideas and principles.[21] In the end, this experiment

[21] See Thomas Knock, *To End All Wars: Woodrow Wilson and the Quest for a New World Order* (New York: Oxford University Press, 1992); Lloyd E. Ambrosius, *Wilsonianism: Woodrow Wilson and His Legacy in American Foreign Relations* (New York: Palgrave, 2002); and John Milton Cooper, Jr., *Breaking the Heart of the World: Woodrow Wilson and the Fight for the League of Nations* (New York: Cambridge University Press, 2001).

in liberal order building failed, and the world soon entered an interwar period of closed economic systems and rival imperial blocs.

When the Roosevelt administration found itself in a position to shape the global system after World War II, it initially sought to pursue order building along Wilsonian lines. It embraced the vision of an open trading system and a world organization in which the great powers would cooperate to keep the peace. Beyond this, American architects of postwar order—drawing lessons from the Wilsonian failure and incorporating ideas from the New Deal period—also advanced more ambitious ideas about economic and political cooperation embodied in the Bretton Woods institutions. But the weakness of postwar Europe and rising tensions with the Soviet Union pushed liberal order building toward a much more American-led and Western-centered system. As the Cold War unfolded, the United States took command of organizing and running the system. In both the security and economic realms, the United States found itself taking on new commitments and functional roles. Its own economic and political system became, in effect, the central component of the larger liberal hegemonic order.

In these instances, we can distinguish various features of liberal international order. Liberal order can be relatively flat, as it was envisaged by Wilson after 1919, or built around institutionalized hierarchical relations, as it eventually came to be after 1945. Liberal international order can be universal in scope or operate as a regional or an exclusive grouping. It can be constructed between Western democracies or within the wider global system. Liberal international order can affirm and embody principles of state sovereignty and national-self-determination or champion more supranational forms of shared sovereignty. It can be highly institutionalized with formal legal rules, or it can operate with more informally structured expectations and commitments. Liberal international order can be narrowly drawn as a security order—as the League of Nations was on collective security—or developed as a more ambitious system of cooperative security and shared rights and obligations.[22]

[22] These various dimensions of liberal order are explored in G. John Ikenberry, "Liberal Internationalism 3.0: America and the Dilemmas of Liberal World Order," *Perspectives on Politics* 7, no. 1 (March 2009), 71–87.

Third, liberal international order—and the successive waves of liberal order building—has been built upon the modern states system and evolving frameworks for managing great power relations. That is, liberal order, in each of its nineteenth- and twentieth-century formations, has been built on realist foundations. This is true in two respects. Most generally, over the last two centuries, the construction of open and rule-based relations has been pursued by liberal great powers as they operated in the wider system of states. At a deep or foundational level in the modern era, the Westphalian system of states has prevailed, defined in terms of the multipolar or bipolar organization of great powers and shared norms of state sovereignty. It has been leading states, operating within this system of states, that have pursued liberal order building.

Over the last two centuries, the great powers within this Westphalian system have evolved principles and practices to manage and stabilize their relations. Beginning in 1815, successful settlements were increasingly understood to be based on a set of principles of restraint and accommodation. Embodying this "society of states" approach to international order, the Vienna settlement integrated the defeated French, recognized legitimate French national and security interests, and put in place a diplomatic process for resolving emerging problems on the basis of shared principles and understandings.[23] The resulting Concert of Europe is widely seen as a model of a stable and successful international order. The failure of the Versailles settlement in 1919 to embody these restraint and accommodation principles is widely seen as a critical source of the instability and war that followed. In contrast, in the settlement of World War II, the United States undertook the comprehensive reconstruction of Germany and Japan as liberal democratic states and their integration into the postwar American-led liberal international order—incorporating principles and practices of great-power restraint and accommodation brought forward from earlier eras of order building within the Westphalian system.[24]

[23] On the society-of-states approach to international order, see Hedley Bull, *The Anarchical Society*. A more detailed survey of these ideas is presented in chapter 2.

[24] For a discussion of principles of great-power restraint and accommodation as they were manifest in the Cold War settlement, see Daniel Deudney and G. John Ikenberry, "The Unraveling of the Cold War Settlement," *Survival* (December/January 2009–10).

Taken together, we can see several distinct eras of liberal order building, and across these eras we can trace evolving ideas and practices of
liberal international order. The American-led liberal hegemonic order is
only one type of liberal order. Liberal international order itself has been
pursued on the foundation of a state system in which the great powers
have evolved principles and practices of restraint and conflict management. These various "waves" and "layers" of international order coexist
within the contemporary global system.

Imperial and Liberal Rule

The United States emerged in the mid-twentieth century as the world's
most powerful state. It had the power not just to pursue its interests but to
shape its global environment. It made strategic choices, deployed power,
built institutions, forged partnerships, and produced a sprawling order.
It was an order with many parts, features, and layers—global, regional,
economic, political, military, social, and ideological. But together, the
parts constituted a political formation—that is, a more or less coherent political order with a distinct logic and character. As Charles Maier
argues, the American order—much like empires and other political
orders of the past—has had a distinctive set of characteristics or "institutional markers."[25]

But what sort of order was it? If the American postwar order has
been a mix of command and consent, what is the nature of this mix and
how has it changed over time? Is the American political formation an
empire, or do its liberal features give it a shape and organization that is
distinct from the great empires of the past? Put simply, has the United
States been engaged in imperial rule or liberal rule?

The empire debate is an old one—shadowing the rise of American
power itself. In the early postwar years, in the 1960s, and again in the

---

[25] Charles Maier, *Among Empires: American Ascendancy and Its Predecessors* (Cambridge:
Harvard University Press, 2006).

post–Cold War decades, scholars and commentators have debated the character of American domination, arguing about whether it is a modern form of empire.[26] The British writer and labor politician Harold Laski evoked a looming American empire in 1947 when he said that "America bestrides the world like a colossus; neither Rome at the height of its power nor Great Britain in the period of economic supremacy enjoyed an influence so direct, so profound, or so pervasive."[27] Later, during the Vietnam War, critics and revisionist historians traced what was seen as a deep-rooted impulse toward militarism and empire through the history of American foreign policy. Some writers saw the underlying motive for empire as essentially economic, tracing this impulse back to the Open Door policy of the turn of the nineteenth century.[28] Others saw imperial ambition rooted in a logic of security and geopolitical control, given impetus by the Cold War. As one prominent critic of American foreign policy argued during this period: "Since 1945 this country, not content with being *primus inter pares* among the nations, has sought not the delicate balance of power but a position of commanding superiority in weapons technology, in the regulation of the international economy, and in the manipulation of the internal politics of other countries."[29]

In recent years, the empire debate has returned, focusing on America's global ambitions under conditions of unipolarity. With the collapse of the Soviet Union, geopolitical rivals to the United States all but disappeared. Yet, a half century after their occupation, the United States still provides security for Japan and Germany—until recently, the world's second- and third-largest economies. American military bases and carrier battle groups project power into all corners of the world—and

[26] For surveys of these waves of empire debate, see Michael Cox, "Empire in Denial? Debating U.S. Power," *Security Dialogue* 35, no. 2 (2004), 228–36; and Cox, "The Empire's Back in Town—Or America's Imperial Temptation—Again," *Millennium* 32, no. 1 (2003), 1–27.

[27] Harold Laski., quoted in Niall Ferguson, *Colossus: The Rise and Fall of the American Empire* (New York: Penguin, 2004), 68.

[28] See the works by William Appleman Williams, especially *The Tragedy of American Diplomacy* (New York: Norton, 1959).

[29] Richard Barnet, *Intervention and Revolution: America's Confrontation with Insurgent Movements Around the World* (New York: World Publishing, 1968), 25.

indeed the United States possesses a near monopoly on the use of force internationally. Upon this unipolar foundation, the Bush administration came to power and, after the attacks of September 11, 2001, pursued a "war on terror," invaded Afghanistan and Iraq, expanded the military budget, and put forward a controversial 2002 National Security Strategy articulating a doctrine of military preemption in the face of self-defined threats. American power was once again thrust into the light of day—and it deeply unsettled much of the world. Not surprisingly, the concept of empire was invoked again to describe America's global ambitions and exercise of power in a one-superpower world.[30]

But is the American political formation—in the postwar decades or more recently—really an empire? The term "empire" refers to the political control by a dominant state of the domestic and foreign policies of weaker peoples or polities. The European colonial empires of the late nineteenth century were the most direct, formal kind. The Soviet "sphere of influence" in Eastern Europe entailed an equally coercive but less direct form of control. The British Empire included both direct colonial rule and informal empire. If empire is defined loosely, as a hierarchical system of political relationships in which the most powerful state exercises decisive influence, then the American-led order indeed qualifies.

What the American postwar political formation shares with empires is that it is an order organized, at least loosely, around hierarchical relations of domination and subordination. But the American postwar order is multifaceted. The most salient aspect of American domination in the

[30] The historian Niall Ferguson captured this widely held view, noting that "the British Empire is the most commonly cited precedent for the global power currently wielded by the United States. America is heir to the Empire in both senses: offspring in the colonial era, successor today." Ferguson, *Empire: The Rise and Demise of the British World Order and the Lessons for Global Power* (New York: Basic Books, 2002), xii. For surveys of the large and growing list of books and essays on the United States as global empire, see G. John Ikenberry, "The Illusions of Empire," *Foreign Affairs* 82, no. 2 (March/April 2004), 144–54; Alexander J. Motyl, "Is Empire Everything? Is Everything Empire?" *Comparative Politics* 39 (2006), 229–49; and Charles S. Maier, "Empire Without End: Imperial Achievements and Ideologies," *Foreign Affairs* 89, no. 4 (July/August 2010), 153–59.

postwar era is its mixed character. The United States built hierarchical relations but also mutually agreed-upon rules and institutions. There are both command-based and consent-based logics embedded in the postwar American-led order. The more general point is that hierarchical systems of domination and subordination can vary widely in their logic and character. Hierarchical political orders can have imperial characteristics, or they can have liberal characteristics — or they can be a mix.[31] Thus, it is useful to think of hierarchical political orders as existing on a continuum between imperial and liberal hegemonic ideal types.[32]

Empires are hierarchical political systems in which the dominant state exercises direct or indirect sovereign control over the decisions of subordinate states. "Empire," as Napoleon's foreign minister, Charles Maurice de Talleyrand, said, is "the art of putting men in their place." Political control is extensive. The imperial state asserts control over both the internal and external policies of subordinate states—or at least it maintains the right to do so. At the same time, the imperial state imposes the rules of hierarchical order but is itself not bound by those rules. In an empire, the dominating state has the final say over the terms of the relationship—its control may be disguised and obscured, but it has ultimate and sovereign control over the subordinate units within the order. Historically, imperial systems have been manifest in a wide variety of ways, ranging from direct colonial rule to looser types of informal empire.[33]

[31] In efforts to capture the distinctive blend of liberal and imperial features of America's postwar political formation, scholars have used terms such as "empire by invitation," "consensual hegemony," "empire by consent," and "empire of trust." These terms have been invoked, respectively, by Geir Lundstadt, *The American "Empire"* (Oxford: Oxford University Press, 1990); Charles S. Maier, "Alliance and Autonomy: European Identity and U.S. Foreign Policy Objectives in the Truman Years," in Michael Lacey, ed., *The Truman Presidency* (Cambridge: Cambridge University Press, 1991); John Lewis Gaddis, *We Now Know: Rethinking Cold War History* (New York: Oxford University Press, 1997); and Thomas F. Madden, *Empires of Trust: How Rome Built—and America Is Building—a New World* (London: Plume, 2009).

[32] See David Lake, *Entangling Relations: American Foreign Policy in Its Century* (Princeton, NJ: Princeton University Press, 1999); and Lake, "Anarchy, Hierarchy and the Variety of International Relations," *International Organization* 50, no. 1 (1996), 1–35.

[33] The literature on empire is vast. For studies of the logic of empire, see Michael Doyle, *Empires* (Ithaca, NY: Cornell University Press, 1984); and Herfried Munkler, *Empires: The*

In contrast, liberal hegemony is hierarchical order built around political bargains, diffuse reciprocity, provision of public goods, and mutually agreeable institutions and working relationships. The liberal hegemonic state asserts more limited control over subordinate states, primarily directed at shaping the terms of their external policies. The liberal hegemonic state dominates the order by establishing and maintaining its rules and institutions—but in doing so, it operates to a greater or lesser extent within those rules and institutions. The liberal hegemonic state establishes its rule within the order by shaping the milieu in which other states operate.

In the case of the American postwar order, as we shall see, there are several features that—at least in its ideal form—give it a more consensual and agreed-upon character than imperial systems. One is the sponsorship and support of a loose system of rules and institutions that it has itself operated within. Another is its leadership in the provision of public goods—including security and maintenance of an open economic system. As an open system organized around leading liberal democratic states, states that operated within it have opportunities to consult, bargain, and negotiate with the United States. In effect, subordinate states have access to decision making at the center. Institutions for joint or concerted leadership span the liberal hegemonic landscape. These features of the American-led order do not eliminate hierarchy or the exercise of power, but they mute the imperial form of hierarchy and infuse it with liberal characteristics.

To be sure, variations in hierarchy exist across the various regional realms of American domination. Liberal characteristics of hegemonic order are most extensive within the advanced liberal democratic world, particularly in U.S. relations with Western Europe and Japan. In other parts of East Asia and across the developing world, American-led order

Logic of World Domination from Ancient Rome to the United States (London: Polity, 2007). For recent comprehensive histories, see John Darwin, *After Tamerlane: The Global History of Empire Since 1405* (New York: Bloomsbury Press, 2008); and Jane Burbank and Frederick Cooper, *Empires and the Politics of Difference in World History* (Princeton, NJ: Princeton University Press, 2010).

is hierarchical but with much fainter liberal characteristics.[34] While American hegemony within the Western world tends to be organized around agreed-upon multilateral rules and institutions, American hegemony in East Asia is organized around a "hub-and-spoke" security system of client states. In some parts of the developing world—including in Latin America and the Middle East—American involvement has often been crudely imperial.[35]

If this liberal hegemonic order is in crisis, can the bargains and institutions that support it be renegotiated and reestablished? This is in part a question about American willingness and capacity to continue to operate within a liberal hegemonic framework—providing public goods, supporting and abiding by agreed-upon rules and institutions, and adjusting policies within an ongoing system of political bargaining and reciprocity. It is also a question of the interests and ambitions of other established and rising states in the system. Was the American liberal hegemonic order a historical artifact of the long postwar era, now breaking down and giving way to a different type of international order? Or can it be reorganized and renegotiated for the next era of world politics?

Plan for the Book

This book explores the long "arc" of the American liberal order-building experience—its origins, logic, growth, crisis, and coming transformation.

---

[34] For an important exploration of regional variations within the American "imperium," see Katzenstein, *A World of Regions*. Katzenstein argues that the character of Europe and East Asia as regions has been influenced by America as a global geopolitical presence. In particular, the intermediary role of Germany and Japan as supporters of United States power and purpose have shaped in complex and divergent ways the institutions and political organizations of these regions. My study draws upon several of Katzenstein's insights, including the importance of Europe and East Asia and the differential ways in which they have extended and institutionalized American power in their regions but also set limits on it as well.

[35] This study focuses primarily on the international order created by the United States and the other great powers. It does not fully illuminate the wider features of world order that include America's relations with weaker, less developed, and peripheral states.

Chapter 2 takes up the issues of anarchy, hierarchy, and constitution-alism in international relations. It looks at the three major mechanisms through which order is established and perpetuated, namely, balance, command, and consent. To understand the logic and character of the American postwar order, it is necessary to explore the logic of hierarchy. In contrast to anarchical forms of order, hierarchical orders entail ongoing relations of domination and subordination between polities. But hierar-chical systems of domination and subordination can vary widely in their logic and organization, involving different mixes of domination and con-sent. I will offer a distinction between types of hierarchical political orders and focus in particular between imperial and liberal forms of hierarchy.

Liberal forms of hierarchical order require that the leading state engage in institutionalized forms of restraint and commitment. Power and domination are channeled through more or less agreed-upon rules and institutions. Chapter 3 explores state power and the logic of rule-based order. A powerful state has incentives to shape and control the international system in which it operates. While weak and subordinate states are "order takers," powerful states are on occasion "order makers." The type of order that a powerful state seeks to construct will flow from its interests and its geopolitical position in the global system. But the order that emerges will also reflect the tools and strategies that the lead-ing state has available to it to assert control over other states.

I offer what might be called a "political control" model of rule-based institutions. Rules and institutions are tools by which states gain some measure of political control over the behavior of other actors in the global system. Doing so involves trade-offs between policy autonomy and rule-based commitments. A state bargains away some of its policy autonomy to get other states to operate in more predictable and desirable ways—all of it made credible through institutionalized agreements. The shifting incentives, choices, and circumstances surrounding this "institu-tional bargain" help explain variations in state commitments to rules and institutions. The degree to which the leading state sponsors and operates within multilateral rule-based relations determines the degree to which the global hierarchy has imperial or liberal characteristics.

Chapter 4 probes the prospects for rule-based order under conditions of unipolarity—and how this logic shifts as unipolarity wanes.
Unipolarity does shift the incentives that a leading state has to operate under multilateral rules and institutions. Two strategies of unipolar
governance are identified—"rule through rules" and "rule through relationships." The first entails traditional multilateral commitments to rule-
based governance—and it has been most fully manifest in U.S. relations
with Europe. The other involves building order around patron-client
relations—and it is most fully manifest in America's "hub-and-spoke"
relations with East Asia. Under conditions of unipolarity, the United
States has incentives to move toward a hub-and-spoke system. However,
to the extent that the leading state calculates that its unipolar power is
waning or is rendered less effective in securing control over its environment because of a loss of legitimacy and the acquiescence of weaker
states, it will find incentives to remain tied to other states through multilateral rules and institutions.

Chapter 5 provides a survey of the logic and character of the American postwar liberal hegemonic order. The core of this new order was
established among the Western democracies, but its ideas and institutions were potentially universal in scope. The vision behind this order
was expressed in a sequence of declarations and agreements—the Atlantic Charter of 1941, the Bretton Woods agreements of 1944, the U.N.
Charter in 1945, the Marshall Plan in 1947, and the Atlantic Pact in 1949.
Together, these agreements provided a framework for a radical reorganization of relations among the Western democracies—and a basis for the
wider integration of much of the postwar world. Between 1944 and 1951,
American leaders engaged in the most intensive institution building the
world has ever seen—global, regional, security, economic, and political.
The United States took the lead in fashioning a world of multilateral
rules, institutions, open markets, democratic community, and regional
partnerships—and it put itself at the center of it all.

Chapter 6 examines the great transformation and the crisis of the
American order. It looks at the long-term shifts in the global system that
have eroded the foundations upon which the United States constructed

the postwar order. These shifts amount to an inversion of the Westphalian system in which great powers maintained order through an equilibrium of power and the norms of state sovereignty. Under conditions of unipolarity and eroded norms of state sovereignty, American power has become a problem in world politics. In effect, there has been a shift over time in the character and mix of modes of American domination. The rise of American unipolarity after the end of the Cold War—together with other long-term shifts in the global system—have altered the incentives, costs, bargains, and institutions that form the foundation of the American postwar order. These shifts have rendered more problematic America's commitment to liberal hegemony and rule-based order.

I also explore the failed efforts of the Bush administration to embrace this post-Westphalian moment to impose a new system of order on the world. The Bush administration sought to build on the transformations on the global system—the rise of unipolarity and the flipping of the Westphalian order—and articulate a new vision of American-centered order. Fundamentally, the Bush administration offered up a vision of order that was, in important respects, hegemony with imperial characteristics. The United States was to step forward and provide rule and order based on its unilateral assertion of power and rights. It is a vision of American as a conservative Leviathan. This post-Westphalian logic of order has failed. The world has rejected it, and the United States cannot sustain it.

The experience of the Bush administration shows that there are limits to the ability of powerful states to operate outside the norms and institutional frameworks of liberal international order. The Bush experience shows that the world's leading state can break out of institutional and normative constraints—even those that it has itself helped create—but that there is a price to be paid for it. Lost legitimacy, partnerships, cooperation, and credibility do have consequences.

Chapter 7 explores alternative pathways away from the current crisis. I identify three different possible futures. One involves a renegotiated American-led liberal hegemonic order. Another possibility is the building of a post-hegemonic liberal order in which the United States plays a more "normal" role within the context of declining unipolarity. A third possibility is that the crisis of the American-led order could give way to fragmentation and a general decline in order itself. Regional blocs, spheres of influence, and complex patterns of hubs and spokes could emerge in ways that leave the international order both radically less open and less rule-based.

I argue that there are several factors that will shape the pathway forward. One is the actual willingness of the United States to cede authority back to the international community and accommodate itself to a system of more binding rules and institutions. Short of a radical shift in the international distribution of power, the United States will remain the world's most powerful state for several decades to come. So there is reason to think that other countries would be willing to see the United States play a leading role—and provide functional services—if the terms are right. A second factor is the degree to which America's security capacities can be leveraged into wider economic and political agreements. The United States has extraordinary advantages in military power. The question is, to what extent can the United States use these assets to strike bargains with other states on more general rules and institutions of global order? If it can, the United States will find opportunities to renegotiate a modified hegemonic system. Finally, the degree of divergence among the lead states in their visions of global order will matter in how the crisis plays out. The question is whether non-Western rising states such as China and India will seek to use their increasing power to usher in a substantially different sort of international order.

In the end, I argue that despite America's imperial temptation, it is not doomed to abandon rule-based order—and rising states are not destined to reject the basic features of liberal international order. The United States ultimately will want to wield its power legitimately in a world of rules and institutions. It will also have incentives to build and strengthen regional and global institutions in preparation for a future after unipolarity. The rising power of China, India and other non-Western states presents a challenge to the old American-led order that will require new, expanded, and shared international governance arrangements.

If America is smart and plays its foreign policy "cards" right, twenty years from now, it can still be at the center of a one-world system defined in terms of open markets, democratic community, cooperative security, and rule-based order. This future can be contrasted with less-desirable alternatives familiar from history: great-power-balancing orders, regional blocs, or bipolar rivalries. The United States should seek to consolidate a global order where other countries "bandwagon" rather than balance against it—and where it remains at the center of a prosperous and secure democratic-capitalist order, which in turn provides the architecture and axis points around which the wider global system turns. But to reestablish this desired world order, the United States must work to re-create the basic governance institutions of the system—investing in alliances, partnerships, multilateral institutions, special relationships, great-power concerts, cooperative security pacts, and democratic security communities.

Part One
Theoretical Foundations

Two
Power and the Varieties of Order

The order created by the United States in the decades after World War II is a curious amalgam of logics, institutions, roles, and relationships. It is an order that has been given various names—the free world, the American system, the West, the Atlantic world, Pax Democratica, Pax Americana, the Philadelphian system. It took shape in the early decades of the Cold War, organized in part as an alliance aimed at countering and containing Soviet power. The United States quickly became a pole or organizing hub within the emerging bipolar global system. American postwar order building was, in this sense, an outgrowth or facet of geopolitical competition and bipolar balancing. Along the way, this American-led order took on hierarchical characteristics. The United States was vastly more powerful than other states within the order. It organized and led the order, underwriting security, stability, and economic openness. A global array of weaker and secondary states became junior partners and client states. But, at the same time, the order was also—at least within its Western core—a community of liberal democracies. These democracies shared a vision of liberal order that predated the Cold War, and they worked together to organize open and loosely rule-based relations that were not simple reflections of power hierarchies. Complex and institutionalized forms of cooperation of increasing depth and breadth marked the order—cooperation that continues today.

How can we make sense of this American-led order? An international order is a political formation in which settled rules and arrangements exist between states to guide their interaction. How can we describe and situate the American postwar order within the wider array of types of international orders? This chapter develops a framework for the theoretical and historical depiction of international orders.

The postwar American-led order plays havoc with prevailing understandings of international relations. The traditional image of world politics is one in which a group of roughly equally capable states— so-called great powers—shape the system as they compete, cooperate, and balance with each other. States operate in a decentralized system where order is established through an equilibrium of power among the major states. The anarchical character of the international system is manifest in the decentralization of power and authority. States are sovereign and formally equal. No state—not even a powerful one—"rules" the global order under conditions of anarchy. The insecurity and competition that flow from this anarchical situation drives state behavior and gives international politics its distinctive and enduring features.

This theoretical perspective, however, has a hard time making sense of the American-led international order. This is true in several respects. First, the relations between states within this order are not based on a balance-of-power logic or even overtly marked by anarchy-driven power politics. Bargains, institutions, and deeply intertwined political and economic relations give the American-led order its shape and character. The extensiveness of interdependence, specialization of functions, and shared governance arrangements are not easily understood in terms of anarchy and power balancing. Second, the end of the Cold War did not return international order to a multipolar great-power system, but rather it led to a unipolar system in which a single state overshadows and dominates the functioning and patterns of global politics. States—both those inside the American-led order and outside—have not responded to unipolarity with clear and determined efforts to balance against the United States. The result has been several decades of world politics marked by the commanding presence of a leading state and the absence of a return to a multipolar balance-of-power system.

In effect, the anarchy problematic misses two features of the American-led international order—hierarchy and democratic community. First, the order does in fact look more like a hierarchy than like an anarchy. In critical respects, the order is organized around superordinate and subordinate relationships. States have differentiated roles and capacities. Several leading states—Japan and Germany—do not possess the full military capacities of traditional great powers. Rules and institutions in the global system provide special roles and responsibilities for a leading state. Although a formal governance structure does not exist, power and authority is informally manifest in hierarchical ways. The United States is situated at the top of the order and other states are organized below it in various ways as allies, partners, and clients. Second, the order is marked by the pervasiveness of liberal relationships. At least in the Western core of this order, other liberal democratic states engage in reciprocal and bargained relations with the United States. The order is organized around an expanding array of rules and institutions that reduce and constrain the prevalence of power politics. The United States shares governance responsibilities with other states. In these various ways, the American-led order has characteristics of a hierarchy with liberal features.

To make sense of the American-led order and the transformations under way, we need to expand our theoretical vision. I do so in several steps. First, I look at the background conditions that shape and limit the ways in which political formations are manifest. Here the focus is on variations and shifts in the distribution of power. I identify various types of power distributions, and I distinguish them from the political rules and relationships that might arise in the context of different arrays of material capabilities among leading states. It is in this context that we can see the ways in which the American postwar order has traveled through the era of Cold War bipolarity into the recent decades of unipolarity.

Second, I look at the three general ways in which international order can be organized. These are orders built on balance, command, and consent. Each of these logics of order is rooted in a rich theoretical tradition. Each tradition offers a sweeping account of the logic and character of international order. Each offers a grand narrative of the rise and transformation of the modern international system. And importantly, each offers a major argument about the way in which stable international order is formed and maintained.

These logics direct attention to the shaping of international order as it occurs at periodic historical turning points, particularly in the aftermath of major wars. Settlements of great-power wars have often turned into ordering moments when the rules and institutions of the international order are on the table for negotiation and change. The principal components of settlements are peace conferences, comprehensive treaties, and postwar agreements on principles of order. These ordering moments not only ratify the outcome of the war. They also lay out common understandings, rules and expectations, and procedures for conflict resolution. As such, these settlements have played a quasi-constitutional function, laying the foundation and enshrining the organizational logic of international order.

Finally, I look more closely at the ways in which these logics of order have been manifest in the American-led postwar order. In particular, I explore the continuum that exists between imperial and liberal forms of hierarchy and rule. This continuum seeks to capture variation in the degree of formal and coercive control by the leading state over the policies of weaker and secondary states. Several aspects of hierarchical order shape the degree to which it takes on liberal characteristics. These include the degree to which the leading state provides and operates within a set of agreed-upon rules and institutions; the degree to which the leading state provides public goods to other states; and the degree to which the leading state provides "voice opportunities" for weaker and secondary states in the order. The American-led order did manifest these liberal features—and its overall logic and character can be described as liberal hegemony.

The Distribution of Power

Relations between states are built on foundations of power. International order has come in many varieties over the centuries, but in each instance it has been shaped and constrained by the distribution of power. Indeed, the first questions we typically ask about international order are about power. How is power distributed? Does one state or a few dominate the system, or is power diffused more broadly? What are the material capabilities that matter in world politics? How do relations between states change as power shifts? In asking these questions, we are making a distinction between the distribution of power and the political formations that are built on top of the distributed capabilities of states. The distribution of power refers to the way in which material assets and capabilities are arrayed among states and other actors. The distribution of power tells us who has power but not how it will be used. The distribution of power provides opportunities and constraints for states within the system. But it does not, in itself, determine the way power is exercised or how order is created.

The international distribution of power can vary widely. Power capabilities can be more or less concentrated in the hands of one, a few, or many states.[1] These variations are typically described in terms of polarity. A multipolar system is one in which power is spread out or diffused among several states. In a bipolar system, power is concentrated in the hands of two states. A unipolar system is one in which one state possesses

[1] Power distributions are defined in terms of the aggregate material capabilities that states possess relative to other states. This definition of power as material capabilities, rather than power as control over outcomes, follows the distinction made in the literature of power. See David Baldwin, *Paradoxes of Power* (New York: Basil Blackwell, 1989). For methodological challenges in measuring and comparing the distribution or concentration of power in international systems, see James Lee Ray and J. David Singer, "Measuring the Concentration of Power in the International System," *Sociological Methods and Research* 1, no. 4 (May 1973), 403–37.

substantially more power capacities than other states. In multipolar and bipolar systems, power capabilities among two or more states are more or less in balance or equilibrium. These multiple "poles" provide competing centers of power, and the character of their cooperation and competition shapes the overall international order. In a unipolar system, power is concentrated and unbalanced—the unipolar state has no peer competitors.[2] It alone is a pole of global power.

Realist theory offers the most systematic characterizations of state power and polarity. In the realist rendering, a pole is a state that is powerful by virtue of its aggregation of various material capabilities: wealth, technology, military capacity, and so forth. Kenneth Waltz provides the classic definition of a pole. A state takes on the position of a pole within the larger system if it possesses an unusually large share of resources or capabilities and if it excels in all the various components of state capabilities, including, most importantly, the "size of population and territory, resource endowment, economic capacity, military strength, political stability and competence."[3]

This conception of power and polarity has been invoked by scholars who offer general depictions of the global distribution of material capabilities over many centuries. In these accounts, the modern state system has tended to be multipolar from its European beginnings in the seventeenth century into the mid-twentieth century. During these centuries, a small group of major states organized the system and competed for influence and control. After World War II, the era of great-power multipolarity gave way to a bipolar global system dominated by the United States and the Soviet Union. The power structure became unipolar in the

[2] A peer competitor is a rival state that has the military, economic, technological, and geopolitical capabilities to match those of the leading global power. A peer competitor to the United States today would be a state that could project its military force into any region of the world in a sustained fashion and, more generally, compete with the United States on a global basis. None currently exist. See John Mearsheimer, *The Tragedy of Great Power Politics* (New York: Norton, 2001); and Thomas S. Szayna, Daniel L. Byman, Steven C. Bankes, et al., *The Emergence of Peer Competitors: A Framework of Analysis* (Washington, D.C.: RAND Corp., 2001).

[3] See Kenneth Waltz, *Theory of International Politics* (Reading: Mass.: Addison-Wesley, 1979), 131.

1990s with the collapse of the Soviet Union and the continuing growth of America's material capabilities relative to the other major states.

These broad differences in the international distribution of power are captured in aggregate measures that combine economic and military size. These percentage indicators provide measures of both economic capacity and military might. The gross national income (GNI) measure—particularly utilizing measures of both aggregate and per capita GNI—provides the single best measure of power capabilities.[4] In contrast, military spending captures effort, not potential.[5] The multipolarity of the earlier periods is contrasted with the bipolarity of the Cold War and the unipolarity of the last two decades. (See figure 2-1.)

These measures of aggregate power show the distinctiveness of the postwar era of bipolarity and the last two decades of unipolarity. In previous centuries, power was shared more or less evenly among a group of great powers. Leading states were only slightly set apart from the other great powers. Moreover, in these earlier periods the leading states were either great commercial and naval powers or great military powers on land, but they were never both. Great Britain emerged as the leading economic and naval power in the nineteenth century, but other major states matched or exceeded British capabilities in some areas. As Brooks

[4] Before a change in terminology by the World Bank, GNI was formerly referred to as gross national product (GNP). This study cites GNI statistics calculated using the World Bank's "Atlas" conversion factor, according to the World Bank "to reduce the impact of exchange rate fluctuations in the cross-country comparison of national incomes." See World Bank "Methodologies," http://data.worldbank.org/about/data-overview/methodologies (accessed July 14 2010).

[5] There are many ambiguities in measures of the distribution and concentration of power. As noted, one issue is how to weight disparities in military spending, which is a reflection of a policy decision and not underlying capacity. There is also the problem of how to treat empires. If we measure "Britain's" power, do we include India? Finally, there is the problem of whether to measure power distributions between the great powers or the power capacities of the leading state (and/or the great powers) in relation to the wider world. The United States may be more capable relative to the other great powers than Britain was in the nineteenth century, but great powers today may be relatively less capable vis-à-vis the non–great powers taken as a whole. Recognizing that no approach is perfect, this study will employ consistent and unadjusted measures of the distribution of power across eras, as arguably this facilitates the simplest comparisons while still capturing major trends.

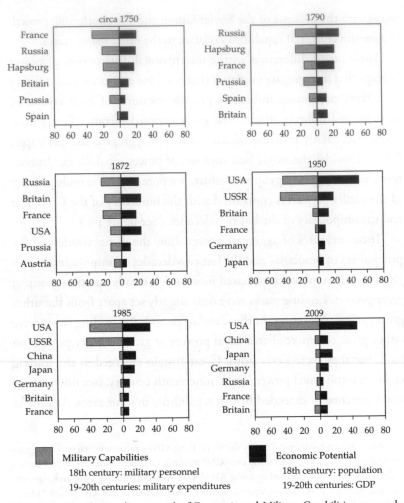

Figure 2-1: Distribution (Percentage) of Economic and Military Capabilities among the Major Powers[a] (17th–21st Centuries)

Sources: Eighteenth-century data: Paul M. Kennedy, *The Rise and Fall of the Great Powers* (New York: Random House, 1987). GDP for 1870–1985: Angus Maddison, *Monitoring the World Economy, 1829–1992* (Paris: OECD, 1995); GDP for 2009: sources from Table 1.2; military expenditures for 1872–1985: National Material Capabilities data set v. 3.02 at http://www.correlates ofwar.org. The construction of these data is discussed in J. David Singer, Stuart Bremer, and John Stuckey, "Capability Distribution, Uncertainty, and Major Power War, 1820–1965," in Bruce Russett, ed., *Peace, War, and Numbers* (Beverly Hills, Calif.: Sage, 1972), 19–48. Military exenditures 2009: sources from Table 1.1

[a]Russia = USSR in 1950 and 1985; Maddison's estimates are based on states' modern territories. For 1872, Austria, Hungary, and Czechoslovaikia are combined, as are Russia and Finland.

and Wohlforth observe, "[e]ven at the height of the Pax Britannica, the United Kingdom was outspent, outmanned, and outgunned by both France and Russia."[6] Similarly, the United States emerged from World War II as the world's leading economy, and it was unrivaled in many areas of military power, including air and naval capabilities. But during the Cold War, the Soviet Union matched the United States in overall military capabilities, reinforced by its vast territorial holdings and military investments. During the Cold War, the United States and the Soviet Union were both poles in a geopolitically divided world.

Seen in this light, a global unipolar distribution of power is historically unique. In the last two decades, the United States has stood alone at the top of the worldwide power hierarchy, commanding an especially large share of the material capabilities and unique in possessing the full range of economic, technological, military, and geopolitical assets.[7] Only the United States has had the attributes of a pole.

Unipolarity is reflected in the distribution of economic, military, and technological capabilities.[8] In 2008, the United States accounted for over a quarter of global GNI and over 49 percent of GNI among the traditional great powers. This is greater than the economic position of

---

[6] Stephen G. Brooks and William C. Wohlforth, *World Out of Balance: International Relations and the Challenge of American Primacy* (Princeton, NJ: Princeton University Press, 2008), 31.

[7] As a leading scholar of long-cycle theory notes: "The current U.S. position is unprecedented in some ways. Two important ones come immediately to mind. One is that the current system leader has no major power rivals. That condition may be temporary, but it is certainly unprecedented. It is also closely related to the unipolar outcome. The emergence of a genuine rival may end US military unipolarity, although there are other ways that the unipolar status may end. A second novelty is that the United States currently possesses the world system's lead army—not necessarily in size but in terms of lethality, technological competence, and ability to project force at long distance. Not all of these characteristics are entirely novel, but the total package is unusual. Normally, the leading whale is not also the leading elephant." William R. Thompson, "Systemic Leadership, Evolutionary Processes, and International Relations Theory: The Unipolarity Question," *International Studies Review* 8 (2006), 14.

[8] This empirical depiction of American unipolarity draws on work by William C. Wohlforth. See Wohlforth, "Stability of a Unipolar World," *International Security* 21, no. 2 (Summer 1999), 5–41; Wohlforth, "U.S. Strategy in a Unipolar World," in John Ikenberry, ed., *America Unrivaled: The Future of the Balance of Power* (Ithaca: Cornell University Press, 2002); and Brooks and Wohlforth, *World Out of Balance*, chap. 2.

any other state in history—aside from America's own relative economic size after World War II when the economies of the other major were temporarily depressed.[9] The U.S. share of world GNI among the great powers has remained relatively stable over the postwar decades. In 1992, the U.S. share of great-power GNI was approximately 41 percent and in 2002 it was 48 percent. (See table 2-1.)

While its share of total world GNI has declined slightly (as a result mainly of economic growth in Asia and the developing world), the United States continues to possess economic capacity far greater than that of the other great powers. Indeed, since the end of the Cold War, these economic disparities have intensified between the United States and the other advanced industrialized countries—Western Europe and Japan. Over the last twenty years, American GDP growth has averaged over 2.7 percent, while Japan has averaged 1.48 percent growth, Germany and France have averaged less than 1.9 percent, and the United Kingdom has averaged 2.37 percent.[10]

The American advantage in economic size is extended by its advantages in per capita GNI. The other democratic great powers—Japan, Germany, France, and Britain—have a per capita GNI roughly 10 to 20 percent below the United States', while China—a potential geopolitical rival—has only a fraction of the American total. This comparison is useful as a measure of relative potential taxable income that a state has at its disposal.[11]

Militarily, the disparities between the United States and the rest of the world are even more pronounced. At the end of the Cold War, the

[9] According to the World Bank, in 2008, the United States accounted for 20.5 percent of world GNP calculated using purchasing price parity (PPP) and 25 percent using market exchange rates. The other leading states employing the PPP measure were China (11.5 percent), Japan (6.5 percent), India (4.8 percent), and Germany (4.3 percent). See World Bank, *World Development Indicators*, http://data.worldbank.org/data-catalog (accessed July 14, 2010).

[10] The World Bank records annual growth in GNP but not GNI. A back-of-the-envelope calculation suggests that this trend is also present in GNI.

[11] Per capita GNI matters as a indicator of power capacity: the greater a country's per capita GNI, the greater its economic and technological advancement and, everything else equal, the greater the ability of its government to extract resources to invest in military and high-tech capacity.

Table 2-1
Great Power GNI, 1986–2008[a]

	1986	1992	1996	2002	2008
France	605.605	1,310.153	1,578.624	1,378.321	2,695.615
Germany	810.304	1,927.204	2,457.974	1,895.913	3,506.923
Japan	1,532.028	3,477.065	5,200.504	4,236.594	4,869.121
United Kingdom	499.198	1,043.401	1,208.155	1,556.371	2,827.343
United States	4,289.871	6,072.35	7,805.278	10,145.806	14,573.576
China	315.752	435.424	788.443	1,406.922	3,888.082
Russian Federation	n/a	435.125	386.295	305.799	1,371.173

Source: World Bank, World Development Indicators 2010.
[a] In current US dollars (billions), Atlas method.

Table 2-2
Great Power Defense Expenditures 2009

	Defense Expenditures ($b)	% of great powers	% of world
United States	661	63.98	43.17
China	100	9.68	6.53
France	63.9	6.19	4.17
United Kingdom	58.3	5.64	3.81
Russia	53.3	5.16	3.48
Japan	51.0	4.94	3.33
Germany	45.6	4.41	2.98

Source: Stockholm International Peace Research Institute, Military Expenditure Database 2010.

United States cut its expenditures less sharply than other major states—including, most importantly, the former Soviet Union—and it rapidly expanded its defense budget after 2001. As a result, the United States today spends on defense approximately as much as the rest of the world combined. In 2009, America's share of world defense expenditures was approximately 43 percent, and it was about 64 percent of defense expenditures by the great powers. (See table 2-2.)

These combined economic, military, and technological advantages give the United States "command of the commons." Barry Posen argues that it is the ability of a leading state to militarily dominate the global commons—that is, mastery of sea and space areas—that provides the defining feature of unipolar military power. He notes that it is this mastery of the global commons that is the key to American global power:

> Command of the commons is the key military enabler of the
> U.S. global power position. It allows the United States to exploit
> more fully other sources of power, including its own economic
> and military might as well as the economic and military might of
> its allies. Command of the commons also helps the United States
> to weaken its adversaries, by restricting their access to economic,
> military and political assistance.... Command of the commons
> provides the United States with more useful military potential
> for a hegemonic foreign policy than any other offshore power
> has ever had.[12]

What is clear is that power distributions—and the concentration of power in the hands of a leading state—vary widely across the last centuries, and from this comparative-historical perspective, the current system is uniquely unipolar. What is remarkable about American power is that it has been so durable and multifaceted. The United States has accounted for roughly a quarter to a third of world GNP for most of the last hundred years. As Brooks and Wohlforth observe, no other economy today or in the near future "will match its combination of wealth, size, technological capacity, and productivity."[13] To be sure, the U.S. power advantages are most pronounced in the area of military capacity. This is a problematic feature of power because military spending is a reflection of a government's policy effort, not its underlying potential. Nonetheless, the prevailing distribution of power is unipolar in character and this is unique in world-historical terms.

The polarity of the international system provides important but limited information about the character of international order. It is a description of the distribution of power capabilities. That is all. It is not a description of the political formation that is built on and around these

---

[12] Barry Posen, "Command of the Commons: The Military Foundation of U.S. Hegemony," *International Security* 28 (2003), 9.

[13] Brooks and Wohlforth, *World Out of Balance*, chap. 2.

distributed capabilities. Multipolar systems of power have provided the setting for both stable and unstable, peaceful and conflict-ridden, relations among states. During the Cold War, a bipolar power distribution existed, but the actual relations between the United States and the Soviet Union varied from intense conflict and security competition to periods of and negotiated peace. The post–Cold War era of unipolarity has also provided the setting for a wide variety of American policies and patterns of conflict and cooperation. We need to look more closely at the various ways that states can build international order.

Order and the Balance of Power

States have built international order in many different ways, doing so around various configurations of power. International order refers to the settled rules and arrangements that guide the relations among states. These rules and arrangements can differ in many ways. They can be regional or global, they can be more or less institutionalized, and they can be built around more or less agreed-upon rules and institutions. International order can be dominated by one or a few states or organized around more far-flung forms of cooperation among powerful and weak states. Most fundamentally, international order can differ in terms of the underlying source of order; that is, in the mechanisms that give shape to order and render it stable. In this regard, there are three general logics of order: order built on balance, command, and consent. Each offers a general account of the origins and changing character of the modern international system. Each has a conception of the sources and locations of political authority within the system.[14] Table 2-3 summarizes key characteristics of these logics.

One of the oldest and most studied sources of international order is the balance of power. This is order built around either a multipolar or

[14] These three logics of order are ideal types. Actual historical cases of international order, as we shall see, often combine several logics.

Table 2-3
Logics of Order

	Balance	Command	Consent
Source of authority	State sovereignty	Material power	Rule of law
Moral purpose	Preservation of autonomy	Interests of dominant states	Creation of public goods
Hierarchy/nature of hierarchy	No/great power co-equals	Yes/rulers and subjects	Sometimes/leaders and followers

bipolar distribution of power. No one state dominates the system. States compete and counterbalance each other. When one state grows increasingly powerful or aggressive, other states respond by aggregating power. Out of the resulting stalemate of power, order arises. Balance can be achieved through internal mobilization of resources within a state, the building of alliance coalitions, or both. Through this ongoing power-aggregating and -balancing process, relations among states are rendered stable. In effect, order is the result of an equipoise or equilibrium of power between competing states.

This logic of international order is richly theorized within the realist tradition. States exist in a world of anarchy. No authority or governance institutions operate above the state to enforce agreements or maintain order. Sovereign states compete in a self-help system. In Kenneth Waltz's seminal statement of this view, the parts of the system are made up of states that are alike ("like units") in their fundamental character, undifferentiated by function.[15] When there is no guarantee that contracts will

---

[15] Waltz, *Theory of International Politics*, 95. In Hobbes's classic formulation, so long as "men live without a common power to keep them all in awe, they are in that condition which is called Warre." In such a condition, individuals cannot trust that their contracts will be honored and must provide for their own security, preventing the development of a robust division of labor: "In such condition there is no place for industry, because the fruit thereof is uncertain; and consequently no culture of the earth; no navigation, nor use of the commodities that may be imported by sea; no commodious building; no instruments of moving and removing such things as require much force; no knowledge of the face of the earth; no account of time; no arts; no letters; no society; and which is worst of all, continual fear, and danger of violent death; and the life of man, solitary, poor, nasty, brutish, and short." Thomas Hobbes, *Leviathan*, first quote in chap. 13, para. 62.

be enforced, prudent actors ensure that they can provide for as many of their own needs as possible. States are under strong pressure to fulfill the same functions. States are left to their own devices to secure themselves and protect their interests. State power—defined as material capabilities—is the coin of the realm. States can protect themselves and achieve their goals to the extent that they have the power to do so. In a condition of anarchy, states do not stand in any fixed, formal, or hierarchical relation with one another. The last word in political authority is state sovereignty, which constitutes the formal rejection of hierarchy.

It is under these conditions that incentives exist for states to balance. States can never be fully certain of the intentions of other states and so cannot rely on commitments and guarantees to ensure their security. States rise and fall in material capabilities, triggering responses by other states. When powerful states emerge, weaker states will seek protection in countervailing coalitions. The alternative is to risk domination. "Secondary states, if they are free to choose, flock to the weaker side; for it is the stronger side that threatens them," Waltz argues. "On the weaker side they are both more appreciated and safer, provided, of course, that the coalition they join achieves enough defensive or deterrent strength to dissuade adversaries from attacking."[16] As the distribution of power shifts, coalitions will shift as well. International order, therefore, is the result of balancing by states seeking to ensure their survival in an anarchical system.

This notion of order and the balance of power provides the basis for a sweeping narrative of the rise and fall of international order. International relations are marked by a succession of global struggles over power, with each cycle of history returning the system to a settled order based on an equilibrium of power among the leading states. States are in a constant competition for security. Great powers rise up and seek domination, or they ally with other states to prevent their domination by other

[16] Waltz, *Theory of International Politics*, 127. As Stephen M. Walt defines balance-of-power theory, it is "the proposition that states will join alliances in order to avoid domination by strong powers." Walt, "Alliance Formation and the Balance of World Power," *International Security* 9, no. 4 (1985), 5.

great powers. War comes when powerful states seek to overturn the state system and replace it with universal empire—the Hapsburg Empire, the France of Louis XIV, the France of Napoleon, and Hitler's Germany—all of which suffered the same fate. In the face of these imperial ambitions, a coalition of threatened states came together to restrain and subdue the would-be dominating state. Security and order was returned to the system as power again became decentralized among competing states who reaffirmed their rights to independence and sovereignty.[17]

The European continent has been the central stage for this great historical drama. France, Great Britain, Prussia, Russia, Spain, and other major powers and imperial states are the *dramatis personae* of this grand narrative. Over the centuries, aggrandizing states have grown powerful, weakened and declined, acquired and lost empires, gone to war, and made peace. Despite the many variations of specific historical circumstance, the European—and later, worldwide—great powers have operated according to a common logic. In each era, powerful states have risen up to challenge the balance of power—perhaps seeking domination or simply growing more powerful as other states have gone into decline—in turn threatening other states that respond by mobilizing their national capacities and allying themselves with others to confront and resist the challenge. War and peace settlements have marked these moments when power is brought back into balance.

Going beyond this basic logic, some scholars have explored the historical evolution of the system of states and balance-of-power politics. These moderate realists and society-of-states theorists have identified

---

[17] On the balance-of-power politics that marked European history and the failure of attempts to establish hegemony, see Ludwig Dehio, *The Precarious Balance: The Politics of Power in Europe, 1494–1945* (London: Chatto and Windus, 1963). As Herbert Butterfield writes, "the eighteenth century looked back to the Roman Empire as a thing that must never be allowed to happen again. They realized, what the twentieth century forgot sometimes, that there are only two alternatives: either a distribution of power to produce equilibrium or surrender to a single universal empire like that of ancient Rome. And this development in their theory became extremely relevant when Napoleon overthrew the balance and seemed to be creating a new Roman Empire." Herbert Butterfield, "The Balance of Power," in Herbert Butterfield and Martin Wight, eds., *Diplomatic Investigations: Essays in the Theory of International Politics* (Cambridge, MA: Harvard University Press, 1969), 142.

long-term changes in the institutional arrangements and practices of great-power relations.[18] From the early modern era to the present, the great powers have engaged in repeated episodes of war and peacemaking. In the aftermath of these conflicts, the great powers have found themselves grappling with the terms of postwar settlement. Inevitably, these settlements have been not just about the ending of war but also about the organization of the peace. They have been "ordering moments," when the great powers have struggled over the basic rules and principles of international order. The result has been the rise and evolution of the so-called Westphalian system of states. The great powers compete, cooperate, and balance each other within a wider framework of rules and norms. In the background, Westphalian norms of sovereignty enshrine states as formally equal and independent, possessing the ultimate authority over their own people and territory.[19]

Over the centuries, the Westphalian system has evolved as a set of principles and practices and expanded outward from its European origins to encompass the entire globe. Despite this unfolding, however, states have retained their claims of political and legal authority. The founding principles of the Westphalian system—sovereignty, territorial integrity, and nonintervention—reflected an emerging consensus that states were the rightful political units for the establishment of legitimate rule. Norms

[18] Moderate realist accounts of great-power balancing and the evolution of its practices and principles include Henry Kissinger, *A World Restored: Metternich, Castlereagh and the Problem of Peace, 1812–22* (Boston: Houghton Mifflin, 1957); Gordon A. Craig and Alexander L. George, *Force and Statecraft: Diplomatic Problems of Our Time* (New York: Oxford University Press, 1981); and Paul Schroeder, *The Transformation of European Politics, 1763–1848* (Oxford: Oxford University Press, 1994). For society-of-states perspectives on the evolution of the state system see Hedley Bull, *The Anarchical Society: A Study of Order in World Politics* (London: Macmillan, 1977); Barry Buzan and Richard Little, *International Systems in World History: Remaking the Study of International Relations* (Oxford: Oxford University Press, 2000); Barry Buzan, *From International to World Society: English School Theory and the Social Structure of Globalization* (Cambridge: Cambridge University Press, 2004); Ian Clark, *The Hierarchy of States: Reform and Resistance in the International Order* (Cambridge: Cambridge University Press, 1989); and Andrew Hurrell, *On Global Order: Power Values, and the Constitution of International Society* (Oxford: Oxford University Press, 2007).

[19] For depictions of the Westphalian state system, see F. H. Hinsley, *Power and the Pursuit of Peace* (Cambridge: Cambridge University Press, 1963); and Bull, *Anarchical Society*.

and principles that subsequently evolved within the Westphalian system—such as self-determination and nondiscrimination—served to further reinforce the primacy of states and state authority.[20] To be sure, the resulting norms and principles of sovereignty and nonintervention have not been inviolable. As Stephen Krasner argues, state sovereignty norms have been systematically violated by great powers in each of the eras that followed 1648. They were honored primarily in the breach.[21] Nonetheless, these norms and principles have served as the organizing logic for Westphalian order and provided the ideational source of political authority within it. Under the banner of sovereignty and self-determination, political movements for decolonization and independence were set in motion in the non-Western developing world. Westphalian norms have been violated and ignored, but they have, nonetheless, been the most salient and agreed-upon rules and principles of international order in the modern era.

The succession of postwar settlements also provided moments for the great powers to develop principles and practices that have shaped and updated the functioning of great-power relations.[22] Particularly

[20] In Henry Kissinger's realist account, stable international order emerges when there is a balance among the great powers and a shared sense of the legitimacy of the order. See Kissinger, *Diplomacy* (New York: Simon and Schuster, 1994).

[21] Stephen D. Krasner, *Sovereignty: Organized Hypocrisy* (Princeton, NJ: Princeton University Press, 1999). Krasner argues that the seeming sense of novelty in the 1990s that norms of sovereignty were eroding is based on a false historical baseline. The norms of sovereignty and nonintervention have been articulated and affirmed by states, but these norms have never stood in the way of interventions by powerful states when it has suited their interests. Krasner makes the important point that Westphalian norms did not emerge full blown in 1648. Indeed, the notions of sovereignty and sovereign equality were not formally referred to in the settlement. Westphalian norms have been contested, ignored, and abridged across the history of the states system. However, as I argue in chapter 6, what does change in the 1990s is the emergence of new doctrines and norms of interventionism and contingent sovereignty, which were given particular salience in the context of the rise of American unipolarity and a transforming global security environment.

[22] On the evolving norms of great power authority, see Osiander, *States System of Europe*. The distinction between great and secondary powers emerged in European diplomacy during the Congress of Vienna era as diplomats negotiated over processes of decision making. See Harold Nicholson, *The Congress of Vienna: A Study in Allies Unity, 1812–1822* (New York: Harcourt, Brace, 1946), 137; and Charles Webster, *The Congress of Vienna, 1814–1815* (London: Thames and Hudson, 1934), 80.

paradigmatic is the Vienna settlement that followed the Napoleonic Wars. This settlement is widely seen as particularly successful because it was based on great-power restraint and accommodation. Embodying the restraint principles of the society-of-states approach to international order, the Vienna settlement integrated the defeated French, recognized legitimate French national and security interests, and put in place a diplomatic process for resolving emergent problems on the basis of shared principles and understandings. The resulting Concert of Europe is widely seen as a model of a stable and peaceful international order.[23] In contrast, the Versailles settlement was famously less successful. Its punitive character violated the restraint principles that had been so critical to the earlier settlement. Although Woodrow Wilson articulated progressive principles of international order, the settlement itself was punitive in that it embodied British and French demands for retribution; imposed heavy reparations, asymmetrical disarmament, and the partial territorial occupation of Germany; and neglected legitimate German national security interests. These punitive features are widely seen as a major reason for its ultimate failure.

The settlement of World War II was more complicated than were previous settlements. There was no negotiation with the defeated adversaries, Germany and Japan. And the negotiations that did occur at Potsdam and Yalta were conducted by the victors, who essentially partitioned Europe among themselves. Nonetheless, within the American sphere, the United States undertook the comprehensive reconstruction of Germany and Japan as liberal democratic states and their integration into the postwar American-led international order. France and West Germany tied themselves together through the Coal and Steel Community and to the other European states in wider European and Atlantic institutions. The great powers of Europe and Japan were integrated into a rebuilt states system. Along this historical pathway—through war and

---

[23] For accounts of the Vienna settlement that emphasize its evolving practices of great-power restraint and accommodation, see Paul Schroeder, *The Transformation of European Politics, 1763–1848* (New York: Palgrave Macmillan, 2002); and Charles A. Kupchan, *How Enemies Become Friends: The Sources of Stable Peace* (Princeton, NJ: Princeton University Press, 2010), 188–217.

settlement, learning and adaptation—it is possible to see an evolution in how the great powers have operated within a multipolar balance-of-power system. The source of order remained rooted in a decentralized states system in which major states compete with and balance each other. But the practices and principles of competition and balance have evolved to incorporate strategic notions of restraint and accommodation.

Taken together, the realist theory of anarchy and the balance of power provides a major statement of the character and functioning of international order. It draws attention to the evolution of great-power relations within the Westphalian system and the long-term shifts in how major states have used and adapted the balance-of-power mechanism in the building and rebuilding of international order. As I will argue later, these innovations in great-power restraint and accommodation have been essential breakthroughs in the twentieth-century construction of liberal international order.

Nonetheless, there are also severe limits on the ability of the anarchy/balance problematic to explain American-led liberal international order. As noted earlier, the relations among states in this order are not imbued with the balancing and security competition that neorealist theory expects. Complex and institutionalized forms of cooperation bind the liberal democracies together. The stability of this American-led order is all the more striking in the decades after the end of the bipolar Cold War struggle. In these decades, the order has remained relatively coherent and expanded outward to integrate states from beyond its Western core. Despite the troubles that currently beset this American-led order, states have not responded to unipolarity by seeking to balance against the United States. The balancing dynamic is not as straightforward or automatic as is implied in neorealist theory. The balance of power is actually not as pervasive across historical eras and regional systems as the neorealist logic suggests.[24] Perhaps most importantly, the contemporary

---

[24] As one major study of the balance of power across historical systems concludes: "[A] survey of 7,500 years of the history of international systems shows that balanced and unbalanced distributions of power are roughly equally common. There is no iron law of history favoring either a balance of power or hegemony." See William C. Wohlforth, Stuart J. Kaufman, and

American-led international order is organized as a loosely hierarchical system. To understand the existing order, we need to ask questions about how great powers become poles and organize hierarchical relations with secondary and weaker states.

Hierarchy and Command

International order can also be organized around the domination of a powerful state. This is order based on command. In these instances, a state rises up and uses its leading position to create and enforce order. International order takes the shape of a hierarchy. Superordinate and subordinate relations are established between the leading state and weaker and secondary political entities that are arrayed around it. Command-based systems have varied widely in terms of the degree to which order is maintained through direct coercion or infused with more bargained and agreed-upon ordering arrangements.

Across world history, states have grown powerful and built hierarchically organized political orders. Indeed, for most of the last two thousand years, world politics has been dominated by major states seeking to extend their rule over other people. For most of these centuries, the vast majority of the world's population has lived—for better or worse—within imperial political orders of one kind or another. In the ancient world, Athens, Rome, China, and the Mongols built far-flung and long-lasting empires that incorporated diverse peoples. In the modern era, the European great powers built empires and colonial systems that extended throughout Africa, Asia, and the Americas.[25] In each instance, a hierarchical political entity ruled from the top. "Violence and day-to-day coercion were

---

Richard Little, "Introduction: Balance and Hierarchy in International Systems," in Kaufman, Little, and Wohlforth, eds., *The Balance of Power in World History* (New York: Palgrave, 2007), 20. States also frequently underbalance and overbalance in the face of rising states or threats. See Randall L. Schweller, *Unanswered Threats: Political Constraints on the Balance of Power* (Princeton, NJ: Princeton University Press, 2008).

[25] For a sweeping history of empires, see John Darwin, *After Tamerlane: The Global History of Empire Since 1405* (New York: Bloomsbury, 2008).

fundamental to how empires were built and how they operated," observe the historians Burbank and Cooper. "But as successful empires turned their conquests into profit, they had to manage their unlike populations, in the process producing a variety of ways to both exploit and rule."[26]

Hierarchical systems are marked by ordered relations between units where power and authority is centralized and the units in the system are functionally differentiated. In a hierarchical international order, states are integrated vertically within well-defined superordinate and subordinate positions. In anarchical systems, order is the equilibrium that results from the balancing of a decentralized array of competing states. In hierarchical systems, order is established or imposed by a leading state wielding concentrated power and authority. Hierarchical orders are characterized by stratified relations between leading and secondary states.[27] Beyond this, hierarchical orders can vary widely in terms of the degree to which superordinate and subordinate roles are established and maintained by such factors as coercive power, legitimate authority, institutionalized relations, and a division of labor.[28]

---

[26] Jane Burbank and Frederick Cooper, *Empires in World History: Power and the Politics of Difference* (Princeton, NJ: Princeton University Press, 2010), chap. 1.

[27] For surveys of the logic of hierarchy in international relations, see David Lake, "Escape from the State of Nature: Authority and Hierarchy in World Politics," *International Security* 31, no. 1 (Summer 2007), 47–79; David Kang, "The Theoretical Roots of Hierarchy in International Relations," *Australian Journal of International Relations* 58, no. 3 (September 2004), 337–52; Jack Donnelly, "Sovereign Inequalities and Hierarchy in Anarchy: American Power and International Society," *European Journal of International Relations* 12, no. 2 (2006), 139–70; and Alexander Cooley, *Logics of Hierarchy: The Organization of Empires, States, and Military Occupations* (Ithaca, NY: Cornell University Press, 2005).

[28] David Lake provides an important theoretical statement of hierarchy in international relations. In his formulation, hierarchies are bargained relations in which the dominant state provides services—such as order, security, and governance—to subordinate states in return for compliance. What distinguishes the various forms of hierarchy, from colonialism to modern alliances, is the amount of sovereignty signed over to the leading state. Lake uses this insight to explore patterns of American-led hierarchy in the security and economic realms, relying on measures such as the presence of U.S. military bases, exchange-rate linkages, and trade dependence. Lake sees hierarchy primarily as voluntary transfer of sovereignty based on "contracts" between state. In contrast, this study seeks to differentiate types of hierarchy—empire and liberal hegemony—in terms of the mix of coercion and consent that infuse superordinate and subordinate relationships. See Lake, *Hierarchy in International Relations* (Ithaca, NY: Cornell University Press, 2009).

In this view, international order is shaped by a succession of powerful—imperial or hegemonic—states that rise up to organize and dominate the system. They create and enforce the rules and institutions that ensure a stable order in which to pursue their interests. Change occurs as great powers rise and decline and as they struggle over the rules and institutions of order. Robert Gilpin provides a classic account of the dynamics of international relations in these terms, arguing that "the evolution of any system has been characterized by successive rises of powerful states that have governed the system and have determined the patterns of international interactions and established the rules of the system."[29] Steady and inevitable shifts in the distribution of power among states gives rise to new challenger states that eventually engage the leading state in hegemonic war. This in turn gives rise to a new hegemonic state that uses its dominant position to establish an order favorable to its interests.

Within a hegemonic order, rules and rights are established and enforced by the power capacities of the leading state. Compliance and participation within the order are ultimately ensured by the range of power capabilities available to the hegemon—military power, financial capital, market access, technology, and so forth. Direct coercion is always an option in the enforcement of order, but less direct "carrots and sticks" also maintain hegemonic control. Gilpin also argues that a wider set of resources—ideology and status appeals—are integral to the perpetuation of hegemonic order.[30] But the authority of the hegemonic state and the cohesion of the hegemonic order are ultimately based on the preeminent power of the leading state.

The hierarchical system is maintained as long as the leading state remains powerful enough to enforce the rules and institutions of order. When hegemonic power declines, the existing order begins to unravel and break apart. As Gilpin contends, "a precondition for political change lies in a disjuncture between the existing social system and the

[29] Robert Gilpin, *War and Change in World Politics* (New York: Cambridge University Press, 1981), 42–43.

[30] Gilpin, *War and Change.*

redistribution of power toward those actors who would benefit most from a change in the system."[31] The power transition leads to geopolitical struggles and security competition that ultimately culminate in hegemonic war—and the emergence of a new leading state that organizes the international system according to a new logic.

A.F.K. Organski offers a similar depiction of this process of making and unmaking of international order. "At any given moment the single most powerful nation on earth heads an international order that includes some other major powers of secondary importance and some minor nations and dependencies as well." Britain and the United States in their respective eras followed this pattern: rising up and establishing international order, defined as a system in which participating states "accept the given distribution of power and wealth and . . . abide by the same rules of trade, diplomacy, and war."[32] The resulting international order "is legitimized by an ideology and rooted in the power differential of the groups that compose it."[33] Over time, international shifts in power and wealth create challengers, and eventually a transfer of "world leadership" takes place. This grand process of power transition will be either peaceful or be accompanied by great-power war, depending on whether the rising state accepts or rejects and seeks to overturn the "working rules" of the existing international order. The basic argument in Organski's grand narrative is the same as Gilpin's—namely, that the international order is most stable when it is commanded by a dominant power.

In another version of this theory, George Modelski argues that the global political system goes through distinct historical cycles of domination by powerful states. According to Modelski, four states have played dominant or hegemonic roles since AD 1500: Portugal until the end of the sixteenth century, the Netherlands in the seventeenth century, Great Britain in the early eighteenth century until the Napoleonic wars and

[31] Gilpin, *War and Change*, 9.
[32] A.F.K. Organski, *World Politics*, 2nd ed. (New York: Knopf, 1969), 354, 361.
[33] Organski, *World Politics*, 364.

again in 1815 to 1945, and the United States since 1945. Modelski argues, as does Gilpin, that each cycle of hegemonic domination ends with war, ushering in a new hegemonic era.[34]

These conceptions all see international order as a project undertaken by leading global states. Order is established and maintained through command. Each era is defined by a powerful state that rises up to organize and dominate the system. It is the power and control exercised by the leading state that gives shape and stability to the order. As the leading state declines—as all leading states inevitably do—the international order begins to unravel.[35] Disorder is manifest in geopolitical competition and war. International order returns when a new leading state rises up and uses its dominant position to organize and run the system. Of course, not all command-based orders are global in scope. Major powers have established and presided over more limited hierarchical orders within regions or maritime systems.

As noted earlier, Britain in the nineteenth century and the United States created and led international orders with a mix of hierarchical characteristics. Each acquired commanding power advantages—economic, technological, military—and used these advantages to establish a global system of diplomatic, political, and commercial relationships. The British world system contained an extraordinary variety of types of hierarchical rule: formal colonial possessions, informal governing

[34] George Modelski, "The Long Cycle of Global Politics and the Nation-State," *Comparative Studies in Society and History* 20, no. 2 (April 1978), 214–35. See also George Modelski and William R. Thompson, *Leading Sectors and World Politics: The Coevolution of Global Economics and Politics* (Columbia: University of South Carolina Press, 1996).

[35] For critiques and extensions of the theory on power transitions, see J. DiCicco and Jack Levy, "The Power Transition Research Program: A Lakatosian Analysis," in Colin Elman and Miriam F. Elman, eds., *Progress in International Relations Theory: Appraising the Field* (Cambridge, MA: MIT Press, 2003), 109–57; Jacek Kugler and Douglas Lemke, eds., *Parity and War: Evaluations and Extensions of the War Ledger* (Ann Arbor: University of Michigan Press, 1996); Woosang Kim and James Murrow, "When Do Power Shifts Lead to War?" *American Journal of Political Science* 36, no. 4 (November 1992), 896–922; and Douglas Lemke and William Reed, "Regime Types and Status Quo Evaluations: Power Transition Theory and The Democratic Peace," *International Interactions* 22, nos. 3–4 (1996), 143–64.

arrangements, and spheres of influence and control.[36] Both Britain and the United States established a set of loosely arranged rules and institutions around which world markets and politics turned. Each used its internal market to promote trade abroad and manage an open system of commerce. Britain championed the gold standard as a mechanism to facilitate worldwide trade and investment. Its naval dominance was used to protect shipping and provide security protection to friends and allies. The United States used its power advantages after World War II to reopen the world economy and create an array of political and alliance institutions that provided the foundation for postwar security and the management of economic openness.[37] But the United States also used its commanding position to discipline and coerce weaker states, particularly in Latin America and the Middle East.[38]

The challenge for theories of hierarchy is to capture the nature of and variation in power relations between the leading state and weaker and secondary states. Hierarchy can come in many varieties, and the

[36] John Darwin describes this remarkable variety of relationships with the nineteenth British world system. "It contained colonies of rule (including the huge 'sub-empire' of India), settlement colonies (mostly self-governing by the late nineteenth century), protectorates, condominia (like the Sudan), mandates (after 1920), naval and military fortresses (like Gibraltar and Malta), 'occupations' (like Egypt and Cyprus), treaty-ports and 'concessions' (Shanghai was the most famous), 'informal' colonies of commercial pre-eminence (like Argentina), 'spheres of interference' (a useful term coined by Sellars and Yeatman) like Iran, Afghanistan and the Persian Gulf, and (not least) a rebellious province at home. There was no agreed term for this far-flung conglomerate." John Darwin, *The Empire Project: The Rise and Fall of the British World-System 1830–1970* (Cambridge: Cambridge University Press, 2009), 1.

[37] For studies of British and American hegemony, Robert Gilpin, "Economic Interdependence and National Security in Historical Perspective," in Klaus Knorr and Frank N. Trager, eds., *Economic Issues and National Security* (Lawrence: University Press of Kansas, 1977); Robert Gilpin, *U.S. Power and the Multinational Corporation: The Political Economy of Foreign Direct Investment* (New York: Basic Books, 1975); Joseph Nye, *Bound to Lead: The Changing Nature of American Power* (New York: Basic Books, 1991); Patrick Karl O'Brien and Armand Cleese, eds., *Two Hegemonies: Britain 1846–1914 and the United States 1941–2001* (Aldershot, UK: Ashgate, 2002); and David Lake, "British and American Hegemony Compared: Lessons for the Current Era of Decline," in Michael G. Fry, ed., *History, the White House, and the Kremlin: Statesmen as Historians* (New York: Columbia University Press, 1991).

[38] For a historical survey of American interventions to overthrown hostile regimes, see Michael Kinzer, *Overthrow: America's Century of Regime Change from Hawaii to Iraq* (New York: Times Books, 2007).

character of domination can be overtly coercive or involve a more complex mix of incentives and constraints. What makes hierarchies of states persist? Is it the simple dominance of the leading state, coercing weaker and secondary states to operate under its command? Or do weaker and secondary states operate within a hierarchical order through a more negotiated process of give-and-take? The rise of unipolarity after the Cold War is a puzzle to realist theories of anarchy and balance. It is less so to theories that see hierarchy as a basic and enduring feature of world politics. But is the American-led international order simply the most recent manifestation of a long sequence of command-based systems, or is there something profoundly distinctive about it? Is it best seen as a modern form of empire, or is it something different? The American-led order is hierarchical but—at least in its Western core—it is also organized around open and loosely rule-based relationships. How does hierarchy and liberal order coexist? We can look more closely at liberal theories of order and variations in the logic and character of hierarchical systems.

Constitutionalism and Consent

International order can also be organized around agreed-upon rules and institutions. This is order based on consent. Here, states and societal groups of various sorts respond to deep impulses and incentives to mutually build structures of exchange and cooperation. Liberal democracies in particular are drawn to this sort of order, finding their security and societal interests advanced through open and rule-based relations. While systems based on balance and command depend fundamentally on state power—either in balance or by preponderance—for the establishment and maintenance of stable order, consent-based order relies on shared interests and the rule of law. In its most developed form, international order is constitutional in character. That is, state power is embedded in a system of rules and institutions that restrain and circumscribe its exercise. States enter the international order out of enlightened self-interest, engaging in self-restraint and binding themselves to agreed-upon rules and institutions. In this way, order is based on consent.

This liberal conception of order is attached to a grand narrative about the rise and transformation of the modern international system. It is an account of the "liberal ascendancy." In the late eighteenth century, liberal states emerged and began two centuries of experiment and innovation in order building, championing open and rule-based relations. Triumphs and setbacks followed. In this liberal ascendancy, the Western democracies became more powerful and prosperous. Their numbers and share of world power increased and took a huge jump with the defeat of fascist and totalitarian challengers in the twentieth century. These liberal states also made efforts to construct a congenial international order. At postwar moments, led by Great Britain and the United States, they put forward progressive ideas about the organization of global relations. With the end of the Cold War, the last rival organizing logic of world order fell away.[39]

There are several specific bodies of theory that contribute ideas to this liberal vision of order. As Michael Doyle observes, liberal international theory has at least three intellectual wellsprings. The first is commercial liberalism, which dates back to Adam Smith. The spread of capitalism and markets creates economic interdependence, joint gains, shared interests, and incentives for international cooperation. The second is the democratic peace, which traces to Kant. Republican or democratic polities seek affiliation with each other and manifest pacific relations. The third is liberal institutionalism, which dates to Lockean writings on rights and the rule of law. International law and institutions

[39] For general statements of liberal international theory, see Robert O. Keohane, "International Liberalism Reconsidered," in John Dunn, ed., *Economic Limits to Modern Politics* (Cambridge: Cambridge University Press, 1990), 165–94; Mark W. Zacher and Richard A. Mathew, "Liberal International Relations Theory: Common Threads, Divergent Strands," in Charles Kegley, ed., *Controversies in International Relations Theory: Realism and the Neoliberal Challenge* (New York: St. Martin's, 1995); Andrew Moravcsik, "Taking Preferences Seriously: A Liberal Theory of International Politics," *International Organization* 51, no. 4 (Autumn 1997), 513–53; and Daniel Deudney and G. John Ikenberry, "The Nature and Sources of Liberal International Order," *Review of International Studies* 25 (Spring 1999), 179–96.

are outgrowths of liberal societies that establish rule-based expectations and obligations between them.[40] Each of these traditions offers a set of claims about how liberal democracies build and operate within the international system.

Despite its richness and diversity, liberal conceptions of order share a core set of assumptions and expectations. Liberal theories assume that peoples and governments have deep common interests in the establishment of a cooperative world order organized around principles of reciprocity and the rule of law. There is an assumption in liberal theories that states can overcome the constraints of a competitive and decentralized international system and cooperate to solve security dilemmas, pursue collective action, and create an open, stable system. There is also an assumption that powerful states will act with restraint in the exercise of their power and find ways to credibly convey commitments to other states. Liberal theories have shared the view that trade and exchange have a modernizing and civilizing effect on states, undercutting illiberal tendencies and strengthening the fabric of international community. Liberal theories also share the view that democracies are—in contrast to autocratic and authoritarian states—particularly able and willing to operate within an open, rule-based international system and to cooperate for mutual gain. Likewise, liberals have shared the view that institutions and rules established between states facilitate and reinforce cooperation and collective problem solving. Governments and domestic actors have incentives and impulses embedded in the deep structures of society to trade, bargain, negotiate, and seek cooperation for joint gain.[41]

[40] Michael Doyle, *The Ways of War and Peace: Realism, Liberalism, and Socialism* (New York: Norton, 1997).

[41] There are a variety of related theoretical literatures that make up liberal international theory. On power and complex interdependence, see Robert Keohane and Joseph Nye, *Power and Interdependence* (Boston: Little, Brown, 1977). On transnational relations and transgovernmental networks, see Thomas Risse, *Bringing Transnational Relations Back In: Non-State Actors, Domestic Structures and International Institutions* (Cambridge: Cambridge University Press, 1995); and Anne-Marie Slaughter, *A New World Order* (Princeton, NJ: Princeton University Press, 2004). On the democratic peace, see Michael Doyle, "Kant, Liberal Legacies, and Foreign Affairs," *Philosophy and Public Affairs* 12 (1983), 205–35, 323–53. On the domestic sources of state preferences, see Moravcsik, "Taking Preferences Seriously." On international

These assumptions—and the liberal vision—are tied together by the idea that societies are involved in an ongoing process of modernization. Modernization itself is driven by the deep forces of science and technology that are constantly evolving and transforming human capacities. These evolving human capacities have manifold implications for the ways in which power, communication, relationships, interests, community, and political possibilities are arrayed. In this sense, there is directionality to the logic and character of states and international order. Modernization tends to take societies down a common path of political pluralism and market openness. Modernization across societies and cultures tends to produce similar sorts of challenges and responses—and the general movement is toward loosely convergent sorts of political-economic institutions.[42] This developmental logic suggests that international order is not static or tending toward equilibrium. There is a logic of change implicit in the liberal ascendancy. While realists see war as a major engine of change, and Marxists look to revolution, liberals emphasize learning and adaptation.

The liberal claim is that these modernizing forces and movements reinforce each other, pushing and pulling the global system forward in a progressive direction. In particular, the three components of liberal international order—liberal democracy, economic interdependence, and international institutions—are understood to reinforce each other.

---

institutions, see Robert Keohane, *After Hegemony: Cooperation and Discord in the World Political Economy* (Princeton, NJ: Princeton University Press, 1984); and Martha Finnemore and Michael Barnett, *Rules for the World: International Organizations in Global Politics* (Ithaca, NY: Cornell University Press, 2004). On security communities, see Emanuel Adler and Michael Barnett, eds., *Security Communities* (New York: Cambridge University Press, 1998); and Karl Deutsch, et al., *Political Community and the North Atlantic Area* (Princeton, NJ: Princeton University Press, 1957).

[42] On the modernization theory underpinnings of the liberal tradition, see Edward Morse, *Modernization and the Transformation of International Relations* (New York: Free Press, 1976); James Rosenau, *Turbulence in World Politics: A Theory of Change and Continuity* (Princeton, NJ: Princeton University Press, 1991); Craig N. Murphy, *International Organization and Industrial Change: Global Governance Since 1850* (New York: Oxford University Press, 1994); and Deudney, *Bounding Power*, chap. 7. On the American embrace of liberal modernization thinking, see David Ekbladh, *The Great American Mission: Modernization and the Construction of an American World Order* (Princeton, NJ: Princeton University Press, 2010).

Liberal democracies are able to overcome the insecurities generated by anarchical order, at least in their relations with each other. Trade and other forms of exchange are mutually beneficial across the liberal democratic world and create incentives and stakeholders for the continuation of stable international order. International institutions facilitate exchange and cooperation.[43] The expectation is that liberal democracies will thrive in this expanding international order. The liberal international order's open and rule-based character creates advantages for states that operate within it—and places states outside the order at a disadvantage.[44]

The building and rebuilding of liberal international order has taken place at periodic historical junctures when leading liberal states have been in a position to shape global rules and institutions. As noted earlier, realists and "society of states" theorists have emphasized the ways in which great-power relations and the operation of the balance of power have evolved over the centuries through the negotiations over postwar settlements. In the same way, these postwar settlements have been crucial for liberal order building. The old order has been destroyed and opportunities emerge for shaping the principles and organizational arrangements of a new order.

In the twentieth century, these liberal turning points have come after the world wars and the Cold War. At these junctures, the United States and other liberal democracies stepped forward with progressive ideas about the organization of international order. The first great moment of twentieth-century liberal order building came in 1919 with Woodrow Wilson's ambitious agenda at the Versailles conference. The Versailles settlement launched the League of Nations, which its progressive advocates hoped would usher in an entirely new system of interstate relations based on advanced liberal principles. Although the Versailles settlement essentially failed as a framework for international order, its liberal principles

[43] For an exploration of these reinforcing effects, see John Oneal and Bruce Russett, *Triangulating Peace: Democracy, Interdependence, and International Organizations* (New York: Norton, 2000).

[44] G. John Ikenberry, "The Universal Claims of Liberal Internationalism," unpublished paper, 2009.

were taken up again and adapted after World War II. The United States took on a more direct role in organizing international order. The ideas and practical organization of liberal order evolved. It became more hierarchical, institutionalized, and harnessed to an agenda of human rights and economic development. Again, at the end of the Cold War, the United States and other Western democracies articulated liberal principles of order as they negotiated with the Soviet Union (and later, Russia) over the terms of the settlement. Adaptation, innovation, success, and failure have shadowed liberal order building across the last century.

Liberal theories offer rich accounts of the ascendancy of Western democracies to global preeminence. These theories also illuminate the consent-based principles and logic of the international order championed by the United States and other states in the postwar era. But liberal order building has also unfolded alongside the ordering forces captured by theories of anarchy and hierarchy. The Western state system has evolved as the great powers have developed norms and practices of restraint and accommodation. This Westphalian system has provided a foundation for liberal order building. At the same time, the post–World War II innovations in liberal international order involved the direct and ongoing hegemonic leadership of the United States. Liberal theories see stable order built around the consent of the states that operate within it. But the other mechanisms of order—balance and command—also lurk at the edges of liberal international order.

Empire and Liberal Hegemony

It is the mixed character of American dominance that is most striking. The United States has built international order in the postwar era incorporating all three logics. Under conditions of Cold War bipolarity, it led a balancing coalition of states against the Soviet Union. The American-centered hierarchical order that emerged over these decades manifested characteristics of command and consent. In some realms, American domination was crudely imperial; in others, it was built around agreed-upon rules and institutions. We can look more closely at these two ideal types of international order—empire and liberal hegemony. Each offers a distinct logic of hierarchy. In an imperial order, the dominant state operates unilaterally and above the rules and institutions. In a liberal hegemonic order, the lead state establishes agreed-upon rules and institutions and operates—more or less—within them. The lead state negotiates rather than imposes order. In an imperial order, the lead state rules through command and, ultimately, coercion. In a liberal hegemonic order, the lead state rules by shaping the milieu in which states operate. The character of domination and authority varies accordingly.[45]

Empire has many different meanings and manifestations, but in essence, it is a hierarchical order in which a powerful state engages in organized rule over several dispersed weaker and secondary polities.[46] There are several features to this type of order. First, it is indeed hierarchical—manifest as a sort of hub-and-spoke organization where control is exercised from the core. Hence, Alexander Motyl depicts empire

---

[45] For discussions of the distinction between empire and hegemony, see Doyle, *Empires*; Herfried Munkler, *Empires: The Logic of World Domination from Ancient Rome to the United States* (London: Polity, 2007), 40–46; and Daniel Nexon and Thomas Wright, "What's at Stake in the American Empire Debate?" *American Political Science Review* 101, no. 2 (July 2007), 256–61. For skeptical views about the meaningfulness of this distinction, see Chalmers Johnson, *The Sorrows of Empire: Militarism, Secrecy, and the End of the Republic* (New York: Holt, 2004), 30; and Ferguson, *Colossus*.

[46] Munkler provides a challenging alternative to this book's conception of American liberal hegemonic order. Munkler seeks, as do I, to draw a line between "hegemonic supremacy" and "imperial domination." In his formulation, "[h]egemony is supremacy within a group of formally equal political players; imperiality, by contrast, dissolves this at least formal—equality and reduces subordinates to the status of client states or satellites. They stand in a more or less recognizable dependence in relation to the centre." In an imperial order, the rights and sovereign equality of states give way to permeable boundaries and hierarchical gradations of power and influence. Accordingly, Munkler sees the United States presiding over a "world empire," acting according to a "logic of imperial power" seen most clearly in the Bush administration's post–September 11 military interventionism. Munkler, *Empires*, 6. In contrast, this study sees liberal hegemony as a more elaborate form of hierarchical order in which differentiated roles and authority, dependencies, and patron-client relations are manifest in the context of a wider system of negotiated rules and institutions. The state system and its logic of action still operate in the background, providing mechanisms for power restraint and accommodation. Likewise, I argue that America's recent post–September 11 foreign policy misadventures show the limits—not the preeminence—of illiberal hegemony and imperiality.

as a "hublike structure—a rimless wheel—within which a core elite and state dominate peripheral elites and societies by serving as intermediaries for their significant interactions."[47] The peripheral polities are all connected to the core but disconnected from each other. All roads lead to and from Rome.

Second, empire entails the direct or indirect control by the dominant state over the external policies and orientations of the weaker and secondary policies. As Michael Doyle suggests, "empire . . . is a relationship, formal or informal, in which one state controls the effective political sovereignty of another political society."[48] In such an order, de facto (and sometimes de jure) sovereignty resides in the hands of the imperial state. Whether it is established through authoritative law or coercion, the core state exercises control—and has the final sovereign authority—in the functioning of the imperial order. Whether rule by the imperial state is direct or indirect, the secondary or peripheral states do not engage in autonomous foreign relations.

Third, hierarchy is established and control exercised through various sorts of center-periphery elite networks and relationships. As Charles Maier argues, "[e]mpire is a form of political organization in which the social elements that rule in the dominant state—the 'mother country' or the 'metropole'—create a network of allied elites in regions abroad who accept subordination in international affairs in return for security of their position in their own administrative unit (the 'colony' or, in spatial terms, the 'periphery')."[49] In particular, imperial states exercised rule, as Nexon and Wright note, "through local intermediaries over various actors within the domestic sphere of constituent political communities."[50] Weaker peoples and societies on the periphery are dependent on and coercively tied to the imperial center.

[47] Alexander Motyl, *Imperial Ends: The Decay, Collapse, and Revival of Empires* (New York: Columbia University Press, 2001), 4. See also Johan Galtung, "A Structural Theory of Imperialism," *Journal of Peace Research* 8, no. 2 (1971), 81–117.

[48] Doyle, *Empires*, 45.

[49] Charles S. Maier, *Among Empires: American Ascendency and Its Predecessors* (Cambridge, MA: Harvard University Press, 2007), 7.

[50] Nexon and Wright, "What's at Stake," 253.

In actual practice, imperial orders have varied widely in their institutional forms and in their degree of hierarchical domination and control. Dominic Lieven suggests that there are two general types of empire. One is the modern European maritime empire, which is defined in terms of the relationship between the metropolitan center and colonial periphery. Cultural and political domination, along with economic exploitation, are seen as inherent aspects of empire. The other type encompasses the great military and absolutist land empires, which run through world history from Alexander the Great to ancient Rome and China and on through the Hapsburg and Ottoman empires to Russia and the Soviet Union.[51]

The character of the interaction between the imperial state and the peripheral societies varies across empires—ranging from direct to indirect rule. As Motyl notes: "Direct rule means that representatives of the imperial center govern colonial peripheries. Indirect rule means that native administrators under the control of the center govern the colonial peripheries."[52] Direct—or formal—control involves rule over exclusively held colonies, annexed territories, and other sorts of non-sovereign peripheral units. Indirect—or informal—control involves looser arrangements of rule. These informal imperial systems can be organized around commercial domination by the core but backed by local elites who profit and support these exclusive ties. In other cases, informal imperial systems take the form of military protectorates, where the imperial core provides security for a local elite in exchange for allegiance and support. What emerge in these alternative forms of imperial control are differences in the way power is exercised and compliance is secured by the imperial state. In direct forms of rule, force and authority are wielded by proconsuls and colonial administrators. In indirect forms of rule, compliance is achieved through the assistance of peripheral elites and other intermediaries.

---

[51] Dominic Lieven, *Empire: The Russian Empire and Its Rivals* (New Haven, CT: Yale University Press, 2001). On maritime and colonial empires, see Doyle, *Empires*. On the great land empires, see S. M. Eisenstadt, *The Political Science of Empires* (London: Transaction Books, 1992).

[52] Motyl, "Is Everything Empire?" 234.

Empire, in these various forms, can be contrasted with liberal hegemony. Liberal hegemony, as the term is used here, refers to rule and regime-based order created by a leading state. Like empire, it is a form of hierarchical order—but, in contrast, it is infused with liberal characteristics. Weaker and secondary states are formally sovereign and the extent and mechanisms of domination will tend to be looser and less formal. Hegemonic order is established and maintained by the preponderance of power by the leading state. When that power declines or passes to another state, the order will eventually break apart or at least change to reflect the interests of the newly powerful state. Hierarchical order is made stable through a combination of benefits and sanctions that the leading state provides to weaker and secondary states. But what is distinctive about hegemonic order is that it is a bargained order in which the lead state provides services and frameworks of cooperation. In return, it invites participation and compliance by weaker and secondary states. Great Britain in the nineteenth century, in its non-empire-related capacity as a champion of free trade and open navigation, and the United States after World War II are the great historical cases of liberal hegemony.

By virtue of its dominant position, the liberal hegemonic state can act in its long-term interests rather than compete over short-term gains with other states. It can identify its own national interest with the openness and stability of the larger system. The United States thus shapes and dominates the international order while guaranteeing a flow of benefits to other governments that earns their acquiescence. In contrast to empire, this negotiated order depends on agreements regarding the rules of the system between the leading state and everyone else.[53] In this way,

---

[53] This logic is explored in the literature on hegemonic stability theory. For the original statements, see Charles Kindleberger, *The World in Depression, 1929–1938* (Berkeley: University of California Press, 1973); Stephen Krasner, "State Power and the Structure of International Trade," *World Politics* 28, no. 3 (April 1976); and Robert Gilpin, *U.S. Power and the Multinational Corporation: The Political Economy of Foreign Direct Investment* (New York: Basic Books, 1975). For important statements and critiques, see Duncan Snidal, "The Limits of Hegemonic Stability Theory," *International Organization* 39, no. 4 (1985), 579–614; Arthur Stein, "The Hegemon's Dilemma: Great Britain and the United States and the International Economic Order," *International Organization* 38, no. 2 (1985), 355–86; and, more recently,

Table 2-4
Empire and Liberal Hegemony

	Empire	Liberal Hegemony
Institutional form	Rimless hub and spoke	Multilateral
Rules	Imposed	Negotiated
Compliance	Coercion	Consent
Sovereignty	Concentrated	Dispersed

the norms and institutions that have developed around American hege-mony both limit the actual coercive exercise of American power and draw other states into the management of the system.

In a liberal hegemonic order, the leading state is not simply build-ing hierarchical relations around a series of bilateral, hub-and-spoke relations. It is creating a larger order—a political and economic space within the international system—in which participating states operate.[54] In doing so, it provides a basis for weaker and secondary states to make decisions to willingly join and comply with the rules and institutions of the order. These diffuse features of order alter the incentives and oppor-tunities that states across the system face—and so they alter the nature of power and authority associated with hierarchical order. (See table 2-4.)

In particular, three institutional features of liberal hegemony distin-guish it from empire. First, the leading state sponsors and operates within a system of negotiated rules and institutions. Power disparities still give advantages to the hegemonic state, but the arbitrary and indiscriminate exercise of power is reined in. Rules and institutions can take several forms. In an imperial order, the core state enforces the rules of hierarchy while remaining unbound by those rules. In a hegemonic order, the leading state both sponsors rules and institutions of order *and* acts in accordance

Carla Norrlof, *America's Global Advantage: US Hegemony and International Cooperation* (New York: Cambridge University Press, 2010).

[54] In chapter 5, I describe this approach to order building as a milieu-oriented grand strat-egy, in which the lead state attempts to influence the actions of other states by shaping the environment or strategic setting in which they operate. A milieu-oriented grand strategy can be contrasted with a positional grand strategy, in which a leading state seeks to more directly confront, contain, or undercut a rival great power.

with them. These rules and institutions may be more or less formal, states may be more or less bound to abide by them, and the leading state may or may not have special exemptions, privileges, and differential rights within the rule-based system. What is distinctive about liberal hegemonic order is that—despite these variations—the rules and institutions are generally agreed upon by both leading and secondary states. Organized in this way, a rule-based hegemonic order provides advantages for all parties—it is, in effect, a framework of transactions and cooperation that all states can draw upon in building relationships and pursuing their interests across the international order. At the same time, the coercive character of the dominant state is reduced.

Second, in a hegemonic order, the lead state provides some array of public goods, offered in exchange for the cooperation of other states. These sorts of public goods include the provision of security and the support for an open trade regime. Because of its dominant position in the system, the hegemonic state has incentives to organize the international environment within which states operate. This is the observation made in the literature on hegemonic stability: if a state is sufficiently large, it could very well identify its own individual interests with the interests of the larger world economic and security system. Even if it is unable to "tax" other states, the hegemonic state will still be better off over the long term by providing the public goods. The hegemonic order may also be built around various "private" deals between the hegemon and weaker and secondary states. But to the extent that the leading state also supports and upholds the general stability and openness of the order, the order becomes less imperial in character.

Third, the hegemonic order provides channels and networks for reciprocal communication and influence. These liberal "voice opportunities" are manifest as informal access to the policymaking process of the hegemonic state and the intergovernmental institutions that make up the international system. These possibilities for reciprocal interaction and influence further mute the coercive features of hierarchical order. The opportunities for voice are provided in the multiple and many-layered institutional channels that connect states within the hegemonic order. The alliances offer one mechanism for communication and the multilateral institutions provide another. What these architectural features of the order do is provide a multifaceted arena for ongoing "pulling and hauling" between leading and secondary states. Even if formal decision making is not shared, the institutional connections between states provide access points for diffuse forms of collective decision making.[55]

Taken together, these organizational features of liberal hegemony are distinct from those of empire.[56] It is not simply that the rules and institutions within a liberal hegemonic order are more elaborated and consensual. It is also that the leading state itself operates within them. In an imperial order, the core state operates above the law—outside the hierarchical structures that shape and constrain weaker and peripheral units. As Steve Rosen notes: "The organizing principle of empire ... rests on the existence of an overarching power that creates and enforces the principles of hierarchy, but is not itself bound by such rules."[57] What ultimately gives a hegemonic order its liberal character is the fact that all parties are more or less situated inside a system of rules and institutions.

Imperial and liberal hegemonic orders exhibit differences in the character of authority and rule. In an empire, the rule of the imperial center is established and maintained through coercion, at least in the last instance. Rule is enforced—indirectly where possible and directly where

---

[55] See G. John Ikenberry, "America's Liberal Hegemony," *Current History* 98 (January 1999), 23–28; and Ikenberry, "Getting Hegemony Right," *National Interest* (Spring 2001), 17–24.

[56] Niall Ferguson refers to these features of liberal hegemony as "liberal empire," manifest in nineteenth-century British and twentieth-century American efforts to uphold rules and institutions and underwrite public goods by maintaining peace, ensuring freedom of the seas and skies, and managing a system of international trade and finance. But this has the effect of conflating liberal hegemonic leadership with more traditional types of empire associated with colonialism and direct imperial rule. See Ferguson, *Colossus*, 8–12.

[57] Steve Rosen, "An Empire, If You Can Keep It," *National Interest*, no. 71 (Spring 2003), 51–61.

necessary—by the imperial state. In a liberal hegemonic order, order is also established and maintained through the exercise of power by the leading state, but power is used to create a system of rule that weaker and secondary states agree to join. The power of the hegemonic state is also felt in the "carrot and stick" that it wields in efforts to create and maintain the order. Thus, in at least its ideal-typical form, the hegemonic order is based on some measure of acquiescence or consent by secondary and peripheral states. Elites in these states "buy into" the order in some fundamental normative way.[58] That is, participation in the order is seen by these elites as something that is desirable, given the array of choices that they confront. Indeed, elites in key subordinate states actively seek and participate in the creation of the liberal hegemonic order. To be sure, this may be constrained consent—and there will surely be different degrees of consent or approval that may be manifest, ranging from grudging acquiescence to outright normative embrace.[59]

The distinction between empire and liberal hegemony is often most difficult to discern at the specific point of contact between the leading state and the elite in the subordinate polity. Both imperial and hegemonic orders are built around hierarchically ordered networks of elites.[60] Informal empires rely on the compliant cooperation of local elites, whose compliance is at least partially based on benefits that they receive from agreeing to operate as they do within the imperial order. Likewise, in a liberal hegemonic system, the elites in secondary states are

[58] See G. John Ikenberry and Charles A. Kupchan, "Socialization and Hegemonic Power," *International Organization* 44, no. 3 (Summer 1990), 283–315.

[59] For discussions of varieties of consent, see Michael Mann, "The Social Cohesion of Liberal Democracy," *American Journal of Sociology* 35, no. 3 (June 1970), 423–39. Danielle Allen proposes a continuum that ranges from assent (actual affirmation) to acquiescence (agrees quietly but without inward affirmation) to submission (one gives into a stronger power but maintains some resistence) to domination (consistently forced over time into submission through surveillance and or punishment). (Private correspondence with author, October 2007.). In effect, the forms of power exercised by a leading state in creating and enforcing order can run along a continuum from persuasion to rewards to punishment to the use of force. The mix of coercion and consent varies accordingly.

[60] For a discussion of these alternative forms of intersocietal hierarchical networks, see Nexon and Wright, "What's at Stake."

crucial sources of support for the overall order. The hegemonic system operates through the willing participation of these elites who agree to do so in part because of the benefits that accrue to their states through the hegemonic provisioning of public goods but also because of the specific benefits that flow directly to them—the elites and the wider polity—as clients of the hegemonic state. Liberal hegemonic order is built on rules and institutions but also on bargains that are struck bilaterally between superordinate and subordinate states. The ways in which these bargains and the wider array of rules and institutions are constructed shape the degree to which hierarchical orders are ultimately imperial or liberal in character.

Conclusion

International order is built on a multilayered foundation. The distribution of power provides the setting for order building. It determines which states will dominate and which will not. An international system in which power is decentralized among many states offers different challenges for order building than one in which power is concentrated in the hands of one or two states. The problem of order is different in a multipolar system than it is in a unipolar one. At the same time, the polarity of a system refers only to the distribution of material assets among actors. It is not a depiction of the political order that is organized on top of these distributed material capabilities. The distribution of power creates opportunities and constraints for states. It does not determine, by itself, the character of international order.

International order can be manifest in various ways. This chapter has focused on the three major logics or mechanisms by which order is established and maintained: balance, command, and consent. These notions of order are rooted in both theory and history. Each offers a specific set of assumptions and expectations about how relations among states are organized. Each offers a general account of the rise and fall of international order over the centuries. The aftermath of major wars have often provided "order moments" for the global system. At these junctures, great powers have endeavored to establish rules and arrangements for stable intestate relations. And in changing ways over the centuries, these three logics of order have variously informed the principles and practice by which states have engaged in order building.

All three logics of order are relevant to understanding American-led postwar order. The United States has been in the vanguard of liberal order building in the twentieth century. But these efforts have unfolded alongside postwar settlements in which the great powers have negotiated and adapted principles of restraint and accommodation. The Westphalian state system—and its evolved principles and practices—provides the foundation for efforts at building liberal international order. At the same time, the American-led order is deeply hierarchical in character. The United States undertook postwar order building when its power overshadowed the other major states, within the West and beyond. In terms of the prevailing power disparities, the postwar order was, in a sense, doomed to be hierarchical. But it was a hierarchical order infused with liberal characteristics. The theoretical challenge is to understand the changing ways in which balance, command, and consent have operated within and across the political landscape of this expansive order.

This chapter has identified variations in types of hierarchical orders. Hierarchical orders can be established and maintained by coercive domination or through consent. Hierarchies can grow out of economic exchange that create specialization and core-periphery forms of interdependence. They can be built simply on disparities of power capabilities or on more elaborate forms of institutionalized rule—either imposed or negotiated. Out of these dimensions, we can distinguish between imperial and liberal forms of hierarchy. Imperial-oriented hierarchy exists when the dominant state imposes order and establishes its rule, in the final instance, through coercion. Liberal-oriented hierarchy is international order in which the dominant state builds and operates within more or less agreed-upon rules and institutions. The dominant state provides public goods and opens itself up to reciprocal political processes of consultation and negotiation. Along a continuum between these ideal types, hierarchical orders can be arrayed.

Equipped with these concepts and distinctions, we are now in a position to look more closely at the circumstances that lead powerful states to build hierarchy around imperial and liberal logics. What are the incentives that dominant states have to sponsor and operate within an agreed-upon system of rules and institutions? And how do shifts in power and strategic interests alter imperial and liberal logics?

Three
Power and Strategies of Rule

In various eras, powerful states have risen up and shaped the rules and institutions of the global system. They have sought to use their power advantages to alter the international environment to accord with their interests. In doing so, they have—in one way or another—created international order. In the previous chapter, I explored the varieties of international order, and I distinguished between two types of hierarchical orders: empire and liberal hegemony. But the question remains: when do dominant states seek to construct one type of order or the other? This is a question about the logic and instruments of domination. How and to what extent do powerful states, in building international order, turn power into legitimate domination? What are the choices and circumstances that lead powerful states to engage in imperial or liberal order building? Most importantly, when and to what extent do powerful states have incentives to create and operate within a system of agreed-upon multilateral rules and institutions? It is the strategic decision to do so—or not—that ultimately determines whether the resulting international order is imperial or liberal.

As an international-order builder, the United States has been ambivalent about international rules and institutions. In the decade after World War II, the United States was the leading architect and champion of global multilateral governance. It led the way in an unprecedented burst of global institution building—establishing the United Nations, IMF, World Bank, NATO, and an array of other institutions and regimes. The United States pursued a "milieu" strategy of order building, attempting to shape the setting in which other states operated. But the United States has also been deeply reluctant—today and at various moments in the past—to sponsor and participate in international agreements in areas as diverse as security, arms control, human rights, and the environment. So it is necessary to explore the trade-offs and incentives that states like the United States face in building and operating within rule-based international order.

This chapter unfolds in four steps. First, I explore the ways in which dominant states shape their international environment; that is, their strategies of rule. Powerful states have a variety of tools with which to build and manage international order. The two most salient mechanisms for establishing hegemonic order are "rule through rules" and "rule through relationships." The first entails the provisioning of multilateral agreements that specify the rules and institutions through which states are expected to operate. These rules and institutions can be more or less formal, encompassing, and binding. The second entails the forging of bilateral relationships between the lead state and weaker and secondary states. These client-state relationships or "special relationships" involve bargains and agreements in which the leading state offers benefits or services—such as security protection and market access—in exchange for political support and cooperation within the wider international system.

Second, I make a set of claims about why and how states use international rules and institutions—and in doing so, I offer a political-control explanation for institutions. Rules and institutions are mechanisms that allow states to assert some control over their environment by making more predictable the policy actions of other states. In committing to operate within a framework of rules, a state is agreeing to circumscribe its policy autonomy or freedom of action—in various ways and degrees—so as to induce other states to do the same. A state bargains away some of its policy autonomy to get other states to operate in more predictable and desirable ways, all of it made credible through institutionalized agreements. The shifting incentives, choices, and circumstances surrounding this institutional bargain help explain variations in state commitments to rules and institutions.

Third, I argue that this same logic applies to powerful states, such as the United States. Indeed, a dominant—or hegemonic—state has a complex array of incentives to use rules and institutions to shape its environment, including to reduce its enforcement costs, foster legitimacy, and institutionalize a favorable international order for the long term. A leading state should want to establish a favorable set of rules and institutions that shape and constrain the policies of other states. To do so is to create a more stable and predictable environment in which it can pursue its interests. And it reduces the necessity of exercising power to enforce the terms of order. If these rules and institutions are mutually agreeable, the order itself becomes more legitimate, reducing the costs of enforcing order. Moreover, if the rules and institutions are deeply embedded in wider systems of politics and economics, the order itself is made more durable and can last even into the future when the power of the hegemonic state declines. So rules and institutions are not the enemy of powerful states— but there are costs and trade-offs associated with rule through rules, and the incentives for pursuing rule-based order will vary accordingly.

Fourth, I explore the incentives and trade offs relating to various tools of hegemonic rule. The incentives that powerful states have to build and operate within a rule-based order are not absolute. Such states also have opportunities to shape their environment without making international or rule-based commitments. They can avoid and work around rules and institutions. They can act unilaterally outside of institutionalized relationships or strike bargains directly with individual states. Critical to a hegemonic state's choice between these alternatives is the value it attaches to the efficiency and legitimacy of its "rule" over the international order—and its assessment of its future power position.

Overall, this perspective allows us to appreciate the logic of variations in the type of order that a leading state seeks to build. The United States has used a variety of strategies of rule during the postwar era. Relations with Western Europe were based in important ways on rule-based, multilateral agreements, while in East Asia the United States relied primarily on bilateral, clientelistic relationships. In Latin America and the Middle East, the United States was more willing to fall back on traditional imperial tools of control. The logic of when a leading state resorts to one type or another of these strategies is tied to its incentives to exchange reductions in its own policy autonomy for institutional forms of cooperation. The United States wanted a great deal from Europe in the postwar decades, and it was willing to tie itself to these states through a variety of multilateral economic and security agreements. In East Asia, the United States wanted less from its partners and was less willing to restrict its own policy independence. The character of hierarchical order follows from how states—leading and secondary—respond to these incentives and trade-offs associated with rule through rules and rule through relationships.

Order Building and Strategies of Rule

Only rarely are states in a position to shape the basic terms of international order. Great powers typically find themselves operating within an established international order. But on occasion, moments arrive when a leading state finds itself with sufficient power and opportunity to decisively shape the terms of global order. When such moments arrive, these leading states face choices about how to organize the rules and institutions of the system. Either alone or with other states, either through imposition or negotiation—such states are in a position to establish the governing arrangements of the international system. In doing so, they engage in international order building. But what sorts of order might these states seek to build?

In chapter 2, we distinguished between two ideal types of hierarchical order—imperial and liberal hegemonic. These types of order differ in terms of the ways that superordinate power is exercised and authority is established. Each ideal-typical order is organized around a mode of rule or governance. In imperial order, rules are imposed and compliance is ultimately enforced through coercive uses of power. Imperial rule is manifest through coercive domination. At the extreme, this is rule in which the dominant state directly occupies and commands the subordinate state—and indeed the subordinate state is no longer truly a state as such. Sovereign authority is effectively in the hands of the dominant state. The occupied or dominated polity has no independent foreign policy or direct diplomatic relations with other states. This form of rule is most clearly seen in postwar occupations and colonial-style imperialism.

In a liberal hegemonic order, rules are negotiated and compliance is ultimately based on consent. Liberal hegemonic rule is based on bargained and rule-based relations. Weaker and secondary states have voice opportunities, and their agreement to operate within the order is based on the willingness of the dominant state to restrain and commit its power and lead in the provision of public goods. In its most developed form, a liberal hegemonic order is based on the rule of law. Both the dominant and subordinate states operate within a multilateral set of rules that effectively eliminate coercive rule. This is the closest an international order might come to "constitutional" rule—governance through the rule of law rather than the rule of power.[1] No state is above the law. Hierarchy may still exist to the extent to which the rules and institutions provide special rights and exemptions to the leading state. Nonetheless, political authority within the order flows from its legal-constitutional foundation rather than from power capabilities.[2] In this situation, hegemony is manifest essentially as rule-based leadership.

---

[1] On constitutional order in international relations, see G. John Ikenberry, "Constitutional Politics in International Relations," *European Journal of International Relations* 4, no. 2 (1998), 147–77; and Ikenberry, *After Victory*, chap. 2.

[2] This is dominance based on the perceived legitimacy of the rules and institutions that structure the exercise of power. In effect, a hegemonic order organized around the rule of law is, as Max Weber described legal-rational authority, "domination by virtue of 'legality,' by virtue of the belief in the validity of legal statute and functional 'competence' based on rationally created *rules.*" Weber, "Politics as a Vocation," in H. H. Gerth and C. Wright Mills, eds., *From Max Weber: Essays in Sociology* (New York: Oxford University Press, 1958), 79.

Imperial and hegemonic orders in the real world tend to exist well within these two extremes. Imperial orders are rarely based entirely on coercive domination, and liberal hegemonic rule—at least as it is manifest in America's postwar order—is only partially built around multilateral rules and institutions. Imperial and liberal hegemonic states pursue a mix of rulership strategies, and the orders they create also display a mixture of hierarchical governance arrangements and power relations. We can describe the two most basic strategies of rule as rule through rules and rule through relationships.

Rule through rules is the dominant governance strategy of liberal hegemony. Power is exercised through sponsorship of rules and institutions. Rule-based relations are built around multilateral rules and institutions that set out the terms on which relations among a group of states are to operate. Thus, there are several aspects to rule-based relations. One is that it entails the coordination of relations among a group of states, and as such it can be contrasted with bilateral, hub-and-spoke, and imperial arrangements. Second, the terms of a given relationship are defined by agreed-upon rules and principles—and sometimes institutions—so rule-based relations can be contrasted with interaction based on ad hoc bargaining or straightforward power politics. Third, rule-based relations entail some reduction in policy autonomy, since the choices and actions of the participating states are—at least to some degree—constrained by the agreed-upon rules and principles.[3]

As we discuss later in this chapter, building order around rule-based relations can be an attractive strategy of rule for a dominant state. If the rules can be established widely—spread across many states and regions and covering an array of policy realms—it can be an efficient mechanism for ensuring a stable and congenial environment for the leading state to

---

[3] See G. John Ikenberry, "Is American Multilateralism in Decline?" *Perspectives on Politics* 1, no. 3 (September 2003), 533–50. This definition of rule-based relations draws on discussions of the organizational logic of multilateralism, including John G. Ruggie, "Multilateralism: The Anatomy of an Institution," in Ruggie, ed., *Multilateralism Matters: The Theory and Praxis of an Institutional Form* (New York: Columbia University Press, 1993), 3–47; and essays in Stephen Krasner, ed., *International Regimes* (Ithaca, NY: Cornell University Press, 1983).

Table 3-1
Leading States and Strategies of Rule

	Institutional form	Variations
Rule by relationship	Colonial rule Neocolonial rule Client-state relationship "Special relationship"	Defined by power asymmetries, relations of sovereignty, and terms of exchange
Rule by rules	Imposed rules Differential rules Loose multilateralism Legal binding rules	Defined by degree to which they are mutually agreed upon and applied and the degree to which they are binding

pursue its interests. Control is not directly maintained through the exercise of power; it is embedded in the rules and institutions themselves.[4]

These rule-based relationships can take different forms—variations defined in terms of the degree to which the rules are mutually agreed upon and applied and the degree to which they place binding constraints

---

[4] This is the paradox of power: a powerful state can increase its influence and ability to shape outcomes in the international system by voluntarily restraining and institutionalizing its power, at least to some extent. Power and rules are not opposites but work together in complex and reinforcing ways. This paradox is a major theme in the study of power within societies. As many scholars have noted, the rise of modern Western states—and the strengthening of their position relative to social groups and classes—involved gradual steps by absolutist rulers to delimit the powers of the state and embed its authority within legal and political institutions. Institutionalizing state power within constitutional structures had the effect of making state power more authoritative, lasting, and plenary within society. On the ways in which state builders in early modern Europe supported the promulgation of legal and political institutions to facilitate the establishment of stable rule, capitalist markets, extraction of revenue, and the deployment of government authority, see Jean Baechler, *Origins of Capitalism* (Oxford: Blackwell, 1975 [1971]); Ernest Gellner, *Nations and Nationalism* (Ithaca, NY: Cornell University Press, 1983); Douglass C. North and Robert P. Thomas, *The Rise of the Western World: A New Economic History* (New York: Cambridge University Press, 1973); and John A. Hall, *Powers and Liberties: The Causes and Consequences of the Rise of the West* (Oxford: Basil Blackwell, 1985). For an exploration of why "powerful political actors" variously resist and embrace the rule of law, see Stephen Holmes, "Lineages of the Rule of Law," in Jose Maria Maravall and Adam Przeworski, eds., *Democracy and the Rule of Law* (Cambridge: Cambridge University Press, 2003). In this sense, domestic and international realms are not, as structural realist theory suggests, fundamentally different. Institutions matter in the international realm just as power matters in the domestic realm.

on the states involved. At one extreme, a dominant state can impose rules on weaker states but remain unconstrained itself. This is, in effect, the imperial use of rules. Alternatively, the rules could be mutually agreed upon and apply to both the leading state and other states but provide differential rights and obligations based on power position. The dominant state or the great powers might operate under a different set of rules—conveying rights and authority—that other states do not possess. At the other extreme, the rules could be mutually agreed upon and apply equally to all states regardless of their power or position within the system.

Regardless of whether rules are differentially applied or not, the rules themselves can be more or less binding. In their loosest form, rule-based relations can simply entail general consultations and informal adjustment among states. The diplomatic practices of the Concert of Europe were of this sort—where the great powers observed a set of unwritten rules and norms about the balance of power on the continent. In the current era, the World Trade Organization and other multilateral economic institutions entail more formal, treaty-based agreements that specify certain commitments and obligations. But the binding character of these multilateral agreements is still qualified: escape clauses, weighted voting, opt-out agreements, and veto rights are all part of the major post-1945 multilateral agreements. The most binding rule-based agreements are ones where states actually cede sovereignty in specific areas to supranational authorities. The European Union is the most important manifestation of this sovereignty-transferring, legally binding rule-based form of rule.[5]

Rule through relationships entails establishing order by building a series of bilateral arrangements with weaker and secondary states. In each case, power relations are manifest in specific ongoing bargains, exchanges, and instrumental agreements that are established between

---

[5] See Judith L. Goldstein, Miles Kahler, Robert O. Keohane, and Anne-Marie Slaughter, eds., *Legalization and World Politics* (Cambridge: MIT Press, 2001). For rationalist explanations for variation in the form of institutions, see Lisa Martin, "Interests, Power, and Multilateralism," *International Organization* 46, no. 4 (Autumn 1992), 765–92; and James Morrow, "The Forms of International Cooperation," *International Organization* 48, no. 30 (Summer 1994), 387–423.

the dominant state and elites in subordinate states. The resulting order takes the form of a hub-and-spoke system in which a hierarchical array of states are connected to the lead state in separate and distinct relationships, variously unequal, reciprocal, and dependent. The order is not organized around agreed-upon multilateral rules but around a constellation of bilateral relations that together form a system of client states and political dependencies.[6]

In the broadest sense, this sort of strategy of rule involves building interstate patron-client relationships. According to James Scott, the patron and the client form an "instrumental friendship in which an individual of higher socioeconomic state (patron) uses his own influence and resources to provide protection and benefits, or both, for a person of lower status (client) who, for his part, reciprocates by offering general support and assistance, including personal services, to the patron."[7] Various terms have been used to describe these sorts of clientelistic relations—patronage, machine politics, brokerage systems. What they have in common, as Gianfranco Poggi argues, is an exchange between unequal and hierarchically organized actors; a situation where the power wielders exchange the provision of "favor and protection" and receive "allegiance and support" in return.[8] As manifest in international relations, the leading state provides protections and benefits—such as economic aid, market access, and military assistance—in exchange for cooperation and political support.[9]

---

[6] As such, rule through relationships and rule through rules offer distinct and alternative logics of governance. The ideal-typical order built on rule through rules is one where states are sovereign and equal under the law. The ideal-typical order built on rule through relationships is one where states are differentially arrayed around the dominant state—a hub-and-spoke system in which the bilateral relationships are defined by the gradient of power asymmetry and the specific bargain and exchanges that result.

[7] James Scott, "Patron-Client Politics and Political Change in Southeast Asia," *American Political Science Review* 66 (1972), 1142–58. For other discussions of clientelism and patronage politics, see S. N. Eisenstadt and Rene Lemarchand, eds., *Political Clientelism, Patronage, and Development (Beverly Hills, CA: Sage, 1981)*.

[8] Gianfranco Poggi, "Clientelism," *Political Studies* 31 (1983), 663.

[9] See Christopher P. Carney, "International Patron-Client Relationships: A Conceptual Framework," *Studies in Comparative International Development* 24, no. 2 (Summer 1989), 42–55.

These bilateral relationships fall along a continuum defined in terms of the degree of domination as it is reflected in power inequalities, the relations of sovereignty, and terms of exchange. As such, these bilateral ties can range from colonial and neocolonial relationships to more reciprocal and bargained partnerships.[10] Colonial rule is the most direct form of control by the leading state. Domination is nearly complete—a situation where sovereignty in the subordinate state is effectively usurped by the dominant state and coercive enforcement of rule lurks in the background. The governing elites in the subordinate polity are directly under the political and administrative command of the dominant state. As a result, the terms of exchange are essentially one-sided, and subordinate elites are in a highly dependent and nonnegotiable relationship. Neocolonial relations entail a more indirect form of rule in which local elites exercise authority within their own political system but remain directly tied to and dependent on the dominant state.[11] Local elites are co-opted into playing a supporting role within the larger hierarchical political-economic order and rewarded with economic benefits and security protection. In both colonial and neocolonial relations, the coercive enforcement of rule by the dominant state lurks in the background, circumscribing sovereignty and the limits of political choice within the subordinate state.[12]

A dominant state may also build bilateral relations with less weak and dependent states, based on more explicit and reciprocal exchanges

[10] For a discussion of dependency and bargaining models of relations between weak states and strong states, see Bruce E. Moon, "The Foreign Policy of the Dependent State," *International Studies Quarterly* 27 (1983), 315–40.

[11] The term "comprador" is sometimes used to denote this indirect form of dominance. It originally referred to a member of the Chinese merchant class who aided Western traders beginning in the late eighteenth century. These local agents were hired by contract and were responsible for a Chinese staff that facilitated trade and exchange. The term now is used in reference to individuals who aid Western economic trade and investment—and exploitation—in the developing world.

[12] These forms of hierarchical rule are captured in a rich literature on neocolonialism and dependency relations in the developing world. See, e.g., Fernando Henrique Cardoso and Enzo Faletto, *Dependency and Development in Latin America* (Berkeley: University of California Press, 1979); and Jorge Larrain, *Theories of Development: Capitalism, Colonialism, and Dependency* (London: Polity, 1991).

and bargains. The client state retains greater sovereign authority and the terms of exchange are less unequal. Typically, the dominant state forges patron-client relations as part of its larger regional or global political-security goals. The client state is one of an array of junior partners that anchor and support the leading state's global and regional position. The client state ties its own political and economic fortunes to those of the lead state, and in return it receives economic benefits and security. The exchange between the patron and client can vary. As one study indicates: "In the international context, the patron can offer military and intelligence protection. It can offer material aid or crisis insurance in the form of a reliable response when the client is threatened with loss of income, unexpected costs, or its own survival. It can offer brokerage with the outside world, including financial and political institutions as well as multinational banks and businesses. The goods and services offered by the client-state may include investment opportunities, raw materials, exports, military bases and services that support the patron's regional interests, votes in international fora, and other expressions of loyalty."[13]

During the Cold War, the United States developed a wide array of client-state ties with regimes in the Middle East, Asia, Latin America, and Africa. The ties were often established with specific leaders—the shah of Iran, Ferdinand Marcos of Philippines, and the Somoza family of Nicaragua. Many Cold War–era client-state relationships were pursued by the United States as part of its efforts to build a global anticommunist alliance system—and the bargains and exchanges often included security guarantees and the presence of forward-deployed bases. The United States would offer economic assistance and market access to its junior partners, and in return these client states would host military bases and support the American-led international order.[14]

---

[13] Osita G. Afoaku, "U.S. foreign policy and authoritarian regimes: Change and continuity in international clientelism," *Journal of Third World Studies* 17, no. 2 (Fall 2000), 13–40.

[14] On American client states, see David Sylvan and Stephen Majeski, *U.S. Foreign Policy in Perspective: Clients, Enemies, and Empire* (New York: Routledge, 2009); and Odd Arne Westad, *The Global Cold War: Third World Interventions and the Makings of Our Times* (New York: Cambridge University Press, 2007).

In some instances, these bilateral, clientelist ties are elevated to "special relationships." America's relations with Great Britain and Japan are often described in these terms. These are still bilateral ties between unequal states—and patron-client bargains and exchanges still exist. But the ties are given more status equality and the relationships are seen as more genuine partnerships between major states that together occupy leading positions within the larger international hierarchy.[15] In special relationships, the junior partner is understood to have privileged access to the dominant state and its foreign policy decision making. Reciprocity, consultation, partnership, and status equality—these are the norms and expectations of special relationships, and they distinguish these sorts of bilateral relationships from the more traditional patron-client arrangements.

Rule through rules and rule through relationships are based on distinct and divergent logics of order. Both are strategies that a dominant state can use in efforts to assert control over the international environment. But they lead logically to very different sorts of orders. One is an order built around agreed-upon rules and multilateral governance. The other is a hub-and-spoke order in which the dominant state asserts more direct control over other states. One is open and inclusive—states participate on the basis of consensual multilateral rules that diminish the role of the arbitrary and discriminatory exercise of power. The other is a system in which power asymmetries are translated into an array of hierarchically organized bilateral relations and political dependencies.[16]

A leading state can pursue both these sorts of strategies, and indeed the postwar international order bears the marks of both these logics of rule. The United States pursued both rule-based and client-based strategies in the 1940s. Toward Western Europe, the United States pursued

[15] On special relationships, see John Drumbell and Axel Schafer, eds., *America's Special Relationships: Allies and Clients* (New York: Routledge, 2009). On America's special ties with Great Britain, see Duncan Andrew Campbell, *Unlikely Allies: Britain, America, and the Victorian Beginnings of the Special Relationship* (London: Hambledon and London, 2008); and Ferguson, *Colossus*, 216–17.

[16] For a discussion of these alternatives logics, see John Gerard Ruggie, "Multilateralism: The Anatomy of an Institution," in Ruggie, ed., *Multilateralism Matters*, 3–47.

primarily a strategy of rule through rules—working closely with post-war European states in building multilateral economic rules and insti-tutions and agreeing ultimately to multilateral security cooperation. In East Asia, the United States pursued a series of bilateral security pacts, creating a hub-and-spoke system of security cooperation.[17] Out-side of these two regions, the United States established a wide variety of patron-client relationships—in many instances, old-style imperial domination.[18]

Although these strategies offer alternative logics of rule, they also can work together within an international order. Client-based relations between a dominant state and weaker secondary states can provide ways for the dominant state to signal restraint and commitment and chan-nel payments and rewards for cooperation within the wider rule-based international order. Overall, it is the mix of these types of rule that give the international order its imperial or liberal character. We can look more closely at the logic of rule by rules and the limits and trade-offs that a dominant state faces in pursuing strategies of rule.

States and International Rules and Institutions

Why do states—to the extent they do—organize international relations around multilateral rules and institutions? The answer is that institu-tional agreements help states create a predictable and cost-effective environment in which to pursue their interests. In effect, international rules and institutions are potentially useful to states as tools of political control. Their basic value to states is that they affect the levels of state autonomy and political certainty. Rules and institutions alter the envi-ronment in which states operate.

[17] See Galia Press-Barnathan, *Organizing the World: The United States and Regional Coop-eration in Asia and Europe* (New York: Routledge, 2003).

[18] On the creation of America's informal empire of hub-and-spoke client states in the Mid-dle East, see Marc J. O'Reilly and Wesley B. Renfro, "Evolving Empire: America's 'Emirates' Strategy in the Persian Gulf," *International Studies Perspective* 8, no. 2 (May 2007), 137–51.

There are two ways in which institutions act as tools of political control. One is that they help solve collective-action problems by reducing the commitment uncertainties and transaction costs that stand in the way of efficient and mutually beneficial political exchange.[19] In these instances, states are using rules and institutions to reduce the uncertainty about the reliability and intentions of other states, thus overcoming fears of cheating or bad faith. Institutions provide a bundle of functions that make it easier for states to work together for mutual advantage. The institutions facilitate the flow of reliable information that reduces obstacles to transactions that advance the interests of the participating states. The institutions help states assess the reputations of other states by providing benchmarks and standards of behavior against which actual policies of other states can be judged. Likewise, the ongoing presence of the rules and institutions provides a framework for a flow of bargaining and exchange. Institutions provide a forum within which states can obtain evaluative information about other states. In effect, they provide a reliable architecture for cooperation that would be harder to achieve without the rules and institutions. Institutional mechanisms and pathways are put in place for states to conduct mutually beneficial transactions and cooperation.[20]

In a second way, rules and institutions can also be used as more direct instruments of political control. As Terry Moe argues, "political institutions are also weapons of coercion and redistribution. They are the structural means by which political winners pursue their own interests, often at the expense of political losers."[21] A winning political party in Con-

[19] The classic statement of this functional view of institutions is Keohane, *After Hegemony*. For arguments that institutions help states cope with situations of uncertainty, see Barbara Koremenos, "Contracting Around International Uncertainty," *American Political Science Review* 99 (November 2005), 549–65; and Peter Rosendorff and Helen Milner, "The Optimal Design of International Trade Institutions: Uncertainty and Escape," *International Organization* 55, no. 3 (Autumn 2001), 829–58.

[20] For useful summaries of this approach to institutions, see Andreas Hasenclever, Peter Mayer, and Volker Rittberger, *Theories of International Relations* (Cambridge: Cambridge University Press, 1989), chap. 3; and Lisa L. Martin and Beth Simmons, "Theories and Empirical Studies of International Institutions," *International Organization* 52, no. 4 (Autumn 1998), 89–117.

[21] Terry M. Moe, "Political Institutions: The Neglected Side of the Story," *Journal of Law, Economics, and Organization* 6 (Special Issue 1990), 213.

gress will try to write the committee voting rules to favor its interests. Similarly, in international relations, a powerful state will want to make its advantages as systematic and durable as possible by roping weaker states into favorable institutional arrangements.[22] In these instances, states that momentarily have opportunities because of their power to set the rules do so and thereby shape and constrain the options and choices of weaker secondary states. A powerful state may have a variety of advantages that allow it to shape the terms of rules and institutions—it may have won a war, or it may possess the largest and most productive economy. As such, it has opportunities to set down the rules and institutions. Other states—those outside the "enacting coalition"—are faced with the choice of either not participating in the institution and losing all benefits from cooperation or participating on terms that they would not otherwise choose.[23] The advantages that a leading state has can vary—and so, too, will the degree to which its promulgation of rules and institutions is imposed or results from bargaining. In these situations, rules and institutions are used not to promote efficiency and cooperation, as such, but to shape and constrain the policies of other states.

Both these theoretical views about the uses of institutions hinge on the role that institutions play in shaping and constraining the choices and policies of states. States are, in effect, seeking to use institutional agreements to limit and make more predictable the behavior of other states. In the first instance, the rules and institutions are used to alleviate worries about cheating and free riding. The institutional agreement provides a variety of functions that increase information that facilitates cooperation. In the second instance, the effort is to lock other states into patterns of behavior that give the most powerful state ongoing advantages. The goal of the leading state is to translate momentary power

[22] The notion that institutions can be used by states as mechanisms of political control starts with the neo-institutional view of the causal mechanisms at work. That is, institutions shape and constrain state behavior by providing value in terms of commitment and reduction of uncertainty or transaction costs. Political control is exerted through the manipulation of these causal mechanisms, which alter the distribution of gains from institutional agreements.

[23] This argument is developed in Lloyd Gruber, *Ruling the World: Power Politics and the Rise of Supranational Institutions* (Princeton, NJ: Princeton University Press, 2000).

disparities into a durable flow of benefits. But in both cases, the reason that states seek institutional agreement is to reduce the uncertainty of the policy choices of other states. States are seeking to make the ongoing policy actions of other states more predictable and, by doing so, to create a more certain and congenial environment with which to pursue its security and interests.[24]

Cast in this light, states can be seen as engaged in an ongoing effort to use institutional agreements to shape and restrict the range of policy actions of other states. The aim is to reduce the policy autonomy of other states.[25] In return, states use commitments to reduce their own policy autonomy as incentives to get other states to work within a set of rules and institutions that in fact limits their policy autonomy. When a state makes an institutional commitment, it is agreeing to reduce its policy autonomy. Ideally, a state might want to remain unencumbered by international rules and institutional commitments, while operating in a global system in which all other states are bound to rules and institutions. But in order to get other states to make institutional commitments, states need to negotiate and offer restrictions on their own policies so as to achieve agreement.[26]

[24] For a debate on the role and limits of international institutions, see Randall L. Schweller, "The Problem of International Order Revisited: A Review Essay," *International Security* 26, no. 1 (Summer 2001), 161–86; and correspondence by Robert Jervis, Henry R. Nau, and Schweller, "Institutionalized Disagreement," *International Security* 27, no. 1 (Summer 2002), 174–85.

[25] In making binding international agreements, a state is reducing its freedom of action—and in this sense, such agreements are costly to states. Abbott and Snidal describe this reduction of policy autonomy as "sovereignty costs," noting that the "costs involved can range from simple differences in outcome on particular issues, to loss of authority over decision making in an issue-area, to more fundamental encroachments on state sovereignty." Kenneth Abbott and Duncan Snidal, "Hard and Soft Law in International Governance," in Goldstein et al., *Legalization and World Politics*, 52.

[26] The classic statement of the strategic use of commitment, in which states seek to "constrain the other's choices by affecting his expectations," is Thomas Schelling, *Strategy of Conflict* (Cambridge, MA: Harvard University Press, 1960), quotation at p. 122. Schelling has recently restated the basic insight: "Commitment is central to promises and threats, to bargaining and negotiations, to deterrence and arms control, to contractual relations. I emphasize the paradox of commitment—to a relationship, to a promise or a threat, to a negotiating position—entails relinquishing some options, giving up choices, surrendering opportunities,

Thus, when deciding whether to sign a multilateral agreement, a state faces a trade-off. In agreeing to abide by the rules and norms of the agreement, the state must accept some constraints on its freedom of action—or independence of policymaking—in a particular area. But in exchange it expects to get other states to do the same. The multilateral bargain will be attractive to a state if it concludes that the benefits that flow to it through the coordination of policies achieved through rule-based constraints on policy choice are greater than the costs of lost policy autonomy.

A state's willingness to agree to a multilateral bargain will hinge on several factors that shape the ultimate cost-benefit calculation. One is whether the policy constraints imposed on other states (states B, C, D) by the multilateral agreement really matter to the first state (state A). If the unconstrained behavior of other states is judged to have no undesirable impact on state A, state A will be unwilling to give up any policy autonomy of its own. It also matters if the participating states are actually able to credibly restrict their policy autonomy. If state A is doubtful that states B, C, and D can actually be constrained by multilateral rules and institutional agreements, it will be unwilling to sacrifice its own policy autonomy. Likewise, state A will need to convince the other states that it, too, will be constrained. These factors are all continuous rather than dichotomous variables—so states must make judgments about the degree of credibility and the relative value of constrained policies.

When multilateral bargains are made by states with highly unequal power, the considerations can be more complex. The more a powerful state is capable of dominating or abandoning weaker states, the more the weaker states will care about constraints on the leading state's policy autonomy. This is another way of saying that they will be more eager to see some limits and restraints placed on the arbitrary and indiscriminate exercise of power by the leading state. Similarly, the more the powerful state can actually restrain itself in a credible fashion, the more the weaker

---

binding oneself. And it works through shifting the expectations of some partner or adversary or even a stranger of how one will behave or react." Thomas Schelling, *Strategies of Commitment* (Cambridge, MA: Harvard University Press, 2006), vii.

states will be interested in multilateral rules and norms that accomplish this end. When both these conditions hold—when the leading state can use its unequal power to dominate and abandon weaker states and when it can restrain and commit itself—the weaker states will be particularly eager for a deal. They will, of course, also care about the positive benefits that accrue from cooperation. From the perspective of the powerful state, the less important the policy behavior of weaker states, the less the leading state will offer to limit its own policy autonomy. Likewise, the less certain the leading state is that weaker states can in fact constrain their policies, the less the leading state will offer constraints on its policy autonomy.

So the leading state is faced with a choice: how much institutional limitation of its own policy autonomy and exercise of power is worth how much policy lock-in of weaker states? Institutionalization tends to be a two-way street. A powerful state can try to embed other states in a set of rules and institutions, but it will likely need to give up some of its own discretionary power to get the desired outcome. Terry Moe notes this in regard to a ruling party's control of government institutions: "They can fashion structures to insulate their favorable agencies and programs from the future exercise of public authority. In doing so, of course, they will not only be reducing their enemies' opportunities for future control; they will be reducing their own opportunities as well. But this is often a reasonable price to pay, given the alternative. And because they get to go first, they are really not giving up control—they are choosing to exercise a greater measure of it ex ante, through insulated structures that, once locked in, predispose the agency to do the right things. What they are moving away from—because it is dangerous—is the kind of ongoing hierarchical control that is exercised through the discretionary decisions of public authority over time."[27]

Several hypotheses follow immediately from this model of state power and institutions. First, a leading state should try to lock other states into institutionalized policy orientations while trying to minimize its own limitations on policy autonomy and discretionary power. This is the story

[27] Moe, "Political Institutions," 227–28.

that Michael Crozier tells about politics within large-scale organizations. Each individual within a complex organizational hierarchy is continually engaged in a dual struggle: to tie his colleagues to precise rule-based behavior—thereby creating a more stable and certain environment in which to operate—while also trying to retain as much autonomy and discretion as possible for himself.[28] Similarly, leading states will try to lock in other states as much as possible while also trying to remain as unencumbered as possible by institutional rules and obligations. Second, the leading state will make use of its ability—to the extent the ability exists—to limit its capacity to exercise power in indiscriminate and arbitrary ways as a "currency" to buy the institutional cooperation of other states.

The availability of the institutional bargain will depend on several circumstances that can also be specified as hypotheses. First, the amount of "currency" available to the leading state to buy the institutional cooperation of weaker states is determined by two factors: the ability of the leading state to potentially dominate or injure the interests of weaker states and its ability to credibly restrain itself from doing so. Although all states might offer to restrain and commit themselves in exchange for concessions by other states, the willingness and ability of powerful states to do so will be of particular interest to other states. Chad may offer to lock itself into an institutional agreement that lowers its policy autonomy and make its future policy orientation more predictable, but few states will care much about this offer to bind itself and they are not likely to offer much in return to get it. But if a powerful state with the capacity for serious domination and disruption offers to restrain itself, this will get the attention of other states and they are likely to be willing to offer something to get it. Moreover, it is not just the domination and disruption potential of the leading state that generates currency to buy the institutional cooperation of other states. It is also the capacity to actually make good on restraint and commitment. If a powerful state cannot credibly limit its power, its currency will amount to very little.

[28] Michael Crozier, *The Bureaucratic Phenomenon* (Chicago: University of Chicago Press, 1964).

Two other factors will also determine if the leading state—if it has the currency with which to buy institutional cooperation—will in fact want to do so. One is the degree to which the leading state is interested in locking in the policy behavior of other states. This is a question about the extent to which the actions of other states actually impinge on the interests of the leading state. For example, the security policy orientation of European states would tend to qualify as important but the domestic policy orientations of European states—and the wide range of policy orientations of other states around the world—are not significant enough to justify efforts by the leading state to lock in stable and favorable policy behavior, particularly if the price of doing so entails a reduction of policy autonomy. The other factor is simply the ability of weaker states to be locked in. The United States may want to lock in the policy behavior of other states—particularly the security policy behavior—but not have enough confidence that these institutionalized commitments and obligations can be effectively locked in.

Taken together, these considerations allow us to see how a leading state and weaker states might make trade-offs about binding themselves together through multilateral institutions. The four factors are summarized in table 3-2.

The more the leading state is capable of dominating and abandoning weaker states, the more the weaker states will care about restraints on its exercise of power—and the more they are likely to make some concessions to obtain the restraint and commitment. Similarly, the more a potentially dominating state can credibly restrain and commit itself, the more the weaker states will be interested in pursuing an institutional bargain. When both these conditions hold—when the leading state can dominate and abandon other states and when it can restrain and commit itself—that state will be particularly willing and able to pursue an institutional bargain. From the perspective of the leading state, the less important the policy behavior of weaker states is (that is, the less consequential it is) to the leading state, the less likely it is to offer restraints on its own policy autonomy to achieve policy lock-in. Likewise, the less certain the leading state is that policy lock-in of weaker states can in fact be accomplished, the less likely it is to offer restraints on its own policy autonomy.

Table 3-2
Incentives and Opportunities for Asymmetric Institutional Bargains

Variable	Implication
Domination/abandonment potential of the leading state	Weaker states more willing to make concessions to gain restraint
	Leading state has enhanced institutional bargaining advantage
Restraint/commitment potential of the leading state	Weaker states more willing to make concessions
	Leading state has enhanced institutional bargaining advantage
Lock-in importance to leading state	Leading state has greater incentive to offer restraint and commitment
Lock in potential of weaker states	Leading state has greater incentive to offer restraint and commitment

Seen in this way, the ability of the leading state to credibly restrain and commit its power is, ironically, a type of power.[29] It wants to lock other states into specific types of institutional commitments. It could use its power to coerce them, but to do so is costly and eliminates any chance of building a legitimate order. If the leading state can bind itself and institutionalize the exercise of power, at least to some credible extent, offering to do so becomes a bargaining chip it can play as a way to obtain the institutional cooperation of other states.[30] But it is only a bargaining chip when the power disparities make limits and restraints desirable to other states and when the leading state can in fact establish such limits and constraints. It is variations in these diverse enabling circumstances that explain why the United States sometimes seeks to build multilateral institutions and bind itself to other states and sometimes it does not.

These considerations are helpful in understanding America's embrace of multilateral institution building after World War II. The United States emerged as the preeminent global power after the war. It cared greatly about the fates of Western Europe and East Asia, which both hung in

[29] See the discussion by Thomas Schelling of "the power to bind oneself." Schelling, *Strategy of Conflict*, 22–28.

[30] On the notion of institutional power, see Michael Barnett and Raymond Duvall, "Power in International Politics," *International Organization* 59, no. 1 (Winter 2005), 39–75.

the economic and geopolitical balance. It was willing to tie itself to these regions through various sorts of institutional agreements—to give up policy autonomy—so as to gain some leverage on their policy orientation and trajectory of political development. At the same time, countries in these regions worried about American domination and abandonment, and so they too were willing to enter into institutional agreements that entailed long-term commitments to an American-led international order. Judith Goldstein and Joanne Gowa, for example, argue that the United States' agreement to bind itself to the GATT was necessary to encourage smaller states to make a risky move toward market liberalization.[31] The credibility of these institutional commitments was facilitated by the democratic character of the states themselves as well as other more specific steps, such as the stationing of American troops in both regions and complex sorts of institutional agreements.[32]

The logic is also helpful in explaining variations in America's institutional commitments to Western Europe and East Asia. The United States pursued a multilateral strategy in Europe—with NATO as its anchor—while in Asia it pursued a series of bilateral security agreements with Japan, Korea, and several states in Southeast Asia. The United States tied itself more tightly to Europe, embedding its power in a multilateral security order that involved extensive institutionalized restraints and commitments. Because the United States was more dominant and wanted less out of East Asia, as a practical matter, it was less necessary to give up policy autonomy in exchange for institutionalized cooperation there. In contrast, the United States had an elaborate agenda for uniting the European states, creating an institutional bulwark against communism, and supporting centrist democratic regimes. These goals could not be realized simply through the brute exercise of power. To get what it wanted,

---

[31] Judith Goldstein and Joanne Gowa, "U.S. National Power and the Post-war Trading Regime," *World Trade Review* 1 (2002), 154–70.

[32] On the ways in which the democratic character of states facilitates institutional commitments, see Lisa Martin, *Democratic Commitments: Legislatures and International Cooperation* (Princeton, NJ: Princeton University Press, 2000); and Charles Lipson, *Reliable Partners: How Democracies Have Made a Separate Peace* (Princeton, NJ: Princeton University Press, 2005).

the United States had to bargain with the Europeans, and this meant agreeing to restrain its exercise of power. In Asia, the United States did not have goals that were sufficiently important to "purchase" with an agreement to restrain its power. As Galia Press-Barnathan argues, the American military's "specific objective was to attain base rights," and as a result "there was little to gain in that respect from pooling regional resources."[33] Bilateralism was the desired strategy in Asia because multilateralism would have required more restraints on policy autonomy.

The United States had much more unchallenged hegemonic power in Asia than in Western Europe, and therefore it had fewer incentives to secure its dominant position with international institutions. As Peter Katzenstein argues, "the United States was willing to create in Europe multilateral institutions that would restrain U.S. power in the short term only to enhance that power in the long term. It was eager to build bilateral institutions in Asia, where the concept of binding institutions did not seem as attractive as locking in the advantages of the preponderance of power of the United States through bilateral relations."[34] The United States did not need to give up policy autonomy to secure its objectives in East Asia.

Other factors, of course, contributed to and reinforced these divergent American institutional strategies in Europe and Asia. Victor Cha argues that the United States was drawn to bilateral pacts in East Asia out of fears of entrapment and collusion of East Asian states.[35] Bilateral security treaties provided more direct mechanisms for restraining East Asian allies within the region. "The United States created a series of bilateral alliances in East Asia to contain the Soviet threat," observes Cha, "but a congruent rationale was to constrain anticommunist allies in the region that might engage in aggressive behavior against adversaries that could entrap the United States in an unwanted larger war."[36] Also

[33] Press-Barnathan, *Organizing the World*, 61.

[34] Peter J. Katzenstein, *A World of Regions: Asia and Europe in the American Imperium* (Ithaca, NY: Cornell University Press, 2005), 50.

[35] Victor D. Cha, "Powerplay: Origins of the U.S. Alliance System in Asia," *International Security* 34, no. 3 (Winter 2009), 158–96.

[36] Cha, "Powerplay," *International Security*, 158.

contributing to the difference in the level and form of institutionalization in the two regions was the character of the political regimes. While
postwar Western Europe was organized around advanced democracies,
East Asia was a heterogeneous mix of regime types. Consequently, it
was easier for the United States to engage in complex and far-reaching
multilateral agreements with its Western partners. As Stewart Patrick
argues, the "existence of democracy in these [Western European] states
reinforced the U.S. predilection for a consensual style of hegemony and
the egalitarianism of postwar multilateral institutions."[37]

Hegemonic Uses of Rules and Institutions

Why would dominant states want to build international order around
multilateral rules and institutions? When a state is sufficiently powerful to shape the organization of international relations, rules and institutions can serve quite useful purposes, becoming tools for managing
international hierarchy. In the broadest sense, rules and institutions
provide the leading state with instruments of political control. They
are useful in shaping and entrenching a favorable international environment. Rules and institutions are both tools of hegemonic power and
constraints on the exercise of that power. But, importantly, it is precisely
because of the constraining impacts of rules and institutions—on both
the leading state and others—that they are so useful as instruments of
political control. Again, however, costs, benefits, and trade-offs infuse
the calculations of the hegemonic state.

Dominant states should find rules and institutions useful in several
ways. First, the leading state has an incentive to use institutions to reduce
uncertainty and facilitate cooperation and market exchange. If the leading
state has the most advanced productive economy, it has very strong incentives to create a stable open order—and rules and institutions can be useful

[37] Stewart Patrick, *The Best Laid Plans: The Origins of American Multilateralism and the
Dawn of the Cold War* (Boulder, CO: Rowman & Littlefield, 2009), 270–71.

for managing economic openness. Likewise, as global economic independence grows, so do incentives for the multilateral coordination of policies.
The more economically interconnected states become, the more dependent they are on the actions of other states for the realization of objectives.
"As interdependence rises," Robert Keohane argues, "the opportunity
costs of not co-ordinating policy increase compared with the costs of sacrificing autonomy as a consequence of making binding agreements."[38] Thus,
a hegemonic state has a double functional incentive for rules and institutions. It wants them as a tool to create economic openness, and it needs
them as a tool to managing growing economic interdependence.[39]

International rules and institutions provide a contractual environment within which states can more easily pursue joint gains. As the
density of interactions between states increases, so too will the demand
for rules and institutions that facilitate these interactions and cope with
their consequences. In this sense, multilateralism is self-reinforcing. A
well-functioning contractual environment facilitates the promulgation
of additional multilateral rules and institutions.

This argument helps explain why a powerful state might support
multilateral agreements, particularly in trade and other economic

[38] Robert O. Keohane, "Multilateralism: An agenda for research," *International Journal* 45,
no. 4 (1990), 742. See also Daniel Drezner, *All Politics Is Global: Explaining International
Regulatory Regime* (Princeton, NJ: Princeton University Press, 2007), 45.

[39] The literature on hegemonic stability argues that a single powerful state can have incentives to promote and support an open world economy. If the leading state is sufficiently large,
it will identify its interests with the organization of the international system, and it will be
willing to provide the public goods associated with organizing and maintaining an open
world economy even if it alone bears the costs. The seminal statement of this thesis is Charles
Kindleberger, *The World in Depression, 1929–30* (Berkeley: University of California Press,
1973). These ideas are developed further in Robert Gilpin, *U.S. Power and the Multinational
Corporation* (New York: Basic Books, 1975); Robert Gilpin, *War and Change in World Politics*
(New York: Cambridge University Press, 1981); and Stephen D. Krasner, "State Power and
the Structure of International Trade," *World Politics* 28, no. 3 (April 1976), 317–47. During
the 1980s, refinements, extensions, and critiques were put forward. For a summary of these
debates, see David Lake, "Leadership, Hegemony, and the International Economy: Naked
Emperor or Tattered Monarch with Potential?" *International Studies Quarterly* 37 (1993),
459–89. For a recent restatement of the theory, emphasizing the self-interest-based logic of
hegemonic leadership, see Carla Norrof, *America's Global Advantage: U.S. Hegemony and
International Cooperation* (New York: Cambridge University Press, 2010).

policy areas. To return to the cost-benefit logic of rules and institutions discussed earlier, the leading state has a major interest in inducing smaller states to open their economies and participate in an integrated world economy. As the world's leading economy, it has an interest in establishing not just an open system but also a predictable one—that is to say, it will want rule-based economic order. What the dominant state wants from other states grows along with its economic size and degree of interdependence. But to get weaker states to commit themselves to an open and increasingly elaborate rule-based regime, it must establish its own reliability. It must be willing to commit itself credibly to the same rules and institutions. It will be necessary for the dominant state to reduce its policy autonomy—and do so in a way that other states find credible.

Second, the hegemonic state has a more general incentive to use rules and institutions to preserve its power and create a stable and legitimate international order. This logic of institutional restraint and commitment is particularly evident at major historical turning points—such as 1919, 1945, and after the Cold War—when the United States has faced choices about how to use power and organize interstate relations. The support for rules and institutions is a way to signal restraint and commitment to other states, thereby encouraging the acquiescence and cooperation of weaker states. By binding itself to other states within a system of rules and institutions, the leading state makes its power more acceptable to other states, creating incentives for support rather than opposition.[40]

[40] One argument in the literature on hegemonic stability is that the hegemonic state—by virtue of its size and power—is able to act on its long-term interests rather than struggle over short-term distributional gains. In Robert Keohane's formulation, the theory holds that "hegemonic structures of power, dominated by a single country, are most conducive to the development of strong international regimes whose rules are relatively precise and well obeyed." Such states have the capacity to maintain regimes that they favor through the use of coercion or positive sanctions. The hegemonic state gains the ability to shape and dominate the international order, while providing a flow of benefits to smaller states that is sufficient to persuade them to acquiesce. See Keohane, "The Theory of Hegemonic Stability and Changes in International Economic Regimes, 1967–1977," in Ole R. Holsti, Randolph M. Siverson, and Alexander L. George, eds., *Change in the International System* (Boulder, CO: Westview, 1980), 132.

This theoretical perspective begins by looking at the choices that dominant states face when they are in a position to shape the fundamental character of the international order.[41] A state that wins a war or through some other turn of events finds itself in a dominant global position faces a choice: it can use its power to bargain and coerce other states in struggles over the distribution of gains or, knowing its power position will someday decline and that there are costs to enforcing its way within the order, it can move toward a more rule-based, institutionalized order in exchange for the acquiescence and compliant participation of weaker states. In seeking a more rule-based order, the leading state is agreeing to engage in strategic restraint. It is acknowledging that there will be limits on the way in which it can exercise its power. Such an order, in effect, has "constitutional" characteristics. Limits are set on what a state within the order can do with its power advantages. Just as in constitutional polities, the implications of winning in politics are reduced. Weaker states realize that the implications of their inferior position are limited and perhaps temporary. To operate within the order despite their disadvantages is not to risk everything, nor will it give the dominant state a permanent advantage. Both the powerful and weak states agree to operate within the same order despite radical asymmetries in the distribution of power.

When the leading state does in fact circumscribe its behavior, it is giving up some opportunities to use its power to gain immediate returns on its power—it settles for fewer gains at the initial moment of rule creation by operating within institutional rules and obligations than it could otherwise achieve with its brute power. It does this with an eye toward longer-term gains that are specified above. But weaker states may have reason to gain more sooner rather than later. The discount rate for future gains is potentially different for the leading and lesser states, and this makes an institutional bargain potentially more mutually desirable. So the leading state is faced with a choice: how much institutional

---

[41] This logic is sketched in Ikenberry, *After Victory*, chap. 3.

limitation on its own policy autonomy and exercise power is worth how much policy lock-in of weaker states?

But why would weaker states agree to be roped in? After all, they might calculate that it is better to not lock themselves into an institutional agreement at T_1 and wait until T_2 or T_3, when the power asymmetries do not favor the leading state as much. Weaker states have two potential incentives to buy into the leading state's institutional agreement. First, if the institutional agreement also puts limits and restraints on the behavior of the leading state, this would be welcome. In a non-institutionalized relationship, these lesser states are subject to the unrestrained and unpredictable domination of the leading state. If they believe that credible limits could be placed on the arbitrary and indiscriminate actions of the leading state, this might be enough of an attraction to justify an institutional agreement at T_1.

Rules and institutions become mechanisms by which states can reach a bargain over the character of international order. The dominant state uses institutions to restrain and commit its power, establishing an order where weaker states will participate willingly—rather than resist or balance against the leading power. It accepts some restrictions on how it can use its power. The rules and institutions that are created serve as an investment in the longer-run preservation of its power advantages. Weaker states agree to the order's rules and institutions, and in return they are assured that the worst excesses of the leading state—manifesting as arbitrary and indiscriminate abuses of state power—will be avoided, and they gain institutional opportunities to work and help influence the leading state.

Thus, there are three aspects to the logic of the hegemonic use of rules and institutions. One aspect has to do with reducing the costs of enforcement of hegemonic rule. If a hegemon can get other states to buy into a set of rules and institutions, it does not need to spend its resources constantly to coerce other states into following them. The hegemonic state is by definition powerful, so it can engage in power struggles with subordinate states, most of which it is likely to win. It can dominate without the use of rules and institutions. In getting other states to operate within a system of rules and institutions, however, the hegemon reduces the time and energy it must expend to enforce order and get other states to do what it wants. By locking subordinate states into a rule-based order, it reduces its costs of enforcement.[42]

A second aspect is that by agreeing to lead and operate within a rule-based international order, the hegemonic state enhances the legitimacy of the order and its position within it. The logic is simple. Hegemonic support for an order based on rules and institutions signals restraint and commitment—and this makes the order more normatively acceptable. The more multilateral rule-based characteristics the hegemonic order has, the more likely other states in the global system are to seek to join or cooperate with the leading state and see the operation of the hegemonic order as legitimate in some fundamental sense. The more imperial characteristics the hegemonic order has—that is, ruling through the direct and coercive use of power—the less the order will be seen as legitimate.[43]

A third aspect is the use of rules and institutions by the hegemonic state to invest in its future power position. A durable system of rules and institutions can help to safeguard the leading state's interests and preserve its standing even as the distribution of power slowly shifts against it. This is true, at least, to the extent that institutional agreements have some degree of stickiness—that is, if they have some independent ordering capacity. If they do, rules and institutions can continue to provide favorable outcomes for the leading state even after its material capacities

[42] See G. John Ikenberry and Charles A. Kupchan, "Socialization and Hegemonic Power," *International Organization* 44, no. 4 (June 1990), 283–315; Lisa Martin, "The Rational State Choice of Multilateralism," in Ruggie, ed., *Multilateralism Matters*, 91–124; and Lisa Martin, "Interests, Power, and Multilateralism," *International Organization* 46, no. 4 (Autumn 1992), 765–92.

[43] Legitimacy refers to the normative quality of a political relationship. Legitimacy can be said to exist when actors—regardless of the underlying conditions of the relationship—see the terms of the relationship as normatively acceptable. The assumption, however, is that the normative acceptance of the terms of a relationship is related to the actual terms of the relationship. In this instance, the rules and institutions are assumed to have some actual impact on the way in which the sup erordinate and subordinate actors in the hegemonic relationship relate to each other—that is, it reduces the imperial characteristics of rule. But, ultimately, legitimacy hinges on what states believe about the political relationship. For a discussion of the sources and character of legitimacy within international orders, see Ian Clark, *Legitimacy in International Society* (Oxford: Oxford University Press, 2005).

decline in relative terms.[44] Institutions can both conserve and prolong the power advantages of the leading state. If leaders of a hegemonic state believe that their preeminent power position will last indefinitely—or possibly even grow greater—the attraction of establishing an institutionalized order that will last past the state's hegemonic zenith is less compelling. But to the extent that the leaders see relative decline coming, incentives exist for building an institutionalized order with deep roots.[45]

This logic is similar to the "insurance" logic that scholars have identified in studies of the movement toward judicial autonomy and the rule of law in democratizing states. Ruling elites in countries moving toward democracy must worry about the protections of the political system if and when they find themselves out of office. This possibility creates incentives for these power holders to support the rule of law, including the independence of judicial institutions, as insurance against future contingencies. In a wide range of countries, judicial empowerment has emerged from the strategic calculations of ruling parties that foresee their replacement. As threatened governing elites face electoral loss, they move to lock-in their policy preferences and protect themselves politically by strengthening courts and the constitution.[46]

Together, this threefold logic suggests that a leading state has motives to strike bargains with weaker states and arrive at a settled order orga-

[44] See Keohane, *After Hegemony*; and Stephen Krasner, "Structural Causes and Regime Consequences: Regimes as Intervening Variables," in Stephen Krasner, ed., *International Regimes* (Ithaca, NY: Cornell University Press, 1983.

[45] This logic of this argument is developed in Ikenberry, *After Victory*, chap. 3.

[46] See Rebecca Bill Chavez, *The Rule of Law in Nascent Democracies: Judicial Politics in Argentina* (Stanford, CA: Stanford University Press, 2004); Tom Ginsberg, *Judicial Review in New Democracies: Constitutional Courts in Asian Cases* (Cambridge: Cambridge University Press, 2003); and Jodi Finkel, *Judicial Reform as Political Insurance: Argentina, Peru, and Mexico* (Notre Dame, IN: University of Notre Dame Press, 2008). Ran Hirschl describes this logic as "hegemonic preservation." See Hirschl, *Towards Juristocracy: The Origins and Consequences of the New Constitutionalism* (Cambridge, MA: Harvard University Press, 2004). For additional explorations of constitutionalism and judicial authority as tools of political protection, see Rebecca Chavez, "Rule of Law and Courts in Democratizing Regimes," and Thomas Ginsberg, "The Global Spread of Constitutional Review," both in Keith E. Whittington, R. Daniel Kelemen, and Gregory A. Caldeira, *The Oxford Handbook of Law and Politics* (Oxford: Oxford University Press, 2008).

nized around agreed-upon rules and institutions. A rule-based environment is created in which all the participants in the order are given tools with which to protect and advance their interests. In this way, the hegemonic order is rendered stable through an ongoing confluence of interests. But to the extent that the wider system itself is seen as legitimate, the basis of rule—and domination—shifts. Compliance with the rules and institutions of the order is not based directly on calculations of self-interest. Rather, it is based on a broader understanding that the order itself is normatively acceptable and just. As Nico Krisch argues: "Once dominance is regarded as legitimate—and thus turns into authority—obedience is no longer based on calculation, but on a conviction that it is necessary and right."[47] The rules, institutions, bargains, and diffuse reciprocity that are manifest within the order give it legitimacy. As a result, states normatively embrace the order—and the power of the leading state is turned into authority.

A dominant state has incentives to build an order of this sort. But the incentives are not absolute. They operate in specific political contexts in which power and opportunities for institutional bargains vary and evolve. We can examine these choices and trade-offs more closely.

Strategic Choices and Trade-offs

When a dominant state is in a position to build international order, it faces choices about how to do so. If it is the preeminent state in the global system, it will want to use its power to create a stable and congenial international environment in which to pursue its interests. In this situation, there are two general types of strategies with which it can assert influence and control over international order: rule through rules and rule through relationships. As a strategy for building order, creating rules and institutions has attractions. If basic ordering rules and institutions can

[47] Nico Krisch, "International Law in Times of Hegemony: Unequal Power and the Shaping of the International Legal Order," *European Journal of International Law* 16, no. 3 (2005), 374.

be put in place, the leading state is not forced to bargain bilaterally with states directly and continuously exercise power to control outcomes. Such an order provides for relatively organized and efficient rule, and it provides some future protections to the leading state as the distribution of power shifts. But this strategy also has potential costs associated with making binding commitments and reduced policy autonomy. So there are trade-offs and the leading state—together with other states in the system—must make choices about how and when to cooperate.[48]

We can identify a set of general expectations about how the leading state will make these choices. First, a dominant state will try to lock other states into institutionalized policy orientations while trying to minimize its own limitations on policy autonomy and discretionary power. This, as we noted earlier, is the game that all states are playing. All states would like to be relatively unencumbered by rules and institutions while operating in a global system where other states are tightly bound. So it would not be surprising to see the leading state simultaneously agreeing to the creation of a set of institutionalized rules and seeking to exempt itself or at least minimize its own exposure to the constraining effects of those rules.[49]

The strategic question the leading state must ask is: how much restriction on its own policy autonomy is needed—and worth the cost—to gain agreements from other states that restrict their policy autonomy? The question leads to a cost-benefit calculation. Institutionalized agreements are a tool that the leading state can use to gain greater control over its international environment. The leading state has huge incentives

[48] For discussions of the relationship between power politics—including hegemony—and international law, see Richard H. Steinberg and Jonathan M. Zasloff, "Power and International Law," *American Journal of International Law* 100 (2006), 64–87; and Detlev F. Vagts, "Hegemonic International Law," *American Journal of International Law* 95 (2001).

[49] For a discussion of the various ways that the United States has sought to build hierarchy into international law and control the content of international law without becoming subject to it, see Nico Krisch, "More equal than the rest? Hierarchy, equality and US predominance in international law," in Michael Byers and Georg Nolte, eds., *United States Hegemony and the Foundations of International Law* (Cambridge: Cambridge University Press, 2003), 156–66; and Nico Krisch, "Weak as Constraint, Strong as Tool: The Place of International Law in U.S. Foreign Policy," in David Malone and Yuen Foong Khong, eds., *Unilateralism and U.S. Foreign Policy: International Perspectives* (Boulder, CO: Lynne Rienner, 2003).

to encourage the establishment of an international order built around widely agreed-upon rules and institutions. But such an order is built on a variety of specific rules and institutional agreements—and in each case, the leading state will seek to gain as much institutional control with as little loss of its own policy autonomy as possible.

Second, the leading state will also attempt to make institutional commitments that grant it disproportionate influence or decision-making power. The leading state will look for opportunities to introduce differential rules and obligations into agreements. As the dominant state, it will want—ideally, at least—agreements that enable it to retain a privileged position of authority in the institution and greater discretion in its compliance with rules. In effect, it will want the overall hierarchy of power to be reflected in differential rights and obligations within the rule-based order. The leading state will want its unique role and responsibility in upholding the rules and institutions of the international order to translate into special rights and authority.

These differential rights and authority are a basic characteristic of all the major postwar multilateral institutions championed by the United States. The IMF and World Bank give the United States and the other leading shareholder states weighted voting rights in their operation and governance. America's commitment to NATO carries with it the power of supreme command over the combined alliance forces—and within the organization, the United States is "first among equals." The U.N. Security Council also gives the United States and the other postwar great powers rights of membership and veto. In these various ways, the multilateral institutions specify the rights and circumscribe the obligations of the hegemon—thereby ensuring that the rules and institutions reflect as much as constrain hegemonic power.[50]

Third, regardless of any differential rights and obligations, the leading state will look for ways to limit the strength of its commitments to rules and institutions. These different types or degrees of commitment run

---

[50] See Miles Kahler, "Conclusion: The Causes and Consequences of Legalization," in Goldstein et al., *Legalization and World Politics*, 281–82; and Abbott and Snidal, "Hard and Soft Law in International Governance," in Goldstein et al., *Legalization and World Politics*, 63–66.

along a continuum from strong to weak in terms of their legally binding character. Strong commitments are manifest when the leading state agrees to adhere to specific and explicit substantive rules or policy obligations. Weaker commitments take the form of less specific rules or policies—in which monitoring, compliance, and enforcement is less certain.[51] In particular, when the leading state is in fact making commitments to rules and institution, it will seek "loose multilateralism," that is, rules and institutions that provide safeguards, veto rights, and opt-out clauses. How loose would, again, hinge on specific calculations that the leading state would make about its gains from binding other states to rules and agreements and the costs of lost autonomy that it would incur along the way.

Fourth, the leading state can also offer "process commitments" rather than, or in addition to, substantive rule-based commitments. It can agree to formal processes of multilateral consultation. In these instances, it is not—strictly speaking—giving up or reducing its policy autonomy. But it is agreeing to operate in an institutional environment in which other states have opportunities to influence what the hegemon does. The United States has made this a feature of its approach to hegemonic rule. Through NATO and other formal and informal arrangements, the United States offers voice opportunities to other states in exchange for their cooperation and acquiescence.[52] In these circumstances, the dominant state opens its doors to outsiders—offering the opportunity for consultation and influence by weaker and secondary states—while not agreeing to formal limits on its independence of decision making.

Fifth, the dominant state can promote rule-based relations through unilateral steps that do not require it to make binding commitments to others. Specifically, it can also use the size of its economy—and the dependence of other states on it—as a tool to influence the policies of other states. Its domestic rules and regulations become the world's rules and regulations. Its internal regulatory standards are externalized. States with sufficient market size can influence global regulatory rules through the

[51] On institutionalized monitoring and enforcement as measures of regime strength, see Keohane, *After Hegemony*; and Goldstein et al., *Legalization and World Politics*.
[52] See Ikenberry, *After Victory*, chap. 3.

use of market power and coercion.[53] As Nico Krisch argues in regard to the United States, "US rules often exceed their formal confines and begin to function as global rules." This is not simply because of American pressure but also because of "the superior expertise of US agencies, the availability of model norms in US domestic law, and the market dominance of US corporations, especially in the early phases of emerging fields."[54]

In a study of economic regulatory cooperation, Daniel Drezner argues that as levels of economic interdependence grow, so do the benefits of policy coordination. But for a state to adjust its domestic regulatory arrangements to converge with cooperative agreements generates domestic economic and political costs. The greater the divergence from the coordination agreement, the higher the costs. In the struggle over who adjusts—that is, who alters its domestic regulatory standards to converge in an international agreement—great powers tend to win. Drezner notes that because their larger internal markets give them bargaining power, major states are "more likely to achieve regulatory coordination at their preferred level of standards."[55] This logic applies more generally to a dominant state's incentives in supporting global rules and institutions. It will seek to extend its internal rules and institutions to the outside system, exporting the costs of adjustment onto others. All states have an interest in arriving at an agreement that coordinates policy—particularly in areas of business and trade regulation—but the leading state can use its power advantages to get other states to adopt its rules and regulations.[56]

---

[53] See Scott James and David Lake, "The Second Face of Hegemony," *International Organization* 43, no. 1 (Winter 1989), 1–29.

[54] Krisch, "More equal than the rest?" 163.

[55] Drezner, *All Politics Is Global*, 59.

[56] On the export of domestic standards, see also Beth Simmons, "The International Politics of Harmonization: The Case of Capital Market Regulation," *International Organization* 55, no. 3 (Autumn 2001), 589–620; and David Vogel, *Trading Up: Consumerism and Environmental Regulation in the Global Economy* (Cambridge, MA: Harvard University Press, 1995). On the way in which powerful states seek to force "adjustment" onto other states, see Beth Simmons, *Who Adjusts? Domestic Sources of Foreign Economic Policy during the Interwar Period* (Princeton, NJ: Princeton University Press, 1994); and Michael Mastanduno, "System Maker and Privilege Taker: U.S. Power and the International Political Economy," *World Politics* 61, no. 1 (January 2009), 121–54.

Beyond this, the United States has found a variety of ways to use its domestic laws to promote international rules and norms. One is the certification mechanism, in which the American government defines substantive rules and monitors compliance in countries around the world—in areas such as arms control, environmental protection, human rights, narcotics, and terrorism. Developmental aid or military assistance from Washington hinges on whether states meet the American-set standards. As Krisch notes, "the extensive use of the certification mechanism provides a tool for the United States to create law for other States and to monitor its observance, while the United States itself remains unbound and unmonitored. It thereby provides a convenient substitute for treaties and other monitoring bodies."[57] The United States can also impose unilateral sanctions. It can do this to uphold agreed-upon international rules, such as multilateral trade agreements, but sanctions can also be used against specific states—third parties—who do not pursue similar policies toward target states.[58]

Finally, dominant states will find themselves making trade-offs between rule through rules and rule through relationships. The attraction of rule through rules is that a system of multilateral rules and institutions creates a wider space of predictable and efficient state relations. A system of negotiated multilateral rules gives weaker and secondary states greater influence on outcomes than bilateral negotiations do, but it also creates incentives for them to abide by the agreements. The costs to the dominant state of enforcing order are reduced. The legitimacy of the order that is engendered by its multilateral rule-based character reduces opposition and resistance to the leading state's dominant position in it. But there are costs to the leading state in such an order—in the form of lost autonomy and the ability to directly manipulate other states.

[57] Krisch, "More equal than the rest?" 161.

[58] This is the extraterritoriality tool that has been used by the United States with its Helms-Burton law, which sanctions countries that trade with companies and property that have been expropriated by Cuba. See Vaughan Lowe, "United States Extraterritorial Jurisdiction: The Helms-Burton and D'Amato Acts," *International and Comparative Law Quarterly* vol. 46, 378–90.

It is here that bilateral, patron-client relations offer attractions. Bilateral agreements tend to make it easier for dominant states to translate their power into favorable agreements than multilateral rules and institutions do. Krisch explains: "Bilateral negotiations are far more likely to be influenced by the superior power of one party than are multilateral negotiations, in which other states can unite and counterbalance the dominant party—*divide et impera*, as reflected in the forms of international law. The bilateral form is also more receptive to exceptional rules for powerful states. In multilateral instruments, especially *traités lois*, exceptions for powerful parties are always suspicious and in need of justification, as manifest in, for example, the Nuclear Non-proliferation Treaty and the failed attempts of the US with respect to the ICC Statute. . . . Bilateral treaties are thus a much easier tool to reflect and translate dominance than multilateral ones."[59]

Thus, bilateral agreements will be attractive to the leading state when it determines that multilateral agreements will not be as effective at asserting control over other states in the desired way—or that the costs of doing so is too high relative to the gains. The first consideration is really a functional one: what precisely does the leading state want to influence or control? If the outcome it wants is quite specific, bilateral deals are likely. If the other state is very weak, the leading state may be less likely to pay the price of tying itself to multilateral rules and institutions to get what it wants. As I suggested earlier, the United States was more willing to negotiated binding multilateral agreements with Europe than with East Asia after World War II in part because it wanted more from Europe and was willing to make more costly concessions to get the desired outcomes. In East Asia, the United States was much more powerful relative to the other states, and it wanted less from these states—and so it was less willing to entangle itself in multilateral pacts with them.

At the same time, bilateral and multilateral agreements can work together. A leading state's client-based relations with weaker and secondary states can provide mechanisms to channel resources and signal commit

<hr />

[59] Krisch, "International Law in Times of Hegemony," 390.

and restraint. The leading state may use these bilateral relations as a way to make side payments for cooperation by these states in multilateral settings.

In all these ways, the hegemon is confronted with crosscutting incentives. There are powerful incentives for a hegemonic state to establish and operate within a system of rules and institutions: efficiency, legitimacy, and investment in future advantages. The central insight here is that powerful states do have incentives to commit themselves to rules and institutions. Rules and institutions can project and preserve hegemonic power as much as limit and reduce it. But the hegemonic state also has incentives—as do other states—to protect its policy autonomy and freedom of action. The specific incentives, trade-offs, and choices shape the extent to which the hegemon makes commitments and binds itself to other states through rules and institutions—driven by attempts to get the benefits of multilateralism while minimizing the costs.

Conclusion

When powerful states rise up to shape the rules and institutions of the global system, they face choices. The most basic choice is how to make trade-offs between sovereignty and rule-based order. A leading state has incentives to use its position of dominance to shape its environment—and the most efficient, legitimate, and enduring way to do this is through a bargained system of rules and institutions. But to establish such an order—to build hegemonic rule around institutionalized cooperation—the leading state must give up some of its own policy autonomy.

This way of looking at the problem of hegemonic order emphasizes the pragmatic and instrumental character of state choice. The implication is that the dominant state can pick and choose between strategies of rule—that is, between rule through rules and rule through relationships. The choices will be driven by costs and benefits. The leading state will seek to get the most rulership "bang" for the sovereignty- and policy-autonomy-limiting "buck." It will seek to preserve its predominant position—its power and sovereignty—and the advantages that flow from its superordinate position in the global hierarchy. But it will exchange some of this power—or more precisely, discretion over the exercise of power—in various ways to get the long-term advantages of a global system with rules and institutions that facilitate the pursuit of its interests. Efficiency, legitimacy, and durability—these are features of an international order that a leading state will want. The question is, how can it get them and what price must it pay along the way?

An important variable in this framework is also the most difficult to specify. It has to do with legitimacy. A leading state has an incentive to create an international order that is legitimate. Such an order is one where other states cooperate within it willingly. At some basic level, the leaders of weaker and secondary states accept the logic and normative underpinnings of the order. If an order is constituted as such, the leading state will not be required to use its coercive power to enforce rule. The order itself will take on a more cooperative and efficient character. Diffuse reciprocity is more likely under these circumstances. The leading state can pursue its interests without worrying about challenger states that seek to overturn the order. But questions remain. What specific features of the order give it legitimacy? If the leading state wants to establish a legitimate order, how does it go about it?

The implication of my argument is that the more rule-based the order is, the more legitimate it is likely to be. As the character of a hierarchical order moves from imperial to liberal hegemonic, somewhere along this continuum, the order will take on features that will lead participants to see it as legitimate. But how much rule-based character is enough to give the order legitimacy? And what are the costs to the leading state—in terms of cooperation and efficiency of rule—if the overall system declines in legitimacy? The answers to these questions will, in turn, inform judgments by leading states about the value of legitimacy and their willingness to bind themselves to a rule-based international order. These questions have come into focus with the rise of American unipolarity after the Cold War.

Four

Unipolarity and Its Consequences

When one state stands alone as the world's most powerful state—when the world is unipolar—how does this affect its strategies of rule and the character of world order? For most of the modern era, leading states have pursued order building in the company of other powerful states. They have pursued strategies of rule in multipolar and bipolar structures of global power. America's order building after World War II was pursued within an emerging bipolar Cold War system. But how do strate gies of rule shift when the dominant state is unipolar, unrivaled by other powerful states? And how do strategies of rule shift when unipolarity is in decline?

What makes the global system unipolar is the distinctive distribution of material resources. With the end of Cold War, America's primacy in the global distribution of capabilities became one of the most salient features of the international system. The end of the Cold War did not return the world to multipolarity. Instead, the United States—already the world's dominant power—became more so. No other major state has enjoyed such advantages in material capabilities—military, economic, technological, geographical. Other states rival the United States in one area or another, but the multifaceted character of American power places it in a category of its own. The sudden collapse of the Soviet Union and its bloc of allies, slower economic growth in Japan and Western Europe during the 1990s, and America's outsized military spending all intensified these disparities. While in most historical eras, the distribution of capabilities among major states has tended to be bipolar or multipolar—with several major states of roughly equal size and capability—the United States emerged from the 1990s as an unrivaled global power. It became a unipolar state.[1]

The rise of unipolarity over the last two decades involves a shift in the distribution of power in two respects. One is simply a shift toward more concentrated power—the disparities between the leading state and other states are intensified. These heightened power disparities are captured in America's dominance in economic, military, and technological capabilities. The other shift is the disappearance of competing poles of power. The lead state no longer has a global rival—or, to use the term of art, a peer competitor. In the modern era, there have always been several competing poles of power. During the Cold War there were two poles. But beginning in the 1990s there was only one. Defined in these terms, the United States stands above all other states. This commanding position is unprecedented in the modern era.

The global system is unipolar, but this observation does not say anything in particular about the logic of political relations surrounding the unipolar state. The political order built around unipolarity could be coercive or consensual, legitimate or illegitimate. Describing the system as unipolar leaves unanswered questions about the logic and character of hierarchy and the ways in which an American-centered unipolar system operates. What is the character of domination in a unipolar distribution

---

[1] An international system is unipolar if it "contains one state whose overall share of capabilities places it unambiguously in a class by itself compared to all other states." G. John Ikenberry, Michael Mastanduno, and William C. Wohlforth, "Introduction: Unipolarity, State Behavior, and Systemic Consequences," *World Politics* 61, no. 1 (January 2009), 5.

of power? If world politics is always a mixture of force and consent, does movement from bipolarity to unipolarity remove restraints and alter the mix in favor of force? Will a unipolar world be built around rules and institutions, or will it be based on the unilateral exercise of unipolar power? Does unipolarity select for unilateralism, and will it therefore lead to an unraveling of the postwar American-led liberal international order?

In looking at the relationship between unipolarity and liberal international order, we need to look at the impacts of moving in both directions. We need to probe the impact that unipolarity—defined in terms of material capabilities—has had on international order. As we shall see, the connections between the distribution of power and the logic and character of political formations that surround unipolarity are not causally tight. Unipolarity can coexist with various sorts of international orders—defined in terms of imperial and liberal forms of hierarchy. Unipolarity does, however, shift the incentives and constraints associated with various rulership strategies. At the same time, we need to look at the impact that liberal international order has had on the rise and durability of unipolarity. Importantly, unipolarity can be understood not just as the concentration of material capabilities in the hands of one state, but as a more general set of political and institutional characteristics that turn the unipolar state into a "hub" around which other states connect and operate. The presence or absence of other poles in the system hinges not just on whether there are other powerful states in the system but on whether these other states are able or willing to become organizing hubs. Over the last century, the United States—in building liberal hegemonic order—has become the most expansive and far-reaching pole the world has seen. It is the American political formation, together with its power capabilities, that has allowed a unipolar international system to emerge.

This chapter proceeds in five steps. First, I offer a description of the features of unipolarity and explore a central puzzle: why American unipolarity has not triggered a power-balancing reaction by other states. The concentration of material power capabilities is unprecedented, but there are reasons why the traditional response to concentrated power—great-power balancing—has not occurred and is unlikely to. In part, this is because of the extreme concentration of power itself. But it is also because of unique features of the contemporary international system, namely the presence of nuclear weapons and the dominance of capitalist democratic great powers. The shift from a multipolar—and most recently bipolar—distribution of power has effects on the patterns of domination and rule. This is because the oldest and most classical mechanism for constraining and disciplining power—a counterbalancing power coalition—is not present in the current international order.

Second, I explore the impact that the postwar American-led liberal international order has had on the rise of unipolarity. Unipolarity— defined broadly as a one-pole global system—is itself an effect of liberal international order. Unipolarity is created by a distinctive distribution of material capabilities, but it is also created by the absence of other poles. Poles have characteristics that go beyond their material power capabilities. They also have institutional characteristics. In this sense, they can be described as hubs to which other states connect. They provide the organizing infrastructure around which states operate. The United States is not just unipolar in the sense of possessing disproportionate material capabilities. It is also a singularly important hub in the sense that it is the organizational center of a wider system of order. Other countries have connected themselves to the United States and the wider rules and institutions that make up the liberal international order. Unipolarity emerged in the post-Cold War era as alternative hubs fell away or failed to emerge.

In this sense, the unipolar order—a one-pole international system— is an artifact of the American-led political formation. The United States led in the creation of an open and loosely rule-based postwar order. It provided public goods in support of economic openness, stability, and security. More generally, the liberal international order has provided benefits and services for states that operate within it. This order also has institutional characteristics—compared with other types of order—that make it expandable and relatively easy to integrate states into it. The liberal characteristics of the American-led order make it "easy to join and hard to overturn." This has put other states seeking to establish rival poles at a disadvantage, thereby reinforcing and perpetuating unipolarity.

Third, I argue that the rise of unipolarity does, however, generate new dilemmas of rule for the leading state. The shift from bipolarity to unipolarity has implications for the strategies of rule discussed in the previous chapter. It has implications for the incentives that the leading state has to provide public goods, compromise its policy autonomy, and use rules and institutions as strategies of rule. The shift from a bipolar to a unipolar distribution of power has triggered reassessment of the costs and benefits of a wide range of bargains and institutions across the global system—a reassessment by both the leading state and subordinate states. The overall impact of unipolarity is to shift the mix of strategies. During the bipolar Cold War era, the United States pursued both logics of order—rule-based and hub-and-spoke. Under conditions of unipolarity, the hub-and-spoke logic of order has gained greater prominence. In the absence of a common threat—such as was manifest during the Cold War—the United States has incentives to negotiate bilateral bargains on security with countries, creating a wider hierarchical hub-and-spoke system of security protection. At the extreme, this would amount to a so-called East Asianization of world politics. The pattern of America's relations with East Asia would be generalized across the globe.

Fourth, I argue, nonetheless, that the unipolar state still has incentives to operate in a one world system of rules and bargained institutions. The overall character of the order hinges on several key variables—time horizon, legitimacy, and the ability to establish credible commitment and restraint. As a unipolar state, the United States is not destined to completely abandon rule-based order. This is true if only because the alternatives are ultimately unsustainable. An imperial system of American rule—even the hub-and-spoke version that holds sway in East Asia—is costly, fraught with contradictions, and premised on unrealistic assumptions about future American power advantages. There are still an array of incentives and impulses that will persuade the United States to try to organize unipolarity around rules and institutions. The United States will want to renegotiate rules and institutions in some global areas, but it ultimately will also want to wield its power legitimately in a world of rules and institutions.

Finally, based on these considerations, I argue that the global system should retain political characteristics of unipolarity even as the distribution of material capabilities shift away from the United States. A relative decline in American power disparities will not inevitably lead to the formation of new poles or a multipolar balance of power system. The fact that China has taken steps to join this order is evidence of the way in which the logic and character of liberal order reinforces a one-pole system. The pathway toward a return to multipolarity has several stops along the way: the diffusion of power, the rise of new poles, and the igniting of balancing and security competition. The liberal character of the political formation that has emerged around American unipolarity will influence the return to multipolarity. Even if there is a diffusion of material capabilities away from the United States, the rise of new global-scale poles and the return to balancing and security competition is not inevitable.

Unipolarity and the Balance of Power

What are the effects of unipolarity on patterns of cooperation and strategies of rule by the leading state? The most dramatic possibility is offered by realist theory, namely that weaker and secondary states will seek to protect themselves from domination by the leading state by balancing against it. In this classic view, concentrated power tends to be threatening to other states and the most effective way to check this power is by counterbalancing it. Balance of power is the most enduring mechanism to restrain power because it is the most reliable; power checks power. The realist expectation is that the rise of unipolarity—and the movement toward greater concentration of power capabilities in the hands of one state—should invite a power-balancing response.[2]

In a unipolar distribution of power, balance-of-power realism makes a clear prediction: weaker and secondary states will resist and balance

---

[2] See the discussion of anarchy and balance of power theory in chapter 2.

against the predominant state. Security—indeed survival—is the fundamental goal of states, and because they cannot ultimately rely on the commitments or guarantees of other states to ensure their security, states will be very sensitive to their relative power position. When powerful states emerge, secondary states will seek protection in countervailing coalitions of weaker states.

The strategy of counterbalancing is to generate sufficient material capabilities to impose constraints on the most powerful state. This could happen through the efforts of a single state or coalition of states taking steps to generate additional power capacities and deploying them in a way to block or thwart the advances of the lead state. One expects to see a rival state rise up and seek to become a peer competitor, or a coalition of states band together to match and offset the capacities of the leading state. In terms of American unipolarity, the expectation is that traditional allies will distance themselves from the United States and expand their autonomous defense capacities. Waltz suggests that the logic of balance will again take hold as the great powers—including China and Russia—expand their defense capacities and loose alliances of states appear to undercut the global power position of the United States.[3] Christopher Layne suggests that unipolarity is unstable precisely because concentrated American power is threatening to the other major states. He foresees a return to a global system based on an equilibrium of power among traditional and rising great powers.[4]

It remains an interesting puzzle that the rise of American unipolarity has not in fact generated a counterbalancing response, at least as counterbalancing is envisaged in realist theory. A debate continues on what actually constitutes balancing. Some scholars do anticipate a

[3] Kenneth Waltz, "Structural Realism after the Cold War," *International Security* 25, no. 1 (Summer 2000), 5–41.
[4] Christopher Layne, "The Unipolar Illusion: Why Great Powers Will Arise," *International Security* 17, no. 4 (Spring 1993), 5–51; Christopher Layne, "From Preponderance to Offshore Balancing: America's Future Grand Strategy," *International Security* 22, no. 1 (Summer 1997), 86–124; and Christopher Layne, "The Unipolar Illusion Revisited: The Coming of the United States' Unipolar Moment," *International Security* 31, no. 2 (2006), 7–41.

return to traditional security counterbalancing, while others argue that a new form of counter-balancing—or so-called soft balancing—is emerging that conforms to new circumstances while also validating the basic tenets of the theory.[5] But even if soft balancing is occurring, it suggests a very different array of responses to concentrated power than has been seen in the past.[6] Well into the period of American unipolarity, most of the world's major states sought to get closer to the United States—and not to distance themselves. Trade and cooperation among the advanced industrial countries expanded in the post–Cold War 1990s. The United States maintained—and in various ways deepened—its alliance ties to Western Europe and Japan.[7] At least until the crisis triggered by America's military invention of Iraq in 2003, it has been difficult to see systematic efforts by the other major states to actively oppose—let alone—balance against a unipolar America.[8]

Waltz acknowledges that balance-of-power dynamics can be suppressed by hegemony. Acceptance of American hegemonic leadership, for example, has helped prevent the return of a balance of power on the European continent. But from a realist perspective, unipolarity is nonetheless likely to be the least durable of the various types of international order. Two reasons are offered for this view. First, the dominant state will

---

[5] See Robert Pape, "Soft Balancing Against the United States," *International Security* 30, no. 1 (Summer 2005), 7–45; T. V. Paul, "Soft Balancing in the Age of U.S. Primacy," *International Security* 30, no. 1 (Summer 2005), 46–71; and Stephen Walt, *Taming American Power: The Global Response to U.S. Primacy* (New York: Norton, 2005), 126–32. For skepticism about the notion of soft balancing—its presence, significance, and measurement—see Stephen G. Brooks and William C. Wohlforth, "Hard Times for Soft Balancing," *International Security* 30, no. 1 (Summer 2005), 72–108; and Keir A. Lieber and Gerard Alexander, "Waiting for Balancing: Why the World Is Not Pushing Back," *International Security* 30, no. 1 (Summer 2005), 109–39.

[6] For an exploration of the various strategies that weaker and secondary states have adopted to engage and resist American unipolar power, see Stephen M. Walt, *Taming American Power: The Global Response to U.S. Primacy* (New York: Norton, 2005), chaps. 3 and 4.

[7] See Ikenberry, *After Victory*, chap. 7.

[8] For general efforts to grapple with the logic of balance under conditions of unipolarity, see Ikenberry, *America Unrivaled*; and T. V. Paul, James J. Wirtz, and Michael Fortmann, eds., *Balance of Power: Theory and Practice in the 21st Century* (Stanford, CA: Stanford University Press, 2004).

tend to take on more tasks and responsibilities, which over the long term will weaken the state. This argument echoes the thesis of Paul Kennedy that the United States could eventually go the way of all powers—down. Dominant states tend to make mistakes in the exercise of their power, a problem that emerges directly from its concentration.[9] The other reason why unipolar order is unstable follows directly from the underlying condition of anarchy: even if the dominant state acts with moderation, other states will fear the insecurities of unchecked concentrated power. During the Cold War, the United States and the Soviet Union restrained each other, but today the United States is largely unrestrained. As Waltz argues, "Faced with unbalanced power, some states try to increase their own strength or they ally with others to bring the international distribution of power back into balance."[10] Regardless of its good intentions or eagerness to please, the United States is destined to experience the same fate of other dominant states in world history.

But contrary to this view, there are deeply rooted reasons why large-scale balancing against American unipolarity has not occurred. One reason is that even if the great powers wanted to balance, it is hard to do.[11] It is costly to mobilize a countercoalition, particularly when the threat is not that of immediate territorial conquest. At one level, it is a problem of collective action. States would ideally like other states to do the balancing, thereby saving themselves the costs of mobilizing power and building coalitions and incurring risks of retaliation from the unipolar state. That is, there is a tendency to engage in "buck passing."[12] It is also difficult to build coalitions because states do not all experience the threats of domination to the same degree. As Wohlforth suggests,

[9] Paul Kennedy, *The Rise and Fall of Great Powers: Economic Change and Military Conflict from 1500 to 2000* (New York: Random House, 1987).

[10] Waltz, *Theory of International Politics.*

[11] This argument is advanced most systematically by Wohlforth. See William Wohlforth, "The Stability of a Unipolar World," *International Security* 24, no. 1 (Summer 1999), 4–41; William Wohlforth, "U.S. Strategy in a Unipolar World," in Ikenberry, *America Unrivaled,* 98–118.

[12] John Mearsheimer stresses this dynamic in *The Tragedy of Great Power Politics* (New York: Norton, 2001), chap. 6.

states often think about their security in very local terms, and therefore systemwide balancing imperatives are not likely to be as intensely felt by state leaders. The loss of policy autonomy in such coalitions also makes balancing coalitions costly. It can also be dangerous. If balancing is attempted but fails, the dominant state can exact reprisals. These inherent constraints make balancing difficult to produce—and in fact, across historical eras, there are many instances where states underbalance even in the face of what appear to be substantial threats emerging from a rising or dominant state.[13]

Wohlforth, however, goes beyond these organizational problems to argue that the stability of unipolarity is actually locked into the system by the deep structure of unipolar power, which generates a clear and durable array of costs, benefits, and constraints that reinforce the existing order. When material power capabilities are as concentrated as they are under conditions of unipolarity, it is difficult to see how a coalition of sufficient countervailing capabilities can be constructed.[14] If the unipolar state has the dominant economy, spends as much on military capabilities as the rest of the world combined (and does so at a relatively low cost), and has command of the commons—it is difficult to see how a traditional counterbalancing alliance could actually be assembled to create a rival global power center.

The implication of this argument is that even if there is a demand for counterbalancing, there is always a problem with the organization

---

[13] On the puzzle of underbalancing, see Randall Schweller, *Unanswered Threats: Political Constraints on the Balance of Power* (Princeton, NJ: Princeton University Press, 2006). Jack Levy argues that the realist theory of balance of power has quite circumscribed conditions, and therefore it should not be surprising that the logic of balance is not seen in wide stretches of international history. See Jack Levy, "What Do Great Powers Balance Against and When?" in Paul, Wirtz, and Fortmann, *Balance of Power*, 51; and Jack Levy and William R. Thompson, "Hegemonic Threats and Great-Power Balancing in Europe, 1495–1999," *Security Studies* 14, no. 1 (2005), 1–31. For a survey of the balance of power across world history, including in premodern and non-Western settings, see Stuart J. Kaufman, Richard Little, and William C. Wohlforth, eds., *The Balance of Power in World History* (New York: Palgrave, 2007).

[14] See Brooks and Wohlforth, *World Out of Balance*, chap. 2.

of its supply. But also, once the disparities in power grow so great—
that is, when unipolarity emerges—the supply will be next to impossible to provide simply because there is insufficient power capacity
among the would-be balancers (even if they could solve their collective-action problems). At some threshold level of power imbalance,
traditional counterbalancing is no longer a strategic option for other
major states.

A second set of factors that constrain counterbalancing under conditions of unipolarity is the specific features of the current global system.
These factors reduce the demand for balancing. One is the presence of
a large aggregate of democratic great powers. The realist logic of counterbalancing is ultimately driven by concerns over security and survival in the face of a dominant state. But there is reason to believe that
democracies are less likely to respond to this logic in their relations with
other democracies. The democratic-peace theory holds that democracies do not tend to see each other as security threats that could lead to
war.[15] An implication of this theory is that power disparities will be less
threatening to weaker states when both the unipolar state and the weaker
states are democracies—and so democratic states will be unlikely to take
counter-balancing steps against the unipolar state. Beyond this, liberal
democracies are also unusually capable of building stable, peaceful, and
institutionalized cooperative relations among themselves—creating what
are called security communities.[16] These complex and interdependent

---

[15] There is a huge literature on the democratic-peace theory. See Michael Doyle, "Kant, Liberal Legacies, and Foreign Affairs," *Philosophy and Public Affairs* 12 (1983), 205–35, 323–53; and
Bruce Russett, *Grasping the Democratic Peace: Principles for a Post–Cold War World* (Princeton: Princeton University Press, 1994).

[16] The argument is not just that democracies do not fight each other, it is also that they have
"contracting advantages" that allow them to develop more thoroughgoing cooperative relations. These relations, in turn, provide mechanisms to signal restraint and commitment that
reduce insecurity that might otherwise still exist between states in unequal power relations.
See Charles Lipson, *Reliable Partners: How Democracies Have Made a Separate Peace* (Princeton, NJ: Princeton University Press, 2003). On security communities, see Karl Deutsch et al.,
Political Community and the North Atlantic Area (Princeton, NJ: Princeton University Press,

political relationships have the effect of further reducing the demand for full-scale balancing.[17]

As noted earlier, one of the striking features of the contemporary international system is the predominance of democratic great powers. The vast bulk of wealth and military power is in the hands of advanced democratic states that are tied to the United States in tightly bound economic, political, and security relationships. In 1992, the United States, France, Germany, Great Britain, and Japan possessed 96 percent of GNP held by the traditional great powers.[18] Russia and China had—and continue to have—substantially less economic capacity than the aggregate of the advanced democracies. The implication is that a coalition of major states is simply not available—states with sufficient worries about unipolarity—to organize a balancing response.

Another feature of the contemporary international system is the presence of nuclear weapons, which alters the logic of balance. The fact that most of the great powers have nuclear weapons changes the nature of threats posed by concentrated power in two ways. First, because states such as China and Russia have established a nuclear deterrent, they do not need to worry about war and domination by the leading state. American power is rendered more tolerable because in the age of nuclear deterrence, American military power cannot now be used for conquest against other great powers. Deterrence replaces alliance counterbalancing. Second, nuclear weapons also make it harder for these great powers to overturn the existing international order. The status quo international order led by the United States is rendered less easily replaced. War-driven change is removed as a historical process. As Robert Gilpin has noted, great-power war is precisely the mechanism of change that has been used throughout history to redraw the international order. Rising states

---

1957), and Emanuel Adler and Michael Barnett, *Security Communities* (New York: Cambridge University Press, 1998).

[17] On liberal democracies' relative support for American unipolarity and hegemony, see John M. Owen, "Transnational Liberalism and American Primacy: Or, Benignity Is in the Eye of the Beholder," 239–59; and Thomas Risse, "U.S. Power in a Liberal Security Community," 260–83; both in Ikenberry, *America Unrivaled,*.

[18] See data presented in chapter 2.

depose the reigning—but declining—state and impose a new order.[19] Thus, there is a double effect of nuclear weapons. The demand for great-power balancing declines in comparison to that in previous eras. Like-wise, the ability of a countercoalition—should it actually emerge—to overturn the existing order through war also declines as an option. The overall effect is to undercut the logic of great-power balancing.

Finally, world geography has also shaped the way American unipolar power is expressed. The United States is the only great power that is not neighbored by other great powers. This geographical remoteness made the power ascent of the United States less threatening to the rest of the world. The United States could continue to grow without destabiliz-ing great-power relations.[20] America's era of territorial expansion took place without directly threatening other major states. The European powers had stakes in the New World but not fundamental interests or even—at least by the mid-nineteenth century—a direct presence. The United States purchased territory from France rather than acquiring it by conquest. Germany, of course, was not as geographically lucky, and the expansion and unification of Germany unleashed nationalist rival-ries, territorial ambitions, arms races, and ultimately world war.[21] As European great powers grew in strength, they tended to trigger security-dilemma-driven conflict and balancing reactions in their regional neigh-borhoods. But America's remoteness lessened the destabilizing impact of its transition to global prominence.[22]

The geographical remoteness of American power has made it less threatening to other states—something that mattered both during the bipolar Cold War era and under the current conditions of unipolarity. In addition, the way that unipolarity emerged softened its impact on

[19] Robert Gilpin, *War and Change in World Politics* (New York: Cambridge University Press, 1981).

[20] As A.J.P. Taylor notes, from the perspective of Europe during this period, "The United States seemed . . . not merely in another continent, but on another planet." A.J.P. Taylor, *The Struggle for the Mastery of Europe, 1848–1918* (Oxford: Oxford University Press, 1957), xxxiii.

[21] A.J.P. Taylor, *The Course of German History* (London: Hamish Hamilton, 1945).

[22] See G. John Ikenberry, "American Unipolarity: The Sources of Persistence and Decline," in Ikenberry, *America Unrivaled*, 291–93.

great-power calculations. The United States did not become unipolar through a war, and certainly not through a war of territorial aggression. It became unipolar when its bipolar rival collapsed. Unipolarity emerged quietly as the Soviet system fell into disarray and as Western Europe and Japan grew more slowly than the United States and remained closely allied with it.

Unipolarity and Liberal International Order

The polarity of a system is determined by the distribution of power. But what precisely a pole is remains somewhat ambiguous. Waltz's definition is essentially a depiction of material capabilities, yet it also includes political-institutional features such as competence, which presumably entails the ability of a major state to translate its material assets into influence. The original usage of the term by realists also includes the idea that poles are analogies to magnetism, where each pole is a center of attraction and repulsion.[23] This imagery suggests that poles are not just materially capable states but also organizational forces that shape and bend movements and connections between states. The society-of-states literature also talks about poles as more than aggregations of power but as great powers that have roles and functions within the wider international society. Poles are great powers—and great powers play a role in organizing and managing the system.[24] It is a small step from these ideas to talk about poles as organizational hubs within the global system. That is, a pole can be defined in terms of material capabilities. It can be defined as a hub in

[23] A state takes on the position of a pole within the larger system if it possesses an unusually large share of resources or capabilities and if it excels in all the various components of state capabilities, including, most importantly, the "size of population and territory, resource endowment, economic capacity, military strength, political stability and competence." Waltz, *Theory of International Politics*, 131. For a critical survey of the polarity literature, see Barry Buzan, *The United States and the Great Powers: World Politics in the Twenty-First Century* (London: Polity, 2004), chap. 3.

[24] Hedley Bull, *The Anarchical Society: A Study of Order in World Politics* (New York: Columbia University Press, 1977).

reference to its institutional capacity to organize relations among states. A state is a hub to the extent that it provides the organizing infrastructure of international relations within a geographical region, a functional sphere, or, more generally, within the wider global system.[25]

A pole can take on characteristics as an organizing hub in several ways. It can provide goods and services for other states that affiliate with it. The most basic service is security protection. A state is a hub when it builds alliance partnerships and organizes regional and global cooperative security relations. Other states come to rely on the hub for security and stability. A state can take on the characteristics of a hub when it provides rules and institutional arrangements within which other states operate. The hub facilitates cooperation among states that are arrayed around it. More generally, the state can provide a political-institutional venue for commerce, diplomacy, and other forms of international exchange. This is the hub as a geopolitical crossroads location, providing institutional connections and services for regional or global governance.[26]

A hub is not just a reflection of power capabilities. It is also determined by its wider organizational characteristics and roles. Hubs can be more or less comprehensive as centers of power and power. The most fully developed hub would be a powerful state that organized the full range of functional areas: security, economics, politics, and so forth. A

[25] As Barry Buzan argues, "Polarity can be used to move forward into realist assumptions about conflict of interest, balance of power, and war, but it can just as easily fit with international political economy concerns with leadership and the provision of collective goods, Gramscian ones about hegemony, globalist ones about a dominant core, world system ones about world empires and world economies, and English school ones about great power management and international society." Buzan, *United States and the Great Powers*, 32.

[26] I use the term "pole" to refer to states with aggregated material power capabilities, which is the standard definition. I use the term "hub" to refer to the political and organizational character of leading states in the international system. The imagery of polarity often includes organizational features of states—their ability to build alliances and spheres of influence, and thereby compete against other poles. And indeed, the power of a state—and its ability to be a pole—is at least partly defined by its ability to aggregate material capabilities and organizationally engage in power politics. But it is useful to distinguish between the two terms. See Emilie M. Hafner-Burton and Alexander H. Montgomery, "Power Positions: International Organizations, Social Networks, and Conflict," *Journal of Conflict Resolution* 50, no. 1 (February 2006), 3–27.

hub can differ in terms of its regional or global scale. Japan and China have variously played such a role in East Asia over the centuries. France and Britain have played such a role in Western Europe. Other hubs operate at a global level, drawing in states from across geographical areas. Britain in the nineteenth century was perhaps the first global hub. The United States and the Soviet Union during the Cold War were even more globally far-flung in their organizational reach. In these ways, hubs can have more or less expansive and integrative political-institutional characters. They can be imperial in character or liberal hegemonic. They can be quite limited in scope, operating regionally within a narrow functional area, such as trade and monetary relations. Or they can be far-reaching geopolitical entities that operate worldwide and along all the functional dimensions of world politics.

Seen in this light, the United States has created the most comprehensive and far-reaching pole/hub in world history. The extraordinary material capabilities that it possessed at the end of World War II made the notion that it would be a hub in the larger system inevitable. But it was the elaborate order building that the United States pursued with these capabilities that give the American hub its distinctive characteristics and ultimately has made it so expansive, integrative, and durable. More than other great powers or hegemonic states of the past, including Great Britain in the nineteenth century, the United States built order around institutionalized strategic relationships. It was a hub built around multilateral alliances, strategic restraint, cooperative security, and open and institutionalized rule-based relations. It is this order that has expanded outward during the postwar decades, integrating countries along the way, surviving the end of the Cold War and other upheavals to emerge as a unipolar system.

As we shall see in the next chapter, the United States turned itself into an organizational hub through its order building and provision of services and benefits. Security provision was the most important. As the Cold War unfolded, the United States took on expanding commitments to the security of allies in both Europe and Asia. It also made systematic efforts to open the world economy and underwrite rules and institutions for trade and monetary relations. American-sponsored rules and institutions provided the organizational infrastructure for expanding networks of political relationships. Specific countries and regions were beneficiaries of these security commitments and economic ties, but the resulting stability and openness of the system provides a wide organizational expanse within which states could integrate and operate.

The effect of these organizational features has been to make the American pole/hub unusually expansive and integrative. This is true in three ways. First, the unusually dense, encompassing, and broadly endorsed system of rules and institutions reduces the role of brute power—arbitrary and indiscriminate or not—in the operation of the system. It is a more open and rule-based order than previous historical orders. This has made it easier for other states to work with and connect to the United States. The United States is powerful and retains the ability to exercise its power in self-interested ways. But the overall system of rules and institutions puts bounds on that power and makes it less threatening. The United States has bound itself to allies and partners in ways that reduce the incentives that these states might otherwise have to resist and balance against the lead state.[27]

Second, the barriers to entry are relatively low. Unlike imperial systems of the past, the American-led order is built around rules and norms of nondiscrimination and market openness, creating conditions for countries—including rising countries on the periphery of this order—to advance their economic and political goals within it. Across history, international orders have varied widely in terms of whether the material benefits that are generated accrue disproportionately to the leading state or are widely shared. In the American-led system, the barriers to economic participation are low, and the potential benefits are high. States can join by adopting political and economic practices that are congruent with the open world system. Command decisions are not made at the center of the system about whether to include or exclude states. States have it within their own hands to make these decisions.

[27] These features are discussed in Ikenberry, *After Victory*.

This openness of the American hub extends beyond the state system. The low barriers to entry provide opportunities for nongovernmental actors—transnational activists, entrepreneurs, professional groups—to operate in and with others across the order. Anne-Marie Slaughter describes this quality of a country—and its outward organizational characteristics—as its capacity for connectivity.[28] In this sense, the American pole is "network friendly." It is an open and expandable organizational social and political system. It is a hub that attracts partners and participants.

Third is the coalition-based character of its leadership. Past orders have tended to be dominated by one state. The stakeholders of the current liberal international order include a coalition of powers arrayed around the United States—an important distinction. These leading states, most of them advanced liberal democracies, do not always agree, but they are engaged in a continuous process of give-and-take over economics, politics, and security. Unlike an imperial system, governance in this order takes place in a variety of formal and informal venues in which multiple states take the lead or operate in concert. The so-called G-7/G-8 process—and the more recent G-20 process—are emblematic of this open style of multilateral and expandable governance.

In these various ways, the liberal character of the political order that has surrounded the United States has turned it into a hub that is unusually expansive and integrative in character. Other countries have made systematic decisions to connect to and operate within this order rather than resist and oppose it. The economic growth and wealth creation generated within it makes it easier for leading states to provide aid and other benefits for weaker and smaller states. The multilateral rules and institutions within this order also provide mechanisms for states seeking to manage economic crises or reforms. Coordination is facilitated and

[28] Anne-Marie Slaughter, "America's Edge: Power in the Networked Century," *Foreign Affairs* (January/February 2009). See also David Singh Grewal, *Network Power: The Social Dynamics of Globalization* (New Haven, CT: Yale University Press, 2008). For a discussion of networks and international conflict, see Zeev Maoz, Lesley Terris, Ranan D. Kuperman, and Ilan Talmud, "Network Centrality and International Conflict, 1816–2001: Does it Pay to Be Important?" working paper, November 2004.

resources—policy knowledge, standby funds, etc.—are available for participating states. In effect, the liberal order takes on the form of a mutual aid society. States join the order and benefit accordingly. Alternative poles/hubs—existing or imagined—offer fewer attractions. Unipolarity emerged in the post-Cold War decades as alternative poles/hubs fell away or failed to form.

Consequences of Unipolarity

If counterbalancing is not the central response to the rise of unipolarity, what is? The global system remains hierarchical, but does the character of that hierarchy change under conditions of unipolarity, and if so in what ways? In particular, we are interested in knowing how the shift from Cold War bipolarity to unipolarity alters the constraints and incentives on institutional cooperation between the United States and other states in the system. Does the rise of unipolarity alter the incentives for the United States to construct and operate within multilateral frameworks? How does unipolarity alter the incentives for weaker and secondary states to cooperate with the leading state? And how do these shifts change the overall character of international order?

To ask these questions is to probe the changing logic of the institutional bargain between a unipolar state and others around it. As I argued in chapter 3, the state's decision whether to operate within rule-based institutional relationships entails a basic cost-benefit calculation. To make binding agreements is to give up policy autonomy. This is a cost states would prefer not to bear unless doing so generates rules and institutions that yield benefits that are greater than the costs of lost autonomy. Benefits can entail the expected material gains that flow from a stable, rule-based order as well as less tangible gains associated with the enhancement of the legitimacy of the state and the wider international order it dominates. This institutional bargaining model allows us to see how long-term shifts in power and interests can alter the multilateral commitments of the leading state.

The rise of unipolarity is manifest in growing power advantages for the leading state, generated in part by the loss of a competing pole. The leading state has no peer competitor or global rival. This shift in power and polarity appears to give added bargaining advantages to the unipolar state in several ways. First, the lead state has more discretionary power resources because it no longer has a security competitor. It possesses the same power resources as before—and indeed it may increase them—but those capabilities are not now tied down in bipolar security competition. Second, and relatedly, there are fewer external restraints on the leading state's exercise of power because it is not being balanced by the other major states. Power is not actively being deployed—at least on a global scale by a rival great power—to oppose and contain the leading state. Third, secondary and weaker states no longer have an exit option. The lead state has a near-monopoly on the global provision of security protection. Under these circumstances, there is no escape from hierarchy under conditions of unipolarity. A rival hierarchical order to which a weaker state might move does not exist. Finally, and more generally, the unipolar state now has a more encompassing impact on the global system. If there is to be order and the provision of public goods, the unipolar state will need to be involved in their generation. It is harder to work around the leading state than in bipolar or multipolar orders. Other states must therefore worry more about whether or not the leading state will provide public goods and exercise power in ways that promote stability, openness, and rule-based relations. These factors all give the leading state new advantages in institutional bargains.

But unipolarity may also reduce some of the power advantages that the lead state has under Cold War bipolarity. To start, weaker and secondary states are not threatened by a global rival power, and so their security needs decline—and therefore their potential dependence on the lead state for security protection declines. To some extent, this reduces the bargaining advantage of the security-providing unipolar state. The unipolar state has an abundance of military capacity, and so it is in a position to provide security protection around the world. But this protection is not in demand in the way it was before, or at least the demand for unipolar security protection will be more disparate and unevenly manifest in various parts of the world.

More generally, the legitimacy of the lead state is less self-evident. In the eyes of weaker and secondary states, the exercise of power is less easy to see as normatively right or proper. Junior partners in a bipolar coalition see the lead state as a security protector and provider of order. The power of each is seen as good for the well-being of all. In a unipolar order, the power of the lead state is less obviously good for the other states within the order. If there is a decline in the legitimacy of the international order under conditions of unipolarity, the lead state is faced with new problems about how to establish restraints and credible commitments on its power that are necessary for the maintenance of legitimate rule.

These shifts in power advantages and bargaining circumstances allow us to see a variety of possible impacts on the leading state's strategies of rule, on the policy responses of weaker and secondary states, and on the overall patterns of global rules and relationships. We can look at these impacts in turn.

Renegotiation of Institutional Bargains

The first impact of unipolarity relates to opportunities it creates for the leading state to recapture some of its policy autonomy through the renegotiation of institutional bargains. These opportunities emerge from gains in power advantages. If power disparities shift in favor of the lead state, it finds itself with new bargaining advantages. It is potentially less dependent on other states, and so it can walk away more easily from international agreements. Other states are potentially more dependent on the lead state. These changing circumstances create shifts in bargaining advantage, putting the unipolar state in a position to hold on to or regain policy autonomy. It is out of this logic that we can expect that the unipolar state—if the power shifts are sufficiently great and manifest in these ways—will seek to renegotiate its institutional bargains with other states and make adjustments in its strategies of rule.[29]

As I argued in chapter 3, the leading state makes institutional commitments—and in doing so, restricts its policy autonomy—to gain agreements from other states that shape and constrain their policies. The leading state wants to shape and constrain the policies of other states in its efforts to organize a predictable and congenial environment in which it can pursue its interests. It makes commitments to restrict its own policy autonomy so as to gain political control over other states and the wider international system. When power disparities shift in favor of the leading state, it has opportunities to adjust its commitments and strategies to get political control at, in effect, a cheaper price. This should be reflected in the renegotiation of specific institutional bargains and in its choice of governance strategies.

The leading state could use its increased power advantages to make a variety of institutional adjustments that give it the level of international political control it seeks with the least amount of lost autonomy. Building on the discussion in chapter 3, there are several different ways that the leading state can do this. One involves introducing greater differential rules and obligations into agreements. Veto rights, voting shares, and other decision-making rules can be adjusted to give greater rights and authority to the leading state—thereby reducing the constraints that rules and institutions have on its power and policy. A related step involves reducing the strength of the rules and institutions themselves by making the institutional agreements less binding, as manifest in weaker rules concerning monitoring, compliance, and enforcement. Another step is to introduce less formal forms of institutional commitments. The leading state can offer process commitments that involve giving weaker and secondary states voice opportunities rather than formal and substantive rule-based commitments. Finally, the leading state can use its heightened power position to shift toward the more unilateral provision

---

[29] For an interpretation of American foreign policy along these lines, see Dan Drezner, "The New New World Order," *Foreign Affairs* 86 (March/April 2007), 34–46.

of rules. It attempts to externalize its domestic rules into the international system. In doing so, the leading state is using its power position—manifest in, for example, the centrality and size of its domestic market—to force other countries to adjust to its standards and practices. In each of these ways, the rise of unipolarity does not lead to the abrogation of rule-based order but to an adjustment in its terms and conditions. Rules and institutions are renegotiated—in one way or another—to reflect changes in the hierarchy of power.

In addition to renegotiating institutional bargains, the leading state might also make changes in its more basic strategies of rule, which I have described as rule through rules and rule through relationships. During the period of Cold War bipolarity, the United States built order around both these strategies. Each has its attractions as a mechanism to assert political control. Rule through rules involves the negotiation of multilateral agreements that, if successful, can provide a wide-open space of predictable and efficient cooperative relations—and they can help foster a shared sense of legitimacy in the overall international order. The cost to the leading state—depending on how strong and undifferentiated the rules in fact are—is in lost autonomy and the ability to directly manipulate specific states.

Rule through relationships involves negotiating bilateral agreements and building patron-client pacts. The attraction of these bilateral relationships is that the leading state can assert more direct control without incurring the costs associated with making binding rule-based agreements. As noted in chapter 3, this is the logic that helps explain America's different strategies of rule in Europe and East Asia in the postwar era. The United States tended to pursue multilateral strategies with Europe and bilateral strategies with East Asia. With Europe, the United States had a full agenda: it wanted a great deal of ongoing cooperation with its Atlantic partners and was willing to make multilateral institutional commitments. With East Asia, the United States wanted less and dominated these states more, and so it could gain the political control it wanted through bilateral pacts without losing its freedom of action.

In the shift from Cold War bipolarity to unipolarity, the attraction of this sort of bilateral strategy of rule would appear to grow.

With greater power disparities between itself and various other states, the United States will want less from them and therefore will be less inclined to entangle itself in multilateral rule-based arrangements. The end of the Cold War itself also contributes to the strength of the rule-through-relationships logic, at least as it relates to security. Without a common security threat—such as that posed by the Soviet Union—the security needs of states are more differentiated. Some will seek American security protection and others will not. The United States also has more differential sorts of security relations with these states.[30] These considerations appear to make bilateral relations—and rule through relationships—more attractive to the unipolar state. But there are also crosscutting incentives that favor multilateral arrangements. I will return to them later in the chapter.

Provision of Public Goods

A second impact of unipolarity is on the provision of public goods. During the era of Cold War bipolarity, the United States found itself as a provider of public goods in the areas of security provision, maintenance of economic openness and stability, and support for the rules and institutions that formed the order. This willingness of the leading state to act in behalf of the system as a whole—to provide system services to participants within the order—is a key characteristic of liberal hegemony. The question is whether and in what ways the shift to unipolarity alters the willingness or ability of the leading state to provide these goods.[31]

Public or collective goods may be consumed by multiple actors without the actors necessarily having to pay the full costs of producing them. The classic theoretical insight is that if enough actors follow their rational self-interest and choose to free ride on the efforts of others, public

---

[30] Stephen Walt explores the logic of alliance relations under conditions of unipolarity, focusing on the ways that a unipolar state might use alliances to manage relations with other states and the strategies of weaker states to influence the unipolar state. Walt, "Alliances in a Unipolar World," *World Politics* 61, no. 1 (January 2009), 86–120.

[31] This section and the next draw on Ikenberry, Mastanduno, and Wohlforth, "Introduction."

goods will be under-produced or not produced at all.[32] To overcome the free-rider problem requires cooperation among self-interested actors.[33] The literature on hegemonic stability theory hypothesizes that cooperation in international relations requires the leadership of the dominant state.[34] Its preponderance of economic and military resources means the dominant state has the ability to bear disproportionately the costs of providing international collective goods such as an open world economy or a stable security order. The leading state has an interest in bearing these costs because it benefits disproportionately from promoting systemwide outcomes that reflect its values and interests.

During the Cold War, the United States did step forward to provide public goods. It took on the responsibilities that Charles Kindleberger argues were needed to promote international economic stability, such as serving as an open market of last resort and allowing the use of its currency for exchange and reserve purposes.[35] International economic stability among the Western powers reinforced their security alliance against the Soviet Union. The United States also bore disproportionately the direct costs of Western alliance security. In the background, American support for the basic framework of postwar rules and institutions was also a type of public goods provision. The Soviet Union, on its side of the international divide, ultimately shouldered disproportionately alliance costs as well.[36] Kenneth Waltz took the argument a step further, arguing that the United States and Soviet Union may have been adversaries in the bipolar system, but they shared, as the two dominant powers, a mutual interest in system stability that prompted them to cooperate in providing public goods such as nuclear

[32] See Mancur Olson, *The Logic of Collective Action: Public Goods and the Theory of Groups* (Cambridge, MA: Harvard University Press, 1971 [1965]).

[33] Kenneth Oye, ed., *Cooperation under Anarchy* (Princeton, NJ: Princeton University Press, 1986).

[34] See literature cited in chapter 3.

[35] See Charles Kindleberger, *The World in Depression, 1929–1938* (Berkeley: University of California Press, 1973).

[36] See Valerie Bunce, "The Empire Strikes Back: The Evolution of the Eastern Bloc from Soviet Asset to Liability," *International Organization* 39, no. 1 (1985), 1–46.

nonproliferation.[37] Hedley Bull makes a similar point in his classic study of the international system as a society of states.[38]

How might the shift from a bipolar system to a unipolar one affect the inclination of the now singularly dominant state to provide international public goods? Two possible logics present themselves. One possibility is that it would continue to provide public goods—and even increase its responsibilities for the stability, openness, and security of the order. The capabilities of a unipolar state relative to other major states are greater than those of either dominant state in a bipolar system. It has more capacity to provide system services. The unipolar state's incentive should be stronger as well, since it now has the opportunity to influence international outcomes globally, not just in its particular subsystem. In effect, the underlying logic of liberal hegemony should still obtain under conditions of unipolarity. The leading state should try to lock in a durable international order that reflects its interests and values.[39]

The other possibility is the opposite logic. After the shift from Cold War bipolarity to unipolarity, we might expect the leading state to underproduce public goods despite its preponderant capabilities. The fact that it is unthreatened by peer competitors and relatively unconstrained by other states creates incentives for the unipolar state to pursue more parochial interests even at the expense of a stable international order. The fact that it is extraordinarily powerful means that it will be more inclined to force adjustment costs onto others rather than bear disproportionate burdens itself.

It is possible that both these logics will be at play simultaneously. The unipolar state may continue to provide public goods, but in the absence of a common threat or rival pole, the states in the order may increasingly disagree on what public goods should be provided and on what terms. This may be particularly true in the security realm. The leading state may seek fewer rules and institutional constraints in the provision of security protection or otherwise attempt to alter old security bargains. As Michael

[37] Waltz, *Theory of International Politics*, chap. 9.
[38] Hedley Bull, *Anarchical Society*.
[39] Ikenberry, *After Victory*, chap. 3.

Mastanduno argues, a dominant state can be both a "system maker" and a "privilege taker"—it can seek simultaneously to provide public goods and to exploit its advantageous power position for parochial gain. It simultaneously enlists the cooperation of other states and seeks, with varying success, to force adjustment burdens upon them.[40] The shift to unipolarity may alter the mix of these two lead-state tendencies.

If the lead state does use its unipolar position to become more of a privilege taker and to shift adjustment burdens on others, questions emerge. How far will it move in this direction? At what point does diminished and contested provision of public goods alter the fundamental character of the order? More importantly, what are the pressures and incentives that remain—even under conditions of unipolarity—for the leading state to provide public goods and seek consensus over the rules and institutions of liberal hegemonic order?

Status Quo versus Revisionism

Does the shift from Cold War bipolarity to unipolarity alter the leading state's orientation toward upholding the stability of the existing rules and institutions of the system? This is not a question about renegotiating specific institutional bargains; it is about making more basic transformations in the organizational arrangements of the international system. If the transition from bipolarity to unipolarity does represent a power shift in America's favor, will it seek to use that power to preserve and extend the prevailing rules and institutions or seek to transform them?

The stability of any international system depends significantly on the degree to which the major powers are satisfied with the status quo.[41] Robert Gilpin argues that leading states "will attempt to change the

---

[40] Michael Mastanduno, "System Maker and Privilege Taker: U.S. Power and the International Political Economy," *World Politics* 61, no. 1 (January 2009), 121–54.

[41] See E. H. Carr, *Twenty Years' Crisis, 1919–1939: An Introduction to the Study of International Relations* (London: Macmillan, 1951); A.F.K. Organski, *World Politics* (New York: Knopf, 1958); Randall L. Schweller, "Bandwagoning for Profit: Bringing the Revisionist State Back In," *International Security* 19, no. 1 (Summer 1994), 72–107; and Robert Powell, "Stability and the Distribution of Power," *World Politics* 48, no. 2 (1996), 239–67.

international system if the expected benefits exceed the expected costs."[42]
During the long era of bipolarity, the question of whether the cost-benefit calculation of the United States favored the status quo seemed obvious. After all, the postwar international order—that is, the Western pole within the larger bipolar system—was largely organized and led by the United States. With the end of the Cold War, it also appeared that the United States would remain a satisfied lead state—with overwhelming incentives to consolidate and extend the American-led pole under conditions of unipolarity. But is this necessarily so?

Again, two alternative logics seem possible. One logic is that the unipolar state will be a status quo power. It achieved its predominant position in an international system that was already strongly shaped by its power and preferences. It thrives in the existing system and occupies the commanding positions of authority. The expectation is that the leading state would want to hold on to the rules and institutions of this order and make them last for the long term. But there is also a logic of revision. With the shift to unipolarity, the leading state now has a new opportunity to reshape the international system in a way that was unavailable to it during the period of bipolarity. It has unrivaled power capabilities and seemingly few constraints on reshaping its environment. Robert Jervis takes this argument several steps further, arguing that while the unipolar state has power and opportunity—it also has new sorts of threats and insecurities that might lead it to favor a revisionist orientation toward the international system.[43]

Jervis argues that unipolarity does create incentives for revisionism. A state's definition of its interests tends to expand with its power. "Increasing capabilities make it possible to pursue a whole host of objectives that were out of reach when the state's security was in doubt and all efforts had to be directed to primary objectives." The disappearance of balancing constraints and rival geopolitical poles gives the unipolar state

[42] Gilpin, *War and Change in World Politics*, chap. 2.

[43] Robert Jervis, "Unipolarity: A Structural Perspective," *World Politics*, 61, no. 1 (January 2009).

new opportunities to "re-make the world in its own image, or rather in its desired self-image."[44] At the same time, the unipolar state also has the entire world to worry about. It no longer is threatened by a rival super-power, but it has a stake in what happens everywhere. Jervis notes that "the growth of power and influence leads to new positions that have to be defended."[45] At the very least, unipolarity will generate pressures for the leading state to think—and perhaps rethink—its strategies of rule. It no longer has a bipolar rival; it confronts a more diffuse and global array of worries. A revisionist agenda is one possible pathway for a newly powerful but also newly challenged lead state.

Unipolarity, as a structure of power, may not necessarily by itself favor either conservativism or revisionism. More circumstantial fac-tors—such as the character of the state, its ideas about international order and change, and the prevailing rules and institutions of the sys-tem—will matter when shaping incentives and choices. The fact that power is so highly concentrated and unbalanced suggests that the lead-ing state has a great deal of discretion in making grand strategic choices. As Jervis notes, "unipolarity takes states out of anarchy and transforms if not dissolves international politics." In particular, "security concerns are greatly reduced for the superpower and others it protects (although the superpower itself may be a source of threat as well as of protection). Since such concerns are the main drivers of traditional international politics, the implications are likely to be far-reaching."[46] More so than in bipolar or multipolar systems, the leading state has capacities and oppor-tunities to shape the international system. Its range of options is greater. The constraints and discipline generated by the pressures of anarchy are radically abated under conditions of unipolarity. Because of this, it will matter greatly who leads the unipolar state—and the ideas that these leaders have about their security, interests, and what constitutes a desir-able international order.

[44] Jervis, "Unipolarity," 199.
[45] Jervis, "Unipolarity," 200.
[46] Jervis, "Unipolarity," 194.

Shifts in the Character of the Order

How does the shift from Cold War bipolarity to unipolarity alter the overall character of the American-led international order? In chapter 3, I argued that during the postwar era, the United States built a liberal hegemonic order around two strategies of rule—rule through rules and rule through relationships. Both strategies are employed in efforts to assert political control over other states and the wider international order. One strategy is the multilateral, rule-based approach manifest most fully in America's relations with Western Europe and in world economic governance. The other strategy is what might be called hub-and-spoke bilateralism, and it has been pursued in America's relations with countries in East Asia. The choice of strategy is driven by functional incentives and trade-offs. The shift to unipolarity appears to generate some incentives—but also costs—for the United States to pursue the logic of hub-and-spoke bilateralism.

Each of the two strategies offers some advantages over the other, as well as costs. The multilateral rule-based strategy creates rules and institutions that establish ordered relations that are potentially more efficient and legitimate, while the bilateral hub-and-spoke strategy offers the unipolar state fewer restrictions on its policy autonomy and more direct ways to use power to shape the policies of other states. (See table 4-1.)

As noted earlier, the two logics of rule have been manifest, respectively, in America's relations with Western Europe and East Asia. The United States agreed to a multilateral order with Europe because it determined that the restraints on its own power through NATO and other multilateral institutions was worth what it got in return. Britain, France, and other European states were willing to accept multilateral agreements to the extent that they also constrained and regularized U.S. economic and security actions. American agreement to operate within a multilateral economic order and make an alliance-based security commitment to Europe was worth the price: it ensured that Germany and the rest of Western Europe would be integrated into a wider,

Table 4-1
Two Logics of Unipolar Governance

Hub-and-Spoke Bilateralism

Unipolar state builds an array of bilateral relationships with weaker states, each operating as a patron-client relationship<m->or "special relationship"<m->where specific deals, patronage relations, and understandings prevail

Advantages of bilateralism for the unipolar state:

1- The divide-and-rule approach undercuts the rise of "trade union" of weak states.

2- It frees the unipolar state from multilateral rules and binding commitments and increases its freedom and flexibility of action.

3- Unipolar power can be more directly employable to gain favorable outcomes. It is easier to reward and punish other states.

4- Unipolarity creates opportunities for weak states to free ride on the lead state. By making security and economic relations divisible, bilateralism provides opportunities for the unipolar state to share and redistribute costs.

Multilateral Rule-based Order

Unipolar state operates with a set of multilateral rules and institutions that establishes obligations and commitments for both it and weak states.

Advantages of multilateralism for the unipolar state:

1- It reduces transaction costs. Diffuse reciprocity is more efficient in cooperative state actions than bilateral bargaining.

2- It enhances the legitimacy of the unipolar state. Weaker states are more likely to engage rather than resist the policies of the lead state.

3- It's an investment in the future. Rules and institutions can provide favorable order after unipolar power declines.

4- It confers domestic political advantages. Rule-based order comports with liberal polity self-identity and reduces political costs of unipolar governance.

American-centered international order. At the same time, the actual restraints on American policy were minimized through veto rights and first-among-equals status within these institutions. In East Asia, security relations quickly became bilateral. The United States was dominant in East Asia yet it wanted less out of the region, so giving up policy autonomy in exchange for institutionalized cooperation there was less necessary. In Europe, the United States had an elaborate agenda of uniting Europe, creating an institutional bulwark against communism, and supporting centrist democratic governments. These goals could not be realized simply by exercising power directly. To get what it wanted, the United States had to bargain with the Europeans, and this meant agreeing to institutionally restrain and commit its power. In East Asia, the building of order around bilateral pacts was more desirable because multilateralism would entail more restraints on American freedom of action.

In some ways, the shift to unipolarity generates incentives for hub-and-spoke bilateralism on a global scale. Rather than be bound to multilateral frameworks, the unipolar state might want to consider forging an expanding array of patron-client and special relationships around the world. Countries that cooperate with the United States and accept its leadership receive special bilateral security and economic compensation.[47] Several features of unipolarity suggest a strengthening of incentives for this sort of strategy of rule. One is the feature that existed in postwar East Asia. Intensified power disparities create opportunities to exert control bilaterally while minimizing binding institutional constraints. The unipolar state can more fully translate its power advantages into immediate and tangible concessions from other states—and do so without giving up as much policy autonomy. Second, the rise of unipolarity entails the disappearance of rival poles—and, as noted earlier, this reduces the sense of shared and common threat that was so important for multilateral security cooperation during the Cold War. Operating in a security environment where threats are more differentiated and fragmented, the unipolar state will have incentives to negotiate separate security deals with individual states. Finally, to the extent that unipolarity creates added worries among states in the willingness and ability of the leading state to restrain its power, bilateral deals can be a tool of reassurance. Bilateral partnerships provide a mechanism to signal strategic restraint and commitment.

But what is also apparent is that multilateral strategies of rule remain useful as well. If unipolarity has an impact on the overall system

[47] See Jakub J. Grygiel, "Imperial Allies," *Orbis* 50, no. 2 (Spring 2006), 209–21.

of governance—if it alters the character of postwar liberal hegemonic order—it will do so by influencing the mix of strategies. Unipolarity itself as a distinctive international distribution of power does not in itself generate a particular strategy of rule. More circumstantial factors will also matter in the shaping of the choices of unipolar strategies of rule, driven by how the unipolar state calculates its interests and determines costs and benefits of alternative types of governance arrangements.

Legitimacy, Anticipated Power Shifts, and Credible Restraint

To what extent will a unipolar state seek to break out of or renegotiate its old institutional bargains? The argument developed here is that the shift from bipolarity to unipolarity does generate incentives for the leading state to renegotiate old bargains and alter its strategies of rule. Under conditions of Cold War bipolarity, the United States pursued a mix of rule-based and client-state strategies of rule. The rise of unipolarity creates new opportunities for it to step back from formal, rule-based strategies of governance. But, as we have seen, the incentives cut both ways. In this regard, three factors are most important is determining the degree to which the leading state will continue to rely on rule-based strategies—legitimacy pressures, calculations about future power shifts, and the ability to establish credible restraints on power without resort to balancing.

The shift from bipolarity to unipolarity does appear to generate legitimacy problems for the leading state. Under conditions of bipolarity, the leading state is actively providing security and public goods as it engages in balancing against the other pole. The functional role of the leading state as a system balancer makes it easier for other states to see its power as legitimate. The leading state will also have tangible incentives to make its power legitimate as it engages in competition with the other pole—it will want to cultivate coalition partners and keep them as willing members of its bipolar alliance. In doing this, it may use multilateral institutions and commitments to rule-based order as part of its strategy of maintaining its legitimacy and ensuring the willing participation and compliance of other states.[48] With the rise of unipolarity, it may be harder for the leading state to maintain a sense of its legitimacy. If legitimacy is lost or diminished, how will the leading state respond? That is, how costly is lost or diminished legitimacy to the leading state under unipolarity?

If balancing is removed as a restraint on the leading state—and as a potential sanction on its uses of power—does a more diffuse and less tangible cost such as lost legitimacy have any enduring impact as a restraint and a sanction? To the extent it does, the unipolar state will continue to find advantages in using multilateral institutions and rule-based relations in its governance strategy. These legitimacy costs are not easy to measure. Decision makers in the unipolar state may vary in how they perceive lost legitimacy and calculate its costs. But the greater the costs, the more likely it is that the unipolar state will find itself drawn to support liberal, rule-based order.[49]

The judgments that leaders within the unipolar state make about the country's future power position are a second factor. If these leaders believe that the unipolar distribution of power is semipermanent—that is, that it will last into the foreseeable future—they will be less responsive to the lock-in possibilities of rules and institutions. If, on the other hand, leaders believe that unipolarity will give way in the decades ahead to a bipolar or multipolar distribution of power, they are likely to have

[48] Krisch argues that, under conditions of bipolarity, the dominant state may be particularly concerned with its legitimacy, or at least more so than in multipolar and unipolar systems. "In bipolar international systems, for example, the hegemonic powers tend to be more concerned about the stability of their sphere of influence than in multipolar or unipolar systems, because defection usually results in an immediate gain for the other hegemon. Thus, in such settings, we can expect relatively greater efforts at legitimizing dominance, often times through the use of multilateral institutions." Nico Krisch, "International Law in Times of Hegemony," *European Journal of International Law* 16, no. 3 (2005), 369–408.

[49] For explorations of the ways in which legitimacy acts to impose costs and discipline the exercise of unipolarity, see Martha Finnemore, "Legitimacy, Hypocrisy, and the Social Structure of Unipolarity: Why Being a Unipole Isn't All It's Cracked Up to Be," *World Politics* 61, no. 1 (January 2009), 58–85; and Christian Reus-Smit, *American Power and World Order* (London: Polity, 2004).

a different view of the value of these rule-based mechanisms of governance. An optimistic assessment of the durability of unipolar power
will give leaders reasons to ignore losses in legitimacy. The normative
approval of the international order led by the unipolar state can decline,
but if the material basis of unipolar power remains in place, the leaders
can calculate that they can still achieve their goals without the full consent of other states. The costs of lost autonomy associated with making
binding commitments to rules and institutions can be avoided—at least,
to the extent that those commitments are made primarily for cultivating
legitimacy and consent.

But if leaders in the dominant state judge that the unipolar distribution
of power will soon or eventually wane, a different set of calculations about
rules and institutions are likely. There will be incentives for the unipolar
state to put in place a set of rules and institutions that can last beyond unipolarity, creating a favorable institutional environment for the lead state as
its relative power declines. The investment incentive for rules and institutions emerges as a consideration in the thinking of the lead state.[50] This
calculation does not need to stand alone as a factor that shapes the leading
state's views on strategies of rule. It is a consideration that will presumably
weigh in the balance as decisions are made on specific institutional agreements and on the more general orientation of the state to the character of
international order under conditions of unipolarity.

Finally, another factor that will shape the shift in incentives either
toward or away from commitments to rules and institutions is whether
those commitments in fact establish credible constraints and limits on
the exercise of unipolar power. The institutional bargain—whether negotiated under conditions of Cold War bipolarity or unipolarity—hinges
on the credibility of the restraints and commitments that are embedded
in the agreements. A state will not be willing to restrict its own policy
autonomy if it is not reasonably confident that the agreement will have
some shaping and constraining effect on the other state. During the
Cold War, the credibility of the American restraints and commitments

[50] This argument is developed in Ikenberry, *After Victory*, chap. 3.

were backed up by the bipolar structure of the system itself—and the incentives that the United States had to maintain the anti-Soviet coalition. The question that weaker states must ask when the power structure is unipolar is: are institutional restraints on the exercise of arbitrary and indiscriminate power still credible?

Conclusion

Unipolarity is a distinctive distribution of power that the world has not seen until recently. It is an international system in which material capabilities are highly concentrated. A single state stands above other states, commanding the full range of power resources. In bipolar and multipolar systems, there is a diffusion of power among several great powers. In a unipolar system, in contrast, one state stands above others. In the 1990s, the United States emerged as a unipolar state. It was uniquely powerful, positioned at the center on a one-pole global system. This chapter has explored both the causes and consequences of unipolarity. The first observation is that despite the unprecedented concentration of power in the hands of one state, a counterbalancing response did not emerge. This absence of a traditional balancing response is a puzzle. In one sense, the sheer predominance of the United States created constraints on the ability of other great powers to aggregate sufficient capabilities to challenge unipolarity. The constraints on balancing were reinforced by the geography of world politics that created regional blockages on the rise of great-power challenges to the United States. Regional balances of power have constrained the workings of the global balance of power. The United States, in contrast, has been able to rise in power separated by oceans from the other great powers.

But these explanations for the absence of balancing presume that there has been a demand for balancing—and this is not evident. Nuclear weapons have reduced the threat of aggression by the great powers, and this has made unipolarity itself less threatening. That most of the major great powers are democracies also has mattered in reducing the security competition that would otherwise push the system toward a balancing response.

Most importantly, the political-institutional character of the American pole has had consequences for the rise and functioning of unipolarity. Major states around the United States have actively sought to connect to and operate within the organizational space created by American unipolarity. Democratic states that bound themselves to the United States during the Cold War remained tied to the United States under conditions of unipolarity. Other countries—in Asia and Eastern Europe—also integrated into the American-led order. It is not just that the United States is not threatening enough to trigger balancing. It is that the political formation around unipolarity has an open and integrative logic. The United States is the hub in a one-pole global system. The American-led liberal order offers benefits and services to states that alternative orders or spheres cannot offer. In this way, unipolarity is the consequence of the gradual disappearance of alternative organizing hubs in world politics.

Despite the absence of balancing, unipolarity does alter the array of incentives and constraints that bear on the organization of rules and institutions. Incentives exist to redraw the institutional bargains. Conflicts over burden sharing and free riding are associated with unipolarity. The unipolar state has choices and alternative incentives for multilateral and hub-and-spoke logics of order. The choices that the unipolar state makes will hinge on the way it values legitimacy, makes credible commitments, and responds to the prospect of unipolar decline.

Unipolarity—understood as a one-pole global system—is not just a reflection of the distribution of power but of organizational features of liberal international order. If this is true, the global system could retain political characteristics of unipolarity even as the distribution of material capabilities shifts away from the United States. A relative decline in American power disparities will not inevitably lead to the formation of new poles or a balance-of-power system. The critical question is whether the United States, under conditions of unipolarity, will continue to support liberal international order. Ironically, the prospect of a decline in American relative power generates incentives for a renewed commitment by the United States to open and rule-based order. In the end, it is these liberal features of the international order that will slow down and mute the consequences of a return to multipolarity.

Part Two

Historical Origins and Trajectories of Change

Five
The Rise of the American System

In the mid-twentieth century, in the aftermath of depression and war, and in the shadow of the Cold War, the United States emerged as the world's most powerful state and set about building an international order. Through design, adaptation, choice, and necessity, the United States shaped the governing arrangements of the Western system into an order tied together by partnerships, pacts, institutions, and grand bargains and built around multilayered agreements that served to open markets, bind democracies and anticommunist authoritarian regimes together, and create a far-flung security community. Indeed, between 1944 and 1951, American leaders engaged in the most intensive institution building the world had ever seen. They helped launch the United Nations, Bretton Woods, GATT, NATO, and the US-Japan alliance. They assumed costly obligations to aid Greece and Turkey and reconstruct Western Europe. They helped rebuild the economies of Germany and Japan and integrate them into the emerging Western system. And with the Atlantic Charter, the U.N. Charter, and the Universal

Declaration of Human Rights, they articulated a new vision of a progressive international community.

The result was a hierarchical order with liberal characteristics, built around a set of American political, economic, and security bargains with countries in Europe and East Asia. The United States provided security, championed mutually agreed-upon rules and institutions, and led in the management of an open world economy. In return, other states affiliated with and supported the United States as it led the larger order. The United States dominated the order, but the political space created by American domination was organized around partnerships and agreed-upon rules and institutions that facilitated restraint, commitment, reciprocity, and legitimacy.

This order-building project was a remarkable undertaking. It signified the triumph of American internationalism after earlier post-1919 and interwar failures. It fused new forms of liberalism, internationalism, great-power politics, and national security. It marked the beginning of the "long peace"—the longest period in modern history without war between the great powers. It laid the foundation for the greatest economic boom in history. In almost all important respects, we still live in the world created during these dramatic postwar years of international order building.

How do we make sense of this order? This is a question both about its character—its features and logic—and about how we explain it as a historical-political outcome. What sort of order is it, as seen in theoretical and historical perspective? If it is best described as a liberal hegemonic order, what are the bargains and institutions that give it its distinctive logic and character? Beyond this, why did the United States in fact take the lead in creating such an order? No world power had ever sought to build such an order in the past. What was distinctive about America—its power, position, and ideas—that engendered this project?

In grappling with these questions, this chapter makes four arguments. First, the United States led in the creation of a distinctive international order that combined the ordering mechanisms of balance, command, and consent. This order established governance arrangements—formal and informal—for the states that operated within it and a hierarchical system of rule, through both rules and relationships. Hierarchy and domination were infused with consent and the rule of law. Three features in particular gave it a liberal character: public goods provision, rule-based cooperation, and voice opportunities and diffuse reciprocity. This is not empire—it is an American-led open-democratic political order.

Second, the American-led postwar order was actually the fusing of two order-building projects. One was driven by the unfolding Cold War struggle with the Soviet Union, organized around deterrence, containment, alliances, and the bipolar balance of power. The other was aimed at creating an open, stable, and managed order among the Western democracies and was conceived by American officials before the onset of the Cold War—at least as early as the issuance of the Atlantic Charter in 1941—drawing on and updating liberal internationalist ideas. As it emerged, this liberal hegemonic order existed inside the larger bipolar global system. When the Cold War ended, the inside order became the outside order—that is, its logic was extended to the larger global system.

Third, the order was not conceived in a singular vision and imposed on the world. It was cobbled together in a rolling political process. The initial American impulse was to urge upon other states the creation of a rather straightforward open and rule-based order. But the complexity of the vision—and of the resulting order itself—increased as the United States and the other major Western states dealt with an unfolding array of circumstances: the economic weakness and political vulnerability of Europe, a rising Soviet threat, the constraints of domestic politics, and a continuous process of intergovernmental bargaining and institution building. The specific sets of bargains and institutions also differed across the emerging American-led order, particularly in the types of political and security relationships established between the United States and its Western European and East Asian partners. As this process unfolded, the United States increasingly took on hegemonic roles and responsibilities. What was initially conceived as a sort of free-standing, self-regulating international order eventually became a more explicitly American enterprise. The United States was not simply a party to it;

the U.S. economy, polity, and extended partnerships and commitments came to form its core.

Fourth, several circumstances facilitated and reinforced the liberal character of the American-led order. American ideas of postwar order were not imperial; quite to the contrary, the original vision was for a system that would not be directly managed by Washington, D.C. The United States was also offshore—removed from the immediate pressures and insecurities of great-power politics in Europe and East Asia. This meant that when the Cold War emerged, American allies in both regions worried more about abandonment than about domination. The United States could offer security assistance without threatening complete loss of regional autonomy. The fact that the Western core of the order was built among democratic societies and organized around layers of institutions also helped by increasing the opportunities for reciprocity and voice. Finally, the array of client-state relations—which coexisted with multilateral rules and institutions—created mechanism for side payments, reciprocity, bargaining, and mutual adjustment.

The character and logic of the order was different from anything the world had seen before. It was both hierarchical and loosely rule-based. Its terms were more negotiated than imposed. And with a demand for American hegemonic rule, its supply was generated through the provision of rules and institutions and the forging of an array of patron-client relations.

America and Postwar Order Building

No state in history has been so well positioned after a major war to shape international order as the United States was in 1945. It emerged from the most violent and destructive war in history as the most powerful state the world had ever seen. While the other major states—both the Axis and Allied powers—saw their industrial economies damaged and destroyed by the war, wartime mobilization had lifted the United States out of depression. Its gross national product increased 60 percent during the war, by the end of which the United States had become the world's leading military power, producing more arms than the Axis states combined and almost three times the amount generated by the Soviet Union. As Melvyn Leffler notes: "In 1945, the United States had two-thirds of the world's gold reserves, three-fourths of its invested capital, half of its shipping vessels, and half of its manufacturing capacity. Its gross national product was three times that of the Soviet Union and more than five times that of Great Britain."[1] The war diminished the other great powers—at least temporarily—while it turned the United States into a global superpower.[2]

Paul Kennedy captures this postwar reality:

Given the extraordinarily favorable economic and strategical position which the United States thus occupied, its post-1945 outward thrust could come as no surprise to those familiar with the history of international politics. With the traditional Great Powers fading away, it steadily moved into a vacuum which their going created; having become number one, it could no longer contain itself within its own shores, or even its own hemisphere. . . . There were, however, many Americans (especially among the troops) who expected that they would be home within a short period of time, returning U.S. armed-forces deployments to their pre-1941 position. But while the idea alarmed the likes of Churchill and attracted isolationist Republicans, it proved

---

[1] Melvin P. Leffler, "The Emergence of an American Grand Strategy, 1945–1952," in Melvin Leffler and Arne Westad, eds., *Cambridge History of the Cold War*, vol. 1 (New York: Cambridge University Press, 2010), 67–89.

[2] The end of World War II marked the culmination of a half century of extraordinary American economic growth. In 1870, the United States had 8.8 percent of global GNP. In 1913, it had 18.9 percent, and in 1944, its share had grown to 35 percent. See Angus Maddison, *The World Economy: Historical Statistics* (Paris: OECD, 2003), 258. Moreover, the war had left the United States with a extensive worldwide system of bases, airfields, and communication stations. In 1945, Assistant Secretary of the Navy Strue Hensel estimated that the United States had built 443 bases and other facilities during the war, including 195 in the Pacific, 228 in the Atlantic area, and 11 in the Indian Ocean and Middle East. Robert E. Harkavy, *Great Power Competition for Overseas Bases* (Oxford: Pergamon, 1982).

impossible to turn the clock back. Like the British after 1815, the Americans in their turn found their informal influence in various lands hardening into something more formal—and more entangling; like the British, too, they found 'new frontiers of insecurity' whenever they wanted to draw the line. The 'Pax Americana' had come of age.[3]

If wars create opportunities for order building, the Second World War did so in the extreme. The interwar system had collapsed, and the old arrangements for great-power relations were in disarray and discredited. America had become a geopolitical behemoth with new and expansive international interests. Its power had global reach—and so it had the opportunity to structure the wider world in a way few states ever do. As Jeffry Frieden observes: "The fact that American power had grown and European flagged made it clear that the United States would have its way with the rest of the world."[4]

American officials understood this opportunity. Planners and policy architects offered different ideas, but they generally shared the impulse to restructure the overall international environment rather than just to protect and advance U.S. national interests. That is, they pursued a milieu-oriented grand strategy rather than a positional grand strategy. A positional grand strategy is one in which a great power seeks to counter, undercut, contain, and limit the power and threats of a specific challenger state or group of states. Nazi Germany, Imperial Japan, the Soviet bloc—all provoked the United States to pursue positional strategies. A milieu-oriented grand strategy is one in which a great power seeks to make the international environment congenial to its long-term security and interests through building the infrastructure of international cooperation, promoting trade and democracy in various regions of the world, and establishing partnerships.[5]

---

[3] Kennedy, *Rise and Fall of the Great Powers*, 359.

[4] Jeffry A. Frieden, *Global Capitalism: Its Fall and Rise in the Twentieth Century* (New York: Norton, 2006), 262.

[5] I make this distinction in "Liberal Order Building," in Melvyn P. Leffler and Jeffrey W. Legro, eds., *To Lead the World: American Strategy after the Bush Doctrine* (New York: Oxford

The United States was in a historically unique position to pursue a milieu-based grand strategy. The collapse of the old order and its newly acquired global power position gave it an opening to do what few states are ever able to do: shape the global frameworks—rules, institutions, relationships—within which postwar states would operate. The question was what sort of environment it wanted to create.

The building of American postwar order went through several stages. In the first, the Roosevelt administration sought to build on and update the Wilsonian vision. Like Wilson's version, it would be a one-world system in which the major powers would cooperate to enforce the peace. "The United States did not enter the war to reshape the world," the historian Warren Kimball argues, "but once in the war, that conception of world reform was the assumption that guided Roosevelt's actions."[6] The great powers would work together to provide collective security within a new global organization.[7] Roosevelt's vision did anticipate a more hierarchical system than Wilson's. It also included a more developed notion of how international institutions might be deployed to manage economic and political interdependence. Roosevelt's wartime proclamation of the Four Freedoms and the Atlantic Charter advocacy of a postwar order that would support full employment and economic growth gave liberal

---

University Press, 2008). It follows from Arnold Wolfers's classic distinction between "possession" goals and "milieu" goals of states. In Wolfers's rendering, possession goals involve a state "aiming at the enhancement or the preservation of one or more of the things to which it attaches value," whereas milieu goals involve efforts to change the wider international order, influencing the setting within which more narrow national interests are pursued. See Arnold Wolfers, "The Goals of Foreign Policy," in *Discord and Collaboration* (Baltimore: Johns Hopkins University Press, 1962), 67–80.

[6] Warren F. Kimball, *The Juggler: Franklin Delano Roosevelt as Wartime Statesman* (Princeton, NJ: Princeton University Press, 1994), 17.

[7] Roosevelt voiced these aspirations in a report to a joint congressional session on March 1, 1945, following his return from the Yalta conference. The summit of wartime allies, FDR claimed, "ought to spell the end of the system of unilateral action, the exclusive alliances, the spheres of influence, the balance of power, and all the other expedients that have been tried for centuries—and have always failed. We propose to substitute for all these, a universal organization in which all peace-loving Nations will finally have a chance to join." Quoted in Robert Dallek, *The Lost Peace: Leadership in a Time of Horror and Hope* (New York: HarperCollins, 2010), 59.

internationalism a more expansive agenda. But if the great powers and governance institutions would have more authority than Wilson proposed, Roosevelt's system would remain a unified one in which a "family circle" of states would manage openness and stability.[8]

This updated Wilsonian vision of liberal order gave way to a more far-reaching and complex set of arrangements. The ultimate outcome was more Western-centered, multilayered, and deeply institutionalized than originally anticipated, and it brought the United States into direct political and economic management of the system. The weakness of Europe, the looming Soviet threat, and the practical requirements of establishing institutions and making them work transformed the tasks of order building. The updated Wilsonian vision of liberal order turned into true liberal hegemonic order.

Through this unfolding process, American leaders—Roosevelt and, later, Truman—sought to use the country's power advantages to create an international order that would be open, friendly, and stable. An open order would facilitate free trade across regions; trade would help foster American economic growth and prosperity, and it would also have beneficial economic and political effects on other countries and the overall order. A friendly order would ensure that no hostile and revisionist great power would rise up in Europe and Asia and impose hegemony within these regions; the domination of geopolitical spheres would inevitably serve to exclude and threaten the United States and its viability as a great power with expanding global interests. And a stable order would endure over the decades, operating as a semipermanent political system that could foster collective solutions to problems, resist the domination by hostile powers, and provide a congenial environment in which the United States could pursue its interests.

American officials and policy makers were in wide agreement that the postwar order should be open, friendly, and stable. But the specific measures—policy steps, institutions, commitments—remained in

[8] For a discussion of the Wilson and Roosevelt versions of liberal internationalism, see G. John Ikenberry, "Liberal Internationalism 3.0: America and the Dilemmas of Liberal World Order," *Perspectives on Politics* 7, no. 1 (March 2009), 71–87.

debate, and U.S. strategy evolved considerably over the 1940s, through a process of action and reaction, bargaining and adjustment. At the outset, the United States envisioned a mostly self-run system of free trade and open markets, with no country in charge. The postwar security system, as Roosevelt envisaged it, would have the U.N. Security Council as the central mechanism for security cooperation. The United States might play a decisive leadership role in organizing the postwar order, but once the order was in place, Washington would not be responsible for running it.

The practical circumstances that American officials confronted after the war made this aim impossible. Postwar Europe's economic and political weakness, the growing threat of Soviet power, and the ongoing give-and-take between the United States and its would-be partners all had impacts on order building. The problems of rebuilding Western Europe and organizing a response to the encroachments of Soviet power triggered a more protracted and elaborate order-building process, which in turn altered the bargains, institutions, and commitments that the United States undertook. Along the way, the management of the world economy moved from the Bretton Woods vision to one built around the American dollar and domestic market. Security cooperation moved from the U.N. Security Council to NATO and the other U.S.-led alliances. And so the postwar security and economic system became less a global system and more a Western system. Indeed, in many respects, the order itself became an international extension of the United States.

This rolling process of order building encompassed two American-led geopolitical projects. One was the project that dominated the first decades of the postwar era: the Cold War project, which sought to address the problem of Soviet power. The other was the effort to unite the capitalist democracies within an open and stable system, which sought address the problem of the 1930s. This latter liberal vision of order provided the initial inspiration for American architects of postwar order, but as the 1940s unfolded, the Cold War came to overshadow all other aspects of American foreign policy—and liberal order was quietly built inside the bipolar system.

The Cold War order was organized around bipolarity, containment, deterrence, and ideological struggle between the United States and the Soviet Union. By comparison, the order-building strategy relating to the construction of Western liberal order was more diffuse and wide ranging. It was less obvious that the liberal international agenda was a "grand strategy" aimed at advancing America's national security interests. The challenge was not to deter or contain the power of the Soviet Union but to lay the foundations for an international order that would allow the United States to thrive. This impulse existed before, during, and after the Cold War. Even at the moment when the Cold War gathered force, the grand strategic interest in building such an order was appreciated. For example, the famous NSC-68 planning document that laid out a doctrine of containment also articulated a rationale for building a liberal international order. The United States needed, it said, to "build a healthy international community," which "we would probably do even if there were no international threat." The objective was a "world environment in which the American system can survive and flourish."[9]

By the late 1940s, the twin projects of openness and containment came together. The construction of security partnerships and open economic relations with Western Europe and East Asia were essential to fighting the Cold War, while the imperatives of the Cold War reinforced cooperation with America's partners and created domestic support for American leadership. Robert Gilpin argues that the Soviet threat was critical in fostering cohesion among the capitalist democracies and providing the political glue that held the world economy together. Over time, in his view, an elaborate American-led political order emerged that was built on two pillars: the American market and the American security umbrella. The American military guarantee to Europe and Asia provided a national-security rationale for Japan and the Western democracies to open their markets. Free trade helped cement the alliance, and in turn the alliance helped settle economic disputes. In Asia, the

[9] NSC-68, as published in Ernest May, ed., *American Cold War Strategy: Interpreting NSC-68* (New York: St. Martin's, 1993), 40.

export-oriented development strategies of Japan and (in later decades) the smaller East Asian countries depended on America's willingness to accept their imports and live with huge trade deficits; alliances with Japan, South Korea, and other Southeast Asian countries made this politically tolerable.[10]

Logics of Liberal Hegemonic Order

If a central strategic objective of American officials in the 1940s was to build a liberal international order, the specific ways and means of doing so unfolded in the postwar years. Out of this protracted process, seven logics of postwar order can be identified. These came together to form the American-led liberal hegemonic order.

Open Markets

During the war, the Roosevelt administration had various ideas about how best to organize the postwar system, but one idea stood out—that America needed to promote an open world economy. This followed directly from the conviction that the United States could only survive and prosper as a global power if it had access to the resources and markets of other regions of the world. Open markets were necessary to sustain postwar economic growth and employment. The American economy could not operate with trade and resource flows restricted to its own hemisphere. As Roosevelt announced in 1940, the United States must not become "a lone island in a world dominated by the philosophy of force."[11] Economic and geopolitical lessons learned from the 1930s stood behind this conviction. It was the closure of the world economy—

[10] Robert Gilpin, *The Challenge of Global Capitalism: The World Economy in the 21st Century* (Princeton, NJ: Princeton University Press, 2000), chap. 2.

[11] Samuel I. Rosenman, ed., *The Public Papers and Addresses of Franklin D. Roosevelt, 1940* (New York: Macmillan, 1941), 261. Quoted in Leffler, "Emergence of an American Grand Strategy," 68.

protectionism and the formation of hostile regional spheres—that led to the breakdown of order and great-power war. "The next peace," Vice President Henry Wallace said in 1941, "must take into account economics; otherwise, it will serve as the seedbed for aggression."[12]

During the 1930s, the United States saw its geopolitical operating space shrink as the other great powers began to construct closed and competing regional blocs. Germany pursued a series of bilateral trade agreements with Eastern European countries in order to consolidate an economic and political sphere of influence in the region. Japan pursued an even more overt campaign to create a Greater East Asian Co-Prosperity Sphere. In a less obvious or aggressive way, Britain also was pursuing a strategy of discriminatory economic cooperation with its Commonwealth partners—a nonterritorial economic bloc built around the imperial preference system. By the end of the 1930s, the world was effectively carved up into relatively insular economic blocs—antagonistic groupings that American officials understood to be at least partly responsible for the upset of war.[13]

President Truman embraced this same view—at least initially. In an address at Baylor University in March 1947, he laid out his vision of "economic peace" and appealed for support for his policies of lower trade barriers and a postwar trade organization. In his view, the 1930s demonstrated the indivisibility of economics and politics—of trade and statecraft. "As each battle of the economic war of the thirties was fought, the inevitable tragic result became more and more apparent. From the tariff policy of Hawley and Smoot, the world went on to Ottawa and the system of imperial preferences, from Ottawa to the kind of elaborate and detailed restrictions adopted by Nazi Germany. Nations strangled

[12] Wallace quotation cited in Alfred E. Eckes, Jr., *A Search for Solvency: Bretton Woods and the International Monetary System, 1944–71* (Austin: University of Texas Press, 1975), 34.

[13] For arguments that the great midcentury struggle between an open capitalist order and various regional, autarkic challengers, see Bruce Cumings, "The Seventy Years' Crisis and the Logic of Trilateralism in the New World Order," *World Policy Journal* (Spring 1991), 00–000; and Charles Maier, "The Two Postwar Eras and the Conditions for Stability in Twentieth-Century Western Europe," in *In Search of Stability: Explorations in Historical Political Economy* (New York: Cambridge University Press, 1987), chap. 4.

normal trade and discriminated against their neighbors, all around the world." And so an open trading system was one of the "cornerstones of our plans for peace."[14]

The historian Robert A. Pollard describes this general conviction about the reconstruction of an open world economy as a "postwar consensus" within American policymaking circles. American policy makers "agreed that Washington should take the leadership in creating postwar international institutions that would stabilize currencies, ease financial crisis, and promote world commerce, as well as a new collective security organization that would deter aggression. A proper functioning system of world trade would foster interdependence among nations, they reasoned, thereby raising the price of aggression."[15] An open world economy—managed with cooperative institutional arrangements—would give countries equal opportunities for trade and investment. Peaceful economic competition, nondiscriminatory access to resources, and the efficiency gains from open markets would create an international environment that served America's long-term and extended interests.

Open markets would provide the essential foundation for a wider multilateral system organized around the rule of law. This deep conviction about how to organize the global system brought together economic, ideological, and geopolitical strands of thinking among American policy makers.[16] A postwar effort to reopen the world economy united various groups of strategists and policy makers in the Roosevelt and Truman

[14] Harry S. Truman, Address on Foreign Economic Policy, Baylor University, Waco, TX, 6 March 1947.

[15] Robert A. Pollard, *Economic Security and the Origins of the Cold War, 1945–1950* (New York: Columbia University Press, 1985), 7.

[16] As Stewart Patrick notes, this vision of an open, multilateral world economy was infused with liberal internationalist principles: "In short, [the Roosevelt and Truman administrations] sought "a global economic order that would be *open*—discouraging the formation of closed blocs; *non-discriminatory*—according participants equal access to markets, raw materials, and fields of investment; *liberal*—minimizing state barriers to trade and payments; *private*—dominated by private rather than state-owned enterprise; *cooperative*—emphasizing collaboration rather than economic nationalism; *rule-bound*—delineating normative prescriptions for conduct; and *governed*—by international institutions embodying and enforcing shared rules." Patrick, *Best Laid Plans*, 106.

administrations. One group of officials that embraced the logic of open markets as the organizing idea of postwar order were the wartime free traders in the State Department, led by Secretary Cordell Hull. Hull and his colleagues embraced economic interdependence, led by the United States, as the only way to ensure prosperity and stable peace. As Hull said in a speech in November 1938: "I know that without expansion of international trade, based upon fair dealing and equal treatment for all, there can be no stability and security either within or among nations. . . . I know that the withdrawal by a nation from orderly trade relations with the rest of the world inevitably leads to regimentation of all phases of national life, to the suppression of human rights, and all too frequently to preparations for war and a provocative attitude toward other nations."[17] Hull's emphasis was less on free trade, as such, than on nondiscrimination and equal commercial opportunity. Open markets, according to this widely shared American view, would simultaneously advance two objectives. They would ensure that the United States would have access to markets and raw materials around the world, a goal that Washington officials had pursued since the Open Door policies of the turn of the century, and also contribute to economic growth and interdependence, in turn creating shared interests among countries in a peaceful international order. As Assistant Secretary of State Dean Acheson argued in April 1945, there was "wide recognition that peace is possible only if countries work together and prosper together. That is why the economic aspects are no less important than the political aspects of peace."[18]

Another group supporting open markets after the war were strategic planners inside and outside of government. Starting in the 1930s, these thinkers questioned whether the United States could remain as a great industrial power within the confines of the Western Hemisphere. In one important planning exercise during the war, experts studied what was described as the Grand Area—that is, the geographical zone that the

[17] Cordell Hull, "The Outlook for the Trade Agreements Program," speech delivered before the 25th National Foreign Trade Convention, New York, 1 November 1938.

[18] Dean Acheson, "Bretton Woods: A Monetary Basis for Trade," address before Economic Club of New York, 16 April 1945.

United States would need to have access to and some control over in a way that would allow it remain a global power. The War and Peace Study Group—a gathering of economists and political specialists convened by the Council on Foreign Relations—debated what sort of postwar international system would best meet America's growing economic and strategic interests. As the work proceeded, it became increasingly clear to the group that "the only area sufficiently large was the one equivalent to the world economy as a whole and driven by the United States. The coming to this awareness was gradual, proceeding through a series of thresholds."[19] An American hemispheric bloc would not be sufficient: the United States must have security of markets and raw materials in Asia and Europe.[20] In effect, America's Grand Area would need to be the entire world—or at least its major regions. If the rim lands of Europe and Asia became dominated by one or several hostile imperial powers, the security implications for the United States would be catastrophic. To remain a great power, the United States had to seek openness, access, and balance in Europe and Asia.

This view that America must have access to Asian and European markets and resources—and must therefore not let a potential adversary control the Eurasian landmass—was also embraced by postwar defense planners. As the war was coming to an end, defense officials began to see that America's security interests required the building of an elaborate system of forward bases in Asia and Europe. Hemisphere defense would be inadequate.[21] Defense officials also saw access to Asian and European raw materials—and the prevention of their control by a prospective enemy—as an American security interest. Melvyn Leffler notes that "Stimson, Patterson, McCloy, and Assistant Secretary Howard C. Peterson agreed with Forrestal that long-term American prosper-

[19] Carlo Maria Santoro, *Diffidence and Ambition: The Intellectual Sources of U.S. Foreign Policy* (Boulder, CO: Westview, 1992), 94.

[20] The culmination of this debate and the most forceful statement of the new consensus was presented in Nicholas Spykman, *America's Strategy in the World: The United States and the Balance of Power* (New York: Harcourt Brace, 1942).

[21] See Melvyn P. Leffler, "The American Conception of National Security and the Beginning of the Cold War," *American Historical Review* 48 (1984), 349–56.

ity required open markets, unhindered access to raw materials, and the rehabilitation of much—if not all—of Eurasia along liberal capitalist lines."[22] Indeed, the base systems were partly justified in terms of their impact on access to raw materials and the denial for such resources to an adversary. Some defense studies went further, and argued that postwar threats to Eurasian access and openness were more social and economic than military. It was economic turmoil and political upheaval that were the real threats to American security, as they invited the subversion of liberal democratic societies and Western-oriented governments. A CIA study concluded in mid-1947: "The greatest danger to the security of the United States is the possibility of economic collapse in Western Europe and the consequent accession to power of Communist elements."[23] Access to resources and markets, socioeconomic stability, political pluralism, and American security interests—all were inextricably linked.

Economic Security and the Social Bargain

American officials also believed that a new social bargain should underlie this liberal economic order. Progressive notions of New Deal liberalism became part of America's postwar vision. The industrial democracies would provide a new level of social support—a safety net—under the societies of the Atlantic world. If the citizens of these countries were to live in a more open world economy, their governments would take steps to stabilize and protect market society through the welfare state— through employment insurance, retirement support, and other social protections. In this way, architects of the postwar system sought to build domestic support and construct an encompassing political coalition within countries around the new international order. National security and social security were now closely linked.

[22] Leffler, "American Conception of National Security," 358.
[23] CIA, "Review of the World Situation as Its Relates to the Security of the United States," 26 September 1947, quoted in Leffler, "American Conception of National Security," 364.

This effort recognized that an open world economy generates both winners and losers. Economists argue that in an open system, the winners win more than the losers lose, and if there are compensation and adjustment mechanisms it is possible for the whole society to benefit. It was the building of these mechanisms—the modern welfare state—that provided a fundamental support for an economically integrated liberal international order.[24] This was the message that Roosevelt and Churchill communicated in the Atlantic Charter of 1941. The joint statement of principles affirmed free trade, equal access for countries to raw materials of the world, and international collaboration in the economic field so as to advance labor standards, employment security, and social welfare. Roosevelt and Churchill were telling the world that they had learned the lessons of the interwar years—and those lessons were fundamentally about the proper organization of the Western world economy.[25]

In the background, notions about economic security and social protection in the United States and Europe were evolving. The meaning of security—national, social, and economic—was expanding. The Depression and New Deal brought into existence the notion of "social security," and the violence and destruction of world war brought into existence the notion of "national security." It was more than just a new term of art—it was a new and more comprehensive internationalist notion of security. In earlier decades—and during World War I—the idea of national security was not widespread. The term most frequently used was national defense, referring more narrowly to protection of the homeland against traditional military attacks. Sometime during World War II, the new term emerged, and it captured the new vision of an activist and permanently mobilized state security across economic,

---

[24] See John Gerard Ruggie, "International Regimes, Transactions, and Change: Embedded Liberalism in the Postwar Economic Order," in Stephen D. Krasner, ed., *International Regimes* (Ithaca, NY: Cornell University Press, 1983); and Robert Gilpin, *The Political Economy of International Relations* (Princeton, NJ: Princeton University Press, 1987), 131–34. See also Mark Blyth, *Great Transformations: Economic Ideas and Institutional Change in the Twentieth Century* (New York: Cambridge University Press, 2002).

[25] See Douglas Brinkley and David R. Facey-Crowther, eds., *The Atlantic Charter* (London: Macmillan, 1994).

political, and military realms.[26] National security required America to be actively attempting to shape its external environment—planning, coordinating, generating resources, building alliances, and so forth. In a "fireside chat" on January 11, 1944, Roosevelt articulated this more expansive vision of national security: "The one supreme objective for the future, which we discussed for each nation individually and for all the United Nations can be summed up in one word: security. And that means not only physical security which provides safety from attacks by aggressors. It means also economic security, social security, moral security—in a family of nations."[27]

One aspect of this new emphasis on economic security was the Bretton Woods system of agreements, which gave governments new tools to manage economic openness. During the war, Britain had expressed its skepticism of the more unadorned American ideas about economic openness. The U.S. State Department's stark free-trade ideas worried British officials, who were concerned about the stability of their beleaguered national economy. John Maynard Keynes's famous trip to Washington in August 1941 to discuss the terms of America's Lend-Lease aid to Britain brought these differences into sharp relief. American officials wanted to reconstruct an open trading system, and British officials in the wartime cabinet wanted to ensure full employment and economic stability. In the months that followed, British and American officials,

---

[26] Daniel Yergin notes the moment during World War II when the term "national security" made its appearance in Washington. "In the autumn of 1945, civilian and military heads of the different services trooped up to Capital Hill to testify before the Senate committee on the question of unification of the military services. Whereas in an earlier round of such hearings, in spring 1944, 'national security' barely came up at all; in these 1945 hearings, a year and a half later, the policymakers constantly invoked the idea as a starting point. 'Our national security can only be assured on a very broad and comprehensive front,' argued the most forceful advocate of the concept, Navy Secretary James Forrestal. 'I am using the word "security" here consistently and continuously rather than defense.' 'I like your words "national security,"' Senator Edwin Johnson told him." See Daniel Yergin, *Shattered Peace: The Origins of the Cold War and the National Security State* (New York: Houghton Mifflin, 1977), 194.

[27] Quoted in Julian E. Zelizer, *Arsenal of Democracy: The Politics of National Security—From World War II to the War on Terrorism* (New York: Basic Books, 2010), 55.

led by Keynes and Harry Dexter White, focused their negotiations on the terms of postwar monetary and financial relations. In this area, the two officials were able to find common ground, agreeing on rules and institutional mechanisms that would establish convertible currencies and tools with which governments could manage exchange-rate imbalances while facilitating growth-oriented means of adjustment. The Bretton Woods agreements—negotiated among a wider group of countries in 1944—reflected this new consensus and established the implementing rules and mechanisms.[28]

These new attitudes—which contrasted sharply with the views of leaders in earlier eras—were noted by Jacob Viner, a leading American economist and postwar planner, in 1942. "There is wide agreement today that major depressions, mass unemployment, are social evils, and that it is the obligation of governments . . . to prevent them." Moreover, there was "wide agreement also that it is extraordinarily difficult, if not outright impossible, for any country to cope alone with the problems of cyclical booms and depressions . . . while there is good prospect that with international cooperation . . . the problem of the business cycle and of mass unemployment can be largely solved."[29] What British and American experts agreed on was that in organizing the postwar world economy, there would need to be a framework of cooperation. The framework would provide currency convertibility and stability of exchange rates, create international reserves to allow governments to pursue expansionary responses to balance-of-payments deficits, and, most generally, establish new techniques of international economic management that gave governments the ability to reconcile movements of trade and capital with policies that promoted stable and full-employment

[28] For accounts of these negotiations, see Richard Gardner, *Sterling-Dollar Diplomacy in Current Perspective* (New York: Columbia University Press, 1980); Armand Van Dormael, *Bretton Woods: Birth of a Monetary System* (London: Macmillan, 1978); and Eckes, *Search for Solvency*.

[29] Jacob Viner, "Objectives of Post-War International Economic Reconstruction," in William McKee and Louis J. Wiesen, eds., *American Economic Objectives* (New Wilmington, PA: Economic and Business Foundation, 1942), 168.

economies.[30] Political leaders on both sides of the Atlantic embraced this compromise between open markets and social stability.

The other aspect of the social bargain was the progressive reform developments within European and American societies. Across the advanced industrial world—before and after the war—domestic social reforms ushered in a new era of capitalist regulation. Social insurance programs for workers and retirees reflected new commitments by governments to the management of the national economy. The governments in the Western democracies developed bureaucratic capacities for planning, economic management, and industrial policy. The Keynesian revolution brought new thinking about how the modern state could use fiscal policy and other tools of macroeconomic management to foster full employment and economy stability.[31] Governments sought to reconcile commitments to economic openness with support and protection for a stable domestic economic order. "The industrial West rebuilt its political economies on the basis of compromise among nations, classes, parties, and groups," writes Jeffry Frieden. "Governments balanced international integration and national autonomy, global competition and national constituencies, free markets and social democracy. . . . Socialists and conservatives, Christian Democrats and secular liberals worked together to build modern welfare states."[32]

In the years that followed the war, governments increased spending on social protection. By the 1950s, most of the countries within the West had programs responding to the full range of social insecurities—unemployment, old age, health, disability, and poverty. Postwar economic growth and the liberalization of trade went together with the construction of modern social democracy. This unfolding social

[30] See G. John Ikenberry, "Creating Yesterday's New World Order: Keynesian 'New Thinking' and the Anglo-American Postwar Settlement," in Judith Goldstein and Robert O. Keohane, eds., *Ideas and Foreign Policy: Beliefs, Institutions, and Political Change* (Ithaca, NY: Cornell University Press, 1993), 57–86.

[31] For accounts of the rise of state economic management in the postwar Western industrial democracies, see Andrew Shonfield, *Modern Capitalism: The Changing Balance of Public and Private Power* (Oxford: Oxford University Press, 1966); and Frieden, *Global Capitalism*.

[32] Frieden, *Global Capitalism*, 279.

bargain allows governments to operate within an open world economy and simultaneously make good on commitments to manage and protect domestic social and economic life.[33]

What the New Deal and national security liberalism brought to postwar American internationalism was a wider domestic constituency for liberal order building than in earlier eras. The desired international order would need to have more features and moving parts. It would need to be more elaborate and complexly organized. In several senses, the stakes had grown since the end of World War I—more had to be accomplished, more was at risk if the right sort of postwar order was not constructed, and more of American society had a stake in a successful American internationalism project.

Multilateral Institutional Cooperation

In constructing the postwar order, the United States also sought to create new permanent institutions that would manage a widening array of political, economic, and security relationships. American officials believed that it was not enough simply to open up the system. There would need to be a variety of international institutions that would bring government officials together on an ongoing basis to manage economic and political change. New forms of intergovernmental cooperation would need to be invented. This emphasis was remarkable—never before had a major state laid out such an expansive agenda for international institution building.

This American impulse toward institution building was driven by a pragmatic interest in managing international relations in what officials saw as an emerging era when national solutions to economic stability and national security would not suffice. The country could not solve its problems alone. It needed new forms of institutionalized cooperation.

---

[33] See Tony Smith, "National Security Liberalism and American Foreign Policy," in Michael Cox, G. John Ikenberry, and Takashi Inoguchi, eds., *American Democracy Promotion: Impulses, Strategies, and Impacts* (New York: Oxford University Press, 2000); and Ikenberry, "Creating America's World: The Domestic Sources of Postwar Liberal Internationalism," unpublished paper, 2006.

And the fact that the United States was so powerful meant that it could dominate these institutions. It could set the terms for cooperation, and the institutions would for the most part operate in ways that would be congenial to American interests. The United States would need to make some concessions in the form of commitments and restraints on its power, but in return, it would get a stable and cooperative system of postwar order.

The end of the war was a propitious moment for this endeavor. The old arrangements—economic, political, security—were destroyed, and America could step forward to shape the world according to its wishes. To the extent that these rules and institutions were agreed upon by other states, the United States would not be drawn into costly efforts to enforce order through direct forms of domination; to the extent that these rules and institutions were durable, America was making an investment in its long-term security and welfare. All these considerations came together to make institution building both a practical necessity and an enlightened inspiration.[34]

Officials at the U.S, State Department were an important source of support for multilateralism. The conference diplomacy of the interwar period provided experience and lessons for diplomats who were later involved in postwar planning. During the 1920s, the governments of the United States and European nations engaged in a variety of multilateral efforts to tackle issues such as disarmament and debt—the Washington Naval Treaties, the Kellogg-Briand Treaty, and a series of agreements relating to debt and reparations were prominent outcomes of this post-Versailles multilateralism.[35] The stabilization agreements

[34] See chapter 3 for an elaboration of this logic, and see also Ikenberry, *After Victory*.

[35] In his exhaustive study of 1920s Euro-Atlantic conference diplomacy, Patrick Cohrs observes that "what emerged in the 1920s prefigured in many, yet by no means all, respects the rules and foundations of hegemonic pacification, collective security and concerted efforts at Europe's reconstruction that would foster the more permanent stability achieved after World War II." See Patrick O. Cohrs, *The Unfinished Peace after World War I* (Cambridge: Cambridge University Press, 2006), 619. See also David E. Kaiser, *Economic Diplomacy and the Origins of the Second World War: Germany, Britain, France, and Eastern Europe* (Princeton,

and peace initiatives were simply incapable of withstanding the deterioration of economic and political conditions that led to war. But State Department officials—along with many European counterparts—retained the conviction that multilateral mechanisms of cooperation were essential for the management of economics and security. As the historian Kenneth Weisbrode notes, American diplomats engaged in interwar multilateralism "bought into it, claiming credit not only for its achievements . . . but also for passing it on to their successors, thereby contributing to the so-called second chance for a liberal world order after 1945."[36]

In the background, American officials also brought lessons from the New Deal to their vision of an institutionalized postwar order. The heightened role of government during the downturn of the 1930s was relevant to the wider world economy. Governments would need to play a more direct supervisory role in stabilizing and managing economic order. Markets left to their own devices would end in calamity. At the international level, this meant putting in place regulatory and public-goods mechanisms to guard against economic dysfunction or failure—and its spread to other countries and regions.[37]

This view was embraced by the economic officials who gathered in Bretton Woods in 1944. Governments would need to play a more direct supervisory role in stabilizing and managing economic order. As U.S. Treasury Secretary Harry Dexter White warned in 1942, "a high degree of economic collaboration among the leading nations" would be needed in the postwar era to prevent a return to "economic

---

NJ: Princeton University Press, 1980); and Robert A. Divine, *Second Chance: The Triumph of Internationalism in America during World War II* (New York: Atheneum, 1971).

[36] Kenneth Weisbrode, *The Atlantic Century: Four Generations of Extraordinary Diplomats Who Forged America's Vital Alliance with Europe* (Cambridge, MA: Da Capo, 2009), 20.

[37] See Anne-Marie Burley, "Regulating the World: Multilateralism, International Law, and the Project of the New Deal Regulatory State," in John G. Ruggie, ed., *Multilateralism Matters: The Theory and Praxis of an Institutional Form* (New York: Columbia University Press, 1993), 125–56.

warfare."[38] The democratic countries would enmesh themselves in a dense array of intergovernmental networks and loose rule-based institutional relationships. They would create permanent governance institutions—ones that they themselves would dominate—to facilitate the cooperative management of growing realms of economic and political interdependence.[39]

America's identity as a liberal polity organized around the rule of law reinforced its postwar agenda of building order around multilateral rules and institutions. Liberal principles of political order within domestic society were relevant to the world of states. As Stewart Patrick suggests, "One reason that multilateralism was so compelling to the Roosevelt and Truman administrations was that it resonated with the liberal political culture that forms the core of American national identity."[40] In making strategic choices about how to build order, Washington policy makers drew upon American values and political culture to emphasize the organizing principles of liberal rule-based relations—openness, nondiscrimination, and reciprocity.

The United States, as John Ruggie argues, had choices in organizing the postwar order. Relations could have been built around spheres of influence, autarkic blocs, or an imperial system.[41] The fact that the United States was the world's most powerful state and possessed the largest and most competitive economy gave it material incentives to create an open world system. But the political architecture of openness—the emphasis on a system of multilateral rules and institutions—was nonetheless encouraged and reinforced by America's liberal identity. Roosevelt and Truman shared the view evinced by Woodrow Wilson and others that the United States was the carrier of universal political

---

[38] Quotation cited in Van Dormael, *Bretton Woods*, 45.

[39] Cordell Hull gave voice to this basic logic of institutional cooperation in a radio address on May 18, 1941, arguing that multilateral institutions would "establish . . . the foundations of an international order in which independent nations cooperate freely with each other for their mutual gain." Quoted in Patrick, *Best Laid Plans*, 51.

[40] Patrick, *Best Laid Plans*, xx.

[41] Ruggie, *Multilateralism Matters*.

ideas and ideals that could help set the world on a more peaceful and prosperous pathway.[42]

Security Binding

Although not initially in America's vision of postwar order, cooperative security—or security binding—came to be an integral part of the system. Cooperative security is a strategy in which states tie themselves together in economic and security institutions that mutually constrain one another. This was arguably the most important innovation in national security in the twentieth century. It was manifest in the French decision to build binding ties with Germany. It was also manifest in the binding of Western European countries within a common economic community and in the simultaneous binding of Western Europe to the United States within NATO. Rather than balancing against each other as potential security rivals, these Western states would embed themselves within layers of functional institutions that would be difficult to break.

For the United States, this strategy meant agreeing to remain in close alliance with other democratic countries, especially through NATO and the U.S.-Japan alliance. This single security system would ensure that the democratic great powers would not go back to the dangerous game of strategy rivalry and power politics. It helped, of course, to have an emerging Cold War to generate this cooperative security arrangement. But a security relationship between the United States and its allies was implicit in other elements of liberal order. A cooperative security order—embodied in formal alliance institutions—ensured that the power of the United States would be rendered more predictable and restrained.

Security binding can be seen as an alternative to balancing strategies. Rather than aggregating power to counterbalance a threatening or

---

[42] For arguments that stress the importance of American liberal identity and ideals for postwar order building, see John G. Ruggie, *Winning the Peace: America and World Order in the New Era* (New York: Columbia University Press, 1996); Jeff Legro, *Rethinking the World: Great Power Strategies and International Order* (Ithaca, NY: Cornell University Press, 2005); and Patrick, *Best Laid Plans.*

powerful state, states act to overcome insecurities by tying one another down within a common security institution. By establishing institutions of mutual constraint, binding reduces the risks and uncertainties associated with anarchy and unmitigated security competition. It ties potentially threatening states into predictable and restrained patterns of behavior, thereby making it unnecessary to balance against those threats.[43]

Through security binding, states build long-term security, political, and economic commitments that are difficult to retract. Commitments and relationships are locked in, at least to the extent that this can be done by sovereign states. The most obvious is through participation in security alliances. But binding can also be pursued through other institutional forms of cooperation, such as economic agreements and joint participation in multilateral organizations. These institutions and cooperative arrangements raise the costs of exit and create voice opportunities, thereby providing mechanisms to mitigate suspicion, uncertainty, and security dilemmas as sources of conflict. Security alliances, in particular, allow states to keep a hand in the national security policy of their partners.[44]

The binding strategy of order building was most evident in the occupation and reintegration of West Germany and Japan. American troops began as occupiers of the two defeated Axis states and never left. They eventually became protectors but also a palpable symbol of American

[43] For a discussion of security—or institutional—binding, see Ikenberry, *After Victory*, chap. 3. For a major theoretical statement of security co-binding, see Daniel H. Deudney, "The Philadelphia System: Sovereignty, Arms Control, and Balance of Power in the American States-Union, 1787–1861," *International Organization* 49, no. 2 (Spring 1995), 1191–228; and Daniel H. Deudney, *Bounding Power: Republican Security Theory from the Polis to the Global Village* (Princeton, NJ: Princeton University Press, 2007). See also Patricia A. Weitsman, *Dangerous Alliances: Proponents of Peace, Weapons of War* (Stanford, CA: Stanford University Press, 2004); Jeremy Pressman, *Warring Friends: Alliance Restraint in International Politics* (Ithaca, NY: Cornell University Press, 2008); and Andrew G. Long, Timothy Nordstrom, and Kyeonghi Baek, "Allying for Peace: Treaty Obligations and Conflict among Allies," *Journal of Politics* 64, no. 4 (November 2007), 1103–17.

[44] Paul Schroeder argues that the Concert of Europe was an early manifestation of this binding logic. In this and later cases, alliances were created as *pacta de controhendo,* or pacts of restraint. They have served as mechanisms for states to manage and restrain their partners within the alliance. See Paul W. Schroeder, "Alliances, 1815–1945: Weapons of Power and Tools of Management," in Klaus Knorr, ed., *Historical Dimensions of National Security Problems* (Lawrence: University Press of Kansas, 1975), 227–62.

superordinate position. Host agreements were negotiated that created a legal basis for the American military presence, effectively circumscribing West German and Japanese sovereignty. West German rearmament and restoration of its political sovereignty—made necessary and possible in the early 1950s by a growing Cold War—could only be achieved by binding Germany to Europe, which in turn required binding America's security commitment to Europe. Complex and protracted negotiations ultimately created an integrated European military force within NATO and legal agreements over the character and limits of West German sovereignty and military power.[45]

The United States and Europe took other steps to bind the democracies together. The European union movement explicitly sought to achieve economic interdependence between Germany and her neighbors in order to make strategic military competition much more costly and difficult. The first fruit of this effort, the European Coal and Steel Community, effectively pooled these heavy industries that had been essential for war making. In its administration of the Marshall Plan, the United States sought to encourage the creation of joint economic organizations in order to create economic interdependencies that crossed over the traditional lines of hostility between European states. The United States also supported the creation of political institutions of European union, so as to foreclose a return to the dynamics of anarchy and to create European institutions that were more like the United States than like the traditional sovereign-state variety.

Western Democratic Solidarity

The American vision of a liberal international order was also anchored in a sense that there existed a special solidarity among the Western

---

[45] A treaty governing the relationship between the new German state and Britain, France, and the United States was signed in 1952, and specified ongoing "rights and responsibilities" of the three powers. "Convention on Relations between the Three Powers and the Federal Republic of Germany, 26 May 1952, as modified by the Paris Accords of October 1954," reprinted in Department of State, Documents on Germany, 1944–1985 (Washington, DC: Department of State, 1986), 425–30.

democracies. The principles of liberal order would be global and universal, but the most important commitments and core institutions would be established within the West. Walter Lippmann gave voice to this view of the Western system in 1943: "The Atlantic Ocean is not the frontier between Europe and the Americas. It is the inland sea of a community of nations allied with one another by geography, history, and vital necessity."[46] The United States and Europe increasingly seemed to share both a common fate and affinities of value and identity.

The effort to anchor the postwar order in the West was driven by the fact that the newly established global institutions—the United Nations and Bretton Woods mechanisms—were insufficient to deal with the practical economic and security problems that emerged after the war. The rebuilding of European economies and the construction of a security alliance required intense cooperation across the Atlantic. The sense that America and Europe were imperiled by a common threat strengthened the feelings of Western solidarity. But the notion of a Western core to liberal international order also suggested that unusual opportunities existed—because of a common culture and democratic institutions—to cooperate and build postwar institutions. This notion of a shared political community came with the expectation that the actual dealings between the United States and Europe would be based more on consensus and reciprocity than on the imperial or patron-client exercise of American power.[47]

The notion of an Atlantic order was supported by political figures and experts on both sides of the Atlantic. Ideas of an Atlantic union can be traced to the turn of the century and a few British and Ameri-

[46] Walter Lippmann, *U.S. Foreign Policy: Shield of the Republic* (Boston: Little, Brown, 1943). Lippmann first used the term "Atlantic community" in the months before the American intervention in World War I. See Walter Lippmann, "The Defense of the Atlantic World," *New Republic*, 10, no. 120 (1917), 59–61. For a discussion see James R. Huntley, *Uniting the Democracies: Institutions of the Emerging Atlantic-Pacific System* (New York: New York University Press, 1980), 5.

[47] Ronald Steel notes that this expectation of a consensus-based relationship that muted political hierarchy was one reason that Europeans embraced the notion of Atlantic community. See Ronald Steel, "How Europe Became Atlantic: Walter Lippmann and the New Geography of the Atlantic Community," in Marco Mariano, ed., *Defining the Atlantic Community: Culture, Intellectuals, and the Policies in the Mid-Twentieth Century* (New York: Routledge, 2010).

can statesmen and thinkers, such as John Hay, British ambassador to Washington Lord Bryce, American ambassador to London Walter Hines Page, Admiral Alfred T. Mahan, and Henry Adams.[48] These ideas resurfaced during and after World War II, reflecting a variety of convictions: that the failure of the League of Nations revealed the virtues of a less universal security community and that there was a pressing need to protect the shared democratic values and institutions that united the Atlantic world. American elites increasingly saw themselves as part of an Atlantic community, or, as Andrew Johnston observes, "a state that belongs to a political economic community of liberal capitalist states."[49]

There were several layers of shared identity that came into play after the war. One was the sense of a special Anglo-American bond invoked by Roosevelt and Churchill in the 1941 Atlantic Charter meeting. They identified the principles common to their two countries as the working principles for the postwar order. "Meeting to consider broad oceanic strategy and problem of supply," as one contemporary observer noted, "the seagoing statesmen charted also a Pax Anglo-Americana, which was, in point of terms, a broadening of the liberal practice of the Atlantic world—nonaggression, political and economic freedom—into a formula for wide application when the war is ended."[50]

[48] The idea of an "Atlantic system" bringing together the United States and Western Europe was repeatedly advanced at the turn of the century by Henry Adams, a close friend of Secretary of State John Hay. See Henry Adams, *The Education of Henry Adams* (Boston: Houghton Mifflin, [1907] 1918). On the late-nineteenth-century Anglo-American rapprochement, see Lionel M. Gelber, *The Rise of Anglo-American Friendship: A Study in World Politics, 1898–1906* (London: Oxford University Press, 1938); Charles S. Campbell, *From Revolution to Rapprochement: The United States and Great Britain, 1783–1900* (New York: Wiley & Sons, 1974); and Charles Kupchan," Atlantic Order in Transition: The Nature of Change in U.S.-European Relations," in Jeffrey Anderson, G. John Ikenberry, and Thomas Risse, eds., *The End of the West? Crisis and Change in the Transatlantic Order* (Ithaca, NY: Cornell University Press, 2008). On the Christian underpinnings of Atlantic ideas, see Emiliano Alessandri, "The Atlantic Community as Christendom: Some Reflections on Christian Atlanticism in America, circa 1900–1950," in Mariano, *Defining the Atlantic Community*, 47–70.

[49] Andrew M. Johnston, *Hegemony and Culture in the Origins of NATO Nuclear First-Use, 1945–1955* (New York: Palgrave Macmillan, 2005), 10.

[50] Forrest Davis, *The Atlantic System: The Story of Anglo-American Control of the Seas* (New York: Reynal and Hitchcock, 1941), 303.

American officials were also responding to the wider sense of shared Western identity. The United States saw itself as part of this Western community, which made it easier to make commitments and anchor postwar architecture within the Atlantic area. In arguing for economic aid to Europe in 1948, for example, Secretary of State George Marshall told a congressional committee that American assistance was necessary to prevent "economic distress so intense, social discontents so violent, political confusion so widespread, and hopes for the future so shattered that the historic base of Western civilization, of which we are by belief and inheritance an integral part, will take on a new form in the image of the tyranny that we fought to destroy in Germany."[51]

Europeans also invoked this notion of Western civilization in arguing for postwar Atlantic security cooperation. The British Foreign Minister, Ernst Bevin, argued for a European security alliance with the United States as part of a "spiritual union" that would link the Atlantic world: "While, no doubt, there must be treaties or, at least, understandings, the union must primarily be a fusion derived from the basic freedom and ethical principles for which we all stand. It must be on terms of equality and it must contain all the elements of freedom for which we all stand."[52] These officials were giving voice to an evocative political sentiment—that Europe and the United States form a single political community shaped by common history and values. The failure of peacemaking after World War I and the search by the United States for a stable group of like-minded countries with whom to build institutionalized relations made officials on both sides of the Atlantic receptive to these appeals to Western democratic solidarity.[53]

[51] George Marshall, congressional testimony on the European Recovery Program, *Department of State Bulletin*, 18 January 1948, 71.

[52] Ernst Bevin, speech before House of Commons, 22 January 1948, col. 407–8. Quoted in Patrick Thaddeous Jackson, "Defending the West: Occidentalism and the Formation of NATO," *Journal of Political Philosophy* 11, no. 3 (2003), 241.

[53] For an important exploration of the ways in which notions of Western civilization were invoked in the postwar era by the United States and Europe in negotiations over the reintegration of Germany, see Patrick Thaddeus Jackson, *Civilizing the Enemy: German Reconstruction and the Invention of the West* (Ann Arbor: University of Michigan Press, 2006). See also

American support for some sort of Atlantic community or association came from officials pursuing various—and, to some degree, competing—visions and agendas. "Europeanists" at the State Department focused on the unification of Europe as an end in itself, championed the Marshall Plan, and anticipated an independent Europe with loose links to the United States. "Atlanticists" urged the building of a more ambitious functional and political association that would unite the United States and Europe.[54] Differences existed, for example, over whether the United States should be pushing for European "unification" or "integration." Both groups were reaching for an organizational formula that would embody a new trans-Atlantic solidarity. The challenge, as one American diplomat put it, was to figure out "how to develop a form of unity which will avoid either a US-satellite relationship or a flimsy bilateral partnership between two sovereign 'equals.'"[55] The two positions were ultimately more or less complementary. Indeed, by the 1950s they were largely subsumed by a wider consensus about Atlantic political and security cooperation, embodied in the NATO alliance.

Implicit in this emerging American vision was the view that the West itself could serve as the foundation and starting point for a larger postwar order. The West was not just a geographical region with fixed borders. Rather it was an idea—a universal organizational form that could expand outward, driven by the spread of liberal democratic government and principles of conduct. In this sense, the postwar West was seen as a sort of molecular complex that could multiply and expand outward. The most explicit and radical version of this view was perhaps that of Clarence Streit, who proposed a union of the North Atlantic democracies—with the idea that these countries would form a nucleus of a wider and expanding world order. As Streit argued in 1939: "These few democracies suffice

Mary N. Hampton, "NATO at the Creation: U.S. Foreign Policy, West Germany, and the Wilsonian Impulse," *Security Studies* 4, no. 3 (1995), 610–56; and Mary N. Hampton, *The Wilsonian Impulse: U.S. Foreign Policy, the Alliance, and the Reunificataion of Germany* (New York: Praeger, 1996).

[54] See descriptions of these differences in Huntley, *Uniting the Democracies*, 15–16; and Weisbrode, *Atlantic Century*, chap. 5.

[55] Quoted in Weisbrode, *Atlantic Century*, 160.

to provide the nucleus of world government with the financial, monetary, economic and political power necessary both to assure peace to its members peacefully from the outset by sheer overwhelming preponderance and invulnerability, and practically to end the monetary insecurity and economic warfare now ravaging the whole world."[56] Most American officials did not support the idea of an Atlantic union of democracies, but the idea was nonetheless widespread that a unified West could provide a stable and expandable core for postwar order.

Human Rights and Progressive Change

The American vision of postwar order also had progressive aspirations. Officials in the Roosevelt and Truman administrations shared the view that the order they were devising was ultimately universal in scope. The idea of progressive change had two aspects. One was that the liberal international order, although first established within the West, would spread outward to non-Western and the developing societies. Democracy and integration into the open capitalist system would, in time, envelope the emerging regions of the world. The other was that the order would drive social and political advancement within the societies that became part of it.

The notion that the United States wanted to organize the postwar system so as to promote American-held progressive values was evident early in the Second World War. Like Woodrow Wilson before him, Franklin Roosevelt saw American involvement in World War II as part of a grand clash of ideals. Early in the war, he articulated an American commitment to universal human rights, most notably in the Four Freedoms speech and in the promises laid out in the Atlantic Charter in 1941.[57]

[56] Clarence Streit, *Union Now: A Proposal for a Federal Union of the Democracies of the North Atlantic* (New York: Harper and Brothers, 1939).

[57] In his address to Congress on 6 January 1941, FDR called for a world founded on "four essential human freedoms," namely, freedom of speech and expression, freedom to worship, freedom from want, and freedom from fear. Roosevelt argued this would be a "moral order" that was based upon "the cooperation of free countries working together in a friendly, civilized way."

These commitments were later enshrined in the U.N. Charter in 1945 and in the Universal Declaration of Human Rights adopted by the U.N. General Assembly in December 1948, which launched the postwar human rights revolution. Championed by liberals such as Eleanor Roosevelt and others, the declaration articulated a notion of universal individual rights that deserved to be recognized by the whole of mankind and not simply left to sovereign governments to define and enforce.[58] A steady stream of conventions and treaties followed that together constitute an extraordinary vision of rights, social advancement, and global order.[59]

This human rights revolution was deeply rooted in a progressive liberal vision that emerged in the 1940s. Roosevelt and Truman were clearly sobered by the failure of Wilson but convinced that a new global order committed to human rights, collective security, and economic advancement was necessary to avoid the return to war. More generally, American officials understood that a liberal international order would provide a framework for progressive change. There was an implicit sense that American-led order, Westernization, economic integration, and political development were all compatible and connected, together yielding a one-world global system that advanced the life conditions of everyone. Liberal order and modernization of societies went hand in hand. The liberal vision of Roosevelt and Truman was more world-weary than Wilson's, but they nonetheless saw history moving in a progressive direction, helped along by increasingly elaborate and layered frameworks for economic and security cooperation.

American Hegemonic Leadership

The final aspect of this order was American hegemonic leadership. The United States took the lead in organizing and running the order, on terms that were more or less mutually agreeable to states that were inside

---

[58] See Mary Ann Glendon, *A World Made New: Eleanor Roosevelt and the Universal Declaration of Human Rights* (New York: Random House, 2002).

[59] Jack Donnelly, *Universal Human Rights in Theory and Practice* (Ithaca, NY: Cornell University Press, 2002).

it. In effect, the United States had a special functional-operational role. As Dean Acheson told a group of policy makers at the end of 1947, "We are going to understand that our function in the world will require all of the power and all the thought and all the calmness we have at our disposal."[60] The United States stepped in to provide the public goods of security protection, market openness, and sponsorship of rules and institutions. The American dollar became an international currency and the American domestic market became an engine of global economic growth. Alliance institutions and an array of formal and informal inter-governmental institutions provided the international order with mechanisms and channels for consultation and collaboration. The security of each became the security of all. The resulting order was hierarchical—the United States was most powerful and led the order. But the rules and institutions that it promulgated gave the order its liberal character.[61]

These hegemonic functions entail ongoing American involvement in keeping the order open, stable, and loosely rule-based.[62] When the hegemonic state leads in the provision of rules and institutions, it is providing a public good for the wider order. But it is also using these rules and institutions to establish restraints and commitments on the uses of its power. By undertaking these hegemonic tasks, the leading state serves its long-term interests. It facilitates the creation of a relatively congenial environment in which to pursue its interests. It also signals its cooperative intentions to other states. In return, other states agree to cooperate with the leading state. These weaker and secondary states get an international order that is not threatened by the indiscriminate and arbitrary exercise of power. They also gain some access—through the reciprocal political processes of give-and-take that emerge—to the overall management of the order.

The ability of the leading state to construct rules and institutions and exercise leadership is also based on the security and economic assets that

---

[60] Dean Acheson, "Formation of National Policy in the U.S.," lecture, Washington, DC, December 1947.

[61] See Ikenberry, *After Victory*, chap. 6.

[62] See discussion in chapter 3.

it controls. As the most militarily powerful state, the hegemonic state is able to offer security protection to other states in exchange for their cooperation. This security protection may be provided in multilateral security organizations, such as NATO, or in bilateral security pacts, such as the U.S.-Japan alliance. The leading state's economy is also a source of leadership. Offering market access to the world's largest domestic market is a tool that the United States can use to influence the policies and orientations of other states. These states, in turn, experience economic gains through trade and investment with the United States.

From One-World Order to the American System

The American liberal hegemonic order did not spring full blown at the end of the war. There was no singular "moment of creation." There were many moments of creation.

The Roosevelt administration, from the moment it began to plan for peace, wanted to build a postwar system of open trade that would largely run itself. It would be a reformed "one world" global order.[63] But the order that actually took shape in the decades after the war came to have a more far-reaching and complex logic. It was more Western-centered, multilayered, and deeply institutionalized than originally anticipated, and it brought the United States into direct political and economic management of the system. America found itself to be not just the sponsor and leading participant in a new postwar order—it was also the owner and operator of it. The vision of liberal order turned into liberal hegemonic order.

Liberal order, the United States discovered, required the ongoing exercise of direction and control by Washington. Its own economic and political system became, in effect, central components of the larger liberal hegemonic order. America's domestic market, the U.S. dollar, and

[63] On Roosevelt's wartime efforts to forge an internationalist foreign policy, see Divine, *Second Chance*; and Robert Dallek, *FDR and American Foreign Policy, 1932–1945* (New York: Oxford University Press, 1979).

the Cold War alliances emerged as critical mechanisms and institutions through which postwar order was founded and managed. America and the Western liberal order were fused into one system. The United States established itself at the top of a global political hierarchy. It had more power and control than it had originally anticipated—but it also was compelled to take on more far-reaching responsibilities. It had more direct power in running the postwar order, but it was also more tightly bound to the other states within that order. Along the way, tacit bargains—security, economic, and political—were struck between Washington and the states that operated within this evolving American-led order.

Ultimately, the United States got both more and less than it wanted in the postwar settlement. It wanted a universal order; it got an American system.

Constructing Economic Relations

In economic affairs, the Roosevelt administration's initial impulse to establish an open trading system traveled a long diplomatic pathway during the 1940s. As negotiations over postwar economic rules and institutions proceeded, the character of openness—and America's commitments and obligations—evolved into a more managed and American-run system. The negotiations over Lend-Lease assistance to Britain, the Bretton Woods agreements, the Marshall Plan, and the rising role of the American dollar and domestic market all helped shape the terms of postwar order.

At the outset, American wartime assistance to Britain in the summer of 1941 provided the trigger for wider discussions between Washington and London over rules and arrangements of the world economy. The Ottawa Agreements of 1932, which established Britain's network of imperial preferences, were seen by American officials as one of the causes of economic breakdown in the 1930s and a major obstacle to a postwar nondiscriminatory commercial system. If the United States was to lend resources to Britain to win the war, it expected the British not to discriminate against American trade after hostilities ended. At the Atlantic

Charter meeting between Roosevelt and Churchill, the British leader resisted language that would signal a specific and absolute commitment to dissembling its preferential system. But the United States insisted on a British commitment to "[t]he elimination of all forms of discriminatory treatment in international commerce" as part of the Mutual Aid Agreement signed by the two governments in February 1942, establishing Lend-Lease.[64]

The negotiations that ensued over the following years involved a struggle between two objectives. On the American side, the goal was to bring the rest of the world into an open trading system in which barriers to trade and international payments would be lowered and made nondiscriminatory. The war had turned the United States into a global juggernaut—its power and wealth overshadowed all others, and it held the bargaining advantages at every turn. On the other side, Britain and continental Europe were diminished by the war, and political leaders worried about a postwar recession and rising unemployment. Open trade was less critical than the establishment of social protections to guard against social and economic instability. In Britain, the political left wanted to ensure that postwar economic arrangements were consistent with government commitments to full employment, and the political right maintained its defiant embrace of imperial preferences.[65] Thus, Britain sought a variety of assurances and policy commitments from Washington. It wanted a postwar economic settlement that would facilitate full employment, open up the American market for imports, and provide assistance to overcome balance-of-payments difficulties.

The movement away from America's initial open trade position came in several steps. One occurred in the famous Anglo-American negotiations between Keynes and Harry Dexter that culminated in the Bretton Woods agreements. These negotiations—which established the International Monetary Fund and World Bank—moved the debate over the principles and rules of the postwar world economy from trade to

[64] See Kimball, *Juggler*, chap. 3.

[65] Robin Edmonds, *Setting the Mould: The United States and Britain, 1945–1950* (New York: Norton, 1986), 96–97.

monetary and financial arrangements. The agreements that were reached were consistent with Washington's goal of market openness in the sense that monetary rules would ensure the convertibility of currencies. Currency blocs would not be permitted. But Britain and the other European states also got protections. Although creditor countries were not as obligated as Keynes had sought for coming to the assistance of debtor states, monetary arrangements were establish to bias the system in favor of expansionary forms of adjustment. The agreement between British and American monetary planners was particularly important because it served to transcend the stalemate over the postwar trade system. The Bretton Woods proposals represented a middle way that generated support from both the conservative free traders and the new advocates of economic planning. The international economy would be open, but it would also be managed—and governments would be given tools to support domestic full employment.[66] These compromises that were reached at Bretton Woods in 1944 attracted political support on both sides of the Atlantic and, in the process, reshaped the logic of an open liberal system.

But even with the Bretton Woods agreements, the weakness of the British economy—and the failing continental European economies—drove the United States into further actions. In the fall of 1945, Keynes returned to Washington seeking a loan to address Britain's increasingly precarious financial position. Britain's declining gold and dollar balances were undermining the ability of its new Labor government to make good on ambitious economic and social welfare programs. As in the past, American officials tied financial assistance to British movement to trade liberalization and monetary convertibility. The loan was agreed to in return for British willingness to remove currency controls and restrictions on trade. This is the argument that the Truman administration made to Congress in its effort to build domestic support for passage of the loan agreement. British movement toward an open multilateral system depended on American assistance. Treasury Secretary Fred Vinson argued to Congress that without the loan, the

---

[66] See Ikenberry, "Creating Yesterday's New World Order."

British would move back to barter trade and currency blocs, dividing the world yet again—and "rival blocs would mean economic warfare."[67] Yet Congress remained skeptical.

By early 1946, the Truman administration began to add a national security argument to its congressional appeal. In February, Stalin gave his famous "two camps" speech, depicting the struggle between the capitalist West and the socialist world. The next month, Churchill gave his "iron curtain" speech in Fulton, Missouri.[68] Suddenly, the vision of a one-world open system was giving way to one where ideological and geopolitical clashes would continue to divide the world. In these new circumstances, economic support for Britain was necessary to strengthen Western unity in the face of an emerging Soviet threat. As Joseph Jones, a State Department official, argued to a senator in the spring of 1946: "If these areas are allowed to spiral downwards into economic anarchy, then at best they will drop out of the United States orbit and try an independent nationalist policy; at worst they will swing into the Russian orbit."[69]

The loan passed Congress, but the economic circumstances that prompted it continued to worsen. The British government made sterling convertible in July 1947 only to see a massive run on the currency as traders turned pounds into dollars. The loan failed and the government reimposed currency controls. In the meantime, France was also seeking assistance from the United States. Jean Monnet, an adviser to Charles de Gaulle, warned that without American aid, France could not regain "the first rank of industrial powers in Western Europe." The French would need massive financing from Washington to pay for postwar imports of food, raw materials, and capital goods.[70] In the negotiations that followed, Monnet—like Keynes—found Washington insistent on linking aid to a French commitment to trade liberalization. The French, in turn,

[67] Quoted in Gardner, *Sterling-Dollar Diplomacy*, 242–46.

[68] On these early steps toward Cold War, see Melvyn P. Leffler, *For the Soul of Mankind: The United States, the Soviet Union, and the Cold War* (New York: Hill and Wang, 2007), 48–57.

[69] Lloyd Gardner, *Architects of Illusion: Men and Ideas in Foreign Policy, 1941–1949* (Chicago: Quadrangle Books, 1970), 219.

[70] Monnet quoted in Patrick, *Best Laid Plans*, 162.

sought to circumscribe the conditions for trade openness. Liberalization would occur gradually with the reconstruction and modernization of the economy, be made consistent with commitments to social democracy, and be tied to French goals for postwar Europe. Like the British negotiations with the United States, the French aid agreements addressed the immediate problems of postwar economic stabilization and recovery. But they also served, at least indirectly, to advance a longer-term Atlantic consensus over trade and modern democratic society.

These postwar aid agreements ultimately were overtaken by the worsening economic plight in Europe and the coming Cold War. American officials who traveled to Europe in the winter of 1946–47 were struck by the failure of recovery. Undersecretary of State William Clayton returned from a tour of European capitals in the spring of 1947 alarmed by the severe deterioration. Hunger and economic dislocation were widespread, industrial production was declining, and Europe's payments deficit was rising. "If it should [grow]," Clayton wrote, "there will be revolution."[71] Neither the short-term humanitarian aid nor the long-term Bretton Woods stabilization and adjustment mechanisms were adequate to the economic disarray and political troubles in Europe. In the spring of 1947, as relations with the Soviet Union continued to deteriorate, the Truman administration found itself confronting a crisis in Greece and Turkey after Britain had announced that it no longer could maintain its security commitments in the East Mediterranean. On March 12, the American president went before Congress to announce the Truman Doctrine, committing the United States to aid societies struggling against communism.

It was within this transformed political setting that the Truman administration moved to announce a massive new aid program for Europe. This European Economic Program—the so-called Marshall Plan—sent about $14 billion to Europe to rebuild the economies of America's emerging Cold War allies. Additional aid was also sent to

[71] Memorandum by Undersecretary of State for Economic Affairs Will Clayton, "The European Crisis," 27 May 1947, in *Foreign Relations of the United States, 1947*, 3, 230–32.

Japan. This massive commitment of aid was equal to roughly 5 percent of American's 1948 GNP. For most of the beleaguered European countries, it amounted to between 3 and 6 percent of their national incomes in the first years of the program.

The Marshall Plan aid program brought together economic and national security rationales. Clayton and other officials recognized that movement toward an open, multilateral system would be impossible without aggressive steps to put Europe back on a path of economic growth and stability. U.S. officials also worried that economic misery in Europe would feed political instability and create opportunities for communist political inroads.

The objective of the aid program, as Secretary Marshall indicated in his famous address, was "the revival of a working economy in the world so as to permit the emergence of political and social conditions in which free institutions can exist." Without American-assisted European recovery, Marshall contended, "there can be no political stability and no assured peace."[72] It was this emerging Cold War rationale that helped build the domestic support for such costly undertakings. The United States would take responsibility for the revival of Europe, doing so in a way that allowed Europe to reintegrate and participate in a wider open liberal order.

In this evolving strategic setting, two convictions about Europe emerged among Truman administration officials that would persist through the postwar era. One was that European-wide economic recovery could only occur if Germany was also revived. As George Kennan argued, "[t]o talk about the recovery of Europe and to oppose the recovery of Germany is nonsense."[73] The other was that the administration of Marshall Plan aid had to be a collective European undertaking. The United States would give aid not to individual country but to Europe as a whole. This way of running the program would encourage European cooperation and integration—undercutting tendencies toward bilateral-

[72] Secretary George Marshall, commencement address, Harvard University, 4 June 1947.
[73] Quoted in Charles Mee, Jr., *The Marshall Plan: The Launching of the Pax Americana* (New York: Simon and Schuster, 1984), 90.

ism, autarky, and political conflict. A united Europe would provide the necessary foundation for economic and political reconstruction.[74]

Through the Bretton Woods agreements, Europeans succeeded in shifting America's postwar focus on free trade to support for a more general framework of rules and institutions that reconciled openness with government commitments to full employment and social protections. But along the way, the economic weakness of Europe and rising tensions with the Soviet Union brought the United States into a direct role in rebuilding Europe and opening and managing the world economy. The European states, experiencing a "dollar shortage," were unable to take on responsibilities as envisaged under the Bretton Woods agreements. In these circumstances, as Robert Gilpin notes, "the United States assumed primary responsibility for the management of the world monetary system beginning with the Marshall Plan and partially under the guise of the IMF. The Federal Reserve became the world's banker, and the dollar became the basis of the international monetary system."[75] In the years that followed, the dollar became the principal reserve currency, and international liquidity was provided through the outflow of dollars. America's support for an open world economy would entail organizing and running it.

Constructing Security Relations

In security affairs, America's policies and commitments traveled a similar course. The Roosevelt administration's wartime vision was for a global organization in which the leading world powers would collectively

[74] On the role of the Marshall Plan in supporting European integration, see Ernst H. Van Der Beugel, *From Marshall Plan to Atlantic Partnership* (Amsterdam: Elsevier, 1966); Michael J. Hogan, *The Marshall Plan: America, Britain, and the Reconstruction of Western Europe, 1947–1952* (Cambridge: Cambridge University Press, 1987); and Hogan, "European Integration and the Marshall Plan," in Stanley Hoffman and Charles Maier, eds., *The Marshall Plan: A Retrospective* (Boulder, CO: Westview, 1984) . On the twin themes of German inclusion and European integration, see Greg Behrman, *The Most Noble Adventure: The Marshall Plan and the Time When America Helped Save Europe* (New York: Free Press, 2008), 56–57.

[75] Gilpin, *Political Economy of International Relations*, 133–34.

preside over the international system. At the Atlantic Charter conference in 1941, FDR was hesitant to endorse the idea of an international
security organization, but after Pearl Harbor and the American entry
into the war, he became determined to build a framework for postwar
security cooperation. As the historian Warren Kimball writes, "by mid-
1942, much of Roosevelt's plan for the postwar political system was
on the table. The great powers would act as 'guarantors' of the peace,
colonial empires would be disbanded, postwar reconstruction would be
capitalized, and the rest of the world would be disarmed."[76] Over the
next year, FDR continued to refine his notion of a security organization
in which an executive committee of the Four Powers would act together
as "policemen" to ensure peace and stability.

Roosevelt's insistence that American troops would leave Europe after
the war was based on the assumption that a system of cooperative great-
power relations was possible. The great powers would not divide the
world into spheres of influence but do what they had failed to do after
1919: forge a working system of collective security. The embodiment
of this system would be the United Nations. In the summer of 1944,
negotiations over the organization of the new global body took place
at the Dumbarton Oaks conference in Washington, D.C., culminating
in blueprints for a multilayered organization. The General Assembly
was to embody universal principles of membership and sovereign equality, while the great powers would exercise special rights and responsibilities in the Security Council.[77] The architects of the United Nations
worked in the shadow of the failed League of Nations—and its charter
reflected efforts to accommodate the realities of power politics. Unlike
the League's council, which worked on the basis of consensus, the U.N.
Security Council limited the veto to the permanent members while
making these decisions binding on all states. The charter also limited

[76] Kimball, *Juggler*, 85.

[77] For accounts of the drafting of the U.N. Charter, see Paul Kennedy, *The Parliament of Man: The Past, Present, and Future of the United Nations* (New York: Random House, 2006); and Townsend Hooper and Douglas Brinkley, *FDR and the Creation of the U.N.* (New Haven, CT: Yale University Press, 1997).

the nature of obligations to uphold political and territorial guarantees in reaffirming the sovereign rights of member states to make decisions about the collective use of force.

The founding meeting of the United Nations took place in San Francisco in the spring of 1945. Already there were worries that Soviet-American discord would undermine great-power cooperation upon which the United Nations depended. At the University of California in Berkeley, Secretary of State Stettinius reaffirmed the "fundamental unity" of the Big Four. "It is upon this strong and steady rock of unity that our work at San Francisco is firmly based." At the close of the San Francisco meeting, President Truman affirmed the central notion of great-power restraint that lay behind the organization's design. It is the duty of the powerful nations, Truman said, "to assume the responsibility for leadership toward a world of peace. . . . We all have to recognize—no matter how great our strength—that we must deny ourselves the license to do as we please."[78] On his return to Washington, Truman asked Congress to act quickly to approve the charter. "I am anxious to bring home to you that the world is one. . . . It is a responsibility that this great republic ought to lead the way in—to carry out those ideas of Woodrow Wilson and Franklin D. Roosevelt,"[79] he declared.

The charter was ratified. But rather than launching a new era of great-power concert, the U.N. system of collective security gave way to alternative thinking. By 1946, some officials in the State Department began urging a policy that encouraged European unity, building Europe into a third force alongside the United States and Soviet Union. The idea was to foster a multipolar postwar system in which Europe would be a relatively independent and unified geopolitical power center, with Germany integrated within it. George Kennan and the State Department's policy planning staff articulated this view. "It should be the cardinal point of our policy," Kennan argued in October 1947, "to see to it that other elements of independent power are developed on the Eurasian land mass as rapidly as possible in order to take off our shoulders some of the burden

---

[78] President Harry S. Truman, address at the closing session of the United Nations Conference, San Francisco, 26 June 1945.

[79] Quote from Divine, *Second Chance*, 299–300.

of 'bi-polarity.'"[80] The initial reason for urging European unity was less about countering Soviet power than about establishing a stable framework for the revival of Europe. This was the theme of Kennan's memorandum to Acheson in the weeks before the Marshall Plan address. The emphasis of American policy should be "directed not to combatting communism as such, but to the restoration of the economic health and vigor of European society."[81] It was with this objective in mind that Kennan and the policy planning staff urged that Marshall Plan aid be given to the European countries together so as to encourage them, as Kennan argued, to "think like Europeans, and not like nationalists, in this approach to the economic problems of the continent."[82]

The other argument for encouraging a unified Europe was that it was the only way to reintegrate Germany. Kennan was the foremost advocate of tying Germany to Western Europe. "In the long run there can be only three possibilities for the future of western and central Europe. One is German domination. Another is Russian domination. The third is a federated Europe, into which the parts of Germany are absorbed but in which the influence of the other countries is sufficient to hold Germany in her place. If there is no real European federation and if Germany is restored as a strong and independent country, we must expect another attempt at German domination."[83] The following year, Kennan argued that "we see no answer to German problem within sovereign national framework. Continuation of historical process within this framework will almost inevitably lead to repetition of post-Versailles sequence of developments.... Only answer is some form of European union which would give young Germans wider horizon."[84] The same thinking

---

[80] Quoted in John Lewis Gaddis, "Spheres of Influence," in *The Long Peace: Inquiries into the History of the Cold War* (New York: Oxford University Press, 1987), 58.

[81] "The Director of the Policy Planning Staff [Kennan] to the Under Secretary of State [Acheson]," 23 May 1947, *Foreign Relations of the United States, 1947*, 3:225.

[82] George Kennan, *Memoirs, 1925–50*, 337.

[83] "Report of the Policy Planning Staff," 24 February 1948, *Foreign Relations of the United States, 1948*, 1 (pt. 2): 515.

[84] "Question of European Union," policy planning staff paper quoted in Klaus Schwabe, "The United States and European Integration: 1947–1957," in Clemens Wurm, ed., *Western Europe and Germany, 1945–1960* (New York: Oxford University Press, 1995), 133.

was evinced by the American high commissioner for Germany, John McCloy, who argued in 1950 that a "united Europe" would be an "imaginative and creative policy" that would "link Western Germany more firmly into the West and make the Germans believe their destiny lies this way."[85] If Germany was to be bound to Europe, Europe itself would need to be unified and integrated so as to provide the anchoring foundation.

While the United States promoted European unity and the integration of Germany, British and French governments sought to bind the United States to Europe. The evolution of policy in Washington from pushing for a European third force to accepting an ongoing security commitment within NATO was marked by American reluctance and European persistence. At each turn, European leaders agreed to steps toward greater integration in exchange for corresponding assurances and commitments from the United States. NATO and the American security commitment was the solution to multiple interlocking problems—worry about a return of German militarism, British ambivalence about European economic integration, the growing Soviet threat, and uncertainties about American power.

The British and French governments had their specific reasons for resisting European unification and the reintegration of Germany. Britain wanted to maintain its special relationship with Washington and did not want to anchor its security in a united Europe that was independent of the United States. A European third force would also draw on resources the British needed to shore up postwar strains in its Commonwealth system. Like other European countries, Britain also feared that Germany or even the Soviet Union might come to dominate a united Europe. The French were more enthusiastic about a united Europe, which would provide a basis to extend their leadership of the continent. They also saw their own steps to draw Germany into cooperative ties—most importantly, with the Coal and Steel Community—as key mechanisms to gain

---

[85] Thomas A. Schwartz, *America's Germany: John J. McCloy and the Federal Republic of Germany* (Cambridge, MA: Harvard University Press, 1991), 95. See "A Summary Record of a Meeting of Ambassadors at Rome," 22–24 March 1950, *Foreign Relations of the United States, 1950,* 3:817.

some control over the terms of German economic reintegration. But the French government insisted that the rehabilitation of western Germany would only be acceptable within a security framework that involved the United States. American security ties would establish assurances against a resurgent German state while making the United States more pre-dictable and constrained and reducing the burdens on French security expenditures.

If an Atlantic-wide alliance bound western Germany and the United States to Europe, it also reinforced British and French commitment to an open and united Europe. The United States not only wanted to bring Germany back into the European fold, it also wanted to reori-ent Europe itself. In an echo of Wilson's critique of the "old politics" of Europe after World War I, American officials after 1945 emphasized the need for reform of nationalist and imperialist tendencies. And in their view, encouraging integration would achieve this, not only mak-ing Germany safe for Europe but also making Europe safe for the world. The Marshall Plan reflected this American thinking, as did the Truman administration's support for the Brussels Pact, the European Defense Community (EDC), and the Schuman Plan. In the negotiations over the NATO treaty in 1948, American officials made clear to the Europe-ans that a security commitment hinged on European movement toward integration. One State Department official remarked that the United States would not "rebuild a fire-trap."[86] The American goal was, as Dean Acheson put it in reference to the EDC, "to reverse incipient divisive nationalist trends on the continent."[87] American congressional support for the Marshall Plan was also premised, at least in part, on encouraging integrative political institutions and habits.

When Marshall Plan aid was provided to Europe, beginning in 1948, the American government insisted that the Europeans themselves orga-nize to jointly allocate the funds. This gave rise to the Organization for

---

[86] "Minutes of the Fourth Meeting of the Washington Exploratory Talks on Security," 8 July 1948, *Foreign Relations of the United States, 1948*, 3:163–69.

[87] "The Secretary of State to the Embassy in France," 19 October 1949, *Foreign Relations of the United States, 1949*, 4:471.

European Economic Cooperation (OEEC), which was the institutional forerunner of the European Community. This body eventually became responsible for Europe-wide supervision of economic reconstruction, and it began to involve the Europeans in discussion of joint economic management. As one American official recalls, the OEEC "instituted one of the major innovations of postwar international cooperation, the systematic country review, in which the responsible national authorities are cross-examined by a group of their peers together with a high-quality international staff. In those reviews, questions are raised which in prewar days would have been considered a gross and unacceptable foreign interference in domestic affairs."[88] The United States encouraged European integration as a bulwark against intra-European conflict even as it somewhat more reluctantly institutionalized its own security commitment to Europe. As Michael Mastanduno argues: "The Marshall Plan was prompted by proximate and enduring security concerns, including the risk of internal communist subversion or external Soviet aggression against the fragile economic and political systems of Western Europe, and the need to solve the long-standing Franco-German problem by binding West Germany and France into a more integrated European and Atlantic community."[89]

The various elements of the institutional bargain among the Atlantic countries fit together. The Marshall Plan and NATO were part of a larger institutional package. As Lloyd Gardner argues: "Each formed part of a whole. Together they were designed to 'mold the military character' of the Atlantic nations, prevent the balkanization of European defense systems, create an internal market large enough to sustain capitalism in Western Europe, and lock in Germany on the Western side of the Iron Curtain."[90] NATO was a security alliance, but it was also

[88] Lincoln Gordon, quoted in David Ellwood, ed., *The Marshall Plan Forty Years After: Lessons for the International System Today* (Bologna: SAIS Bologna Center, Johns Hopkins University, 1989), 48–49.

[89] Michael Mastanduno, "Economics and Security in Statecraft and Scholarship," *International Organization* 52, no. 4 (Autumn 1998), 192.

[90] Lloyd Gardner, *A Covenant with Power: America and World Order from Wilson to Reagan* (New York: Oxford University Press, 1984), 81.

embraced as a device to lock in political and economic relations within the Atlantic area. After the Atlantic security treaty was signed, Secretary Acheson was asked by Senator Claude Pepper if NATO had given the "Western European nations some confidence against a resurgent Germany as well as Russia?" "Yes," was Acheson's response. "Yes, it works in all directions."[91]

It was thus that the American vision of an open liberal order was transformed into an American-centered hegemonic order. The initial American project—to construct an open liberal order—gave way to a focus on rebuilding and reconstructing Europe, creating a Western-centered order. As the Cold War emerged, America's other project was to build alliances and construct a containment order. By the late-1940s, these two projects became fused. Openness and containment went hand in hand. The type of open system that the United States was drawn into building required more far-reaching commitments and institutional agreements than Washington had anticipated—and the urgency of the Cold War generated the necessary political support for these undertakings. At the same time, the Cold War alliance system and security commitments provided a wider and deeper foundation for cooperation among the "free world" countries. The postwar order that America came to lead was more hierarchical than anyone expected, but it was also more institutionalized and infused with a complex array of bargains and agreements.

Hegemonic Bargains

As the American-led postwar order took shape, it came to rest on a set of strategic bargains between Washington and its European and East Asian partners. Bundled together, these understandings—explicit in some instances, tacit in others—constituted a sort of hegemonic bargain. The United States would lead and manage the international order by providing security, supporting economic openness, upholding its rules

[91] Senate testimony, 1949, quoted in Gardner, *Covenant with Power*, 100.

and institutions, and other countries would agree to operate within this order and acquiesce in American leadership. The United States would provide an array of services—producing and maintaining an agreed-upon set of governing arrangements—and other countries would affiliate with rather than resist the United States. The United States would be first among equals and exercise hierarchical political control over the functioning of the order. It would have privileges and discretionary authority, but other countries would countenance American hegemonic power if it remained within limits.

The American hegemonic bargain with Europe and East Asia differed in specific ways. It evolved over the decades. The United States would export security, import goods, and uphold the rules of order. It would exercise power, but it would do so within institutions and through political processes that involved active interaction with the other participating states. The reciprocity and negotiated nature of these institutions and relationships gave the hegemonic order its liberal character.

Two major bargains underlay the liberal hegemonic order: a security bargain and a political bargain. The security bargain grew out of the Cold War. It dealt with the ways in which the United States would act to provide military protection, facilitate trade and economic growth, and sponsor and support the overall rules and institutions in the context of building strategic partnerships within an American-led order. The political bargain grew out of the asymmetries of power between the United States and its partners. Here the United States consented to operate within agreed-upon rules and institutions—to exercise power through institutions that established restraints and commitments on that power and provided mechanisms for voice and reciprocity in the political hierarchy of wider American-led order.

The Security Bargain

In the security bargain, the United States agreed to provide security protection and access to American markets, technology, and resources within an open world economy. In return, America's partners agreed to be reliable partners that would provide diplomatic, economic, and logistical support for the United States as it led the wider order. As Charles de Gaulle reluctantly noted at the time, "[c]onfronted with its present danger, the free world could do nothing better, and nothing else, than adopt the 'leadership' of Washington."[92] The security bargain was most explicitly embedded in America's security alliances with Europe and East Asia. In both regions, the United States acted in incremental steps to make security commitments, station troops, and establish ongoing strategic partnerships.

The American provision of security was multifaceted. It was aimed in the first instance at establishing security protection against threats that lay outside the American-led order—principally threats from the communist world. But, as noted earlier, American security presence in both Europe and East Asia was also aimed at providing assurance of stable relations among alliance partners. The American security commitment to Europe was in part to facilitate the reconstruction and reintegration of West Germany into Europe and the Atlantic area. The American security pact with Japan was also aimed in part at ensuring that Japan's economic revival would take place without triggering destabilizing conflicts and rivalries within the region. Japan's reemergence would take place within an American-led regional security order. The American security presence in both regions helped solve security dilemmas—providing reassurance that German and Japanese militarism would not be revived and thereby facilitating regional stability and cooperation. In return, Japan and Western European countries would affiliate with the United States and act cooperatively to support its wider global leadership position.

The security bargain also had an economic dimension. The United States would uphold the rules and institutions of the world economy and promote economic integration; in return, European and East Asian partners would again support the United States. Beyond this, the

[92] Charles de Gaulle, *The Complete War Memoirs of Charles de Gaulle,* vol. 3, *Salvation, 1944–1946,* trans. Richard Howard (New York: Simon and Schuster, 1960 [1959]), 906.

United States also actively sought to integrate and promote the growth and stability of its partners. In the initial years, the United States acted primarily to help revive the European economies through Marshall Plan aid and, later, the expansion of trade and investment. It used economic assistance and alliance commitment as leverage to encourage Europe-wide economic integration. In this sense, the NATO pact should be seen as a continuation of the Marshall Plan approach. The resulting European and Atlantic orders facilitated economic revival in Europe and expanding trade and investment between the two regions.

In East Asia, the United States also took systematic steps to integrate Japan into the Western world economy. The occupation of Japan initially focused on introducing democracy and market reform. As the Cold War took hold in Asia after 1948, the United States shifted its emphasis to policies that fostered economic growth and political stability. The failure of economic reform in Japan, worries about political instability, the victory of the communists in China, and the growing strategic importance of Japan all contributed to a new policy orientation stressing economic revival and incorporation into the world economy. The State Department led the way in emphasizing the strategic importance of Japan in the region and placing East Asia within the wider global context of the containment of communist influence. In the ensuing years, Japan was brought into the American security and economic orbit. The United States took the lead in helping Japan find new commercial relations and sources of raw materials in Southeast Asia to substitute for the loss of the Chinese and Korean markets.[93] Like Germany, Japan was now a junior partner of the United States, stripped of its military capacities and reorganized as an engine of world economic growth. Containment in Asia was based on the growth and integration of Japan in the wider, noncommunist Asian regional economy—what Secretary of State Dean Acheson called the "great crescent," referring to the countries arrayed from Japan through Southeast Asia to India. The historian Bruce Cumings

[93] Michael Schaller, "Securing the Great Crescent: Occupied Japan and the Origins of Containment in Southeast Asia," *Journal of American History* 69 (September 1982), 392–414.

captured the logic behind this policy: "In East Asia, American planners envisioned a regional economy driven by revived Japanese industry, with assured continental access to markets and raw materials for its exports."[94] This strategy would link threatened noncommunist states along the crescent, create strong economic links between the United States and Japan, and lessen the importance of the remaining European colonial holdings in the area. The United States would actively aid Japan in reestablishing a regional economic sphere of influence in Asia, allowing Japan to prosper and play a regional leadership role within the larger order. Japanese economic growth, the expansion of regional and world markets, and the fighting of the Cold War went together.

In constructing security partnerships, the United States opened its domestic market and tolerated economic discrimination in an effort to bolster the growth of its Cold War allies and draw them into the American-led system. As Michael Mastanduno observes, "[t]he United States encouraged, indeed demanded, the integration of the Western European economies and the formation of a European customs union, even though the latter discriminated against U.S. exports through a common external tariff. . . . In the case of Japan, in addition to tolerating high tariff and nontariff barriers, U.S. officials accommodated the desire of the Japanese government to minimize U.S. foreign direct investment and thereby granted a significant edge to Japan in the 'rivalry beyond trade.'"[95] Access to the U.S. market bolstered Western European and Japanese economic growth and political stability and tied their governments more closely to the United States. Deepened economic ties, in turn, reinforced the credibility of the American security commitment.[96]

The American security commitment in Western Europe and Japan brought with it specific agreements between Washington and host gov-

[94] Bruce Cumings, "Japan's Position in the World System," in Andrew Gordon, ed., *Postwar Japan as History* (Berkeley: University of California Press, 1993), 38.

[95] Michael Mastanduno, "Economics and Security in Statecraft and Scholarship," *International Organization* 52, no. 4 (Autumn 1998), 192.

[96] See also Robert Gilpin, *U.S. Power and the Multinational Corporation: The Political Economy of Foreign Direct Investment* (New York: Basic Books, 1975), chap. 6.

ernments. American overseas deployments provided protection to these countries, but the bargain involved a sharing of costs and obligations. Agreements over the "status of forces" were negotiated that specified terms of bases, the stationing of troops, and defense cooperation. Beyond this, America's junior security partners were expected to support Washington's wider political-economic leadership position. In particular, West Germany and Japan—highly dependent on the United States for security in the early postwar decades—felt obligations to support American trade and monetary leadership. From the 1950s to the early 1970s, West Germany supported American monetary policy and the role of the dollar in the face of mounting balance-of-payments pressure as part of its perceived obligations under the alliance.[97]

America's hegemonic role in maintaining economic stability and openness gave it privileges. These would be tolerated as long as the United States continued to provide public goods. This is seen in the advantages it has had within the postwar monetary order. As Benjamin Cohen argues, "an implicit bargain was struck" between the United States and its European and Japanese partners. For both economic and political reasons, Western Europe (particularly West Germany) and Japan agreed to finance the American balance-of-payments deficit. "America's allies acquiesced in a hegemonic system that accorded the United States special privileges to act abroad unilaterally to promote U.S. interests. The United States, in turn, condoned its allies' use of the system to promote their own economic prosperity, even if this happened to come largely at the expense of the United States."[98]

[97] In a recent study, Carla Norrlof argues that American postwar monetary hegemony fostered cooperation and provided benefits to other states, but it also allowed the United States to shift costs of adjustment onto these states, costs that the United States would otherwise bear if it did not have these "positional advantages." Carla Norrlof, *America's Global Advantage: US Hegemony and International Cooperation* (New York: Cambridge University Press, 2010). On the relationship between American troop commitments and monetary relations, see Hubert Zimmermann, *Money and Security: Troops, Monetary Policy, and West Germany's Relations with the United States and Britain, 1950–1971* (Cambridge: Cambridge University Press, 2002).

[98] Benjamin Cohen, *Organizing the World's Money: The Political Economy of International Monetary Relations* (New York: Basic Books, 1977), 97. Michael Mastanduno provides an

The Political Bargain

The political bargain was more implicit and addressed the uncertainties associated with America's preeminent power position. The United States would open itself up and bind itself to its partners; in return, European and East Asian states would accept American leadership and operate within the liberal hegemonic order. Through this bargain, the United States would make itself "user-friendly" by creating channels of access to foreign-policy decision making in Washington. The order would remain hierarchical, but it would be made more consensual, cooperative, and integrative than coercive. Under these circumstances, other states would agree to work with the United States rather than resist it.

The character of the United States and its major partners—they were all liberal democracies—facilitated the building of this liberal hegemonic order organized around multilateralism, alliance partnership, strategic restraint, cooperative security, and institutional and rule-based relationships. The institutional underpinnings of this order made America's power position both more durable and less threatening to other states. And the institutional architecture of the order facilitated a consensual style to hegemonic command and control.

In this view, three elements made the political bargain possible. First, the fact that the United States was a large, open democracy and that its major partners were democracies allowed a reciprocal and consensual style of hegemony. The liberal character of the United States as a political system—with its transparency, diffusion of power, and multiple points of access to policy making—helped create a shared decision-making system that opens up the process. An active press and competitive party system also provides a service to outside states by generating information about American policy and determining the seriousness of its purpose.

---

illuminating characterization of the postwar "grand bargain" between the United States and its German and Japanese allies, tracing its evolution as China has risen and replaced these allies as a pivotal partner in the world economy. See Michael Mastanduno, "The Financial Crisis, U.S.-China Relations, and the End of the Grand Bargain," in Daniel Drezner and Kathleen McNamara, eds., *The International Politics of the Financial Crisis* (forthcoming, 2010).

Second, this open and decentralized political process also reduced the worries about American power by creating voice opportunities—opportunities to allies and partners to gain political access and, with it, the potential to speak to and influence the way Washington's power is exercised.[99] Foreign governments do not have elected officials in Washington but they do have representatives. By providing other states opportunities to play in the policy-making process in Washington, the United States draws them into active, ongoing partnerships that serve its long-term strategic interests.

The third element that facilitated the political bargain was the array of international institutions. These institutions, as noted earlier, provide mechanisms for the United States to establish restraint and commitment, bind states together, and provide channels of access and communication. The multilateral institutions and security pacts are not simply functional mechanisms that generate collective action. They are also elements of political architecture that for states within the order to do business with each other. The political, economic, and security institutions that link the hegemonic order support networks of government officials and other elites, creating channels and mechanisms for ongoing processes of voice and consensual decision making. In effect, the political architecture gave the postwar order its distinctive liberal hegemonic character—networks and political relationships made American power more far-reaching and durable but also more predicable and malleable.[100] In championing these postwar institutions and in agreeing to operate within them, the United States was, in effect, agreeing to open itself up to an ongoing political process with other democratic states.

America's postwar system of military alliances—as mechanisms of security binding—provided important sites of this ongoing political process. The alliances, along with the network of bases and forward

[99] For a discussion of "voice opportunities," see Joseph M. Grieco, "State Interests and Institutional Rule Trajectory: A Neorealist Interpretation of the Maastricht Treaty and European Economic and Monetary Union," *Security Studies* 5 (Spring 1996), 176–222.

[100] See Daniel Deudney and G. John Ikenberry, "The Sources and Character of Liberal International Order," *Review of International Studies* 25, no. 2 (1999), 179–96.

military deployments, provided mechanisms for communication and the management of political relations. "Following World War II," Kent Calder argues, "bases took on new political-economic functions, stabilizing national ties across both the Atlantic and the Pacific in political-military alliance relations."[101] The sprawling alliance system provided institutional architecture for political consultation and bargaining.

The basic bargain that informed the NATO alliance was emblematic of the more general and implicit political bargain within the American hegemonic order. The multilateral institutions that formed the order bound the democratic states together and provided voice and access to hegemonic decision making.[102] Mastanduno notes: "Multilateral decision making procedures may be less efficient, and powerful states are often tempted to act unilaterally. But multilateral procedures help to reassure other states that they are not simply being coerced or directed to follow the dictates of the dominant state."[103] The political bargain gave the United States "first among equals" status but it also gave other states the ability to engage in an ongoing political process that generated reciprocity, voice, and—ultimately—legitimacy for the overall hegemonic order.

While the United States pursued a multilateral strategy in Europe—with NATO as the anchor—it pursued a series of bilateral security agreements with Japan, Korea, and several Southeast Asian states.[104] In effect, the political bargain took a slightly different form with Japan and the East Asian partners. The hub-and-spoke character of America's secu-

[101] Calder, *Embattled Garrisons: Comparative Base Politics and American Globalism* (Princeton, NJ: Princeton University Press, 2007), 8.

[102] See Steven Weber, "Shaping the Postwar Balance of Power: Multilateralism in NATO," in Ruggie, *Multilateralism Matters*, 233–92; Thomas Risse-Kappen, "Collective Identity in a Democratic Community: The Case of NATO," in Peter J. Katzenstein, ed., *The Culture of National Security* (New York: Columbia University Press, 1996), 356–71; Thomas Risse-Kappen, *Cooperation among Democracies: The European Influence on U.S. Foreign Policy* (Princeton, NJ: Princeton University Press, 1997); and Patrick, *Best Laid Plans*, chap. 9.

[103] Michael Mastanduno, "Preserving the Unipolar Moment: Realist Theories and U.S. Grand Strategy after the Cold War," *International Security* 21, no. 4 (Spring 1997), 61.

[104] The United States did raise the idea of a multilateral security institution in Asia in the early postwar years that would be a counterpart to NATO.

rity and political ties to East Asia meant that it would not be subject to the same multilateral restraints and commitments that existed within NATO. The hierarchical character of the relationships would be less compromised by agreed-upon regional rules and institutions. To some extent, the absence of a multilateral security institution in East Asia was due to regional circumstances. Japan did not have ready partners in East Asia with which to built multilateral ties as West Germany had within Europe. Europe had a group of roughly equally sized and situated states that were capable of being bound together in a multilateral security institution tied to the United States, while Japan was alone and isolated in East Asia.[105]

Overall, despite these differences, the security and political bargains between Washington and its partners formed the underpinning of the liberal hegemonic order. The United States agreed to extend its security umbrella to East Asia and Western Europe and support an open and integrative world economy. It took steps to stimulate European and Japanese economic growth, encouraging European economic integration and promoting Japanese trade into the American market. The United States enjoyed such an advantage in production, trade, capital, and technology that it could tolerate asymmetrical discrimination and use some of its economic assets to pursue systemwide policies of growth, integration, and openness. It would provide security to its partners who, in return, would affiliate with and support the United States as a hegemonic leader. As security partners, Japan and Western European states would gain the economic advantages of trade and investment within an American-led international economy. The United States also agreed to operate within a framework of alliances and multilateral institutions that made the exercise of American power more restrained and predictable. These institutional frameworks provided channels and mechanisms for states within the order to consult on and influence American policy.

[105] For explorations of America's divergent order building strategies in Asia and Europe, see Peter J. Katzenstein, *A World of Regions: Asia and Europe in the American Imperium* (Ithaca, NY: Cornell University Press, 2005); and Galia Press-Barnathan, *Organizing the World: The United States and Regional Cooperation in Asia and Europe* (New York: Routledge, 2003).

Conclusion

In the decades after 1945, the United States established an international order. Under the cover of the Cold War, a revolution in relations between the Western great powers took place. It was a Western order built around cooperative security, managed open markets, multilateral governance, and American liberal hegemonic leadership. The Cold War facilitated the building of this order—particularly the strategic bargains between the United States and Europe—but the project began before the Cold War and survived its end. Indeed, the Cold War ended as it did in large part because this Western order was so integrated, dynamic, and cooperative.

American postwar order building went through several phases, and in the process, the character of liberal internationalism itself evolved. It was an order cobbled together in a rolling process in which Washington bargained and compromised with its emerging partners in Western Europe and East Asia. In this process, the character of the liberal order was transformed from a free-standing system envisaged by the United States during the war to a hegemonic order in which America's own political and economic system became part of the overall liberal international order. In both the security and economic realms, the United States found itself taking on new commitments and functional roles. America's domestic market, the U.S. dollar, and the Cold War alliances emerged as crucial mechanisms and institutions through which postwar order was founded and managed. America and the Western liberal order became tied into one system. The United States had more direct power in running the postwar order, but it also found itself more tightly bound to the other states within that order. It became a provider of public goods—upholding a set of rules and institutions that circumscribed how American power was exercised and providing mechanisms for reciprocal political influence. In the late-1940s, security cooperation moved from the U.N. Security Council to NATO and other U.S.-led alliances. The global system of great-power-managed collective security became a Western-oriented security community organized around cooperative security. Likewise, the management of the world economy moved from the Bretton Woods vision to an American dollar and market system. In effect, Washington's allies "contracted out" to the United States to provide global governance.

A critical characteristic of liberal hegemony was its Western foundation. The United States found it possible to make binding security commitments as it shifted from Wilsonian collective security to alliance security built around democratic solidarity within the Atlantic region. This shift was twofold. One aspect was the movement toward more circumscribed and explicit security commitments. Alliance partnerships entailed obligations, but they were also limited liability agreements. Commitments were not universal and open-ended; they were tied to specific security challenges with treaty-based understandings about roles and responsibilities. Second, they were commitments that were backed by a political vision of a Western security community. The sense that America and Europe were imperiled by a common threat strengthened the feeling of Western solidarity. But the notion of a Western core to liberal international order also suggested that unusual opportunities existed—because of common culture and democratic institutions—to cooperate and build postwar institutions.

The American-led postwar liberal order also went beyond the Wilsonian vision with its more complex notions of sovereignty and interdependence. Westphalian sovereignty remained at the core of Truman-era liberal internationalism. But there were new understandings about the dangers and opportunities of economic and security interdependence. The economic calamities of the 1930s and the successes of New Deal regulation and governance informed these new views. Advanced societies were seen to be deeply and mutually vulnerable to international economic downturns and the bad policies pursued by other states. States would need to become more involved in more intense and institutionalized forms of joint management of the global system. New institutions would be needed in which states worked together side by side on a continuous basis to regulate and reduce the dangers inherent in increasingly interdependent societies.

In these ways, the hierarchical character of the order was more liberal than imperial. The United States engaged in public goods provision, supported and operated within agreed-upon rules and institutions, and opened itself up to voice opportunities from subordinate states. To be sure, these liberal features of hierarchy differed across regions and over time. The United States was more willing to make multilateral commitments to Western European partners than to others. In East Asia, the United States built a hub-and-spoke set of security pacts that made the regional order more client-based than rule-based. Generally speaking, America's dominant global position made de facto hierarchy an inevitable feature of the postwar order. But its dominant global position—together with Cold War bipolar competition—also gave Washington strategic incentives to build cooperative relations with allies, integrate Japan and Germany, share the spoils of capitalism and modernization, and, generally, operate the system in mutually acceptable ways.

Six

The Great Transformation and the Failure
of Illiberal Hegemony

The geopolitical foundations on which the United States built its postwar order are shifting. Long-term change in the global system—in the distribution of power, the norms of sovereignty, and the scope and character of interdependence—is transforming the problem of order. The United States emerged from the Cold War as a singular world power. Old threats and insecurities associated with great-power competition have given way to new sources of violence and insecurity. The world economy has expanded and deepened, and it has gone through recession and financial crisis—including the recent world economic downturn, the most severe since the Great Depression. The rise of developing countries such as China and India has brought increasingly powerful non-Western states into the system. Long-standing governance institutions dominated by Western powers, such as the G-7/G-8 grouping, have started to give way to more inclusive groupings. Along the way, the old bargains and institutions of the American-led liberal hegemonic order have weakened and eroded.

The most dramatic shift in the foundations of the postwar American-led order was the end of the Cold War. One historical era ended and another opened. But it was a turning point unlike others in the past, such as the great postwar junctions of 1815, 1919, and 1945. In this case, the old bipolar system collapsed peacefully without great-power war. Moreover, unlike past postwar moments, the global system—or at least the dominant core of that system led by the United States—was not overturned. Quite the contrary. The world that the United States and its allies created after World War II remained intact and stood squarely at the center of world politics. The end of the Cold War simply consolidated and expanded that order. The Soviet bloc—estranged from the West for half a century—collapsed and began a slow and uneven process of integration into that order. As such, the end of the Cold War was not the beginning of a new world order but the last gasp in the completion of an old one.

The end of the Cold War began as a consolidation of the American-led postwar order, but deeper and more profound shifts—not immediately apparent—were also set into motion. The globalization of the world economy and the growing market orientation of the developing world were forces of change. A so-called Washington consensus emerged that emphasized policies of market expansion and deregulation. The nature of the security problem in the global system also changed. The threat to international order was no longer great-power war, as it had been for centuries, but violence and instability emerging from weak, failed, and hostile states residing on the periphery of the system. September 11, 2001, dramatically marked this shift. At the same time, America itself emerged preeminent—or unipolar—after the Cold War, and by the end of the 1990s, its power and position in the global system were the defining feature of world politics. A world of competing great powers—manifest as either Cold War bipolarity or a competitive multipolar system of earlier eras—gave way to a system dominated by a single state.

The restructuring of international relations after the Cold War is a tale of two orders. During the Cold War, these two orders coexisted. One was the Cold War bipolar order. The other was the American-led liberal hegemonic order that existed inside the larger bipolar global system. When the Cold War ended, the inside order became the outside order, that is, the logic was extended to the larger global system. In one sense, this can be seen as the triumph of an American-style liberal international order. The collapse of the Soviet bloc was a collapse of the last great challenger to this order—and in the two decades since the end of the Cold War, no rival logics of order have yet appeared. But in another sense, the end of the Cold War can be seen as a sort of slow-motion crisis of authority and governance of this liberal hegemonic order. During the Cold War, the United States asserted its authority and established rule through leadership in bipolar balancing and management of a liberal order organized around strategic bargains, institutions, and the provision of public goods. That order survived the end of the Cold War but the character of rule—tied as it has been to America's hegemonic position—has been thrown into doubt and dispute.

This chapter makes four arguments. First, the end of the Cold War was a conservative world-historical event, a story of the triumph, continuity, and consolidation of the American-led postwar order. In hindsight, it is clear that the United States and its democratic allies had in fact created a deeply rooted, dynamic, and historically unique political order in the shadow of the Cold War. This inside order expanded and deepened during the 1990s and into the new century. Its watchwords were globalization, integration, democratization, and the expansion of liberal international order. NAFTA, APEC, and the WTO were elements of this expansion and deepening process. The expansion of NATO and the reaffirmation of America's alliances in East Asia also amounted to a consolidation of the American-led postwar liberal international order. Adding stability to this globalizing system were nuclear weapons, which made great-power war—and its transforming impact—unlikely, and the democratic character of the leading industrial societies, which gave the system a core of liberal democratic states operating within a democratic zone of peace.

Second, deeper shifts in the post–Cold War global system—in particular, the rise of unipolarity and the evolving norms of sovereignty—have emerged to undermine the stability of the American-led liberal order. In the past, liberal hegemonic order existed within a wider world of bipolarity and traditional state sovereignty. Liberal hegemonic order was built on a Westphalian system in which great powers maintained order through the balance of power and the restraining norms of state sovereignty. But in the decades since the end of the Cold War, under conditions of unipolarity and eroded norms of state sovereignty, this Westphalian system has been turned on its head. These transformed circumstances alter the logic and terms of American-led governance of the system. As the system has changed, so too have the incentives, costs, bargains, and institutions that form the political framework of the American postwar order. These shifts have had the effect of rendering more problematic both America's leadership of a liberal hegemonic order and the acquiescence and support of other states.

Third, other shifts in the global system have reinforced this new predicament for American liberal hegemony. The sources of violence and insecurity have shifted in the post–Cold War international system from the threat of great-power war to more diffuse and decentralized threats from weak states and troubled regions of the world. Old alignments of interests based on Cold War divisions and great-power threats no longer shape the terms of America's hegemonic provision of security. Long-term shifts in the norms relating to military intervention and the use of force—embraced by liberal democracies—also alter the constraints on and costs of the exercise of American power. At the same time, the character of world economic interdependence and America's position as leader have also undergone change, revealed in the recent financial crisis and global economic recession. Rising states from the developing world have become more active participants in the world economy and seek a greater voice in its governance. Together, these grand shifts in the system play havoc with the old American hegemonic bargains and institutions.

Fourth, against this backdrop and in the aftermath of the September 11 terrorist attacks, the George W. Bush administration embarked on the most ambitious rethinking of America's grand strategy since the early years of the Cold War. In effect, Bush-era grand strategy sought to reorient how the United States organized and led the global system. The Bush administration attempted to take advantage of this post-Westphalian system of unipolarity and eroded state sovereignty to reorganize the terms of American global rule. But its efforts were unsustainable and self-defeating. The United States offered to provide global security and enforce order as a unipolar power, operating in various ways above the system of multilateral rules and institutions. The American-led hierarchical order began to take on imperial characteristics. But this strategy of unipolar governance was unsustainable, generating opposition and resistance both abroad and at home.

The shifting character of power, sovereignty, and interdependence in the global system has made the American system of liberal order problematic. This is true, ironically, even though in many respects the transformations are ones that have been encouraged or made possible through the American-centered postwar liberal order. It has been America's preeminence—manifest after the Cold War as unipolarity—not its weakness or failure as the leading state that has unsettled the system. Moreover, the inside Cold War-era liberal order turned into the outside global liberal order precisely because of the attractions of that liberal order and its capacities for expansion and integration beyond its Western core. The erosion of norms of state sovereignty is the result of many forces, but not least among them are the human rights and liberal interventionist aspirations of the United States and other liberal democratic states. In these various ways, American liberal hegemonic order may be at an impasse, but it is an impasse at least partially of its own making and one that flows from the success of the liberal project. This chapter provides an account of these shifts and explores the implications for American liberal hegemonic order.

The End of the Cold War

The Cold War was not a war as such but a sustained period of bipolar rivalry—a militarized geopolitical standoff. It ended peacefully when, in effect, the leaders of the Soviet bloc called a halt to the competition.

This began initially with President Mikhail Gorbachev's articulation of "new thinking" in Soviet foreign policy aimed at relaxing East-West tensions and creating political space for domestic reforms. "Gorbachev cooperated to end the Cold War because he knew that the Soviet Union could not be reformed if the Cold War continued," argues America's last ambassador to the Soviet Union.[1] At the end of 1988, Gorbachev ordered a unilateral reduction of five hundred thousand Soviet troops, half coming from Eastern Europe and the Western parts of the Soviet Union. Gorbachev also signaled a new Soviet tolerance of political change within Eastern Europe itself, declaring that the "use of force" cannot be and should not be used as an "instrument of foreign policy," and that "freedom of choice" was a universal principle that applied to both capitalist and socialist systems. This statement amounted to a de facto repeal of the Brezhnev Doctrine, which had declared it a Soviet right and responsibility to intervene in Eastern Europe to safeguard socialism. In the following year, Soviet forces were withdrawn from Afghanistan. To the United States, Gorbachev offered a vision of *partnyorstvo*, or partnership, that entailed replacing the Cold War's "negative peace" with cooperation between the superpowers in pursuit of joint interests. The ideological basis of the Cold War was fast disappearing.

The Cold War ended with the spectacular unraveling of communist rule in Eastern and Central Europe in 1989 and the collapse of the Soviet Union two years later. The Cold War could have ended without the implosion of the Soviet Union. Indeed this is what its leader, President Gorbachev, had hoped for. His aim was reconciliation between the United States and Soviet Union that would keep communist rule in the Soviet Union and superpower relations intact. But the end of the Cold War took the form of the collapse of bipolarity itself. Soviet bloc countries elected new governments, Germany was united and remained inside of NATO, and the Soviet Union itself disappeared. The old bipolar international order vanished and a new distribution of power took shape.

[1] Jack F. Matlock, Jr., *Reagan and Gorbachev: How the Cold War Ended* (New York: Random House, 2004), 316.

The Cold War ended, as Robert Hutchings observes, "not with military victory, demobilization, and celebration but with the unexpected capitulation of the other side without a shot being fired."[2] After past great wars, the old international order was destroyed and discredited, opening the way for sweeping negotiations over the basic rules and principles of postwar international order. But in this case, the American-led system of order not only survived the end of the Cold War but was widely seen as responsible for Western triumph. Western policy toward the Soviet Union was vindicated and the organization of relations among the advanced industrial democracies remained stable and cooperative. In this sense, the end of the Cold War was a conservative historical event. It entailed the peaceful capitulation of the Soviet Union—reluctant to be sure and not on the terms that Gorbachev had hoped for. But the collapse of the Soviet pole left in place the American pole, and the American-led rules, institutions, and relationships that had been built during the Cold War became the new core of post-Cold War world order.

The manner in which the Cold War ended says a great deal about the nature of the American-led system that grew up during the decades of U.S.-Soviet struggle. The American pole was extraordinarily capable of generating wealth and power that advantaged the West in its competition with the Soviet Union.[3] Yet at the same time, this Western grouping of democracies presented a sufficiently unthreatening face to the Soviet Union during its time of troubles that its leaders were willing to move forward with domestic reform and a reorientation of their foreign policy. The West was both dynamic and, ultimately, defensive.[4] Gorbachev and

[2] Robert Hutchings, *American Diplomacy and the End of the Cold War: An Insider's Account of U.S. Policy in Europe, 1989–1992* (Baltimore: Johns Hopkins University Press, 1997), 343.

[3] See Stephen G. Brooks and William C. Wohlforth, "Power, Globalization, and the End of the Cold War," *International Security* 25, no. 3 (Winter 2000/01), 5–53.

[4] President George H. W. Bush articulated this American—and Western—effort to convey restraint in the face of Soviet troubles in his 1990 New Year's greetings to the Soviet people, stating that "the West seeks no advantage from the extraordinary changes underway in the East." President Bush, "New Year's Message to the People of the Soviet Union," 1 January 1990, *Weekly Compilation of Presidential Documents* 26 (8 January 1990), 1.

other Soviet leaders were convinced that the United States and Western Europe would not exploit their weakness. The pluralistic and democratic character of the countries that formed the Atlantic alliance, the multiple and conflicting positions toward the Soviet Union that existed within and among these countries, and transnational and domestic opposition movements toward hard-line policies all worked to soften the face that the Soviet Union saw as it looked westward. The alliance itself, with its norms of unanimity, made an aggressive policy by one country difficult to pursue. These aspects of Western order all served to make Gorbachev's historic gamble less risky.[5]

If the end of the Cold War was itself a surprise to many observers, so too was what followed: the remarkable stability and continuity of cooperation within the American-led order. Few observers expected this outcome either. Rather than continuity and consolidation of the Western order, the widespread expectation was for its gradual breakdown and movement toward a more competitive multipolar system.[6] One prominent view was that with the end of the Cold War—and the disappearance of bipolarity and the unifying threat of Soviet power—the global system would return to its older pattern of multipolar balance of power. This, of course, was the pattern of international politics that more or less prevailed for centuries—from 1648 to 1945. No single state dominated the system and alliance commitments were flexible. For traditional realist scholars, the bipolar system was a historical anomaly. The expectation was that the global system would return to its old pattern rather than persist as an even more anomalous unipolar system. The classic statement of this logic was articulated by Kenneth Waltz, namely, that states balance against power and, as a result, the appearance of a single dominant state, will stimulate the rise of other great powers or coali-

[5] Daniel Deudney and G. John Ikenberry, "The International Sources of Soviet Change," *International Security* 16, no. 3 (Winter 1991/92), 74–118; and Deudney and Ikenberry, "The Unravelling of the Cold War Settlement," *Survival* 51, no. 6 (December 2009–January 2010), 39–62.

[6] See survey of views by Michael Mastanduno, "A Realist View: Three Images of the Coming International Order," in T. V. Paul and John A. Hall, eds., *International Order and the Future of World Politics* (New York: Cambridge University Press, 1999), 19–40.

tions of states to balance against the leading state.[7] This was the view of John Mearsheimer, who predicted in 1992 that "bipolarity will disappear with the passing of the Cold War, and multipolarity will emerge in the new international order."[8] Kenneth Waltz also speculated on the prospects for the reemergence of an array of great powers—Japan, Germany, China, the European Union, and a revived Russia.[9] Christopher Layne argued that the extreme preponderance of American power would trigger counterbalancing reactions by Asian and European allies, or at least a loosening of the political and security ties that marked the Cold War era.[10] Anticipations also existed for a return to competitive multipolarity in East Asia.[11]

Others also saw the post–Cold War world returning to instability and conflict but argued that it would revolve around geo-economic competition. America, Europe, and Japan in particular would emerge as competing economic blocs, each built around a different type of capitalism and regional order. The new security competition would be over economic gains and divide capitalist states and fragment the global economic system. Richard Samuels and Eric Heginbotham argued that "mercantile realism" was the emerging form of international competition, in which powerful states will pursue "economic balancing" and geoeconomic interests might be pursued at the expense of more traditional political and security objectives.[12] In one version of

---

[7] Waltz, *Theory of International Politics.*

[8] John Mearsheimer, "Disorder Restored," in Graham Allison and Gregory Treverton, eds., *Rethinking America's Security* (New York: Norton, 1992), 227. See also John Mearsheimer, "Back to the Future: Instability of Europe after the Cold War," *International Security* 15 (Summer 1990), 5–57; John Mearsheimer, "Why We Will Soon Miss the Cold War," *Atlantic Monthly*, no. 266 (August 1990), 35–50.

[9] Kenneth Waltz, "The Emerging Structure of International Politics," *International Security* 18, no. 2 (Fall 1993), 45–73.

[10] See Christopher Layne, "The Unipolar Illusion: Why New Great Powers Will Arise," *International Security* 17 (Spring 1993), 5–51.

[11] Aaron L. Friedberg, "Ripe for Rivalry: Prospects for Peace in a Multipolar Era," *International Security* 18, no. 3 (Winter 1993/94), 5–33.

[12] Eric Heginbotham and Richard Samuels, "Mercantile Realism and Japanese Foreign Policy," *International Security* 22, no. 4 (Spring 1998), 171–203.

this argument, by Lester Thurow, the post–Cold War world would be dominated by three regional powers: a U.S.-led bloc centered around NAFTA, a European bloc led by Germany, and an Asian bloc organized by Japan.[13]

Some American government officials at this time also worried about a return to a competitive multipolar system. During the last years of the first Bush administration, Defense Department officials, led by Paul Wolfowitz, came forward with a strategic planning document—the Defense Planning Guidance of 1992—charting America's global security challenges after the Cold War. A draft of the report argued that a central goal of American security policy must be to block the rise of rival states or peer competitors. "Vague as it was, this language seemed to apply to Japan, Germany or a united Europe, as well as to China and Russia," as James Mann observes. "The draft said the United States should discourage the 'advanced industrial nations' from challenging America's leadership, in part by taking their countries' interests into account but also through unmatched military strength."[14] The leaked document triggered criticism from Europeans and others offended by the suggestion that the United States would seek to block the advance of its allies. The revised document dropped this language but the central argument remained that America must maintain its commanding military position and, in the report's words, "preclude any hostile power from dominating a region critical to our interests."[15]

[13] Lester Thurow, *Head to Head: The Coming Economic Battle Among Japan, Europe, and America* (New York: Morrow, 1992); and Fred Bergsten, "America's Two Front Economic Conflict," *Foreign Affairs* 80, no. 2 (March/April 2001), 16–27. For a survey of American thinking as it related to Japan and Asia during this period, see Michael Mastanduno, "Models, Markets, and Power: Political Economy and the Asia-Pacific, 1989–1999," *Review of International Studies* 26 (2000), 493–507.

[14] James Mann, *The Rise of the Vulcans: The History of Bush's War Cabinet* (New York: Viking, 2004), 210. See also Barton Gellman, "Keeping the U.S. First: Pentagon Would Preclude a Rival Superpower," *Washington Post*, 11 March 1992, A1; and Barton Gellman, "Pentagon Abandons Goal of Thwarting U.S. Rivals," *Washington Post*, 24 May 1992, A1.

[15] Secretary of Defense Richard Cheney, *Defense Strategy for the 1990s: The Regional Defense Strategy* (Washington, DC: Office of the Secretary of Defense, 1993), 3. Quoted in Mann, *Rise of the Vulcans*, 212. For a retrospective on the ideas and reactions triggered by

What these and other views reflected was the assumption that the Cold War was an essential glue that held the advanced industrial countries together, dampening conflict and facilitating cooperation. Conflict and instability among major states would return. Order and cohesion in the West are a result of cooperation to balance against an external threat, in this case the Soviet Union, and with the disappearance of the threat, alliance partnership and cooperation will decline. The expectation was that with the end of the Soviet threat, the West, and particularly the security organizations such as NATO, would weaken and eventually return to a pattern of strategic rivalry.[16]

But none of these expectations came to pass. In the years that followed the end of the Cold War, relations among the advanced industrial countries remained stable and open. During the 1990s, the Cold War alliances were reaffirmed. NATO increased its membership and the U.S.-Japan alliance was deepened. Trade and investment across these regions has grown and institutionalized cooperation in some areas has expanded. There are several surprises here about the post–Cold War distribution of power and the responses to it. Rather than a return to a multipolar distribution of power, the United States emerged during the 1990s as a unipolar state. It began the decade as the only superpower, and it grew faster than its European and Japanese partners. Likewise, the realist expectation of a return to the problems of anarchy—great-power rivalry and security competition—did not emerge. Europe and Japan remained tied to the United States through security alliances, and Russia and China did not engage in great power balancing.

---

the 1992 defense planning document, see Eric S. Edelman, "The Strange Career of the 1992 Defense Planning Guidance," in Melvyn P. Leffler and Jeffery Legro, eds., *When Walls Come Down: Berlin, 9/11 and U.S. Strategy in Uncertain Times* (Manuscript, Miller Center of Public Affairs, University of Virginia, forthcoming).

[16] Some scholars did see the liberal international order as the emerging core of the post–Cold War system. Michael McFaul and James M. Goldgeier, "A Tale of Two Worlds: Core and Periphery in the Post–Cold War Era," *International Organization* 46, no. 2 (Spring 1992), 467–92; and Daniel Deudney and G. John Ikenberry, "The Logic of the West," *World Policy Journal* 10 (Winter 1993/94), 17–26.

Expansion and Integration of Liberal Order

With the sudden end of the Cold War, this inside order survived and provided the organizing logic of the post–Cold War global system. The decade of the 1990s became a "liberal moment." Democracy and markets flourished around the world, globalization was enshrined as a progressive world-historical force, and ideology, nationalism, and war were at a low ebb. Russia became a quasi-member of the West, and China was a "strategic partner" with Washington. Existing institutions were strengthened and new ones were built. Alliances were reaffirmed and extended. The European Union was launched and its membership expanded. Newly market-oriented developing countries—what was termed "emerging markets"—became increasingly integrated into the world economy. Championed by the United States, a neoliberal approach, or "Washington consensus," favoring financial deregulation and market integration, grew in influence and spread worldwide.

The first post–Cold War impulse of the George H. W. Bush administration in the early 1990s was in fact to build on this logic of Western order. Across security and economic areas, the United States sought to build and expand regional and global institutions. In relations toward Europe, State Department officials articulated a set of institutional steps: the evolution of NATO to include associate relations with countries to the east, the creation of more formal institutional relations with the European Community, and an expanded role for the Conference on Security and Cooperation in Europe (CSCE). In the aftermath of the collapse of East Germany, negotiations ensued between West Germany and Soviet, French, British, and American leaders. Alternative pathways for a united Germany were proposed, including a German federation that would exist outside of NATO and the reintegration of Germany within a wider pan-European security structure that would also include the Soviet Union. In the diplomatic pulling and hauling that followed, the Western structures proved most useful to the search by all the major states for mechanisms of restraint, reassurance, and integration. The Bush administration championed this logic, as in a Berlin speech by

Secretary of State James Baker, declaring that the three great institutions of Europe—NATO, the EC, and CSCE—should be adapted to provide the multilevel framework to absorb the coming changes. The slogan was a "new Atlanticism for a new era."[17] In the end, it was NATO, the European Community, and the wider international liberal order that shaped and facilitated the flow of events—creating a foundation for the integration of Germany and countries within the former Soviet bloc.[18]

In the Western hemisphere, the Bush administration pushed for NAFTA and closer economic ties with South America. In East Asia, APEC was a way to create more institutional links to the region, demonstrating American commitment to the region and ensuring that Asian regionalism moved in a trans-Pacific direction. These post–Cold War regional trade initiatives were envisaged as steps that would reinforce the expansion, liberalization, and continued openness of the world economy.[19]

This strategy of building on the logic of the existing order—and expanding and integrating countries into it—was continued during the Clinton years. The idea was to use multilateral institutions as mechanisms to stabilize and integrate the new and emerging market democracies into the Western democratic world. In an early statement of this "enlargement doctrine," National Security Advisor Anthony Lake argued that the strategy was to "strengthen the community of market democracies" and "foster and consolidate new democracies and market economies where possible." The United States would help "democracy and market economies take root," which would in turn expand and

[17] See James A. Baker III, *The Politics of Diplomacy: Revolution, War, and Peace* (New York: Putnam, 1995), 172–73.

[18] For detailed accounts of alternative institutional proposals and their eventual fate in the unfolding process of German unification, see Mary Elise Sarotte, *1989: The Struggle to Create Post–Cold War Europe* (Princeton, NJ: Princeton University Press, 2009); and Philip Zelikow and Condoleezza Rice, *Germany Unified and Europe Transformed: A Study in Statecraft* (Cambridge, MA: Harvard University Press, 1995). See also G. John Ikenberry, "German Unification, Western Order, and the Post–Cold War Restructuring of the International System," unpublished paper, 2009.

[19] See C. Fred Bergsten, "APEC and World Trade: A Force for Worldwide Liberalization," *Foreign Affairs* 73, no. 3 (May–June 1994), 20–26.

strengthen the wider Western democratic order.[20] This strategy was targeted primarily at those parts of the world that were beginning the process of transition to market democracy: countries of Central and Eastern Europe and the Asia-Pacific region. Promising domestic reforms in those countries would be encouraged—and locked in if possible—through new trade pacts and security partnerships. In 1994, the Clinton administration provided a formal statement of this strategy of engagement and enlargement, calling for a multilateral approach to major foreign policy challenges: "Whether the problem is nuclear proliferation, regional instability, the reversal of reform in the foreign Soviet empire, or unfair trade practices, the threats and challenges we face demand cooperation, multilateral solutions. Therefore, the only responsible U.S. strategy is one that seeks to ensure U.S. influence over and participation in collective decision-making in a wide and growing range of circumstances."[21]

By the end of the 1990s, a major consolidation and expansion of the U.S.-led international liberal order had been accomplished. The organizational logic of the Western order built during the Cold War was extended to the global level. The first round of NATO expansion was accomplished, providing an institutional basis to stabilize and embed new entrants into the Western order—creating greater security among alliance partners and reinforcing democratic and market institutions. NAFTA and APEC also were pursued as mechanisms to reinforce and lock in the worldwide movement begun in the late 1980s toward economic and trade liberalization. Finally, the creation of the WTO in 1995 provided a further attempt to expand and institutionally strengthen the foundations of liberal international order. Building on the old GATT agreements, the WTO marked a major step forward in establishing a judicial basis for international trade law. A formal organization was established with an independent secretariat, a formal dispute-settlement

[20] Anthony Lake, "From Containment to Enlargement," *Vital Speeches of the Day* 60, no. 1 (15 October 1993), 13–19. See also Douglas Brinkley, "Democratic Enlargement: The Clinton Doctrine," *Foreign Policy*, no. 106 (Spring 1997), 116.

[21] White House, *A National Security Strategy of Engagement and Enlargement* (Washington, DC: White House, July 1994), 6.

mechanism, and an expanded institutional framework for international trade cooperation.[22]

An important impulse behind the foreign policy activity of both the first Bush administration and the Clinton administration was to ensure that the United States would not pull back from global leadership. The Bush administration was determined that NATO stay engaged on the European continent and do so with the United States in the lead, perpetuating its role as a stabilizing presence. Bush administration institution building, under the "Europe whole and free" rubric, was designed to ensure that the conflicts of the early twentieth century would not return. The Clinton administration carried these strategies forward. In addition, as Chollet and Goldgeier argue, Clinton's and Secretary of State Albright's use of the term "indispensable nation" was directed toward a domestic audience. They feared America might turn inward and wanted to encourage the country to stay engaged in the world.[23] Throughout these years, the logic of liberal order building provided a unifying orientation.

Under American leadership, the world economy both broadened and deepened. The market-oriented ideas championed by Reagan and Thatcher in the 1980s were taken up by the Clinton administration and spread worldwide. The advanced economies continued to move in the direction of open trade and the removal of the remaining barriers to the flow of money and capital. Middle-tier developing countries in Asia, Latin America, and the former communist world also emphasized trade and financial liberalization and became more integrated into global markets. The Asian financial crisis that began in 1997 exposed the degree to which emerging market countries had opened up their financial systems to international investment. A policy debate followed in East Asia and elsewhere about the dangers of unregulated and highly integrated financial markets, but the general orientation of governments toward

---

[22] A detailed account of American foreign policy in the 1990s, see Derek Chollet and James Goldgeier, *America Between the Wars: From 11/9 to 9/11: The Misunderstood Years between the Fall of the Berlin Wall and the Start of the War on Terror* (New York: Public Affairs, 2008).

[23] Chollet and Goldgeier, *America Between the Wars*, 146–48.

market integration continued. New technologies in communication and computing facilitated financial and economic exchange and integration. Policies of financial and public sector deregulation and privatization drew countries more fully into the world economy. The constituencies favoring free markets and international integration had triumphed.[24] The result was the neoliberal "Washington consensus," which by the end of the 1990s had become the organizing idea for the post–Cold War world economy.[25]

In fact, during the 1990s, trade and investment expanded across the developed and developing world and emerging countries became more fully integrated into the larger system. The democratic world itself expanded, with countries making the transition from socialist and authoritarian pasts. At the same time, the great powers remained at peace. Japan and Western Europe stayed tied to the United States, and China and Russia were moving closer to rather than further away from the United States. A decade after the end of the Cold War, the world was not divided into warring camps or antagonistic regional blocs. In critical respects, it was a one-world system in which the United States and the organizational logic of the Cold War–era Western order remained at its center. While there was much debate whether the United States had a grand strategy after the Cold War, the Clinton administration did have a liberal orientation—a strategy of multilateral management of a market-oriented globalizing world system.[26]

In the background, the stability and character of the U.S.-led post–Cold War order was reinforced by America's commanding power position—advantages that gave it the ability to exercise hegemonic leadership. There were several aspects to these power advantages. One was

[24] See Jeffry A. Frieden, *Global Capitalism: Its Fall and Rise in the Twentieth Century* (New York: Norton, 2006), chap. 17; and Daniel Yergin and Joseph Stanislaw, *The Commanding Heights: The Battle for the World Economy*, rev. ed. (New York: Free Press, 2002).

[25] The term "Washington consensus" was coined by the economist John Williamson. See John Williamson, "What Washington Means by Policy Reform," in John Williamson, ed., *Latin American Adjustment: How Much Has Happened?* (Washington, DC: Institute for International Economics, 1990), 7–20.

[26] See Robert Wright, "Clinton's One Big Idea," *New York Times*, 16 January 2001.

simply its preeminence in global power capabilities. The United States was the largest economy in the world at the beginning of the 1990s—and it continued to outpace the other advanced economies during the decade. These economic advantages were partly due to the relative weakness of the other traditional great powers—Russia collapsed, the European Union grew slowly, and Japan entered a decade of economic stagnation.

Also, behind the scenes, the reserve position of the U.S. dollar gave Washington a special status as an economic power—rights of seigniorage, which meant that it could run deficits, fight foreign wars, increase domestic spending, and go into debt without fearing the pain that other states would experience. Because of its dominance, the United States did not have to raise interest rates to defend its currency, taking pressure off chronic trade imbalances. During the 1960s, French President Charles de Gaulle understood this hidden aspect of American hegemony and complained bitterly.[27] In the post–Cold War era, it was Asian countries—China and Japan—and OPEC countries that were the primary holders of American debt rather than Europe, although the advantages for Washington remained. These advantages again came into play during the George W. Bush administration, when the United States was able to launch a costly war in Iraq while running budget deficits and cutting taxes—a foreign policy made possible by the United States' ability to sell its debt to foreign countries such as China and Japan.

In addition to its economic dominance, the United States was also the only global military power—that is, the only country capable of projecting military power to all corners of the world. At the end of the 1990s, the United States was responsible for 36 percent of total world military spending. After the September 11 terrorist attacks, Washington boosted its defense expenditures and increased its share to more than 40 percent of the world total—or roughly equal to the expenditures of

---

[27] On the advantages that accrue to the United States from the dollar's role as an international reserve currency, see Gilpin, *Political Economy of International Relations*, 77; and Carla Norrlof, *America's Global Advantage: U.S. Hegemony and International Cooperation* (New York: Cambridge University Press, 2010).

the next fourteen countries. By 2005, the United States was responsible for half of global military spending. At the same time, it retained most of its Cold War–era alliance partnerships and far-flung bases in Europe and Asia. As table 6-1 indicates, the United States began the postwar era with twenty-one alliance partners and this number grew over the decades, increasing rather than contracting after the Cold War. The expansion of NATO membership into Eastern Europe and the former Soviet sphere drove this growth. The result is a global alliance system that has steadily expanded worldwide, increasingly in contrast to the limited alliances of the nondemocratic great powers.

These American power advantages were ones it brought forward from the Cold War era. What was new in the 1990s was that the United States had no serious great-power challengers. But even if there were no great powers able to balance against it, the purpose of balancing was also unclear. Russia and China's nuclear deterrence capabilities meant that these countries did not fear superpower aggression in any traditional sense. Likewise, the other great powers—Germany, France, Britain, and Japan—were also democracies with well-established cooperative security ties to the United States. These democratic great powers formed a security community—that is, a zone of peace in which the use of force was unthinkable. Rival ideologies and great-power challengers were nowhere to be found.[28]

So the twentieth century ended with world politics exhibiting a deeply anomalous character—the United States had emerged as a unipolar power situated at the center of a stable and expanding liberal international order. The other traditional great powers had neither the ability nor the desire to directly challenge—let alone overturn—this unipolar order. This order was built on the realities implicit in the international distribution of material capabilities. But it was also built on the rules, institutions, partnerships, and political norms about how states do business with each other, aspects of the system that had been built up during the Cold War.

[28] See Ikenberry, *America Unrivaled*, 288–99.

Table 6-1
Alliance Partners: United States, People's Republic of China, and the Soviet Union/Russia[a]

Year	United States	China	USSR/Russia[b]
1946	21	—	8
1951	37	1	10
1956	42	1	10
1961	43	2	11
1966	43	2	11
1971	45	2	10
1976	47	2	10
1981	50	1	9
1986	52	1	9
1991	53	1	8
1996	52	1	10
2001	55	1	9
2003	62	1	8

Source: Brett Ashley Leeds, Jeffrey M. Ritter, Sara McLaughlin Mitchell, and Andrew G. Long, "Alliance Treaty Obligations and Provisions, 1915–1944," *International Interactions* (2002) 28, 23–260.

[a] A state is an alliance partner if it has a defensive obligation toward another state during the year of observation. (This variable captures whether the state has promised to defend another state, not whether the defense obligation is reciprocal.)

[b] The alliance partners of the Soviet Union and of Russia are different, except for North Korea. Soviet alliance partners in 1989 were: East Germany, Poland, Hungary, Czechoslovakia, Bulgaria, Romania, Finland, Mongolia, and North Korea. Russian alliance partners in 1995 were: Belarus, Armenia, Georgia, Azerbaijan, Turkmenistan, Tajikistan, Kyrgyz Republic, Uzbekistan, Kazakhstan, and North Korea.

Transformation of the Westphalian Order

The rise of American unipolarity after the Cold War was part of a deeper and multifaceted shift in the character of power and sovereignty over the last decades—a shift with consequences for American liberal hegemony. Most generally, it was a shift in the underlying logic of the Westphalian system. That is, it was a shift away from international order organized around multiple and competing power centers—an order maintained by ensuring an absence of an overarching power—and the enshrinement of norms of state sovereignty. It was a movement toward an order with one overarching power operating in a global system in which norms of state sovereignty were increasingly contested and abridged.

In the modern era, international order has been marked by a diffusion and equilibrium of power among major states—manifest as either bipolarity or multipolarity. Multiple states with roughly equal capabilities—the so-called great powers—balanced each other or operated in concert. Order existed as a sort of rough equilibrium of power. Domestically, countries have been sovereign, deploying what the German sociologist Max Weber called "a monopoly on the legitimate use of physical force within a give territory."[29] This was the classic understanding of the modern, sovereign nation-state. Together, these two dimensions are what constitute the Westphalian system: a balance and equilibrium of power internationally and sovereign states with supreme legal authority in their own territory.[30]

These features of the Westphalian system are ideal-typical and not an exact reflection of the logic of order over the last five centuries. But they do capture a deep logic. The diffusion of power among several leading states meant that there would not be a single "center" to international order. There would be several powerful and competing centers—or poles of power. Great powers may have spheres of influence, client states, and even far-flung empires. But within the wider world, they operate in a system where power is diffused among several great powers. Likewise,

[29] Max Weber, "Politics as a Vocation," in H. H. Gerth and C. Wright Mills, eds., *From Max Weber: Essays in Sociology* (London: Routledge, 1970), 78.

[30] For discussions of the logic and evolution of the Westphalian system, see Keo Gross, "The Logic of Westphalia, 1648–1948," in Richard A. Falk and Wolfram Hanreider, eds., *International Law and Organization* (Philadelphia: Lippincott, 1968), 45–67; Hedley Bull, *The Anarchical Society* (London: Macmillan, 1977); Hedley Bull and Adam Watson, eds., *The Expansion of International Society* (Oxford: Clarendon, 1984); F. H. Hinsley, *The Pursuit of Peace* (Cambridge: Cambridge University Press, 1963); and K. J. Holsti, *Peace and War: Armed Conflicts and International Order, 1648–1989* (Cambridge: Cambridge University Press, 1991).

states—large and small—claimed rights of sovereignty. State sovereignty is a norm or shared understanding in which states claim for themselves and cede to other states the right of autonomy and independence as a political entity. States are responsible for what goes on inside their sovereign territorial borders. No political entity above the state has the legal right or authority to intervene or make claims on what goes on within the state.[31]

This Westphalian system has been significantly transformed in recent decades, particularly since the end of the Cold War. And in the last decade, the two essential features of that system—diffusion and equilibrium of power among major states and sovereign states with a monopoly on authority over their territory—has been to some extent inverted. The United States, under conditions of unipolarity, has enjoyed a near monopoly on the worldwide use of military power, while norms of Westphalian sovereignty have eroded with rising acceptance of intervention into the internal affairs of states.[32] These dual shifts in the underlying character of the international system places American power at the center of international order—triggering new sorts of insecurities and controversies over power and authority. We can look at these dual shifts away from the Westphalian logic of order.

Power Balancing to American Unipolarity

As noted earlier, the end of the Cold War did not return the world to a multipolar system. Instead, the preeminent power position of the United States was strengthened. This was partly due to the relative weakness of

---

[31] Chris Brown offers a summary of Westphalian norms: "The actors in the Westphalian System are sovereign states—territorial polities whose rulers acknowledge no equal at home, no superior abroad; except in very exceptional and restricted circumstances individual human beings have no standing in international society. States are legally equal, differing in capabilities ('Great Powers, Medium Powers, Small Powers') but with the same standing in international society, which means that the norms of non-intervention is central—no sovereign has the right to intervene in the affairs of another." Brown, *Sovereignty, Rights and Justice: International Political Theory Today* (Cambridge: Polity, 2002), 35.

[32] The Italian scholar Vittorio Emanuele Parsi has called it a transition from *pace d'equilibro* ("peace of equilibrium") to *pace egemonica* ("hegemonic peace"). Parsi, *L'alleanza Inevitabile: Europa e Stati Uniti oltre l'Iraq* (Milan: Universita Bocconi Editore, 2003).

the other traditional powers, as Russia collapsed, the European states grew slowly, and Japan entered a decade of economic stagnation. The United States had the largest and most vibrant economic in the system. The American dollar was the world's reserve currency. The United States was also the only global military power—the only country capable of projecting military power to all corners of the world. It retained most of its Cold War–era alliance partnerships and far-flung bases in Europe and Asia. Rival ideologies and great-power challengers were nowhere to be found.[33]

The international distribution of power favored the United States, the last remaining superpower. At the same time, there were liberal features (discussed in chapter 4) that made American unipolarity more than simply a highly concentrated aggregation of power. The binding security partnerships and "penetrated" character of American hegemony made unipolarity more acceptable and legitimate to other states. Power disparities were tempered by institutionalized and reciprocal processes of doing business. The United States did provide some public goods, such as alliance security, protection of the flow of oil, markets, and a willingness to use its good offices to help settle regional disputes. It was the chief sponsor of rules and institutions of the system, and it more or less operated within that consensual and loosely arrayed governance system. In all these ways, the United States seemed to be uniquely positioned to keep world politics on a stable and cooperative course.[34]

In the last years of the Clinton administration, however, worry about how the United States would exercise unipolar power was already spreading. The American-led NATO bombing of Serbia in 1999 provided a revealing glimpse of the new patterns of world politics in the post-Cold War era: despotic states and hostile regimes in peripheral regions generate threats that challenge the old rules and institutions of the postwar

---

[33] For documentation on America's power preponderance, see William Wohlforth, "The Stability of a Unipolar World," *International Security* 21, no. 1 (Summer 1999), 5–41; Barry Posen, "Command of the Commons: The Military Foundations of U.S. Hegemony," *International Security* 28, no. 1 (Summer 2003), 5–46; and Paul Kennedy, "The Eagle Has Landed," *Financial Times*, 2 February 2002.

[34] See Ikenberry, *America Unrivaled*.

Western order and provoke the controversial use of American military force. Secretary of State Madeleine Albright described America as the "indispensable nation"—the only global power that could provide enlightened and forceful leadership across regions and realms of world politics.[35] But others around the world worried, such as French Foreign Minister Hubert Verdrine, who described the United States as a "hyperpower." When asked in an interview with *L'Express* about what could be done to resist the overbearing power of the United States, Verdrine said: "Through steady and persevering work in favor of real multilateralism against unilateralism, for balanced multipolarism against unipolarism, for cultural diversity against uniformity."[36]

Even without American policies and pronouncements that might aggravate the situation, the shift from Cold War bipolarity to American unipolarity carried with it risks and uncertainties—and a decade after the Cold War, it triggered a global geopolitical adjustment process that continues today. As discussed in chapter 4, the first implication of a shift to unipolarity is that it enhances the power position of the United States. This is true for several reasons. The unipolar state has more discretionary resources—more unspent power—than before because it no longer faces a peer competitor. Likewise, the absence of a great-power coalition balancing against it also reduces the external constraints on American power. Weaker and smaller states have fewer exit options. Overall, the unipolar state has a more encompassing impact on the global system. If there is to be order and the provision of international public goods, the United States will need to lead the way.

But the disappearance of the Cold War threat also removes some leverage for the unipolar state. Weaker states—and long-standing alliance partners—are no longer threatened by a rival global power. Some countries—such as Japan—still build their security around tight alliance

---

[35] Albright's remarks were: "If we have to use force, it is because we are America! We are the indispensable nation. We stand tall, and we see further into the future." NBC "Today" Show, February 19, 1998.

[36] "To Paris, U.S. Looks Like a 'Hyperpower,'" *International Herald Tribune*, 5 February 1999, 5.

ties with the United States, but America's global role as security provider is not as uniformly felt or widely appreciated as it was during the Cold War. The centralizing security problem of the Cold War—manifest in the bipolar competitive struggle—is gone, and security problems have inevitably decentralized into regional ones. The United States continues to play a role in many of these regional security trouble spots, but its overall leverage as global security provider is diminished.

It is the impact of unipolarity on the general framework of Western and global rules and institutions that has triggered the most worries. At the very least, the shift in power advantages in favor of the United States would help explain why it might want to renegotiate older rules and institutions. In this sense, America after the Cold War entered into its second "hegemonic moment." After World War II, it translated its power advantages into a set of global and regional institutions; it created a liberal hegemonic order. By the end of the 1990s, America's unipolar advantages put it in a position to engage in a similar sort of adjustment process. During the Clinton years, this adjustment and renegotiation of the liberal hegemonic order primarily entailed expanding and deepening liberal international order. But the expansion and integration of the global system—a byproduct of the old order—have also brought new issues and new demands for rules and institutions as well as new controversies and conflicts. Out of these circumstances, America appeared to some observers to be a revisionist unipolar state—driven by its power advantages to pursue an ambitious agenda of global transformation.[37]

The shift from Cold War bipolarity to unipolarity gives the United States incentives to renegotiate its hegemonic bargains with other states. But—more profoundly—unipolarity may also be creating conditions that reduce the willingness of the United States to operate within frameworks of agreed-upon rules and institutions. The unique global position that the United States occupies leads it to demand special status

[37] See Robert Jervis, "The Remaking of a Unipolar World," *Washington Quarterly* 29, no. 2 (2006), 7–19; and G. John Ikenberry, "Global Security Trap," *Democracy: A Journal of Ideas* 1, no. 2 (September 2006), 8–19.

and exemptions from multilateral rules and institutions. For example, the United States cannot be party to the anti–land mine convention because its troops are uniquely deployed in harm's way—such as along the Korean DMZ. The United States has also argued that it cannot sign the International Criminal Court treaty because its global security presence makes Americans unusually vulnerable to politically inspired prosecutions. The result is that unipolarity leads to demands by the lead state to be treated differently, and this reduces its willingness to operate within multilateral rules and institutions.[38]

Unipolarity also creates more opportunities for the lead state to influence or control the policies of other states without resort to commitment to multilateral rules and institutions. Its preponderance of power creates opportunities for it to push adjustment off on other states. The United States can set its own domestic regulatory standards in some areas—and this puts pressure on other countries and regions to adopt similar standards. The United States does not need to compromise its policy autonomy to get agreement from other states. Likewise, the market power of the United States can be used to influence or control the policies of others states. An example is the use of third-party sanctions. If countries do not adopt similar policies toward a target state, the United States will threaten sanctions against these countries.[39]

The fundamental implication of the rise of unipolarity is that it has brought a shift in the underlying logic of order and rule in world politics. In a bipolar or multipolar system, powerful states rule in the process of leading a coalition of states to balance against other states. When the system shifts to unipolarity, this logic of rule disappears. Power is no longer based on balancing and equilibrium but on the predominance of one

[38] See John Gerard Ruggie, "American Exceptionalism, Exemptionalisim, and Global Governance," in Michael Ignatieff, ed., *American Exceptionalism and Human Rights* (Princeton, NJ: Princeton University Press, 2005), 304–38.

[39] For example, the Nonproliferation Act passed by the U.S. Congress in 2000 outlines sanctions against countries and firms who supply weapons technology to Iran (and in 2005, it was expanded to include Syria).

state. This is new and different—and potentially threatening to weaker and secondary states. As a result, the power of the leading state is rendered salient and worrisome. Unipolar power itself becomes a problem in world politics. As John Lewis Gaddis argues, American power during the Cold War was accepted by other states because there was "something worse" over the horizon.[40] With the rise of unipolarity, that "something worse" disappears.

Eroding Norms of State Sovereignty

A more gradual and quiet transformation of the Westphalian system involves the unfolding of the postwar human rights revolution and the erosion of the norms of state sovereignty. The international community is increasingly seen to have legitimate interests in what goes on within countries. Sovereignty is more contingent, increasingly a legal right that must be earned.[41]

The human rights revolution is deeply embedded in the postwar liberal international project. It was liberals—wielding liberal ideas about world order—who pushed forward the campaign for international recognition of human rights. The breakthrough was the Universal Declaration of Human Rights adopted by the U.N. General Assembly in December 1948. Championed by liberals such as Eleanor Roosevelt and others, this document articulated a notion of universal individual rights that deserved recognition by the whole of mankind and not simply left to sovereign governments to define and enforce.[42]

---

[40] John Lewis Gaddis, *Surprise, Security and the American Experience* (Cambridge, MA: Harvard University Press, 2004), 66–67.

[41] As Beth Simmons observes: "[F]rom its apogee in the nineteenth century, the idea of exclusive internal sovereignty has been challenged by domestic democratic movements, by international and transnational private actors, and even by sovereigns themselves. The result today is an increasingly dense and potentially more potent set of international rules, institutions, and expectations regarding the protection of individual rights than at any point in human history." Simmons, *Mobilizing for Human Rights: International Law in Domestic Politics* (New York: Cambridge University Press, 2009), 3.

[42] See Mary Ann Glendon, *A World Made New: Eleanor Roosevelt and the Universal Declaration* (New York: Random House, 2002).

A steady stream of conventions and treaties followed that together constitute an extraordinary vision of rights, individuals, sovereignty, and global order.[43]

The international human rights movement was effectively launched in the 1940s. American postwar planners brought to their tasks notions of security, justice, and governance forged within the United States during the New Deal. Roosevelt and Truman were clearly sobered by the failure of the League of Nations but convinced nonetheless that a new global order committed to human rights, collective security, and economic advancement was necessary to avoid the return to war. In various postwar institutional initiatives—the United Nations, Bretton Woods, and the human rights conventions—a new synthesis of ideas about security, human rights, international law, and institutional cooperation informed American efforts.[44] In this way, the notion was established that Westphalian sovereignty was not absolute and that the international community had a moral and legal claim on the protection of individuals within states.

In the 1990s, this contingent character of sovereignty was pushed further. The international community was seen to have a right—even a moral obligation—to intervene in troubled states to prevent genocide and mass killing. NATO's interventions in the Balkans and the war against Serbia were defining actions of this sort. As diplomatic negotiations at the U.N. Security Council over the crisis in Kosovo unfolded in 1998, Russia refused to agree to authorization of military action in what was an internal conflict. In the absence of U.N. approval, an American-led NATO operation did intervene. In framing this action, U.N. Secretary-General Kofi Annan articulated a view of the contingent nature of norms of sovereignty and nonintervention as enshrined in the U.N. Charter. As Strobe Talbott recounts Annan's views:

[43] On the unfolding of the postwar human rights revolution and its implications for Westphalian sovereignty, see Jack Donnelly, *Universal Human Rights in Theory and Practice*, 2nd ed. (Ithaca, NY: Cornell University Press, 2002).

[44] Elizabeth Borgwardt, *A New Deal for the World: America's Vision for Human Rights* (Cambridge, MA: Harvard University Press, 2004).

[I]f the behavior of a regime toward its own people is egregious, it is not just outsiders' business to object but their responsibility to step in, stop the offenses, and even change the regime. "State frontiers," Annan said, "should no longer be seen as a watertight protection for war criminals or mass murderers. The fact that a conflict is 'internal' does not give the parties any right to disregard the most basic rules of human conduct." He acknowledged that "the Charter protects the sovereignty of peoples," and that it prohibits the UN from intervening "in matters which are essentially within the domestic jurisdiction of any State." However, he added, that the principle "was never meant as a licence for governments to trample on human rights and human dignity. Sovereignty implies responsibility, not just power."[45]

A year later, Annan observed that "[s]tate sovereignty, in its most basic sense, is being redefined." Modern states, he argued, are "now widely understood to be instruments at the service of their people, and not vice-versa. . . . When we read the Charter today, we are more than ever conscious that its aim is to protect individual human rights, not to protect those who abuse them."[46] This notion that sovereignty entails responsibilities as well as rights and protections was the leading edge in a gradual and evolving redefinition of the meaning of national sovereignty. The idea was further developed by an International Commission on Intervention and State Sovereignty, which advanced the idea of the "responsibility to protect."[47] The international community had new obligations to see that basic human rights were protected within countries, particularly when faced with mass atrocities and other acts of organized violence.[48]

[45] Annan's remarks were made in a speech at Ditchey Park in June 1998. Strobe Talbott, *The Great Experiment: The Story of Ancient Empires, Modern States, and the Quest for a Global Nation* (New York: Simon and Schuster, 2008), 313.

[46] Kofi Annan, "Two Concepts of Sovereignty," *Economist*, 18 September 1999.

[47] See International Commission on Intervention and State Sovereignty, *The Responsibility to Protect* (Ottawa: International Commission on Intervention and State Sovereignty, 2001).

[48] For a statement of these views by one of the architects of this new doctrine, see Gareth Evans, *The Responsibility to Protect: Ending Mass Atrocity Crimes Once and For All* (Washington, DC: Brookings Institution Press, 2008).

The norms of state sovereignty were further eroded in the aftermath of September 11. The American-led intervention in Afghanistan—where outside military force was used to topple a regime that actively protected terrorist attackers—was widely seen as a legitimate act of self-defense. The outside world had a legitimate claim to what goes on within a sovereign state if that state provides a launching pad, breeding ground, or protected area for transnational violence. The Bush administration pushed the limits of this principle in its invasion of Iraq. Now it was the anticipatory threat of a state itself—and its ambitions to gain weapons of mass destruction—that provided the justification for intervention.

This new thinking was captured at the time by an American official at the State Department. There is, argued Richard Haass, "an emerging global consensus that sovereignty is not a blank check. Rather, sovereign status is contingent on the fulfillment by each state of certain fundamental obligations, both to its own citizens and to the international community. When a regime fails to live up to these responsibilities or abuses its prerogatives, it risks forfeiting its sovereign privileges including, in the extreme, its immunity from armed intervention."[49] Haass argued that there are three circumstances when exceptions to the norms of nonintervention are warranted: when a state commits or fails to prevent genocide or crimes against humanity; when a state abets, supports, or harbors international terrorists or is not capable of controlling terrorists operating within their borders; and when a state takes steps—such as attempting to acquire weapons of mass destruction—that are a clear threat to global security, particularly a state with a history of aggression and support for terrorism.

There are several implications of these developments. First, eroded norms of sovereignty have created a new license for powerful states to intervene in the domestic affairs of weak and troubled states. The norm of sovereignty has less "stopping power" in world politics. Sovereignty really was born as a legal doctrine and international norm in early

[49] Richard Haass, "Sovereignty: Existing Rights, Evolving Responsibilities," lecture at Georgetown University, 14 January 2003.

modern Europe as a way to prevent the intrusion of transnational religious and imperial authority into newly evolving nation-states. It spread around the world and became, in many ways, the single most universal and agreed-upon norm of international politics. It underlies international law, the United Nations, and the grand historical movements of anticolonialism and national self-determination. So when the norm weakens, it is not surprising that there are consequences. And indeed, with the erosion of Westphalian sovereignty, there are fewer international legal or political inhibitions on intervention and the use of force across national boundaries.

Second, the erosion of norms of sovereignty has not been matched by a rise of new norms and agreements about who and how sovereignty-transgressing interventions can proceed. The international community has more authority than it had in the past to act inside troubled states—but who precisely is the international community? To some extent, the answer is: ideally, the United Nations. But there is unresolved disagreement on the standards of legality and legitimacy that attach to the actions of powerful states acting on behalf of the international community.

As a result, the erosion of norms of sovereignty has ushered in a new global struggle over the sources of authority in the international community. This problem is made worse by the rise of American unipolarity. Only the United States really has the military power to systematically engage in large-scale uses of force around the world. The United Nations has no troops or military capacity on its own. The problem of establishing legitimate international authority grows.

Violence, Insecurity, and Democratic Legitimacy

Another deep change that erodes or challenges the Westphalian logic of order is in the sources of violence and insecurity. The security problem at the heart of the Westphalian system is great-power war. But as noted earlier, various developments in the modern global system have diminished this threat to security. Nuclear deterrence and the fact that most of the great powers are liberal democracies together make war among these states less likely. It is now the threat of violence projected out of weak states—wielded by nonstate actors—that shapes how the advance countries organize themselves and engage in security cooperation.

This new development might be called the privatization of war or the rise of informal violence. In the past, only states—primarily powerful states—were able to gain access to means of violence that could threaten other societies. Now we can look out into the future and see the day when small groups—or transnational gangs of individuals—might be able to acquire weapons of mass destruction. The technologies and knowledge almost inevitably will diffuse outward. Determined groups of extremists will increasingly be in a position to obtain increasingly lethal violence capabilities.

This is a transformation in the ways and means of collective violence in international politics that is driven by technology and the political structure of the system itself. The effect of this transformation is to render more problematic the old norms of sovereignty and the use of force. It raises troubling new questions about the relationship between domestic politics and international relations and raises to greater national security significance parts of the world that previously could be ignored. It also creates new functional challenges that inevitably will influence patterns of security cooperation.

What does seem clear is that the privatization of war alters how states conceptualize security and cooperate to protect against new threats and insecurities. "Effective wielding of large scale violence by nonstate actors reflects new patterns of asymmetrical interdependence, and calls into question some of our assumptions about geographical space as a barrier," Robert Keohane argues. "Contemporary theorists of world politics face a challenge similar to that of this earlier generation [who had to make sense of the nuclear revolution]: to understand the nature of world politics and its connections to domestic politics, when what Herz called the 'hard shell' of the state has been shattered. Geographical space, which has been seen as a natural *barrier* and a locus for human barriers, now must be seen as a *carrier* as well."[50] A global consensus does not exist on how to deal with this new type of diffuse nonstate threat. But it plays havoc with old notions of deterrence, alliance, and self-defense, and with Article 51 of the United Nations Charter (which affirms the right of individual and collective self-defense).

A final background shift in the global system has been the rise and maturation of democratic society within and beyond the Atlantic world. As noted earlier, this is a defining feature of the liberal ascendancy. There are several ways this worldwide democratic community might be labeled, such as the Western security community, the democratic complex, or simply the community of democracies. This alliance has been around for most of the last century, but it has been evolving, expanding, and deepening. Indeed, the most powerful and rich countries in the world are now all democracies.

This fact of democratic community has two important implications for world politics. First, it has the effect of creating a stable, cooperative, and interdependent core of major states. Democracies are unusually willing and able to cooperate, at least with other liberal democracies. As argued in chapter 5, the United States and the other Western democracies built an international order around multilateralism, alliance partnership, strategic restraint, cooperative security, and institutional and rule-based relationship. The institutional underpinning of this order made America's power position both more durable and less threatening to other states—rising, declining, or otherwise. It is the order that came to dominate the global system for half a century, surviving the end of the Cold War and other upheavals.

Second, the fact of democratic community sets some constraints on how powerful states can operate within it. Put simply, coercive domination and realpolitik behavior have their limits and liabilities in a world of democracies. Attempts at bullying or strong-arming fellow democratic countries are likely to backfire. As Robert Cooper argues, "power with

---

[50] Robert Keohane, "The Globalization of Informal Violence, Theories of World Politics, and 'The Liberalism of Fear,'" in Craig Calhoun, Paul Price, and Ashley Timmer, eds., *Understanding September 11* (New York: Norton, 2002), 78, 80 (emphasis in original).

calculation and restraint is no longer sustainable in democratic age. Nor is the exercise of hegemony by force, which has been the other source of stability in the international system. In a democracy, domination by the ruthless use of force ceases to be an option in the international field as it is in domestic—as Gandhi well understood when he began the process of dismantling the British Empire."[51] This environment of democratic community has paradoxical effects on American foreign policy. On the one hand, it gives the United States the ready access to partners and the ability to pursue complex forms of cooperation. American power itself is seen as more benign and accessible. The United States is surrounded by affluent, capable, and friendly states. On the other hand, these democratic states are not likely to respond to domination or coercion by the United States. Indeed, they will expect the United States to operate within the rules and institutions of the democratic community.

Overall, the global system has evolved away from the Westphalian order. It is no longer a system built on equilibrium and balance among the great powers. The unipolar distribution of power and the spread of democracy have made this older model problematic as an organizing logic. The building of a liberal international order was more successful— and during the Cold War, largely unnoticed—than anyone in the 1940s really imagined was possible. But the erosion of the old norms of sovereignty, the spread of international norms of human rights, and the rise of new sorts of threats of collective violence have generated problems with the functioning of that liberal order.

In a fundamental sense, there is an authority crisis within today's liberal order. The international community is the repository for new human rights and national security norms—but who can legitimately act on its behalf? American leadership of liberal international order was made acceptable to the other states during the Cold War because it was providing security protection—and, over the horizon, there was "something worse." American power and authority are not one and the same anymore. How to establish legitimate authority for concerted

<hr />

[51] Robert Cooper, "Imperial Liberalism," *National Interest*, no. 79 (Spring 2005), 12–13.

international action on behalf of the global community—and do so when the old norms of order are fading away—is the great challenge of international order. The events of September 11 and the Bush revolution crystallized and intensified these new post-Westphalian controversies over power and authority.

The Rise and Fall of the Bush Revolution

In the aftermath of the terrorist attacks on September 11, the Bush administration embarked on an ambitious rethinking of American grand strategy—the most sweeping since the early years of the Cold War. Controversial ideas about preventive war, "coalitions of the willing," and hegemonic dominance were enshrined as doctrine. Bush administration officials also sent signals to the world about basic shifts in America's postwar national security policies regarding the use of force, deterrence, and alliance partnership. President Bush announced a "war on terror" and a determination to "take the battle to the enemy, disrupt his plans, and confront the worst threats before they emerge."[52] The American invasion of Iraq in the spring of 2003—a preventive war launched over the opposition of many Western allies—was the definitive expression of this strategic reorientation.

The Bush administration embraced the evolving post-Westphalian order—marked by unipolarity, eroded sovereignty, and nonstate sources of violence and insecurity—and proposed a new hegemonic bargain with the world. But in the years that followed, the Bush administration's grand strategic proposal to alter the terms of the American hegemonic leadership were rejected by allies and other states around the world— rejected quite emphatically, in many instances. The Bush administration proposed a system of hegemonic order with fewer liberal characteristics and more imperial characteristics, and the world—for the most

---

[52] "Remarks by the President at 2002 Graduation Exercise of the United States Military Academy," White House Press Release, 1 June 2002.

part—rejected this system. Global worries about how an American-dominated unipolar world, organized around the "war on terror," would work followed the Bush administration to the end of its term. We can look at both the elements of Bush's grand strategy and the causes and consequences of its failure.

Bush's Unipolar Grand Strategy

At the heart of the Bush Doctrine was the proposition that the United States would act directly—and alone, if necessary—in pursuit of global security threats that it itself identified, and in this struggle countries were either with the United States or against it. The United States would be a global security provider, but it would also be less encumbered by rules and institutions. The Bush administration's more general impulse toward unilateralism and resistance to international rules, institutions, treaties, and commitments reinforced this far-reaching shift in America's global position. The United States would stand above the global order and use its unrivaled power to enforce security and order. In a post-Westphalian world of anarchy, the United States proposed to step forward and act as an order-creating Leviathan. Where in previous eras the problem of order could only be solved by the balancing of power, the administration asserted, it would now be solved by American dominance. The dangers of anarchy and balance of power were to be replaced by the stability of American-directed global hierarchy.[53]

The Bush administration was, in effect, making a grand offer to the rest of the world. The United States would serve as the unipolar provider of global security, but in return the world would be expected to treat the

[53] For the formal statement of Bush grand strategy, see *The National Security Strategy of the United States* (Washington, DC: White House, September 2002). For discussions of the NSS report and Bush national security strategy, see John Lewis Gaddis, "A Grand Strategy of Transformation," *Foreign Policy* (November/December 2002), 50–57; Philip Zelikow, "The Transformation of National Security," *National Interest* (Spring 2003), 17–28; Robert Jervis, "Understanding the Bush Doctrine," *Political Science Quarterly* 118 (Fall 2003), 365–88; and G. John Ikenberry, "America's Imperial Ambition," *Foreign Affairs* 81, no. 5 (September/October 2002), 44–60.

United States differently. The United States would not be obliged to play by the same rules as other states. Such was the price the world must pay for the American provision of the global public good of order and peace.

The attacks of September 11 had revealed new threats to the United States and others around the world. It was a cruel paradox. The United States had begun the new century at the zenith of its power. But the terrorist attacks in 2001 dramatically revealed a whole new world of threats and insecurity. In the view of the Bush administration, the United States could not remain content simply to preside over the old rules and institutions of the global system. It would need to redefine and transform America's position and the terms of its leadership. The new threats to America and global security came from small networks of terrorists with a growing ability to gain access to weapons of mass destruction and inflict them on the civilized world. According to Bush administration officials, these new threats required a radical rethinking of American grand strategy—how the United States deploys power, works with other states, and seeks to shape its security environment.

There are six components to this Bush unipolar grand strategy.[54] The first aspect of the Bush grand strategy, as noted, was a fundamental commitment to maintaining a unipolar world in which the United States has no peer competitor. No coalition of great powers without the United States would be allowed to achieve hegemony.[55] President George W. Bush made this point the centerpiece of American security policy in his West Point speech in June 2002: "America has, and intends to keep, military strength beyond challenge, thereby making destabilizing arms

[54] This is a composite depiction of Bush grand strategy. It is meant to illuminate the assumptions and convictions behind administration thinking and policies. I draw in particular on analyses by Robert Jervis and Ian Shapiro. See Robert Jervis, "Understanding the Bush Doctrine," *Political Science Quarterly* 118, no. 3 (2003), 365–88; and Robert Jervis, "The Remaking of a Unipolar World," *Washington Quarterly* 29, no. 3 (2006); and Ian Shapiro, *Containment: Rebuilding a Strategy against Global Terror* (Princeton, NJ: Princeton University Press, 2007).

[55] As such, the Bush vision brought forward ideas advanced by Pentagon officials in the earlier George H. W. Bush administration at the end of the Cold War, arguing that the United States must act to prevent the rise of peer competitors in Europe and Asia. As noted in an earlier section, these ideas were articulated in a Pentagon memorandum written by Assistant Secretary of Defense Paul Wolfowitz. See Mann, *Rise of the Vulcans*, 363.

races pointless and limiting rivalries to trade and other pursuits."[56] The United States would preside over a global hierarchy in which no state or coalition of states could ever challenge it as global leader, protector, or enforcer. The United States would be so much more powerful than other major states that strategic rivalries and security competition among the great powers will disappear, leaving everyone—not just the United States—better off. As such, American unipolar power was seen by the Bush administration as a global public good. American power was to be used to transform international politics itself, making old balance-of-power rivalries obsolete.

As many observers noted at the time, this was a remarkable statement of American global ambition. It shared with American liberal visions of the past a desire to move beyond the balance-of-power system of order to a world undivided by geopolitical blocs and competitive great powers. Fareed Zakaria observes that President Bush's vision was the most Wilsonian statement since Wilson himself announced the American power would be used to "create a dominion of right."[57] But what distinguished Bush from Wilson is that in the new conception, the United States would stand above other countries within the global power structure, aggregating and deploying unipolar military power to maintain order. Unlike Wilson's, the Bush vision did not involve efforts to strengthen the rule-based character of international order.

The second element in the Bush grand strategy was the universal scope of America's security domain. The United States would need to be prepared—and would assume the right—to use military force throughout the world. This imperative followed from the nature of the new security threats. The grim new reality was that small groups of terrorists—possibly aided by hostile states—might soon acquire highly destructive nuclear, chemical, and biological weapons that could inflict catastrophic destruction. These terrorist groups cannot be appeased or

---

[56] "Remarks by the President at 2002 Graduation Exercise of the United States Military Academy," White House Press Release, 1 June 2002.

[57] Fareed Zakaria, "Our Way: The Trouble with Being the World's Only Superpower," *New Yorker*, 14 and 21 October 2002.

deterred, so they must be eliminated—which requires the ability to pursue them wherever they may be. Under these conditions, the Bush administration asserted a claim to the right to use military force anywhere and on a global scale. "The war on terrorists of global reach is a global enterprise of uncertain duration," argued the 2002 National Security Strategy report.[58] It was a war that the United States would need to take to the terrorists—not simply defend itself and its allies but seek out and destroy its enemies where they lay in wait—and so the United States must be able to act militarily worldwide. As Bush put it succinctly at West Point in 2002, "the military must be ready to strike at a moment's notice in any dark corner of the world."[59]

This claim that the world itself was a global battlefield in which the United States must be able to operate freely and effectively went beyond previous official conceptions. As Ian Shapiro argues, "Before the advent of the Bush Doctrine, no U.S. government had ever asserted the right to act militarily anywhere in the world."[60] To be sure, in earlier eras, the U.S. government had had expansive notions of its rights and commitments to use force. Since the early nineteenth century, the United States has asserted a right to use force in the Western Hemisphere to resist encroachments from outside great powers. During the Cold War, the United States also deployed military force in all corners of the world and engaged in covert interventions abroad. It continues to have major military commitments to countries in all regions of the world. What is distinctive—and more expansive—in the Bush strategic doctrine was the notion that the United States must be able to act anywhere and everywhere at a moment's notice to attack enemies before they unleash deadly violence.

The third element in the Bush grand strategy follows directly, that the United States must have the right and capacity to act preemptively—and even preventively—to thwart enemies before they can act. The new sorts

[58] Letter accompanying *The National Security Strategy of the United States* (Washington, DC: White House, September 2002), i.
[59] "Remarks by the President at 2002 Graduation Exercise of the United States Military Academy," White House Press Release, 1 June 2002.
[60] Shapiro, *Containment*, 17.

of security threats are not organized armies massing on territorial frontiers. They are terrorist groups that lurk in the shadows, and because the new threats cannot be appeased or deterred, they must be eliminated. The old defensive strategy of building missiles and other weapons that can survive a first strike and be used in a retaliatory strike to punish the attacker will no longer ensure security. As the 2002 National Security Strategy report argued, in "an age where the enemies of civilization only and actively seek the world's most destructive technologies, the United States cannot remain idle while dangers gather."[61] The only option, then, is offense.

To act preemptively is to strike an enemy as it prepares to strike. But the Bush administration went beyond this notion to claim a right to wage preventive wars. As President Bush argued, "as a matter of common sense and self-defense, America will act against such emerging threats before they are fully formed."[62] In the post–September 11 security environment, the notion of "imminent threat" had to be redefined. To wait until the threat was fully formed would be too late. The Bush administration argued that "[t]he greater the threat, the greater is the risk of inaction—and the more compelling the case for taking anticipatory action to defend ourselves, even if uncertainty remains as to the time and place of the enemy's attack."[63] The notion that states have a right of self defense in the face of an "imminent threat" was widely recognized in international law and diplomacy. What the Bush administration sought to do was adapt and redefine the concept of "imminent threat" in a world where the "destructive technologies" wielded by "rogue states and terrorists" required action before the threats became fully formed.

The fourth element was the conviction that the United States would act alone if necessary—or with "coalitions of the willing"—in pursuing threats. The role of security treaties and alliance partnerships were to be diminished in favor of more informal American-led efforts. "While the United States will constantly strive to enlist the support of the international community," the Bush administration's official strategy report

---

[61] *National Security Strategy*, 2002, 15.

[62] Letter accompanying *National Security Strategy*, 2002, ii.

[63] *National Security Strategy*, 2002, 15

indicates, "we will not hesitate to act alone, if necessary."[64] The United States would seek the assistance of others, but the Bush administration made it clear, as Robert Jervis observes, that they would "forgo the participation of any particular country rather than compromise."[65]

This tendency toward unilateralism followed in part from the new threats themselves: if the stakes are rising and the margins of error are shrinking in the war on terrorism, multilateral norms and agreements that sanction and limit the use of force are obstacles to action. The United States would need to play a direct and unconstrained role in responding to threats.[66] It was also a conviction partially based on a judgment that no other country or coalition—even the European Union—has the force-projection capabilities to respond to terrorist and rogue states around the world. A decade of U.S. defense spending and modernization had left allies of the United States far behind. In combat operations, alliance partners found it increasingly difficult to mesh with U.S. forces. This conviction was also based on the judgment that joint operations and the use of force through coalitions tend to hinder effective operations. To some observers, this lesson became clear in the allied bombing campaign over Kosovo. The sentiment was also expressed during the U.S. and allied military actions in Afghanistan. Secretary of Defense Rumsfeld explained this point in 2002 when he said: "The mission must determine the coalition; the coalition must not determine the mission. If it does the mission will be dumbed down to the lowest common denominator."[67] The Bush grand strategy did not advocate the dismantling of alliances or multilateral security mechanisms.[68] Rather,

[64] *National Security Strategy*, 2002, 6.

[65] Jervis, "Understanding the Bush Doctrine," 374.

[66] The Bush administration's doctrine of preventive wars, as Robert Jervis observers, also reinforces American unilateralism, "since it is hard to get a consensus for such strong actions and other states have every reason to let the dominant power carry the full burden." See Jervis, "Understanding the Bush Doctrine," 373–74.

[67] Donald Rumsfeld, remarks on *Face the Nation*, CBS, 23 September 2001.

[68] The 2002 National Security Report did express rhetorical support for America's system of alliances. For the view that the Bush administration grand strategy was not intrinsically unilateralist, see Philip Zelikow, "The Transformation of National Security," *National Interest* 71 (Spring 2003), 24–25.

the view was that these forms of security cooperation were less useful in confronting new threats.[69]

This impulse toward unilateralism was also expressed more generally in Bush's foreign policy. After he took office, his administration famously stepped back from a series of pending multilateral agreements, including the Kyoto treaty combating global warming, the International Criminal Court, and the protocol implementing the ban on biological weapons. The Bush administration also withdrew from the Anti-Ballistic Missile (ABM) Treaty, which many observers see as the centerpiece of the global arms-control system. In the national security area, officials across the Bush administration evinced a general skepticism of arms control and multilateral security agreements, arguing instead, as one report indicated, that "the United States must rely on its own capabilities rather than treaties to protect its interests and sovereignty."[70] As we will see later, this unilateral orientation toward security protection resonated with and was reinforced by a broader administration resistance to rule-based, multilateral cooperation.

The fifth element of Bush grand strategy was the view that the United States would not just dominate and lead the existing order— it must actively transform it. To fully become secure, the United States must pursue an ambitious agenda of state building and democracy promotion. President Bush's most sweeping statement of this view came in his second inaugural address when he argued that "[t]he survival of liberty in our land increasingly depends on the success of liberty in other lands."[71] In his State of the Union address of the same year, Bush elaborated on this conviction. "In the long term," he said, "the peace we seek will only be achieved by eliminating the conditions that feed radicalism and ideologies of murder. If whole regions of the world remain in

[69] This tendency toward unilateralism in the Bush grand strategy is reinforced by more a general skepticism that Bush administration officials had toward the role of treaties and multilateral forms of cooperation. This more general tendency is discussed in the next section.

[70] Nicole Deller, Arjun Makhijani, and John Burroughs, eds., *Rule of Power or Rule of Law: An Assessment of U.S. Policies and Actions Regarding Security-Related Treaties* (New York: Apex, 2003), xvii.

[71] President George W. Bush, Second Inaugural Address, 20 January 2005.

despair and grow in hatred, they will be the recruiting grounds for terror, and that terror will stalk America."[72] The administration's national security strategy called for the employment of an array of tools and efforts to promote transitions around the world to democracy—or at least to rule-abiding and accountable regimes. Past American presidents had also championed freedom and democracy. The Bush administration's formulation was distinctive in the linkages it drew to national security. In the post–September 11 era, the United States was "now threatened less by conquering states than we are by failing ones."[73] A global agenda for transformation was tied directly to American national security.

Terrorist groups were threats in part because states in troubled parts of the world were weak and failing, providing havens for these groups. Other states—such as Iraq under Saddam Hussein—were autocratic states that posed a threat both directly if they acquired weapons of mass destruction and indirectly if they passed weapons or materials off to terrorist groups. Out of these new security worries grew the agenda for regime transformation. Threats by terrorists and hostile autocratic states could only be confronted by altering the character of the states themselves.[74] Secretary of State Condoleezza Rice captured the essence of the Bush administration's new view in a January 2006 speech at Georgetown University: "Since its creation more than 350 years ago, the modern state system has rested on the concept of sovereignty. It was always assumed that every state could control and direct the threats emerging from its territory. It was also assumed that weak and poorly governed states were merely a burden to their people, or at most, an international humanitarian concern but never a true security threat. Today, however, these old assumptions no longer hold. . . . The fundamental character of regimes

---

[72] President George W. Bush, State of the Union address, 2 February 2005.

[73] *National Security Strategy*, 2002, 1.

[74] America cannot be safe until threatening despotic states join the democratic world. Robert Jervis captures this new logic: "[A]s long as many countries are undemocratic, democracies everywhere, including the United States, cannot be secure. President Woodrow Wilson wanted to make the world safe for democracy. Bush extends and reverses this, arguing that only in a world of democracies can the United States be safe." See "Remaking of a Unipolar World," 13.

now matters more than the international distribution of power."[75] The United States could not render itself safe in the existing system. States would variously need to be confronted, strengthened, and democratized.

Finally, the Bush administration made the support of other states to America's war on terror the preeminent determinant of the quality and character of relationships within the global order. "Over time it's going to be important for nations to know they will be held accountable for inactivity," President Bush asserted soon after the September 11 terrorist attacks. "You're either with us or against us in the fight against terror."[76] Soon after, at an international conference on terrorism in Warsaw, Bush remarked that "[n]o nation can be neutral in this conflict, because no civilized nation can be secure in a world threatened by terror."[77] In effect, countries would not be allowed to remain on the sidelines. The United States would determine if countries—allies or otherwise—were supportive of the new American-led global security order and, in particular, its war on terrorism. States had a simple choice: they could work with the United States or they could be part of the problem, and rewards and punishments would follow accordingly.

This was a remarkable foreign policy message to the world. The United States was the dominant global power with vast, far-flung, and multifaceted relations with almost all states in the system. After September 11, the United States proclaimed that countries would now be seen as friend or foe depending on their fidelity to Washington's anti-terrorism campaign.[78] The war on terror was a struggle between "civilization" and "chaos" and no nation could remain neutral. States would be required to toe the American line or pay the price.

[75] Condoleezza Rice, "Transformational Diplomacy," speech at Georgetown University, 18 January 2006.

[76] President George W. Bush, "You Are Either with Us or against Us," CNN.com, 6 November 2001.

[77] Quoted in Shapiro, *Containment*, 27.

[78] Ian Shapiro argues, "[t]he Bush Doctrine in effect declares null and void the international law on neutrality that stretches back to the nineteenth century and was codified in the Hague Convention of 1907—to which the United States is a signature." Shapiro, *Containment*, 27.

Taken as a whole, the Bush grand strategy attempted to redefine America's global role. It was a strategic vision in which the United States would occupy the center of a unipolar world, providing security, determining threats, using force, and transforming the system. It was a vision in which sovereignty would become more absolute for the United States even as it became more conditional for other countries. The Bush administration embraced the logic of a post-Westphalian world order organized around unipolarity, eroded state sovereignty, and a security system geared to respond to the new threats of terrorism and hostile states. The United States would both command the system and actively seek to transform it. The old American hegemonic bargains with other states would give way to a more direct form of rule. Within this redefined hierarchical order, states throughout the system would gain the benefits of security but it would come at a price of more severe subordination to the United States.

Conservative Nationalism versus Liberal Internationalism

As the Bush administration articulated its vision of a unipolar security order, it also shifted the general orientation of American foreign policy away from liberal internationalism toward more conservative nationalist ideas. This was a departure from the past. As we have seen, at the great turning points of 1919, 1945, and 1989, American leaders tended to invoke liberal internationalist ideas and to talk about international order as a progressive, liberal project. American power was to be used to construct rules and institutions for managing global problems, strengthen the fabric of international community, and bind the United States more closely to other democratic states. International rules and institutions were seen as tools to project American ideas and authority into the global system and embed them there. In one way or another, the international community was seen as a collective body—a repository of rules and norms—with some weight and significance. Most generally, while the United States would protect its sovereignty, it would also make commitments that tied it to other states.

In contrast, the Bush administration resisted these liberal internationalist notions. The making of American foreign policy during the Bush years brought to the foreground a conservative nationalist orientation toward international order.[79] First, and most implicitly, the Bush administration downplayed the role and importance of international institutions and rules as tools of American foreign policy. This was seen in the new unilateralism of the administration. Across a wide array of policy domains, the administration indicated that it would apply a new and more severe cost-accounting calculation to international treaties and agreements. Along the way, it signaled a new resolve to resist recently negotiated multilateral agreements in areas of climate control, international justice, and arms control. Each agreement had its specific liabilities from the viewpoint of the administration, but the resistance was also a more general orientation that a full range of old and new multilateral agreements imposed unacceptable constraints on American sovereignty, interests, and freedom of action.[80]

This orientation that the Bush administration brought to office has been described as the "new unilateralism." "After eight years during which foreign policy success was largely measured by the number of treaties the president could sign and the number of summits he could attend, we now have an administration willing to assert American freedom of action and the primacy of American national interests," wrote the conservative essayist Charles Krauthammer. "Rather than contain power within a vast web of constraining international agreements, the new unilateralism seeks to strengthen American power and unashamedly deploy it on behalf of self-defined global ends."[81] In this view, rules

[79] For a survey of these ideas and their rise within the American foreign policy establishment, see Peter J. Spiro, "The New Sovereigntists: American Exceptionalism and Its False Prophets," *Foreign Affairs* 76, no. 6 (November/December 2000), 9–15. For a spirited defense of the doctrine of sovereignty and of American unilateralism, see Jeremy A. Rabkin, *Law without Nations? Why Constitutional Government Requires Sovereign States* (Princeton, NJ: Princeton University Press, 2005).

[80] See Jonathan Monten, "Primacy and Grand Strategic Beliefs in U.S. Unilateralism," *Global Governance* 13, no. 1 (January–March 2007), 119–38.

[81] Charles Krauthammer, "The New Unilateralism," *Washington Post*, 8 June 2001, A29.

and institutions were primarily useful for weak states that want to try to constrain powerful states, most particularly the United States. In one of the most sweeping critiques, for example, Bush administration official John Bolton argued before becoming Under Secretary of State that a great struggle was unfolding between what he called "Americanists" and "globalists." Globalists were depicted as elite activist groups who seek to strengthen "global governance through a widening net of agreements on environment, human rights, labor, health, and political-military affairs and whose agenda is to enmesh the United States in international laws and institutions that rob the country of its sovereignty."[82] The postwar growth of multilateral treaties and agreements—the so-called global governance movement—was perceived as the result of a primarily liberal agenda that threatened American sovereignty and self-rule. Accordingly, Bolton and others argued for an agenda of prudent resistance to entanglement in multilateral agreements and institutions. The rise of American power after the Cold War provided an opportunity to restore American policy autonomy and sovereign control of its affairs.[83]

Second, there was a deep skepticism about anything that might be called the "international community." So to try to use American foreign policy to strengthen the international community or to adjust policy to abide by its norms and precepts was misguided—even dangerous. The United States operates in a system of states where power politics prevails. Condoleezza Rice articulated this conservative realist view during the 2000 presidential campaign to describe how a Republican administration policy would differ from Clinton's liberal internationalism. Many in the United States are "uncomfortable with the notions of power politics, great powers, and power balances," Rice observed. "In an extreme form, this discomfort leads to a reflexive appeal instead to

[82] John Bolton, "Should We Take Global Governance Seriously?" *Chicago Journal of International Law* 1, no. 2 (2000), 205–22.

[83] This view is expressed, for example, by the neoconservative pundit Max Boot, who argued that the growth of American power in the 1990s inevitably reduced its incentives to operate in a multilateral order. "Any nation with so much power always will be tempted to go it alone. Power breeds unilateralism. It is as simple as that." Max Boot, "Doctrine of the 'Big Enchilada,'" *Washington Post*, 14 October 2002, A29.

notions of international law and norms, and the belief that the support of many states—or even better, of institutions like the United Nations—is essential to the legitimate exercise of power." In contrast to this view, which she describes as deeply rooted in Wilsonian ideas and for which "there are strong echoes in the Clinton administration," a Republican foreign policy would be internationalist but it would also "proceed from the firm ground of the national interest, not from the interests of an illusory international community."[84] The notion of an international community is a polite fiction.

Finally, conservative discourse suggests that the source of legitimacy in American foreign policy is domestic, rooted in popular sovereignty and the constitution. The rectitude of American actions is ensured by the legitimacy of the nation's democratic process and not by the opinions of other governments. States around the world may approve or disapprove of what the United States does but they do not speak for some vague international standard of legitimacy; on the contrary, their views reflect their own national interests and nothing more lofty or virtuous. Giving voice to this view, President Bush asserted in his State of the Union address in 2004 that "America will never seek a permission slip to defend the security of our people."[85] This was both a legal claim and a proclamation about the sources of legitimacy in America's pursuit of its interests and national security.

In practical terms, this view simply restates what is generally accepted as true. The United States retains its sovereignty in regard to the use of force. But in more general terms, it reflects a position that stands in contrast with liberal notions of American foreign policy and international order. John Bolton again offers the essential critique of liberal notions: "The question of legitimacy is frequently raised as a veiled attempt to restrain American discretion in undertaking unilateral action, or multilateral action taken outside the confines of an international organization, even when our actions are legitimated by the operation of that

---

[84] Condoleeza Rice, "Rethinking the National Interest: American Realism for a New World," *Foreign Affairs* (July/August 2008), 2–26.

[85] President George W. Bush, State of the Union address, 20 January 2004.

Constitutional system. The fact, however, is that this criticism would delegitimize the operation of our own Constitutional system, while doing nothing to confront the threats we are facing. Our actions, taken consistently with Constitutional principles, require no separate, external validation to make them legitimate."[86]

Conservative nationalist ideas about international order have always coexisted with liberal ones in the American experience, but they did not guide Washington policy at the most critical order-building junctions of the last century.[87] In the hands of the Bush administration, these themes all led in the same direction—toward an old-style conservative national-ist foreign policy. The United States would attempt to defend itself and get what it could in a competitive state system while also protecting its national sovereignty. It presented itself to the world as a self-regarding actor. The United States does not have any special obligation to uphold the international order, provide public goods, or abide by global norms. It is out for itself like all other states. The United States is a great power in a world of competing great powers seeking security and advantage for itself. Together, its unipolar grand strategy and these conserva-tive nationalist ideas offered a new and provocative way in which the United States would operate in the world. And, in the end, it was simply unsustainable.

The Failure of the Bush Revolution

The Bush administration, galvanized by the 2001 terrorist attacks, artic-ulated a dramatic reorganization of the world's security order. It was a vision of order that built on deep and ongoing post-Westphalian shifts in the global system. The Bush administration found itself in a world in

[86] John Bolton, "'Legitimacy' in International Affairs: The American Perspective in Theory and Operation," remarks before the Federalist Society, Washington, DC, 13 November 2003.
[87] Walter Russell Mead describes this foreign policy orientation as Jacksonian. See Mead's *Special Providence: American Foreign Policy and How It Changed the World* (New York: Knopf, 2001). This Jacksonian or conservative-nationalist orientation should be distinguished from a classical realist orientation, which can actually be quite internationalist, as manifest in the Nixon-Kissinger policy of détente, for example.

which the United States was preeminent, the norms of sovereignty had eroded, and new security threats appeared to render outdated the older logics of deterrence and great-power balancing. Facing this new world of threats and opportunities, the Bush administration articulated a grand strategy in which the United States would provide order and security from the center of the system. The United States would be the global Leviathan. That is, it would be the global security provider, identifying threats and deploying force worldwide. It would also stand above other states, less constrained by multilateral rules and institutions. The United States would have an open-ended license to deploy power and intervene around the world—and do so with fewer checks and balances. The Iraq war and the American-led "war on terror" were the cutting edge of this new global security order. In effect, the United States was offering a new hegemonic bargain to the world. In the end, however, the world did not accept the terms of the new bargain. As a grand conception of a reorganized world order, it was ultimately unwelcome and unsustainable, and it gave way with the end of the Bush administration.[88]

The failures of Bush's grand strategy were multiple, involving problems of coherence, capability, and legitimacy. To begin with, the Bush conception was built on a political contradiction between its unipolar security project and its conservative nationalist impulses. In effect, the Bush administration wanted it both ways. It wanted the United States to be a provider of global security—to provide "system functions" for the international system—and to also assert conservative nationalist claims as a great power. But this double move is impossible to sustain unless the United States would be willing, and able, to enforce order through the systematic exercise of coercion, operating a unipolar system with little or no consent or legitimacy.

In Bush's unipolar logic, the United States is to provide security to the world. It upholds and enforces order as a public good. In return, the rest of the world accepts American dominance. After all, it is not an

---

[88] As many observers note, even before the end of its term, the Bush administration began to retreat from its strong version of this unipolar grand strategy.

inherently bad deal for most states. But when fused with conservative ideas about order, it results in a global hegemon that is fundamentally above the law and out for itself. The idea is to use American unipolar power to replace the risks and dangers of a balance-of-power system with the peace and stability made possible in a single, unified order. Liberals who never liked the balance-of-power system can understand the attraction of this vision, particularly when it is coupled with a commitment to promote democracy and human rights. This is a vision that is not that far away from the progressive international ambitions of Wilsonian liberalism. But when coupled with conservative nationalist ideas about the use of American power—manifest as profound skepticism about international community, multilateral institutions, and legitimacy—it becomes unipolarity with no strings attached. It is a unipolar bargain in which there is no bargaining. The United States was offering a hegemonic order with more command and less consent. It is a vision of a conservative Leviathan—and it is both intellectually and politically untenable.

The contradiction in the Bush foreign policy is that it offered the world a system in which America rules the world but does not abide by rules. This is, in effect, empire. As such it is both unsustainable at home and unacceptable abroad. A unipolar order without a set of rules and bargains with other countries leads to a system of coercive unipolar American dominance. As the Iraq war shows, under these circumstances other countries will tend to under-supply cooperation. They will do so because they decide to free ride on the American provision of security, because they reject the American use of force that is untied to mutually agreed-upon rules and institutions, or because they think that the United States is wrong to use force in the first place. So the United States will find itself—as it did during the Bush years—acting more or less alone and incurring the opposition and resistance of other states. This is the point when the conservative unipolar vision becomes unsustainable inside the United States. The American people will not want to pay the price for protecting the world while other countries free ride and resist.

Second, the Bush vision of a unipolar security order was also pre-mised on a misreading of functional power realities. To be sure, Amer-ica's power advantages—massive, usable, and enduring—are what gave rise to the ambitions of Bush's grand strategy. Indeed, extraordinary power is needed if the United States is to simultaneously pursue a strat-egy of unipolar rule and reduce its exposure to global rules and institu-tions. To get other countries to bend to its goals, America must be able to successfully threaten, induce, coerce, and punish other states—and it must be able to go it alone when other states refuse to cooperate. The emergence of the United States as an unrivaled global power did give Bush administration officials confidence that they could lead a global order on their own terms.[89] Washington could do so not by operating within consensual rules and cooperative frameworks but by wielding a big stick.[90]

Although the United States is powerful, it is doubtful it could sustain its rule through power alone. The flipping of the Westphalian system does give the United States extraordinary global influence. Its military power is without peer or precedent. But in economic and political realms, the world is not unipolar at all.[91] The failure of the Bush administration to get Turkey and Russia to cooperate in the run-up to the Iraq war is revealing. In the end, American leverage over Russia and Turkey was extraordinarily limited. Both countries have more important trade and economic relationships with the European Union than with the United States. They are also fledgling democracies that are sensitive to heavy handed pressure tactics. Even Bush officials must have been sur-prised at how little of America's unipolar power could be turned into

---

[89] The leading figures in the Bush administration, as James Mann notes, shared an "extraor-dinary optimistic assessment of American capabilities.... They had been arguing for thirty years that America was not in decline and that it had vastly more power in reserve for interna-tional affairs than others believed." Mann, *Rise of the Vulcans*, 362–63.

[90] On the Bush administration's misreading of power realities, see Joseph Nye, *The Paradox of American Power: Why the World's Only Superpower Can't Go It Alone* (Oxford: Oxford University Press, 2002); and Michael Mann, *Incoherent Empire* (London: Verso, 2003).

[91] See Nye, *Paradox of American Power*.

useable diplomatic and political influence. More generally, the administration's overestimation of American power reinforced the contradiction in Bush's grand strategy between its unipolar and nationalist visions. In an echo of the classic problem of great-power overextension, overconfidence in American power led to bold imperial-hegemonic ambitions that foundered because that power was insufficient to overcome foreign resistance and dwindling domestic support. These failures, in turn, reinforced American nationalism and global disengagement.

Third, there are more specific problems associated with the Bush grand strategy of preemption and regime change. As the Iraq war demonstrates, the use of force to eliminate WMD capabilities or overturn dangerous regimes is never simple, whether it is pursued unilaterally or by a concert of major states. After the military intervention is over, the target country has to be put back together. Peacekeeping and state building are inevitably required, as are long-term strategies that bring the U.N., the World Bank, and the major powers together to orchestrate aid and other forms of assistance. This is the costly and often forgotten underside to military interventionism. Peacekeeping troops may be required for many years, even after a new regime is built. Regional conflicts inflamed by outside military intervention must also be attended to. This is the "long tail" of burdens and commitments that comes with every major military action. It is unclear that the United States would be able to either pay the price for these undertakings itself or generate cooperation with other states to share the burdens.

Beyond this, it is also unclear that Bush's unipolar grand strategy could generate the cooperation needed to tackle the wider array of global challenges. In the fight on terrorism, the United States needs cooperation from Europeans and Asian countries in intelligence, law enforcement, and logistics. Outside the security sphere, realizing U.S. objectives depends even more on a continuous stream of amicable working relations with major states around the world. It needs partners for trade liberalization, global financial stabilization, environmental protection, deterrence of transnational organized crime, management of the rise of China, and a host of other thorny challenges. But it is impossible to expect would-be partners to acquiesce in America's self-appointed global security protectorate and then pursue business as usual in all other domains.[92]

Finally, there is the fundamental problem of establishing consent from other countries for Bush's unipolar security order. This is a problem that emerges in particular from other democratic countries, particularly in Europe—ironically, countries that are most closely allied with the United States. In these democratic countries, popular sentiments against old-style power politics and the use of force places a constraint—sometimes large and sometimes small—on the ability of their leaders to cooperate with the United States. The failure of the Bush vision of a unipolar security order is that it is an order that cannot legitimate itself within the bounds of the wider democratic world. Legitimacy in the eyes of the democratic public—in the West and beyond—appears to require some deference to the rule of law. Foreigners, after all, are not bound to the U.S. Constitution. It is not the use of force itself or the American exercise of power that is objectionable. It is the absence of a commonly agreed-upon framework or set of norms about how military force and power will be exercised.

As I discussed in chapter 4, the United States was able to legitimate its massive power advantages during the postwar decades. Its leaders understood that American interests would be advantaged by the construction of a global framework of rules and institutions that lock in a favorable international environment and legitimate American power. Power is most profound and durable when it is manifest in the rules and principles of order itself. In the face of Bush's grand strategy, European Union diplomat Javier Solana tried to remind Washington officials: "A rule-based approach is not a ploy to constrain the US. America wrote much of the great body of international law that has served us so well

---

[92] The key policy tool for states confronting a unipolar and unilateral America is to withhold cooperation in day-to-day relations with the United States. The United States may be a unipolar military power, but economic and political power are more evenly distributed across the globe. The major states many not have much leverage in directly restraining American military policy, but they can make the United States pay a price in other areas.

in the post-war period. Upholding and strengthening the rule of law is the best means for America to preserve her position as the benign world power and to continue to protect her values."[93]

The rule-based sources of consent were revealed during the Iraq war. Large majorities of European public opinion were strongly opposed to the Bush administration's decision to invade Iraq. In turn, this opposition made it politically appealing for European leaders to also resist Bush policy. But public opinion polls suggest that if the United States were to get authorization for the use of force from the United Nations, the public would be more supportive.[94] The opposition was less about the use of force, as such, and more about the principles and procedures for using military power. To the extent that the United States seeks the consent of other governments—particularly that of its traditional allies—for the use of force, it has incentives to operate within United Nations and other multilateral forums.

In this sense, a great deal of the opposition to the Iraq war was not directly related to the merits of the war itself but to what it meant in terms of the wider rules and principles of world order. The war was emblematic of an imperial turn in American global strategy, and it was this turn that leaders in many countries opposed. Reflecting this view, a French diplomat noted at the time: "France is not interested in arguing with the United States. This is a matter of principle. This is about the rules of the game in the world today. About putting the Security Council in the center of international life. And not permitting a nation, whatever nation it may be, to do what it wants, when it wants, where it wants."[95] If the Iraq war had been a unique adventure, it is quite possible that world opposition—at least the opposition of leaders from Europe and the other major powers—would have been less severe. But because

[93] Javiar Solana, "Mars and Venus Reconciled: A New Era for Transatlantic Relations," Albert H. Gordon Lecture, Kennedy School of Government, Harvard University, 7 April 2003.

[94] European public opinion polls indicate that opposition to the Iraq war would have been lessened if it had gained full Security Council authorization.

[95] Quoted in Maggie Farley and Doyle McManus, "To Some, Real Threat Is U.S.," *Los Angeles Times*, 30 October 2002.

the war was tied to Bush's grand efforts to redefine America's global security role, the stakes grew and so, too, the opposition.

Taken together, the rise of unipolar American power is paradoxical: the collapse of the Soviet Union and the end of the Cold War did make the United States a superpower without peer, but it also eliminated a geopolitical threat that made countries in Europe and East Asia fully dependent on American security protection. To go back to our post-Westphalian town: the United States is the town's only sheriff and the locks are off the doors—but in addition to this, the town's biggest menace to public safety has disappeared. So the town worries a great deal about the sheriff's conduct while their dependence on him for protection has decreased. Old bargains and restraints erode. The United States is powerful enough to block, disrupt, and punish. But in the absence of cooperation by other states, Washington is doomed to a cycle of foreign policy failure and declining public approval, which further reduces the availability of usable American power—and the entire grand strategic vision is thrown into crisis.

Conclusion

The end of the Cold War was less the beginning of a new era than the completion of an old era. It was the continuation of a liberal ascendancy that had begun two centuries before and struggled through the world wars and bipolar rivalry in the twentieth century. With the collapse of the Soviet Union, the Western system—built in the shadow of the Cold War—emerged as the organizational logic for the larger global system. The inside liberal order became the outside order. The American-led system provided the organizational logic for the expansion of democracy, markets, and liberal international order. By the end of the century, it was possible to see the globe as a one-world system bound together by multilateral rules and institutions, a globalizing form of capitalism, and American political leadership.

At the same time, and at a deeper level, the global system was also transforming. These shifts that have unsettled the American-led liberal hegemonic order are, ironically, developments that largely flow from the logic of that order. The Western liberal order was expanding outward, but it was also evolving. The logic of this transformation is captured in the imagery of the Westphalian system. The older logic of order—the Westphalian order—was defined by a balance and equilibrium of power among several major states. It was either a multipolar system, shaped by a grouping of five or six great powers, or a bipolar system, defined by the rivalry between two superpowers. After the Cold War, this logic gave way to a unipolar system. At the same time, slowly over the decades, the norms of state sovereignty have also evolved and eroded. The old normative protections of sovereignty are not fully extinguished, but they have given way to the human rights revolution and new ideas about the responsibility to protect and contingent sovereignty for weak countries. A world of states has evolved into a political formation with a center and a more complex array of norms about legitimacy and authority.

It was at this juncture that the Bush administration, in the wake of September 11, launched its efforts to overhaul the global security system. The new administration embraced the logic of a post-Westphalian world and offered a new hegemonic bargain with the world. It was a vision that did not just put the United States at the center of the global system but also above its rules and institutions. The United States would use its unrivaled power to enforce order and seek out security threats. Other states would be obliged to follow. This new security system would also be the capstone of the wider world order. The character of America's relations with states in other domains—economic, social, political—would hinge on whether these states were "with us or against us." The result would be a unified global system, but one that was effectively ruled from the center and from the top.

The Bush vision combines post-Westphalian unipolar thinking and conservative national policy ideas where American power is used directly to attack the new threats. But this strategy is built on a contradiction that leads to free riding or resistance by other states—or both. Its greatest attraction is that it provides an easy unilateral solution to security threats. But it is ultimately an unwelcome and unsustainable vision of order. To the outside world, this vision of order looks like modern-day empire. It is a vision of order that cannot gather the consent of other peoples and governments. It does not have the making of a legitimate system of global rule. But even if the Bush administration's unipolar security order had been seen as legitimate by other states, it still is not clear the United States could afford to lead such a system into the future. The hidden costs of the Bush-era transformational agenda are potentially unlimited. Yet, the logic of rule proposed by Bush certainly is not legitimate. It was not a system of rule that received the consent of other peoples and governments, even among allies and friends. So the costs of perpetuating American dominance would be even higher—costs that are well beyond anything that even a preeminent America can afford.

The multiplicity of shifts in the international system would play havoc with any American grand strategy. A traditional realist strategy of reconstructing a Westphalian balance-of-power order that reaffirms state sovereignty is not an easy proposition, particularly given the continuing unipolar distribution of power and the new security threats. In some sense, there is no going back. A global-governance grand strategy of turning questions about the use of force over to the United Nations or other global groupings is consistent with the search for legitimacy and the transformed character of sovereignty—indeed, liberals have championed this rethinking of sovereign norms—but this strategy has great difficulty in dealing with unipolar American power. The United States has the capacity to dominate but not the legitimacy to rule. In other words, it has power but not authority. It would appear we need to move beyond balance of power and empire toward a new international order that combines American unipolar power with widely agreed-upon rules and institutions.

Seven
Dilemmas and Pathways of Liberal
International Order

The American liberal hegemonic order established in the post–World War II decades has reached a turning point. Underlying shifts within the system—in power, sovereignty, the sources of security, and the scale and scope of interdependence—have eroded the stability of the order and the authority of the United States as hegemonic leader. The bargains and institutions of the old order are under stress. This liberal hegemonic order was created inside the West during the period of Cold War bipolarity. Surprisingly, this order survived the end of the Cold War and spread outward. The inside liberal order of the bipolar Cold War decades became the outside order—the organizing logic for the entire global system. But, as we have seen, the triumph of this American-led system was also its slow undoing.

Amidst these transformations, the Bush administration stepped forward with a new vision of American-led order. It was a unipolar order in which the United States would stand above other states—less encumbered by rules and institutions—to provide security and guide the system. It was a logic of order that was more imperial than liberal. And, ultimately, this post-Westphalian vision of American-led order was unacceptable, even to close allies and partners, and unsustainable.

So what comes next? The answer hinges on how deep the crisis of the American-led system is. Is the failure of the Bush vision of a unipolar security order also a failure, more generally, of the basic organizational logic of American-led liberal hegemony? And if it is, is the failure of American-led liberal hegemony also a sign of a deeper crisis of liberal international order itself? The argument advanced here is that the American-led liberal hegemonic order has reached an impasse. It is a crisis of authority within the liberal international order, but it is not a crisis of liberal international order itself. The character of hierarchy and rule within the worldwide liberal international order is in dispute. This is a way of saying that the problems that beset the American-led order are deeper than the Bush administration's failed efforts. The American role itself within the global order is being contested. The terms of hegemony are in dispute. Some sort of liberal international order will emerge on the other side of this crisis. The question is whether or not the next era of liberal order will continue to be shaped and led by the United States, and if so, in what ways.

American dominance within the order will certainly give way to a more diffuse and shared system of authority and rule. But will the United States continue to play a decisive role? Can the liberal order make a transition away from a hierarchical, American-dominated system to a flatter and more shared system of governance? How much of a reduction in America's hegemonic role is necessary to make the system functional and legitimate again? How much of a reduction in America's hegemonic role will make the system *less* functional and legitimate? Does liberal international order require some measure of hierarchically organized authority and control? If so, how much is too much and how much is too little? These are the questions we pursue in this chapter.

This chapter unfolds its argument in four steps. First, I suggest that there are a series of dilemmas in the organization of liberal international order. These are dilemmas—or tensions—between rule-based order and the balance of power, hegemony and democratic community, autonomy and universal human rights, and sovereignty and international authority. These are dilemmas that are never fully reconciled in any of the great eras of the liberal ascendancy. They are always lurking under the surface. And indeed they are tensions that have historically driven states—the United States and its allies and partners—to bargain and negotiate over rules and institutions. But they are also dilemmas or tensions that have been dramatically exposed in recent years as the American-led liberal hegemonic order has entered into crisis. The next era of liberal international order will necessarily need to grapple with these dilemmas in a new round of negotiations and bargains over rules and institutions.

Second, I argue that there are three general pathways that lead away from the current era of American-led liberal hegemonic order. One pathway is simply a renegotiated American-led system. This is an evolution away from the existing order, with the United States continuing to provide unique system functions for the larger order while it also moves to operate within more inclusive and concert-based great power institutions. A second pathway is really the move to a post-American liberal international order. This is a much flatter system of shared authority and rule. Collective institutions and universal rules are at the center of this evolved liberal order. Finally, a third pathway is toward a more fragmented system of rival spheres or blocs. This entails not just the diffusion of power and authority away from the United States but a breakdown of rules and institutions on a global scale.

Third, I argue that the degree to which the order remains a united, one-world order with the United States at its center depends on several key variables. These include the ability of the United States to use its commanding global military position to strike bargains with regional powers across security, economic, and political realms. The key is whether the United States can provide—and be seen as providing—public goods in the area of security (and perhaps in other areas). If so, it will continue to be able to offer system functions and thereby be able to negotiate liberal hegemonic agreements over global rules and institutions. If security becomes a good provided increasingly on a bilateral basis to individual states, the American-centered order moves more in the direction of a hub-and-spoke system that is less universal and more fragmented. A second variable is the ability of the United States to actually agree to reductions in its rights and privileges, sharing rule and authority. This is both a question of domestic politics—that is, can the United States politically agree to be a more normal state in regard to rules and institution—and a question of its ability to credibly make commitments and signal restraint. Finally, a third variable is the degree to which other major states—rising powers such as China and India—in fact want to operate within a liberal international order (of one kind or another). To the extent that their demands on the system are primarily about the distribution of authority and rights, and not about the underlying principles of liberal order as such, it will be more likely that new bargains and agreements can be reached that preserve the basic framework of the existing system.

Finally, I return to the question of whether the United States has basic interests and incentives for operating in a rule-based order. There are reasons to think it does, reasons relating to the preservation of its hegemonic position, the functional organization of the system for the pursuit of economic gain, and the search for a fit between its identity and the principles and logic of international order.

The American-led system of liberal order is evolving toward something new and different. We do not know how different it will be or, indeed, whether the liberal character of the system will endure. But there is reason to think that the liberal character will persist. After all, the liberal order may have emerged first in the West, but it has spread worldwide. Within its cooperative frameworks, the world's democratic capitalist countries are engaged in unprecedented cooperation—policy coordination, investment and exchange, social and cultural entanglement, and strategic partnership. This is what liberal internationalist thinkers of the twentieth century envisaged, and this is what they got. But dilemmas and tensions infuse this order. In many ways, they are inherent in the unresolved intellectual and political tensions within liberalism itself. But they have been sharply revealed anew in the controversies and political disputes that have erupted in the wake of American unipolarity and America's global actions following September 11.

Dilemmas of Liberal International Order

Liberal international order is defined by its open and rule-based character. Openness is reflected in the relatively low barriers to trade and exchange between states. In a liberal order, states—and their societies— have access to each other. Goods, people, and ideas can flow across borders. Liberal international order is rule-based in the sense that order is based on agreed-upon rules and institutions. The rules and institutions themselves may bear the marks of power disparities that allow some states more influence in shaping and operating the rules and institutions. But the rules and institutions still are more or less consensual and legitimate. They emerge from bargaining and agreement between states and they operate—at least to some significant extent—independently of state power. Overall, liberal international order is multilateral in the sense that openness and rules are inclusive and nondiscriminatory. All states within the liberal international order can expect something close to equal access and equal treatment.

This vision of liberal international order, as we have seen in earlier chapters, has been championed by leading liberal states at various junctures across the last two centuries. It is a vision of order that has been more fully realized in some decades and eras than others, and its logic has been reflected in some regions of the world more than others. The agenda of liberal order building has also changed and evolved. Woodrow Wilson's vision was different from Harry Truman's, and the contemporary agenda is different still. Liberal order—as a vision and real-world project—has also coexisted with other visions. Likewise, the organizational logic of liberal order has coexisted with other organizational logics. If liberal order is—at its heart—open and rule-based order based on consent, it has in the real world also drawn upon and coexisted with other organizational logics of order, namely balance and command.

It is not surprising, therefore, that dilemmas and tensions attend the liberal vision and its real-world political formations. These are intellectual tensions but also political ones. These dilemmas and tensions have always existed. But in the last decade, they have come to the surface in new and particularly visible ways that have called into question the logic and viability of liberal international order. The shape and character of liberal order in the next era will be determined in part as states grapple with these dilemmas and tensions.

Liberal Internationalism and the Balance of Power

The liberal project, in all its various manifestations, is animated by a vision of a one-world system of rule-based order. But the emergence of law and institutionalized cooperation in the modern era has also rested on a Westphalian system of balanced power and sovereign states. These traditional pillars of realist international order are, for liberal internationalists, both a blessing and a curse. Today, the balance-of-power underpinnings of the system have diminished, and this is a problem for liberal internationalism. Historically, the balance-of-power state system provided a foundation for international law and rule-based order in two ways. One is by solving the power problem through an equilibrium of power among the major states. An international system organized around a balance of power restricts the ability of any one state to dominate the whole system. The other is that states themselves sought law and rules to strengthen their position and capacities within the international order. When a state system based on the balance of power disappears and norms of state sovereignty erode, these foundational supports disappear.[1]

International law emerged in the modern era as a way of protecting and enshrining the sovereignty and supreme legal authority of the state.

[1] The legal scholar Lassa Oppenheim argued that a balance of power among states is "an indispensable condition of the very existence of international law.... If the Powers cannot keep one another in check, no rules of law will have force, since an overwhelming State will naturally try to act according to discretion and disobey the law." Lassa Oppenheim, *International Law*, 2nd ed. (London: Longmans, Green, 1912), 193.

Treaties and legal doctrines as well as the wider array of international rules and institutions emerged inside the West and the global system over the centuries as tools by which states could signal restraint, commitment, and mutual recognition.[2] At the same time, this emerging infrastructure of laws and rules was built upon a shifting great-power system where power was diffused and balanced among major states. In effect, laws and rules did not check power—it was the underlying balance-of-power system that did the checking. When power was checked and in a stable equilibrium, the circumstances were present to construct and operate within a loosely rule-based order.

Of course, there are compensating features that the liberal order itself provides. If the great powers themselves are democracies, power disparities are of less significance. Binding strategies of security cooperation can also reduce the threats otherwise inherent in unbalanced power disparities.[3] But when one country is overwhelmingly powerful and the protections of balance are lost, uncertainties do emerge over the commitment of that unipolar state to law and rule-based order. The system itself does not generate protections at it does within a balance of power order. The protections are based not on the functioning of the system but on the willingness and capacity of the leading state to act in a restrained and enlightened self-interested way. This is a different logic—and it is arguably a weaker foundation for law and rule-based order. At the very least, states within the liberal order are put in a position to reassess the new risks and rewards that come with a system in which power is not balanced and where restraints and protections are offered instead by the unipolar state.

The foundations of liberal order are weakened—or at least thrown into question—in a second sense. In the postwar era, international law and institutions flourished in the West and around the world partly because this resulting liberal order created rules and institutions that

---

[2] Various scholars have emphasized the connection between the rise of the sovereign state and the state system and the rise of international law and institutions. See Leo Gross, "The Peace of Westphalia, 1648–1948," *American Journal of International Law* 53 (1959), 1–29; and Bull, *Anarchical Society*. This theme is also explored in Krasner, *Sovereignty*.

[3] See Ikenberry, *After Victory*, Chap. Two.

strengthened the capacities of states. For example, the postwar economic rules and institutions—starting with the Bretton Woods agreements—provided mechanisms by which Western governments could strengthen their ability to stabilize and manage their economies. A great deal of contemporary international rules and institutions are still of this sort—facilitating states' ability to open up to flows of goods and investments and manage complex interactions.

But where state sovereignty is eroded and states themselves are highly penetrated and embedded in wider international networks, this statist impulse for capacity-enhancing rules and institutions is lost. More than liberal internationalists might admit, the postwar system of rules and institutions was embraced by political leaders in advanced industrializing states because it strengthened the ability of governments to realize their liberal goals. When the liberal internationalist agenda shifts its attention to the management of post-Westphalian global relations, this underlying political support for rule-based order is not brought into play.[4] The recent global financial crisis and economic downturn has exposed these destabilizing dangers and revealed anew the tensions between the international openness and national stability. The social bargain that was built into the foundation of liberal hegemonic arrangements has given way to a more freewheeling, neoliberal world market system.[5] Under these more recent conditions, liberal order—or at least

[4] A variation of this problem is noted by Stanley Hoffmann. He argues that liberal internationalism has been particularly good at "negative tasks." In the economic area, liberalism's great goal has been to open up markets and tear down trade barriers. In the political arenas, liberalism has battled against colonialism and imperialism, and during the Cold War, it struggled against communism. As Hoffmann argues, liberalism is political thinking that was forged in the effort to protect the individual against tyranny, aggression, and illegitimate violence. It runs into difficulties when it sets about tackling positive tasks. See Hoffmann, "The Crisis of Liberal Internationalism," in his book of essays, *World Disorders: Troubled Peace in the Post–Cold War Era* (Oxford: Rowman & Littlefield, 1998), 75–77.

[5] On the erosion of "embedded liberalism," see Jonathan Kirshner, "Keynes, Capital Mobility and the Crisis of Embedded Liberalism," *Review of International Political Economy* 6, no. 3 (Autumn 1999), 313–37; Mark Blyth, *Great Transformations: The Rise and Fall of Embedded Liberalism* (New York: Cambridge University Press, 2002); and Robert Skidelsky, *Keynes: The Return of the Master* (New York: Public Affairs, 2009).

the market features of this order—seems to undercut rather than support the state's ability to make good on its domestic social and political responsibilities.

If this argument is correct, the best pathway forward for liberal international order is, perhaps ironically, to emphasize rules and institutions that strengthen the state. A rule-based international order will be more stable if its rules enhance rather than erode the ability of states to protect their borders and govern their economies and societies.

State Sovereignty and Universal Rights

Liberal internationalism has been a great champion of state sovereignty and self-determination. At the same time, it has also offered grand visions of a global order united by universal rights and protections—universal principles that are potentially quite subversive of the legal and political claims of state sovereignty. Therein lies the tension. Is liberal international order fundamentally committed to the rights of nations and peoples to sovereign self-determination? Or it is committed to more transcendent political rights and aspirations that turn state sovereignty into a more contingent and circumstantial arrangement? State sovereignty puts legal-normative limits on the ability of the international community to intervene and interfere inside other states. In contrast, universal rights and protections—lodged within the international community—put limits on the claims of states to sovereign noninterference. A challenge for the liberal international project is to find ways to reconcile these divergent visions.

In the nineteenth century and even more so in the twentieth century, liberal internationalism was a body of ideas—and a political project—aimed at giving peoples around the world the right of political independence and self-determination. At the end of World War I, liberal internationalism embraced Westphalian state sovereignty. The nation-state was championed. Ideas of progressive liberal order during this period were closely associated with anti-imperial movements and struggles for national self-determination. Woodrow Wilson and other liberals did not see the liberal project involving a deep transformation of states themselves as sovereign legal units. Nationalism was a dominant force in world politics, and Wilson's support for rights of national self-government gave voice to it. In May 1916, for example, Wilson proclaimed that "every people has a right to choose the sovereignty under which they shall live." He argued that "small states" as well as "great and powerful nations" should enjoy sovereignty and territorial integrity free from aggression.[6] To be sure, at the Paris peace conference, Wilson was hesitant to recognize new nations, particularly outside of Europe. As the historian Lloyd Ambrosius observes: "As in the Philippines earlier, he [Wilson] applied the principle of national self-determination with great caution. He did not undermine British rule in Ireland, Egypt, and India, or French rule in Indochina. Wilson recognized only new nations that emerged from the collapse of the Russian, German, Austro-Hungarian, and Ottoman empires."[7] Wilson's notion of national self-determination was decidedly developmental—and patronizing. Sovereign self-rule required the emergence of an "organic" nation in which the people were politically mature enough to independently govern themselves. Hence the mandate system—a League of Nations innovation to replace foreign colonial rule—that would operate to maintain order in backward areas until national self-rule was possible.

The political reality and preconditions for sovereign self-determination had not fully developed in some parts of the world, but the liberal vision was clear. A world order built on liberal principles would ultimately be a world of sovereign states. The international community would not wield power and authority. Sovereign states would interact in a system defined by open trade and rule-based collective security.

As we noted in chapter 5, in the postwar decades a more universal and interventionist notion of rights and protections emerged that has offered a more complex and restrictive notion of state sovereignty. One

---

[6] Wilson, speech to the First Assemblage of the League to Enforce Peace, Washington, DC, 27 May 1916.

[7] Lloyd E. Ambrosius, *Wilsonianism: Woodrow Wilson and His Legacy in American Foreign Relations* (New York: Palgrave, 2002), 130.

of the shifts was to new understandings about the dangers and opportunities of economic and security interdependence. The economic
calamities of the 1930s and the successes of New Deal regulation and
governance informed these new views. Advanced societies were seen
to be deeply and mutually vulnerable to international downturns and
the bad policies pursued by other states. This new imperative led to an
expansive agenda of rule and institution building in the postwar period
for the management of complex interdependence. The other shift that
challenges the old norms of sovereignty was the unfolding human rights
and "responsibility to protect" revolution. The international community
was seen as having a legitimate interest in what goes on within countries.
As noted, this growing interest on the part of the international community in the domestic governance practices of states is driven by both
considerations of human rights and security.[8] The result is that norms of
sovereignty are seen as more contingent.

It is clear that liberal internationalism does not have a simple and
principled view of state sovereignty. Liberals have both embraced and
rejected it in different times and settings. The importance of the norms
of sovereignty and self-determination to liberal internationalism is at
least twofold. First, the sovereignty of a nation or people seems to be
a necessary step for the realization of individual rights. People should
have the right to have their own government—and thereby the right to
determine for themselves how they will live and be governed. Second,
state sovereignty provides a legal-normative protection for a people
against external domination. It is integral to the Westphalian system of
restraint and protection. A balance of power limits the ability of one
state to dominate others, and state sovereignty creates legal-normative
barriers to outside interference. At the same time, liberal internationalism embraces a universal vision of its principles and practices. States can

---

[8] See discussion in chapter 5. For a survey of shifting norms of state sovereignty, see Haass,
"Sovereignty." The emerging doctrine of the responsibility to protect is the most systematic notion that captures the changing terms of sovereignty and interventionism. See International Commission on Intervention and State Sovereignty, *Responsibility to Protect*; and
Evans, *Responsibility to Protect*.

advance and protect individual rights, but they can also ignore and abuse those rights. If rights are universal, the global political order must be organized in a way to protect and advance these deep and fundamental aspects of humanity. The growth of economic and security interdependence only serves to intensify the contingency of sovereignty norms. The liberal internationalist dilemma is to find a way to reconcile or manage these conflicting claims and imperatives.

The Limits and Dangers of Interventionism

Another dilemma faced by liberal internationalism follows directly from its commitment to universal rights and protections. It relates to the limits and temptations of interventionism and the use of force. If there are universal rights that impel the international community to intervene with force across sovereign borders, who speaks and acts for the international community? How can the international community be sure that states that act on its behalf are in fact upholding universal rights and protections? This is the question of whether liberal internationalism can safeguard against abuses that turn enlightened intervention into imperialism. There are two problems here: the problem of choice and capacity to act and the problem of imperial opportunism.

The first problem is that the norms and principles that establish the legitimacy and moral obligation for the international community to intervene in troubled countries far outstrip the capacity of states as a collective to agree on when and how to act. The international community—or the United Nations as its operational voice—does not itself possess capacities to act. So states must make good on these universal rights and obligations, and a variety of thorny issues immediately emerge. There is the problem of how the international community makes decisions about when and where to act. While the U.N. Security Council is the authoritative voice of the international community, it is also a forum for great-power politics and it often cannot overcome divisions to pass authorizing resolutions. If the United Nations does not authorize action, can or should states act anyway? There is also the problem of collective action. The international community may find its voice and urge action, but sustained military action is costly and so it is not certain that states will in fact respond to all legitimate and pressing circumstances. Principles and rights go undefended. The danger here is not simply that people will continue to suffer. When the norms and principles that establish the legitimacy and moral obligation of countries to act outstrip the capacity or willingness of states to act, this erodes the legitimacy of the liberal order that upholds these norms and principles.[9]

There is no neutral and independent global government that determines when and where interventions will take place, so major states themselves decide—and they inevitably act when their more parochial or strategic interests are at stake. Bosnia and Kosovo were on the doorstep of Europe, and so NATO acted. Rwanda suffered mass killings, but the international community did not respond. The weakly established international arrangements to deal with humanitarian emergencies and the selectivity of the interventions threaten the legitimacy of the norms and principles themselves.

The second problem is the danger that liberal internationalism can turn into "liberal imperialism." Historically, liberals have often embodied both impulses—an awkward duality that continues within the liberal vision today.[10] For Woodrow Wilson, the liberal imperial impulse was on display in his interventions in Mexico in 1914 and 1916. Wilson said that America's deployment of force was to help Mexico "adjust her unruly household." Regarding Latin America, Wilson said: "We are friends of constitutional government in America, we are more than its friends, we are its champions. I am going to teach the South American republics to elect good men." Indeed, Wilson used military force in an attempt to

---

[9] This problem is analyzed in Leslie H. Gelb, "Quelling the Teacup Wars," *Foreign Affairs* 73, no. 6 (November–December 1994), 2–6.

[10] For discussions of the problem of liberal imperialism, including reflections of John Stuart Mill's classic arguments, see Stephen Holmes, "Making Sense of Liberal Imperialism," in Nadia Urbinati and Alex Zakaras, eds., *J. S. Mill's Political Thought: A Bicentennial Reassessment* (New York: Cambridge University Press, 2007); and Alan Ryan, "Liberal Imperialism," in R. K. Ramazani and Robert Fatton, eds., *The Future of Liberal Democracy* (New York: Palgrave Macmillan, 2004).

teach Southern republics, intervening in Cuba, the Dominion Republic, Haiti, Honduras, Mexico, and Nicaragua. The liberal internationalist impulse was articulated later during World War I in Wilson's Fourteen Points address and in proposals for collective security and the League of Nations. This sentiment was stated perhaps most clearly in the summer of 1918 as the war was reaching its climax. Wilson gave his July 4 address at Mount Vernon and described his vision of postwar order: "What we seek is the reign of law, based on the consent of the governed and sustained by the organized opinion of mankind."[11]

There is often a fine line between the two impulses—and the danger is that liberal internationalist principles and norms can provide a cover for powerful states to exploit weak ones.[12] David Rieff makes this argument, namely that the human rights movement provides unwitting intellectual and political support for imperial-style interventions, a problem seen most clearly, in Rieff's view, in the Bush administration's invasion of Iraq. Reiff writes: "[T]he endless wars of altruism posited by so many human rights activists (no matter what euphemisms like 'peace-keeping,' 'humanitarian intervention,' 'upholding international law,' or the like they may care to use) or the endless wars of liberation (as they see it) proposed by American neoconservatives—Iraq was supposed to be only the first step—can only lead to disaster."[13] Tony Smith also argues that contemporary neoliberal incarnations of liberal internationalism

[11] The historian Mark Mazower provocatively argues that even the League of Nations and the United Nations bear the marks of Victorian-era "imperial internationalism." See Mazower's *No Enchanted Palace: The End of Empire and the Ideological Origins of the United Nations* (Princeton, NJ: Princeton University Press, 2010). This account misses the progressive vision that American officials brought to the League and United Nations enterprise and the affirmations of racial equality and universal rights in the U.N. Charter and the 1947 Universal Declaration. Moreover, the United Nations as a political body evolved after its founding, with the colonial rebellions of the 1950s and '60s transforming the center of gravity of the General Assembly into what it is today—the voice of the Global South.

[12] For an exploration of the tensions between liberalism's universalist vision of equality and historical complicity in hierarchy and empire, see Jeanne Morefield, *Covenants without Swords: Idealist Liberalism and the Spirit of Empire* (Princeton, NJ: Princeton University Press, 2005).

[13] David Rieff, *At the Point of a Gun: Democratic Dreams and Armed Intervention* (New York: Simon and Schuster, 2005), 8.

create a slippery slope for American policy makers, built on optimistic assumptions about promoting democracy and peace, that inevitably leads to imperialist adventures. There is much to be admired in the liberal tradition that dates back to Woodrow Wilson, Smith argues, but the problem is that it cannot contain its own excesses. The neoconservatives who championed the Iraq war, he contends, are heirs to the liberal international tradition, distorting it but nonetheless using its ideas to justify preemptive war.[14]

Liberal internationalists think that the international community can distinguish between good and bad interventions. The Iraq war, after all, was not originally justified as a humanitarian intervention. It was a preventive war. Anne-Marie Slaughter argues that the dangers identified by David Rieff, Tony Smith, and others do not go to the heart of liberal internationalism. A mechanism does exist—or can be devised—to separate good interventionism from bad. She suggests that it is a mechanism that grows out of the Wilsonian vision—namely a process of ongoing and institutionalized consultation among the leading democracies.[15] But this shifts the problem back to the United States and its capacity and willingness to work with and listen to its democratic partners. The challenge remains to develop agreed-upon standards and practices for intervention—and the capacities to back them up. Whether this can be done in a way that makes good on liberal international norms and principles but stops short of disasters and abuses remains an open question.

Democracy and International Authority

Another dilemma in the organization of liberal international order is the tension that exists between democracy at home and strengthened

---

[14] See Smith's *A Pact with the Devil: Washington's Bid for World Supremacy and the Betrayal of the American Promise* (New York: Routledge, 2007); and "Wilsonianism after Iraq: The End of Liberal Internationalism?" in G. John Ikenberry, Thomas J. Knock, Anne-Marie Slaughter, and Tony Smith *The Crisis of American Foreign Policy: Wilsonianism in the Twenty-first Century* (Princeton, NJ: Princeton University Press, 2009), chap. 2.

[15] Anne-Marie Slaughter, "Wilsonianism in the Twenty-first Century," in Ikenberry et al., *Crisis of American Foreign Policy*, chap. 3.

authority of international institutions. Here the question is, how does international order build up authority and capacity at the international level—in international bodies and agreements—without jeopardizing the popular rule and accountability built into liberal democratic states? Can the authority and capacity of the international community to act be strengthened without sacrificing constitutional democracy as home?

This is an unresolved problem in the liberal international project. Liberals anticipate a growing role for the international community in the functioning of the global system. The postwar era itself has seen a sharp increase in the norms and cooperative efforts launched on behalf of the international community. The human rights revolution and the rise of international norms relating to arms control and security cooperation carry with them expectations that the outside world will act when governments fail to act properly. The growing economic interdependence of states also creates rising demands for governance norms and institutions. But how do states square the domestic and international liberal visions? That is, how do they reconcile the international liberal vision of increasing authority lodged above the nation-state—where there is a sharing and pooling of sovereignty—with domestic liberal democracy built on popular sovereignty?[16]

This is an old problem, of course. International cooperation is a process, as I argued in chapter 3, where states make commitments to other states that involve giving up some policy autonomy in exchange for similar commitments. Rules and institutions are embodiments of these reciprocal commitments that circumscribe states' freedom of action.[17] In the postwar

---

[16] See Robert Keohane, "Global Governance and Democratic Accountability," in David Held and Mathias Koenig-Achibugi, eds., *Taming Globalization: Frontiers of Governance* (London: Polity, 2003), 130–59; and Robert Keohane and Joseph S. Nye, Jr., "Redefining Accountability for Global Governance," in Miles Kahler and David A. Lake, eds., *Governance in a Global Economy: Political Authority in Transition* (Princeton, NJ: Princeton University Press, 2003), 386–411. For a philosophical inquiry into these issues, see Alan Gilbert, *Must Global Politics Constrain Democracy? Great-Power Realism, Democratic Peace, and Democratic Internationalism* (Princeton, NJ: Princeton University Press, 1999).

[17] In addition to chapter 3, see also G. John Ikenberry, "State Power and the Institutional Bargain: America's Ambivalent Economic and Security Multilateralism," in Rosemary Foot, S. Neil MacFarlane, and Michael Mastanduno, eds., *U.S. Hegemony and International*

era, the world saw a massive expansion of institutionalized cooperation that entailed such commitments. These institutional agreements varied widely in regard to the degree to which they entailed legally binding commitments. Generally speaking, the more states wanted other countries to behave in predictable and rule-based ways, the greater their own requirements to bind themselves to a set of multilateral rules and institutions. This entire logic is at the heart of the liberal internationalist vision.

To be sure, some types of international agreements and institutions actually give states greater capacity to make good on domestic democratic governance. Advanced states have been able to offer greater stability and protections against economic downturns because of international agreements that discipline other states and provide resources for states to manage economic adjustments. In effect, states use international agreements to strengthen their ability to deliver socioeconomic services to their people.[18] International treaties and agreements can also entail governmental commitments to uphold the rule of law at home, which serve to strengthen the institutions of liberal democracy. For example, membership in the World Trade Organization hinges on the ability of states to uphold the domestic rule of law in areas of business, trade, and investment. This, in turn, strengthens state institutions—such as regulatory and judiciary bodies—that are central to liberal constitutional rule.[19] For transitional states that are making small steps toward liberal democracy, international agreements can facilitate additional steps and reinforce rule-based governance itself.[20]

Organizations: The United States and Multilateral Institutions (Oxford: Oxford University Press, 2003), 49–70; and G. John Ikenberry, "Is American Multilateralism in Decline?" *Perspective on Politics* 1, no. 3 (Fall 2003), 533–550.

[18] G. John Ikenberry, "A World Economy Restored: Expert Consensus and the Anglo-American Postwar Settlement," *International Organization* 46 (Winter 1991/92), 289–321.

[19] See Robert Keohane, Stephen Macedo, and Andrew Moravcsik, "Democracy-Enhancing Multilateralism," *International Organization* 63, no. 1 (Winter 2009), 1–31.

[20] For discussions of these trade-offs, see Louis W. Pauly and William D. Coleman, eds., *Global Ordering: Institutions and Autonomy in a Changing World* (Vancouver: University of British Columbia Press, 2008); and Steven Bernstein and Louis W. Pauly, eds., *Global Liberalism and Political Order: Toward a New Grand Compromise?* (Albany: State University of New York Press, 2007).

But when these commitments bind states to international bodies that have realms of autonomous authority, the cost in the form of lost state autonomy goes up. Countries within the European Union have indeed made fundamental trade-offs of this extreme sort. When the European Court can hand down rulings that require national governments to alter their domestic laws, domestic judicial governance—and indirectly domestic democratic governance—is compromised. External courts and judges are setting the parameters for domestic courts and judges. The postwar human rights revolution pushes democracies in this direction—toward transnational justice and supranational judicial authority. This was the subversive move implicit in the U.N. Universal Declaration of Human Rights in which peoples rights were now seen as embedded in the international community and not simply defined and defended by national governments.[21] The liberal international project foresees a future where there will be a fuller realization of universal rights and standards of justice, and the obligations and commitments of national governments will need to adjust accordingly. International authority—in the form of courts and collective governance mechanisms—will be expanded. So the old problem of the trade-offs between national autonomy and popular sovereignty and rule-based global order will intensify. And with it, so too will the questions of lost democratic accountability and popular sovereignty.

Hegemony and Democratic Community

The last dilemma facing the organization of liberal international order is perhaps the most important, at least in terms of shaping the choices that face liberal-order builders today. This is the tension between the dominance of a powerful state in running the liberal order and shared norms of democratic community. On the one hand, the United States has used its preponderant power to organize and manage the system.

---

[21] For a conservative argument that "global governance" threatens national constitutional democracy, see Rabkin, *Law without Nations?* See also Eric A. Posner, *The Perils of Global Legalism* (Chicago: Chicago University Press, 2009).

Liberal international order did not spontaneously emerge. It had to be created and ruled. Taking on this role has given the United States a privileged position within the order. On the other hand, the liberal order was also built with a core group of Western democracies that shared norms and expectations of respect, reciprocity, and consensual rule. The order that emerged was both hierarchical and liberal in character. But conflicts have persisted in the awkward reconciliation—or at least management—of these tensions between hierarchy and liberal rule. And, as I have argued, these tensions have intensified in the last decade with the rise of unipolarity and the erosion of norms of state sovereignty.

The postwar American-led liberal international order was built around both hierarchy and democratic community. As we noted in chapter 5, efforts were made during World War II—as they had been after World War I—to launch a postwar order that was both global and relatively "flat." The great powers would operate in concert to uphold an order built around open trade and collective security. But the exigencies of the postwar years shifted the character and center of gravity of this liberal international project. Order building came to be centered in the West—around the Atlantic world—and to be organized and led by the United States. Liberal order was turned into liberal hegemonic order, with its core institutions and commitments anchored among the advanced democracies. Hegemony and democratic community were both added to the more skeletal—and unsustainable—framework of a global system of open trade, collective security, and great-power concert. In this way, the tensions and contradictions of the system were built into its foundation.

As a result, for half a century, the United States led the liberal international order. As we have seen, this order has had a particular logic. The underlying idea was that if America engages in the right amount of commitment and restraint—anchoring its power in partnerships, alliances, multilateral institutions, special relationships, and governance regimes—the overall international system will tend to remain stable, open, and integrated. The world, in effect, "contracted out" to the United States to provide global governance. The United States provides public goods, frameworks of cooperation, "good offices," and an enlightened but U.S.-centered system of rules and modes of doing geo-political business. In return, the world "bandwagons" with the United States rather than resists or balances against it. This special type of open or liberal American hegemony was more attractive to leading demo-cratic states—and to other states inside and outside the West as well—than the available alternatives. So no rival democratic state or regional grouping has had an incentive to challenge or overturn this liberal hege-monic order.

A grand bargain has stood behind this American-led liberal order. The United States is to provide global services—such as security protec-tion and support for open markets—which makes other states willing to work with rather than resist American preeminence. The public goods provided tended to make it worthwhile for these states to endure the day-to-day irritations of American dominance. The United States would operate within a system of rules and institutions that reduced its ability to engage in the arbitrary and discriminate exercise of power. The fact that the states that operated within this hegemonic system were Western democracies also infused the operation of the order with consensual and reciprocal features of interaction. In these ways, hierarchy and demo-cratic community were reconciled, at least to an extent that made the order more or less stable and legitimate.

What we have seen is that this trade-off seems to be shifting—and thereby exposing the tensions between hierarchy and democratic com-munity. Today, the United States appears to be providing fewer public goods while, at the same time, the irritations associated with American dominance appear to be growing. It is useful to think about the changing dynamic in this way. The United States is unique in that it is simultane-ously both a provider of global governance—through what has tended in the past to be the exercise of liberal hegemony—and it is a great power that pursues its own national interest. America's liberal hegemonic role is manifest when it champions the WTO, engages in international rule and regime creation, or reaffirms its commitment to cooperative security in Asia and Europe. Its great-power role is manifest, for example, when

it seeks to protect its domestic steel or textile industry. When it acts as a
liberal hegemon, it is seeking to lead or manage the global system of rules
and institutions; when it is acting as a nationalist great power, it is seeking to respond to domestic interests and its relative power position. The
danger today is that these two roles—liberal hegemon and traditional
great power—have been in increasing conflict. The grand bargain that
sustained liberal hegemonic order is in danger of unraveling, exposing
the old tensions and contradictions buried within.[22]

So the danger to liberal internationalism lies with its greatest champion. The United States does not appear to be doing as much today as
in the past to sponsor and operate within a system of consensual rule-
based order. The 2008 financial crisis and global economic downturn
has exposed the changed position of the United States. In previous
postwar economic crises, the United States played a role—directly or
indirectly—in stabilizing global markets. The most recent financial crisis
was unique in that the United States was the source of the instability.
Whether it can return to the position of global economic leader remains
uncertain. This is a question of both America's willingness and its ability
to manage the system. Why the United States might be less willing to
play the role of liberal hegemon is complex, rooted in domestic politics.
Some of it is very specifically associated with the Bush administration,
which has left the scene. But America's global position and the structure
of incentives that this setting generates is also part of the explanation.
American unipolarity and the wider set of shifts in the norms of sovereignty and the nature of security and interdependence have also created
a new setting for how the United States thinks about the provision of
international rules, institutions, and public goods.

---

[22] The dilemma is that hegemony may be put at the service of creating an open and rule-
based order but hegemony is itself not democratic. Even when infused with liberal and consent-based relationships, disparities in power remain. In this sense, as Lea Brilmayer argues,
hegemony is, even if organized around democratic polities, "quintessentially autocratic." Lea
Brilmayer, *American Hegemony: Political Morality in a One-Superpower World* (New Haven,
CT: Yale University Press, 1994).

Three Pathways of Liberal International Order

The old American-led liberal hegemonic order is in transition. There are growing pressures and incentives for its reform and transformation. As in the past, the liberal international project is evolving. But what sort of new order will emerge? What would be the organizational logic of a post-hegemonic liberal international order? Will the coming order be a new type of liberal international order or something different altogether? It is easier to identify the pressures and incentives for change than to specify the organizational logic of an evolved or transformed world order. We can, however, identify the issues that will be important in shaping what comes next, and we can sketch alternative pathways of change.

One set of issues concerns scope and hierarchy. A reformed liberal international order will need to become more universal (less Western-centered) and less hierarchical—that is, the United States will need to cede authority and control to a wider set of states and give up some of its hegemonic rights and privileges. But a flatter international order will also be one in which the United States plays a less central role in providing functional services—generating public goods, stabilizing markets, and promoting cooperation. So the questions are several. What is the logic of a post-hegemonic liberal order—and is it viable? Can these functional services be provided collectively? Will the United States agree to relinquish the special rights and privileges built into the older hegemonic form of liberal order? Of course, it is possible for more incremental shifts away from liberal hegemony. The United States could continue to provide functional services for liberal order but do so in wider concert with other major states. Liberal order can be endangered if there is too much hierarchy—indeed hierarchy in its extreme form is empire. But it might also be endangered if there is too little hierarchy, as the Wilson-era experiment in liberal order revealed.

A second issue concerns legitimate authority and post-Westphalian sovereignty. A reformed liberal international order will need to find a way to reconcile more intrusive rules and institutions with legitimate international authority. The human rights revolution makes the international community increasingly concerned with the internal workings of states. So too does the new international-threat environment—a situation where growing security interdependence is making each country's security increasingly dependent on what goes on elsewhere, including inside other states. The international community is going to need capacities and legitimate authority to intervene in weak and troubled states.[23] It is going to need monitoring, surveillance, and inspection capacities to ensure that increasingly lethal technologies of violence do not get into the hands of dangerous groups. These developments suggest that the liberal international order will find itself more and more concerned with the internal governance of states. Unless globalization and the advancement and diffusion of technology are reversed, it is almost inevitable that the erosion of Westphalian sovereignty will continue. Nonetheless, finding consensus on the norms of intervention in a post-Westphalian world is deeply problematic—yet short of establishing such legitimate authority, the international order will continue to be troubled and contested.[24]

A third issue relates to liberal democracy and the international rule of law. Here the question is, how do you build up authority and capacity at the international level—in international bodies and agreements—without jeopardizing popular rule and accountability built into liberal democratic states? Can the authority and capacity of the international community to act be strengthened without sacrificing constitutional democracy at home? As we noted above, this is an unresolved problem in the liberal international project. Liberals anticipate a growing role for

[23] For discussions of post-Westphalian forms of international supervision and management of weak or collapsed states, see Stephen Krasner, "Sharing Sovereignty: New Institutions for Collapsed and Failing States," *International Security* 29, no. 2 (Fall 2005), 85–120; James Fearon and David D. Laitin, "Neotrusteeship and the Problem of Weak States," *International Security* 28, no. 4 (2004), 5–43; and Robert O. Keohane, "Political Authority after Intervention: Gradations in Sovereignty," in J. L. Holzgrefe and Robert O. Keohane, eds., *Humanitarian Intervention: Ethical, Legal, and Political Dilemmas* (Cambridge: Cambridge University Press, 2003). See also Ferguson, *Colossus*.

[24] For an effort to identify norms around which a new consensus might emerge, see Bruce Jones, Carlos Pascual, and Stephen John Stedman, *Power and Responsibility: Building International Order in an Era of Transnational Threats* (Washington, DC: Brookings Institution Press, 2009).

the international community in the functioning of the global system. The postwar era itself has seen a radical increase in the norms and cooperative efforts launched on behalf of the international community. The human rights revolution and the rise of international norms of deviance carry with them expectations that the outside world will act when governments fail to act properly.[25]

Out of these tensions and dilemmas, the next phase of liberal international order will be shaped. There are at least three pathways away from the American-led liberal hegemonic order. Each pathway involves a different mix in the way sovereignty, rules, institutions, and authority are arrayed.

Post-Hegemonic Liberal International Order

The first possibility is a post-hegemonic liberal international order. This would be a far-reaching reworking of the American postwar system. This would be an order in which the United States exercised less command and control of the rules and institutions. America's special rights and privileges would contract as other states gained more weight and authority at the high table of global governance. The "private" governance that the United States provided through NATO and its dominance of multilateral institutions would give way to more "public" rules and institutions of governance. At the same time, the intrusiveness and reach of liberal order would also continue to expand, placing demands on governance institutions to forge consensual and legitimate forms of collective action.

In this post-American liberal order, authority would move toward universal institutions—or at least to international bodies that included wider global membership. These include a reformed United Nations with a reorganized Security Council that expanded permanent membership to rising and non-Western countries such as Japan, India, Brazil,

---

[25] On the evolving norms of "deviance" in international relations, see Miroslav Nincic, *Renegade Regimes: Confronting Deviant Behavior in World Politics* (New York: Columbia University Press, 2007).

and South Africa. Other bodies that would grow in importance include the G-20, which—unlike the G-8—includes representatives from both developed and emerging states. The Bretton Woods institutions—the IMF and World Bank—would also expand and reapportion rights and membership. Countries such as China and India would gain significant voting shares in the governance of these institutions while the United States and Europe would see their voting shares contract.[26]

This post-American liberal order would also see a further erosion of norms of Westphalian sovereignty and the continuing spread of the notion of a responsibility to protect. The idea that the international community has a right—and indeed a responsibility—to intervene inside states for human rights and security reasons would be increasingly embraced worldwide. But this movement toward post-Westphalian norms of sovereignty leaves unanswered the question of which states—and international bodies—would acquire the rights and authority to decide where and how to act. Who is to speak for the international community on questions of responsibility to protect? It is difficult to see a liberal internationalism that has settled this question. The logical move would be to turn to the authority of a reformed U.N. Security Council. But if the recent past is a guide, the ability of the Security Council to actually reach agreement and sanction the use of force is highly problematic.[27] Other less universal bodies—such as NATO or a proposed League or Concert of Democracies—may provide alternative sources of authority for intervention, but the legitimacy of these bodies is only partial and contested.[28] The new liberal international order might solve

[26] On the problem of rising states and the reform of global institutions, see G. John Ikenberry and Thomas Wright, *Rising States and International Institutions* (New York: Century Foundation, 2008).

[27] There is a large literature that explores the problems of legitimacy and the use of force. For the classic exploration of these issues, see Inis L. Claude, *Power and International Relations* (New York: Random House, 1966).

[28] Several proposals for a new grouping of democracies have been advanced. See Ikenberry and Slaughter, *Forging a World of Liberty under Law* (Princeton, NJ: Princeton Project on National Security, 2006); and Ivo Daalder and James Lindsay, "Democracies of the World Unite," *American Interest* 2, no. 3 (January–February 2007). Generally speaking, these proposals for a new democracy grouping are aimed at providing support for the reform of the

this problem by fostering greater agreement among the Security Council permanent member states over the rights and obligations of the international community to act. More likely, questions about intervention and the use of force will remain contested. Regional bodies and nonuniversal groupings of like-minded states will continue to offer alternative sources of authority on these questions.

Beyond questions of humanitarian intervention and the responsibility to protect, security threats coming from the potential diffusion of violence technologies into the hands of terrorist groups will continue to generate incentives for more intrusive international arms control and counterproliferation capacities. The International Atomic Energy Agency is the leading organizational edge of these multistate efforts. In the last two decades, the IAEA has developed scientific and technical competence and legal frameworks for monitoring and inspections of nuclear programs around the world. As nuclear, biological, and chemical weapons technologies grow more sophisticated and diffuse into troubled parts of the world, governments will no doubt seek to expand IAEA-type capacities for monitoring, inspection, verification, and safeguarding. Pressures will grow for norms of Westphalian sovereignty to continue to incrementally give way to intrusive international security regimes.[29]

The hierarchical character of post-hegemonic liberal internationalism will change. It will, generally speaking, be flatter—but hierarchy will remain, it simply will not be American-dominated hierarchy. The hierarchy of a post-hegemonic liberal order will be found in the expanded grouping of leading states that will occupy positions in the U.N. Security

United Nations and, in the absence of U.N. reform and action, they are to provide supplemental authority for international action. A proposal has also been advanced for a League of Democracies, which seeks to organize the democracies for sustained geopolitical struggle with nondemocracies. See Robert Kagan, "The Case for a League of Democracies," *Financial Times*, 13 May 2008.

[29] For discussions of the evolving technical and legal frameworks for arms control monitoring and enforcement, see Joseph Cirincione, Jon B. Wolfshal, and Miriam Rajkmar, *Deadly Arsenals: Nuclear, Biological and Chemical Threats*, 2nd ed. (Washington, DC: Carnegie Endowment for International Peace, July 2005); and J. Christian Kessler, *Verifying Nonproliferation Treaties: Obligations, Process, and Sovereignty* (Washington, DC: National Defense University Press, 1995).

Council, the Bretton Woods institutions, and other less-formal international bodies. It is this group of states that will collectively take over the various functional services previously provided by the United States—maintaining security, upholding open markets, and so forth. In some ways, the character of hierarchy will look similar to the Rooseveltian vision in liberal internationalism. A group of leading states will claim authority and institutional positions to oversee the stability and peace of the global system. But in this new liberal internationalism, their leadership responsibilities will multiply to include a wider array of security, economic, and political governance duties.

The character of the rule of law will also evolve. In some areas, such as trade and investment, the rule-based character of the order will continue. Indeed, the World Trade Organization is already a post-hegemonic type of global system of rules. The United States does not have special rights or privileges under international trade law. The leading trade states do exercise power in various ways. This is due to their market size and overall standing in the international order. But the norms of trade law are fundamentally based on notions of equality and reciprocity. All contracting parties have access to opt-out and escape-clause rights. Mechanisms exist for dispute resolution.[30] In areas where economic interdependence generates incentives for states to coordinate and harmonize their policies, rule-based order should increase. But in other areas where states resist legal-institutional forms of cooperation, less formal networks of cooperation will likely grow.[31] Such network-style cooperation allows states to circumvent politically difficult or costly formal, treaty-based commitments. Network cooperation will appear particularly attractive to the United States as it loses its power advantages and rights and privileges under the older liberal hegemonic order. The United States

[30] On the rule-based character of the World Trade Organization, see P. J. Lloyd, "The Architecture of the WTO," *European Journal of Political Economy* 17 (2001), 327–53.

[31] The leading study of network-based international cooperation is Anne-Marie Slaughter, *A New World Order* (Princeton, NJ: Princeton University Press, 2004). See also Anne-Marie Slaughter, "Governing the Global Economy through Government Networks," in Michael Byers, ed., *The Role of Law in International Politics* (Oxford: Oxford University Press, 2000), 177–206.

will find itself forced to give up its hegemonic ability to foster cooperation on its own terms. It was able to dominate rules and institutions, and
through weighted voting and opt-out agreements, it was able to reduce
its exposure to sovereignty-reducing commitments. In a post-hegemonic
position, the United States will find informal and network-oriented
agreements to be tolerable substitutes that allow it to gain the benefits
of cooperation without offering up formal, legal restrictions on its sovereign independence.

Overall, the post-American liberal international order would draw
on the logics of both its predecessors. Like the post-1945 liberal order, it
would be a governance system that does a great deal of work. The policy
domains in which states would cooperate would be expansive—indeed,
even more so than under the American-led liberal international order.
The breadth and depth of the rules and institutions of liberal order would
continue to grow. But as a nonhegemonic order, the actual functioning
of the system would look a lot like Wilsonian-style liberal internationalism. It would be a universal order that is less tied to the United States or
the West. But also like the Wilsonian version, it would be an order in
which cooperation depended upon shared norms that fostered collective action. It remains a question whether the norms—or ideology of
liberal order—are sufficiently coherent and widely enough embraced to
make this post-hegemonic order function effectively over the long haul.

A Renegotiated American-Led Liberal Order

A second pathway is also possible in which liberal internationalism is less
fully transformed—this would be a reformed American-led liberal hegemonic order. In this adaptation, the United States would renegotiate the
bargains and institutions of the past decades but retain its position as
hegemonic leader. Indeed, this appears to be what the Obama administration is attempting to do. In some sense, this is what is already happen-
ing today. In this reformed liberal hegemonic order, the United States
would continue to provide functional services for the wider system, and
in return, other countries would acquiesce in the hierarchical rules and

institutions presided over by Washington. The order would remain hierarchical but the terms of hierarchy—the bargains and rules—would be altered in ways that are mutually acceptable to states within the order.[32]

In this reformed American-led order, the United States would give up some of its hegemonic rights and privileges but retain others. In economic and political realms, it would yield authority and accommodate rising states. The United States would share authority within the reformed Bretton Woods institutions. In the aftermath of the recent financial crisis, the United States would also work with other liberal market states to fashion a new post-neoliberal consensus on the rules and regulation of an open world economy. In security realms, however, the United States would retain its hegemonic position. It would offer security to other states in a worldwide system of alliances. The American economy would remain a leading source of markets and growth—even if its relative size declined. The United States would remain positioned to support and uphold the renegotiated rules and institutions of the liberal order.[33]

In some respects, the Bush administration sought to save the American hegemonic order by renegotiating its bargains. As we noted in chapter 6, it envisioned the United States as the unipolar provider of global security, upholding an international order of free and democratic states.[34] In this version, the United States would provide functional services to the world—but in return the United States would ask for new rights and privileges. It would remain aloof from various realms of rule-based order. It would not join the International Criminal Court and other

[32] For discussions of American efforts to renegotiate hegemonic bargains, see Bruce W. Jentleson, "America's Global Role after Bush," *Survival* 49, no. 3 (2007), 179–200; Daniel Drezner, "The New New World Order," *Foreign Affairs* 86, no. 2 (March/April 2007), 34–46; and Kori N. Schake, *Managing American Hegemony: Essays on Power in a Time of Dominance* (Stanford, CA: Hoover Institution Press, 2009).

[33] Ian Clark argues that in order to rebuild its hegemonic position the United States must emphasize both its special capacities to provide functional services for the system and the distinctive coalitional and consensual character of American-style hegemony. Ian Clark, "Bringing Hegemony Back In: The United States and International Order," *International Affairs* 85, no. 1 (2009), 23–36.

[34] The best statement of this vision is President George W. Bush's commencement speech at West Point, 1 June 2002.

sovereignty-restraining treaties and international agreements. It was a new hegemonic bargain. The United States would provide security and stable order, but it would receive special dispensation to remain unattached to the multilateral, rule-based system. In the end, as I argued in chapter 5, this was a bargain that the rest of the world did not accept. The question is whether a different set of bargains might be acceptable, in which the United States does provide functional services—particularly security protection—but also agrees to operate within a renegotiated system of rules and institutions. The Bush administration tried to use America's unrivaled military capabilities to reduce its exposure to rule-based order. Is it possible for the United States to increase its exposure to rule-based order as a way to retain aspects of authority and privilege within a renegotiated hegemonic order? If so, this would lead down a pathway of reformed American liberal hegemony.

The Obama administration has also sought to renegotiate hegemonic bargains and rebuild the American position within the global system. It has done so in several ways. First, it has reaffirmed the special roles and responsibilities that the United States still has in the maintenance of international security and order. "[T]he world must remember that it was not simply international institutions—not just treaties and declarations—that brought stability to a post–World War II world," President Obama argued in his 2009 Nobel Peace Prize speech. "Whatever mistakes we have made, the plain fact is this: the United States of America has helped underwrite global security for more than six decades with the blood of our citizens and the strength of our arms."[35] The implication is that the world still needs the United States at the center of the global system, where it continues to provide support for stable and cooperative relations. This message has been reinforced in statements by the administration emphasizing the importance of America's alliance partnerships and other strategic commitments. The United States is not relinquishing its hegemonic duties. Second, the Obama administration has reaffirmed the United States' commitment to operate within agreed-upon rules and

---

[35] President Barack Obama, "Remarks of the U.S. President in Oslo," 10 December 2009.

institutions. Speaking to the doubts raised in the Bush years over this key component of the hegemonic bargain, Obama has asserted that "America cannot insist that others follow the rules of the road if we refuse to follow them ourselves." In the use of military force, "we have a moral and strategic interest in binding ourselves to certain rules of conduct."[36] In his 2010 West Point commencement address, President Obama again claimed that "America has not succeeded by stepping out of the currents of cooperation—we have succeeded by steering those currents in the direction of liberty and justice."[37] Finally, the Obama administration has acknowledged the demand for the reform of global institutions, adapting them to new global challenges and providing a greater role for rising states. "The international order we seek is one that can resolve the challenges of our times," President Obama indicated in his West Point speech. "As influence extends to more countries and capitals, we also have to build new partnerships, and shape stronger international standards and institutions."[38] These declarations by the Obama administration suggest a desire to rehabilitate and adapt the American hegemonic system.

There are several variants to a renegotiated hegemonic bargain. In all instances, the United States would agree to greater sharing of authority and decision making within global security and economic institutions. At the same time, it retains a "first among equals" role in organizing and leading some features of the order, especially within the alliance system as a security provider. The variation would come in the mix of rule through rules and rule through relationships. That is, a renegotiated American hegemonic order could entail simply a shrinkage of the disparities in authority and control that the United States has within the system. Or it could involve a retraction of the realms in which the United States plays the hegemonic role. As a security provider, the United States might find itself emphasizing bilateral security pacts and special relationships as the tools of order, rather than leadership over multilateral security alli-

---

[36] Obama, "Remarks in Oslo."

[37] President Barack Obama, "Remarks by the President at the United States Military Academy at West Point Commencement," 22 May 2010.

[38] Obama, "Remarks at West Point."

ances and regional cooperative security agreements. It is in this way that America's general hegemonic orientation would look increasingly like the hub-and-spoke system of alliances in East Asia.

Breakdown of Liberal International Order

A final possibility is a breakdown of liberal international order. This would occur if the order were to become significantly less open and rule-based. The system of open, multilateral trade could collapse, ushering in a 1930s-style world of mercantilism, regional blocs, and bilateral pacts. The political and security rules and institutions of American-led hegemonic internationalism could also fragment into competing geopolitical blocs. Such a breakdown does not necessarily need to entail a complete collapse of order—it simply means there is an end to its open, rule-based, multilateral character. The American hegemonic order could simply yield to an international system where several leading states or centers of power—for example, China, the United States, and the European Union—establish their own economic and security spheres. The global order would become a less unified and coherent system of rules and institutions, while regional orders emerge as relatively distinct, divided, and competitive geopolitical spheres.[39]

A trigger for such a breakdown could be a conflict between leading states over how best to organize the world economy. The recent financial crisis and global recession provide a portent of this possibility. Unlike previous postwar global economic crises, this episode began in the United States, which found itself less capable than in the past at managing it. The American model of global capitalism has been tarnished—if not discredited—by the recent events. The United States is no longer seen as the indispensable and reliable provider of economic stability. Out of these circumstances, major states will seek alternative arrangements. If no state is able to step forward to reestablish global rules and

[39] For essays exploring a wide array of post-liberal orders, see Greg Fry and Jacinta O'Hagan, eds., *Contending Images of World Politics* (New York: St. Martin's, 2000).

institutions, the system will gradually devolve into decentralized and fragmented regional groupings.

This fragmented order might devolve into several competing subsystems, each connected to its own leading state. These could be regional blocs, or they could be nongeographical coalitions of states that trade and affiliate. The borders of these groupings could be more or less exclusive and preferential. The breakdown in liberal international order might be relatively mild, whereby preferential barriers between groups of states are low but still consequential.[40] One image of such an order is the modern airline system. Airlines are divided up into commercial alliances. It is easier to operate within one of these alliances, and passengers accrue benefits from doing so. Although it is possible to move across these alliances, the incentives discourage doing so.[41] Each of these airlines has its own hub-and-spoke routes. Alliances have their shared clubs and facilities. Passengers are free to travel as they wish. The barriers are not absolute. None of the airline alliances dominates the global system. Over time, travelers find themselves operating within networks. In the same way, the global system could fragment into rival political-economic strategic networks. States—and the groups and firms within them—are able to operate both within and across these networks. But over time, political and economic affairs become increasingly routed through these rival coalitions. The global system is not closed or devoid of multilateral rules, but it is fragmented into subsystems of networked relationships.

Some observers describe a coming fragmentation of the American-centered unipolar order as a "return to multipolarity." This is a vision of a world order organized around one dominant power transforming into a system in which several powers exist and compete. The system loses its core. The United States loses its centrality to the operation of the wider

[40] David Calleo offers one vision of such an order, emphasizing movement toward regional groupings based on economic affinities: "Countries with relatively compatible economies will probably group into blocs, perhaps built around a dominant or common currency, or a relatively stable monetary union." David Calleo, *Follies of Power: America's Unipolar Fantasy* (New York: Cambridge University Press, 2010), 107.

[41] See Mika Aaltola, "The International Airport: The Hub-and-Spoke Pedagogy of the American Empire," *Global Network* 5, no. 3 (2005), 261–78.

global order.[42] But it is useful to distinguish among at least three steps along the way.[43] One step toward multipolarity is simply a diffusion of power away from the unipolar state. Unipolarity is, after all, a depiction of the distribution of power. So the distribution of power could simply and slowly evolve toward a system in which power is more widely shared. The unipolar distribution of power could shift toward a system in which two or three states become peers. Or power could diffuse even more widely into the hands of many states—perhaps a dozen or more— that possess similar shares of world material capabilities. Regardless, what is occurring is a redistribution of power away from the unipolar state. This does not imply anything in particular about the character of the political formation that sits atop these shifts in the power distribution. An open and rule-based international order might survive this shift in power—indeed, it might be reinforced by the return of a group of leading states. A second step away from unipolarity would involve the emergence of rival poles. This is what most observers mean by a return to multipolarity. It is not just that several states gain parity with the United States in power capabilities, but they also become global hubs. That is, they project power and influence and organize parts of the global system

---

[42] The National Intelligence Council's recent survey of global change sees the "return to multipolarity" as the master trend of the coming decades. As the report argues: "[B]y 2025 the international system will be a global multipolar one.... Power will be more dispersed with the newer players bringing new rules of the game while risks will increase that the traditional Western alliances will weaken." See National Intelligence Council, *Global Trends 2025* (Washington, DC: National Intelligence Council, 2008), iv. The Defense Department's strategic-planning review makes a similar observation: "The distribution of global political, economic, and military power is shifting and becoming more diffuse. The rise of China, the world's most populous country, and India, the world's largest democracy, will continue to reshape the international system." U.S. Department of Defense, *Quadrennial Defense Review Report* (February 2010), 7. A similar view is articulated by the British Foreign Office's Director for Strategy, Planning and Analysis. See David Frost, "Atlantis Rediscovered: New Hope for Transatlantic Relations?" keynote speech, RUSI's Global Leadership Forum, London, 11 June 2009. For a discussion of the logic and implications of a "return to multipolarity," see Barry Posen, "Emerging Multipolarity: Why Should We Care?" *Current History* 108 (November 2009), 347–52.

[43] Randall Schweller describes the transition away from unipolarity as process of entropy, in which the organizing power and energy of the center gives way to a slower devolution in organizational coherent and control. See Schweller, "Ennui Becomes Us," *National Interest*, no. 105 (January/February 2010).

around themselves. Each pole has its strategic partners, special relationships, and economic and political realms of influence. It might also be that each pole has its own ideology and vision of global order. A final step away from unipolarity would involve the emergence of a balance of power and security competition between these poles. This is the classic system of rival great powers dividing the world into competing spheres and geopolitical blocs. The great powers are not just rival poles but also competing for security.

The point is that the return to multipolarity does not need to go the full distance toward a competitive security system. To get to this outcome, the world does need to pass through the two prior stops. But unipolarity can devolve into rival poles without fragmenting into a full-blown divided world of security competition, and it can sustain a diffusion of power without turning into a system of rival poles. In this sense, the return to multipolarity has several stops along the way, each with distinct and progressively more serious implications the functioning of an open and rule-based international order.

Variables, Linkages, and Contingencies

There are several factors, or variables, that will shape the pathway away from American-led liberal hegemonic order. One is the actual willingness of the United States to cede authority back to the international community and accommodate itself to a system of more binding rules and institutions. Short of a radical shift in the international distribution of power, the United States will remain the world's most powerful state for several decades to come. So there is reason to think that other countries would be willing to see the United States play a leading role—and provide functional services—if the terms are right. Under almost any circumstances, these terms would entail a reduction in America's hegemonic rights and privileges while operating within agreed-upon rules and institutions. The United States might also come to believe that this renegotiated hegemonic arrangement is better than any of the alternatives. So the question is, could the United States in fact make the political commitments implicit in this renegotiated liberal international order? If there is uncertainty whether the United States can make compromises that are necessary to move to reformed liberal hegemonic international-ism, there is even more uncertainty about whether it can reconcile itself to a post-hegemonic liberal order. It might, in the end, opt for a more fragmented system in which it builds more selective partnerships with key allies that remain tied to its provision of security.

A second variable is the degree to which America's security capaci-ties can be leveraged into wider economic and political agreements. The United States has extraordinary advantages in military power. Its expenditures on military capacity are equal to the rest of the world's expenditures combined. It operates a worldwide system of alliances and security partnerships. It "commands the commons," in that it alone has the power to project force in all regions of the world. This situation will not change anytime soon, even with the rapid economic growth of countries such as China and India. The question here is, to what extent do these advantages and disparities in military capabilities translate into bargaining power over the wider array of global rules and institutions? If the answer is "very little"—the United States will increasingly need to reconcile itself to a post-hegemonic world. But if other countries do, in fact, value security protection, the United States will have more oppor-tunities to negotiate a modified hegemonic system.

A final variable is the degree of divergence among the leading states in their visions of global governance. Europe is clearly more interested in moving to a post-American liberal internationalism than the Chinese—at least to the extent that this entails further reductions in Westphalian sovereignty. But the question really is whether non-Western countries such as China and India will seek to use their rising power to usher in a substantially different sort of international order.[44] One possibility is

[44] Robert Jervis makes this point as it relates to the degree to which the unipolar state will be supported or resisted by other states. "Whether others will comply also depends on non-structural factors, especially the coincidence or discrepancy between the worlds they prefer and the one sought by the superpower." Robert Jervis, "Unipolarity: A Structural Perspec-tive," *World Politics* (January 2009), 192.

that they are not as inclined to embrace the open, rule-based logic of liberal internationalism, hegemonic or otherwise.[45] But another possibility is that they actually see that their interests are well served within a liberal international order.[46] If this second possibility is the case, the character of the negotiations on movement away from American-led liberal hegemonic internationalism will be focused more on participation and the sharing of authority—and less on shifts in the substantive principles of liberal order.

American Incentives for Liberal International Order

The United States will remain the dominant state in the global system for several decades to come. As such, its strategic orientation toward the logic and organization of the system will shape decisively what comes next. So what are its underlying interests and incentives in the maintenance of an open, rule-based international order? The United States might want simply to hold on to the old order. It was, after all, one of the great beneficiaries of that order, occupying its center, with all the authority and privileges that conveyed. But if the maintenance of the old hegemonic order is not possible, the United States will want to help shape a follow-on order that retains its open and rule-based character. It will surely struggle over how authority, sovereignty, hierarchy, and institutions are arrayed within the order. But it will also seek to preserve the order's underlying liberal features. The Bush administration's efforts to transform the system into a unipolar security order in which the United States disentangled itself from multilateral rules and institutions failed—and the lessons have not been lost on its successor administration. Moreover, if unipolarity is, in fact, in a slow process of decline, the incentives are actually intensified for putting in place and reinforcing

---

[45] See Mark Leonard, *What Does China Think?* (New York: Public Affairs Press, 2008).

[46] I make this argument in G. John Ikenberry, "The Rise of China and the Future of the West," *Foreign Affairs* 87, no. 1 (January/February 2008), 23–37.

a reformed liberal order, even if this entails a reduction of American hegemonic rights and privileges.

The rise and fall of unipolarity—and the underlying transformation of the Westphalian system—do not destine the United States to disentangle itself from a multilateral rule-based order. There continue to be deeply rooted incentives for the United States to support multilateralism—incentives that may actually be increasing.[47] These sources of support for open, rule-based order stem from the functional demands of interdependence, strategic calculations about the preservation of American influence and control in a transforming world, and the American political tradition and identity.

Interdependence and Functional Cooperation

American support for open, rule-based order is likely to be sustained and even grow. The United States will find increasing functional reasons—in both economic and security areas—to reaffirm and expand its commitment to multilateral cooperation. The international environment in which even a unipolar state operates is growing more complex and interdependent. America's ability to achieve its economic and security goals increasingly depends on the policies and practices of other states. Inevitably, the United States will be drawn outward to negotiate and build new realms of institutionalized cooperation.

In the economic realm, the more that states become interconnected, the more dependent they are on the actions of other states for the realization of their objectives. As the global economic system in which states

---

[47] An ongoing debate exists on whether long-term shifts in American domestic politics are eroding support for liberal internationalist foreign policy. See Jonathan Monten, "Without Heirs? Assessing the Decline of Liberal Internationalism in U.S. Foreign Policy," *Perspectives on Politics* 6, no. 2 (2009), 451–72; Charles Kupchan and Peter Trubowitz, "Dead Center: The Demise of Liberal Internationalism in the United States," *International Security* 32, no. 2 (Fall 2007), 7–44; Stephen Chaudoin, Helen Milner, and Dustin Tingley, "The Center Holds: Liberal Internationalism Survives," *International Security* 35, no. 1 (Summer 2010), 75–94; and Charles Kupchan and Peter Trubowitz, "The Illusion of Liberal Internationalism's Revival," *International Security* 35, no. 1 (Summer 2010), 95–109.

operate becomes more interdependent, states increasingly gain or lose depending on what other states do. The ability of even large, powerful states to ensure prosperity on their own diminishes. More specifically, as interdependence grows between states, the costs of not coordinating policies increase in relationship to the costs of reduced policy autonomy that comes with making binding commitments.[48] In the postwar decades, the United States and the other liberal capitalist states acted on this logic. They consistently sought to open markets and reap the economic, social, and technological gains that derive from integration into the world economy. And these countries also consistently made efforts to establish rules and institutions that would allow governments to manage this growing interdependence. If the United States and other leading states continue to see open markets as an integral part of economic growth and modernization, it is easy to predict that the demands for multilateral agreements—even, and perhaps especially, by the United States—will increase and not decrease.

Liberal theories of institutions provide an explanation for the rise of multilateral institutions under these circumstances. Institutions perform a variety of functions, including reducing uncertainty and the costs of transactions between states.[49] Mutually beneficial exchanges are missed in the absence of multilateral rules and procedures that help states overcome problems of collective action, asymmetrical information, and the fear that other states will cheat or act opportunistically. In effect, multilateral rules and institutions provide a contractual environment within which states can more easily pursue joint gains. Likewise, as the density of interactions between states rise, the demand for rules and institutions that facilitate these interactions will also increase. In this sense, multilateralism is self-reinforcing. A well-functioning contractual environment facilitates the

---

[48] On the relationship between increased globalization and the demand for international rules, see Jeffrey L. Dunoff and Joel P. Trachtman, "A Functional Approach to International Constitutionalization," in Jeffrey L. Dunoff and Joel P. Trachtman, eds., *Ruling the World? Constitutionalism, International Law, and Global Governance* (New York: Cambridge University Press, 2009), 5–9.

[49] Keohane, *After Hegemony*.

promulgation of additional multilateral rules and institutions. As Robert Keohane argues, the combination of growing interdependence and successful existing institutions should lead to the expansion in the tasks and scope of multilateralism in the relevant policy area.[50]

It is not just economic interdependence but security interdependence that is creating a demand for multilateral rules and institutions. As I argued in chapter 6, one of the deep shifts in the global system is related to the changing sources of violence and insecurity. The United States and the other major states are less threatened today by mass armies marching across borders than by transnational-born dangers. Some of these transnational dangers are nontraditional threats, such as climate change and pandemic disease. In these cases, what goes on in other states—carbon emissions or public health failures—increasingly has the potential to impinge on the health and safety of other countries. Clearly, rising security interdependence is also manifest in the activities of transnational groups of terrorists who may eventually gain access to weapons of mass destruction and unleash this violence in established modern societies.[51] Globalization and the growing ability of small nonstate groups to gain access to technologies of violence threaten the United States and other states in new and insidious ways. The threat environment in which the United States exists is growing more global and complex, creating new and growing incentives to work with other states to manage and control that environment.

Security interdependence is a measure of how much a state's national security depends on policies of other actors. A country is security independent if it is capable of achieving an acceptable level of security through its own actions. Others can threaten it, but the means for coping with these threats are in its own national hands. This means that the military intentions and capacities of other states are irrelevant to a state's

[50] Keohane, "Multilateralism: An Agenda for Research," 744–45.

[51] For a survey of these new sorts of transnational threats and their implications for American national security, see Ikenberry and Slaughter, *Forging a World of Liberty under Law*; and Neyla Arnas, ed., *Fighting Chance: Global Trends and Shocks in the National Security Environment* (Washington, DC: Potomac, 2009).

security. This is true either because the potential military threats are too remote and far removed to matter or because if a foreign power launches a war against the state, it has the capabilities to resist the aggression.[52] With rising security interdependence, a state's security depends more on the policy and choices of other actors. Security is established by convincing other actors not to attack. During the Cold War, the United States and the Soviet Union were in a situation of supreme security interdependence. Each had nuclear weapons that could destroy the other. It was the logic of deterrence that established the restraints on policy. Each state knew that a nuclear strike on the other would be followed by massive and assured retaliation. Under these circumstances, states cannot protect themselves or achieve national security without the help of other states. There is no solution to the security problem without active cooperation—even if that cooperation is based simply on mutual deterrence.[53] What this means, as Zbigniew Brzezinski argues, is that "[t]he traditional link between national sovereignty and national security has been severed."[54] When states are in a situation of security interdependence, they cannot go it alone. They must negotiate and cooperate with other states and seek mutual restraints and protections.

In a world of diffuse and transnational threats, the problem of security interdependence becomes even more severe. Put simply, there are more people in more places around the globe who can matter to American security. So what these people do and how they live matter in ways that were irrelevant in earlier eras—at least irrelevant in relation to national security. The ability of states in all parts of the world to maintain the

[52] The Reagan-era vision of missile defense reflected an aspiration to reestablish security independence. To be able to shoot down any incoming missile assault is to regain the state's ability to protect itself—regardless of the policies and intentions of others. See Francis Fitgerald, *Way Out There in the Blue: Reagan, Star Wars, and the End of the Cold War* (New York: Simon and Schuster, 2000); and Richard Rhodes, *Arsenals of Folly: The Making of the Nuclear Arms Race* (New York: Vintage, 2008).

[53] For an exploration of the logic of security interdependence and its implications for international cooperation, see Daniel Deudney, *Bounding Power: Republican Security Theory From the Polis to the Global Village* (Princeton, NJ: Princeton University Press, 2007).

[54] Zbigniew Brzezinski, *The Choice: Domination or Leadership* (New York: Basic, 2004), 13.

rule of law, uphold international commitments, and engage in monitoring and enforcement of security agreements matters. The presence of weak or failed states in remote regions of the world matters. The socioeconomic fortunes of states—that is, the ability of states to satisfy their citizens—matter.[55] Given these circumstances, the United States has an incentive to seek greater cooperation with other states. It will want to rebuild and expand the authority and capacities of the international community to engage in multifaceted collective action—ongoing tasks that include arms control, state building, economic assistance, conflict prevention, WMD safeguarding, disaster relief, and technology sharing. It will find itself increasingly involved with other states to create more extensive forms of security cooperation and capacity building.

The Obama administration appears to have put the problem of security interdependence at the center of its foreign policy vision. President Obama has argued consistently and repeatedly in speeches and policy declarations that American national security is increasingly tied to the security of others. The United States and other countries cannot be secure alone; they can only be secure together. Around the world, what people do and how they live matter in ways that were irrelevant in earlier eras. The Obama administration's focus on reviving the Non-Proliferation Treaty and its agenda for radical reductions in nuclear weapons, together with its emphasis on development, human security, and multilateral cooperation, are markers in the Obama administration's attempt to craft American foreign policy for an era of escalating security interdependence.[56]

Rising economic and security interdependence is creating incentives for the United States to seek new and more extensive forms of multilateral cooperation. Other states will also find themselves responding to these incentives for cooperation. Major states disagree on the specific

[55] As Robert Cooper puts it: "The world may be globalized but it is run by states. Spaces with no one in control are a nightmare for those who live there, a haven for criminals and a danger to the rest of us." Robert Cooper, "Picking Up the Pieces," *Financial Times*, 25–26 October 2008, Life and Arts, 17.

[56] See G. John Ikenberry, "The Right Grand Strategy," *American Interest* (January/February 2010), 12–14.

ways in which economic and security cooperation should proceed. Nonetheless, the United States and these other leading states will have reasons to avoid a breakdown in multilateral order itself. They will increasingly find reasons to experiment in new and more extensive forms of formal and informal collaboration.

Hegemonic Power and Strategic Restraint

American support for rule-based order will also stem from a grand-strategic interest in preserving its power and creating a stable and legitimate international order. Whether unipolarity is long lasting or in slow decline, the United States has incentives—as it has had in the past—to facilitate the building of rules and institutions that reinforce and legitimize its power. The last decade has shown that American power can be more or less welcome within the global system. States can solicit American leadership and defer to its authority as the most powerful state in the system, or they can resist it and seek alternative partners and systems of order. The United States has an incentive to stay—to the extent that it can—within the center of the international order. It would prefer to operate in a system in which other states are willing partners. And it would like to build or reinforce the rules and institutions of order in such a way as to ensure that the order persists even as American power declines. All these considerations relate to the preservation and management of American power assets—and they all lead the United States to favor an open, rule-based order.

As noted in 3, this perspective begins by looking at the choices that dominant states face when they are in a position to shape the fundamental character of the international order. A state that wins a war or through some other turn of events finds itself in a dominant global position faces a choice: it can use its power to bargain and coerce other states in struggles over the distribution of gains or, knowing that its power position will someday decline and that there are costs to enforcing its way within the order, it can move toward a more rule-based, institutionalized order in exchange for the acquiescence and compliant participation of weaker

states. In seeking a more rule-based order, the leading state is agreeing to
engage in strategic restraint. It is acknowledging that there will be limits
on the way in which it can exercise its power. Such an order, in effect, has
constitutional characteristics. Limits are set on what a state within the
order can do with its power advantages. Just as in constitutional polities,
the implications of winning is reduced. Weaker states realize that the
implications of their inferior position are limited and perhaps temporary—to operate within the order despite their disadvantages is not to
risk everything nor will it give the dominant state a permanent advantage. Both the powerful and the weak states agree to operate within the
same order despite radical asymmetries in the distribution of power.[57]

A multilateral system of rules and institutions becomes the outcome
of bargaining between leading and weaker states over the character of
international order. In agreeing to relations organized around multilateral rules and institutions, the dominant state reduces its enforcement
costs and succeeds in establishing an order where weaker states will participate willingly rather than resist or balance against the leading power.[58] It accepts some restrictions on how it can use its power. The rules and
institutions that are create serve as an investment in the longer-run preservation of its power advantages. Weaker states agree to the order's rules
and institutions, and in return they are assured that the worst excesses
of the leading state—manifest as arbitrary and indiscriminate abuses of
state power—will be avoided, and they gain institutional opportunities
to work with and help influence the leading state.[59]

As noted in chapter 6, the Bush administration attempted to extract
the United States from parts of this postwar system of restraints and
commitments—and costs were incurred. As a result, it paid a price in
lost authority and diminished cooperation. The architects of America's

[57] For a discussion of constitutional logic and international relations, see Ikenberry, "Constitutional Politics in International Relations," 147–78.

[58] For sophisticated arguments along these lines, see Martin, "Rational State Choice
of Multilateralism," 91–121; and David Lake, *Entangling Relations: America in Its Century*
(Princeton, NJ: Princeton University Press, 1999).

[59] See chapter 3 and also Ikenberry, *After Victory*.

national security strategy after September 11, 2001, articulated a new vision of American primacy. As provider of global security, the United States would operate more or less above other states, making choices and deploying forces outside agreed-upon alliances and cooperative security frameworks. The Bush administration also rejected pending international treaties and agreements, including the Kyoto Protocol on Climate Change, the Rome Statute of the International Criminal Court, the Germ Weapons Ban, and the Programme of Action on Illicit Trade in Small and Light Arms. It also unilaterally withdrew from the 1970s ABM treaty, which many experts regard as the cornerstone of modern arms-control agreements. The Bush administration also triggered a global uproar over its torture and detention politics. Together with the Iraq war, these actions by the Bush administration effectively constituted a sharp and unprecedented departure from America's long-standing postwar approach to international order. America's allies and partners—along with many other governments around the world—pushed back. The repositioning of the United States was unwelcome and unsustainable.

The costs that the Bush administration sustained were both specific and diffuse. On the eve of America's invasion of Iraq, a chorus of voices from the United States and abroad warned of the costs of acting unilaterally. Some of the expected costs were seen as practical: if the United States went in alone it would not have sufficient support after the war to engage in the expensive and lengthy process of reconstructing Iraq. As one commentary noted: "As long as the United States stays engaged in the United Nations, it tacitly accepts boundaries on its power in exchange for the benefits of multilateral backing. With U.N. approval, other nations would share the cost of an attack on Iraq and the long-term nation building that must occur afterward. If the U.S. goes it alone, fewer countries will be willing to share the burden—not only for Iraq but for other international ventures, such as anti-terrorism drives."[60] It is difficult to measure the costs of lost cooperation in Iraq or the wider war on ter-

[60] Farley and McManus, "To Some, the Real Threat is U.S."

rorism—but the controversy and hostility that Bush's foreign policy generated certainly diminished world support for the United States. More
general and diffuse costs in lost American legitimacy were also incurred,
as was noted at the time.[61] The Bush administration's movement back to a
more traditional foreign policy in its last years is also an indication that it,
too, recognized the costs of its earlier grand-strategic vision.

The Obama administration has clearly acknowledged the failures
of Bush-era unilateralism and in its first years in office has charted a
return to the restraints and commitments of America's postwar orientation toward order.[62] As a candidate for president, Senator Obama noted
the importance of restraint and institutional cooperation as a feature of
effective American diplomacy. In a 2007 interview with the journalist
Roger Cohen, Obama argued: "We can and should lead the world, but
we have to apply wisdom and judgment. Part of our capacity to lead is
linked to our capacity to show restraint."[63] In other speeches after taking office, Obama also stressed the need to learn from the failures of
the Bush administration and renew America's commitment to a multilateral, rule-based system. Secretary of State Hillary Clinton has also
emphasized the need to return to the liberal hegemonic logic of fostering collective action and partnerships for problem solving. "We will lead

[61] American and European officials and commentators reminded the Bush administration
that strategic restraint and multilateral diplomatic process were vital to preserving the long-
term leadership position of the United States. See, e.g., Philip Stephens, "America Should
Take the Offer of Legitimacy as Well as Power," *Financial Times*, 27 September 2002; Chris
Patten, "America Should Not Relinquish Respect," *Financial Times*, 3 October 2002; and
John F. Kerry, "We Still have a Choice in Iraq," *New York Times*, 6 September 2002.

[62] The European Union's chief foreign policy official wrote a commentary piece on the day
that the new American president was inaugurated, sending a message about his hopes for the
coming administration, emphasizing the need for diplomacy and rule-based order building:
"Ultimately, the objective of diplomacy is to create agreed rules. Rules on political participation, demarcation of borders or movements of military equipment. Rules to end conflicts
within or between states. Rules to help us address the big issues of our time: climate change,
non-proliferation and a sustainable and open global economy. The accumulation of rules,
procedures and institutions sounds like dreary work but it is what global civilization is built
on. Agreed rules make states secure and people free." Javier Solana, "Five Lessons in Global
Diplomacy," *Financial Times*, 21 January 2009, 11.

[63] Roger Cohen, "Obama and the American Idea," *New York Times*, 9 December 2007.

by inducing greater cooperation among a greater number of actors and reducing competition," Clinton argued in her first major speech, "tilting the balance away from a multi-polar world and toward a multi-partner world."[64] These are indications of a recognition within the American foreign policy community that the United States moved dangerously off course in the recent past, leaving the country in a weakened position to pursue its interests.

Finally, a return to a pre–Bush era foreign policy of strategic restraint and multilateral commitments is further reinforced by new assessments of the trajectory of American power. The Bush administration's strategic unilateralism was premised on a very optimistic view of American power. It appears to have calculated that the United States had the unipolar capabilities to go it alone and to cover the costs associated with lost authority and legitimacy. As one top advisor to President Bush is famously reported to have remarked to a journalist, "We're an empire now, and when we act, we create our own reality."[65] In retrospect, it is clear that this assessment of American power was simply not accurate. The Obama administration does not need to be declinist to make more modest assessments of power and costs. Even if a return to multipolarity is a distant and slowly emerging future possibility, calculations about the relative decline of American power reintroduce the importance of making investments today for later decades when the United States is less preeminent. For these reasons, incentives exist—and are perhaps growing—for the United States to rebuild and expand the rules and institutions through which it exercises power and pursues its interests.[66]

[64] Secretary of State Hillary Clinton, speech before the Council on Foreign Relations, Washington, DC, 15 July 2009.

[65] Quoted in Ron Suskind, "Faith, Certainty, and the Presidency of George W. Bush," *New York Times Magazine*, 17 October 2004, http://www.nytimes.com/2004/10/17/magazine/17BUSH.html (accessed 8 November 2010).

[66] The U.S. Defense Department's most recent strategic planning statement makes this point: "While the United States will remain the most powerful actor, it must increasingly cooperate with key allies and partners to build and sustain peace and security. Whether and how rising powers fully integrate into the global system will be among the century's defining questions, and are thus central to America's interests." *Quadrennial Defense Review Report* (February 2010), 7.

Political Identity and the Rule of Law

A final source of American support for open, rule-based order is from the polity itself. The United States has a distinctive self-understanding of its own political order. This has implications for how its leaders and citizens think about international political order. To be sure, there are multiple political traditions in the United States that reflect divergent and often competing ideas about how the United States should relate to the rest of the world.[67] These traditions variously counsel isolationism and activism, realism and idealism, aloofness and engagement in the conduct of American foreign affairs. But behind these political-intellectual traditions are deeper aspects of the American political identity that inform the way the United States seeks to build order in the larger global system. The Enlightenment origins of the American founding have given the United States an identity that sees its principles of politics as having universal significance and scope.[68] The republican democratic tradition that enshrines the rule of law reflects an enduring American view that polities—domestic or international—are best organized around rules and principles of order. America's tradition of civil nationalism also reinforces this notion—that the rule of law is the source of legitimacy and political inclusion. This tradition provides a background support for a multilaterally oriented foreign policy.[69]

[67] See surveys by Walter A. McDougall, *Promised Land, Crusader State: The American Encounter with the World Since 1776* (New York: Houghton Mifflin, 1997); and Walter Russell Mead, *Special Providence: American Foreign Policy and How It Changed the World* (New York: Knopf, 2001).

[68] See Samuel Huntington, *American Politics: The Promise of Disharmony* (Cambridge, MA: Harvard University Press, 1983).

[69] There are, of course, political ideas and traditions in the American experience that give support for unilateral and isolationist policies—and these flourished from the founding well into the 1930s and still exist today. But these alternatives to multilateralism, as Jeff Legro argues, were discredited in the face of the events of World War I and II and opened the way to internationalist and multilateral ideas and strategies. Jeff Legro, "Whence American Internationalism," *International Organization* 54, no. 2 (2000), 253–89. These multilateral ideas and strategies, in turn, are given support by the deeper American rule of law and civic national traditions.

The basic distinction between civic and ethnic nationalism is useful in locating this feature of the American political tradition. Civic identity is group identity that is composed of commitments to the nation's political creed. Race, religion, gender, language, and ethnicity are not relevant in defining a citizen's rights and inclusion within the polity. Shared belief in the country's principles and values embedded in the rule of law is the organizing basis for political order, and citizens are understood to be equal and rights-bearing individuals. Ethnic nationalism, in contrast, maintains that individual rights and participation within the polity are inherited—based on ethnic or racial or religious ties.[70]

Civic national identity has several implications for the multilateral orientation of American foreign policy. First, civic identity has tended to encourage the American projection outward of domestic principles of inclusive and rule-based international political organization. The American national identity is not based on ethnic or religious particularism but on a more general set of agreed-upon and normatively appealing principles. Ethnic and religious identities and disputes are pushed downward into civil society and removed from the political arena. When the United States gets involved in political conflicts around the world it tends to look for the establishment of agreed-upon political principles and rules to guide the rebuilding of order. Likewise, when the United States promotes rule-based solutions to problems, it is strengthening the normative and principled basis for the exercise of its own power—and thereby making disparities in power more acceptable.

Second, because a civic political culture is shared with other Western states it tends to be a source of cohesion and cooperation. Throughout the industrial democratic world, the dominant form of political identity is based on a set of abstract and juridical rights and responsibilities that coexist with private ethnic and religious associations. Just as warring states and nationalism tend to reinforce each other, so too do Western civic

[70] This distinction is made by Anthony D. Smith, *The Ethnic Origins of Nations* (Oxford: Blackwell, 1986).

identity and cooperative political relations.[71] Political order—domestic and international—is strengthened when there exists a substantial sense of community and shared identity. It matters that the leaders of today's advanced industrial states are not seeking to legitimate their power by making racial or imperialist appeals. Civic nationalism, rooted in shared commitment to democracy and the rule of law, provides a widely embraced identity across most of the advanced industrial world. At the same time, potentially divisive identity conflicts—rooted in antagonistic ethnic or religious or class divisions—are dampened by relegating them to secondary status within civil society.[72] This notion that the United States participates in a wider Western community of shared values and like-minded states reinforces American multilateral impulses.[73]

Third, the multicultural character of the American political identity also reinforces internationalist—and ultimately multilateral—foreign policy. John Ruggie notes that culture wars continue in the United States between a pluralistic and multicultural identity and nativist and

[71] Leaders of the advanced democracies have periodically made affirmations of their shared identity, rooted in liberal governance and a commitment to the rule of law. See, for example, the Declaration of Democratic Values issued by the G-7 countries at their 1984 summit: "We believe in a rule of law which respects and protects without fear or favor the rights and liberties of every citizen and provides the setting in which the human spirit can develop in freedom and diversity." Declaration reprinted in the *Washington Post*, 9 June 1984, A14.

[72] See Deudney and Ikenberry, "Nature and Sources of Liberal International Order."

[73] While Woodrow Wilson sought to justify American postwar internationalism on the basis of American exceptionalism and a duty to lead the world to democratic salvation, advocates of internationalism after World War II emphasized that the United States belonged to a community of Western democracies that implied multilateral duties and loyalties. See Anders Stephanson, *Manifest Destiny: American Expansionism and the Empire of Right* (New York: Hill and Wang, 1995), 114–15. For the claim that this wider Western community has reinforced American internationalism and multilateral commitments, see Risse-Kappen, "Collective Identity in a Democratic Community"; Risse-Kappen, *Cooperation among Democracies*; Mary N. Hampton, *The Wilsonian Impulse: U.S. Foreign Policy, the Alliance, and German Unification* (Westport, CT: Praeger, 1996); and Henry R. Nau, *At Home Abroad: Identity and Power in American Foreign Policy* (Ithaca, NY: Cornell University Press, 2002). This insight about Western community has also been used to explain the rise of NATO in the Atlantic and the absence of a similar postwar multilateral security organization in East Asia. See Hemmer and Katzenstein, "Why is There No NATO in Asia?" *International Organization* 56, no. 3 (Summer 2002), 575–607.

parochial alternatives but that the core identity is still "cosmopolitan lib-eral"—an identity that tends to support instrumental multilateralism: "[T]he evocative significance of multilateral world order principles—a bias against exclusive bilateralist alliances, the rejection of discrimina-tory economic blocs, and facilitating means to bridge gaps of ethos, race, and religion—should resonate still for the American public, insofar as they continue to reflect its own sense of national identity."[74] The Ameri-can society is increasingly heterogeneous in race, ethnicity, and religion. This tends to reinforce an activist and inclusive foreign policy orienta-tion and a bias in favor of rule-based and multilateral approaches to the conduct of American foreign policy.[75]

To be sure, American leaders can campaign against multilateral trea-ties and institutions and win votes. But this has been true across the last century, as manifest most dramatically with the rejection of the League of Nations treaty in 1919 but also reflected in other defeats, such as that of the International Trade Organization after World War II. When President Bush went to the United Nations to rally support for his hard-line approach to Iraq, he did not articulate a central role for the world body in promoting international security and peace. He told the General Assembly: "We will work with the U.N. Security Council for the necessary resolutions." But he also made clear: "The purposes of the United States should not be doubted. The Security Council resolutions will be enforced ... or action will be unavoidable."[76] In contrast, just twelve years earlier, when the elder President Bush appeared before the General Assembly to press his case for resisting Iraq's invasion of Kuwait, he offered a "vision of a new partnership of nations ... a partnership based on consultations, cooperation and collective action, especially

[74] John Gerard Ruggie, *Winning the Peace: America and World Order in the New Era* (New York: Columbia University Press, 1996), 170.

[75] On the ways in which American ethnic groups encourage foreign policy activism, see Tony Smith, *Foreign Attachments: The Power of Ethnic Groups in the Making of American Foreign Policy* (Cambridge, MA: Harvard University Press, 2000).

[76] President George H. W. Bush, address to the U.N. General Assembly, 12 September 2002.

through international and regional organizations, a partnership united by principle and the rule of law and supported by an equitable sharing of both cost and commitment."[77] It would appear that quite divergent visions of American foreign policy can be articulated by different presidents—each resonating in its own way with ideas and beliefs within the American polity. If this is true, it means that American presidents do have political and intellectual space to shape policy—and that they are not captives of a unilateralist-minded public.

Recent public opinion findings confirm this view and actually suggest that the American public is quite willing and eager to conduct American foreign policy within multilateral frameworks. In a comprehensive poll of American and European attitudes on international affairs, the German Marshall Fund study found that a clear majority of Americans actually favored joining the European Union in ratifying the Kyoto accord on global warming and the treaty creating an ICC. American public attitudes reveal a general multilateral bent. When given three alternatives about the role of the United States in solving international problems, most Americans (71 percent) said that it should act to solve problems together with other countries, and only 17 percent said that "as the sole remaining superpower the United States should continue to be the preeminent world leader in solving international problems." There was also high—and increased—support for strengthening the United Nations, participating in U.N. peacekeeping operations, and using diplomatic methods to combat terrorism. On the unilateral use of American military force, when asked if, in responding to international crises, the United States should or should not take action alone if it does not have the support of allies, the proportion saying that the United States should not act alone was 61 percent. Only a third of the American public indicated that the United States should act alone.[78]

The manner and extent to which America's liberal political culture and civic national identity shapes or constrains the general orientation

[77] President George H. W. Bush, address to the U.N. General Assembly, 1 October 1990.

[78] German Marshall Fund, "A World Transformed: Foreign Policy Attitudes of the U.S. Public After September 11," report of public opinion survey, 4 September 2002.

of its foreign policy can be debated. American leaders certainly draw upon it in articulating their grand-strategic visions. As we have seen in chapter 6, American political culture also has ideas about national independence and sovereign self-rule, brought forward from the founding, which, together with the tradition of constitutionalism, also inspire conservative opponents of international law, treaties, and binding rule-based commitments. The United States has always evinced a certain ambivalence about the primacy of international law and multilateral commitments. But what is remarkable about the last century of American foreign policy is how central liberal ideas of rule-based order and institutionalized cooperation have been to America's global orientation, and the experience of the Bush administration has tended to reinforce the attractiveness of those ideas today.

Conclusion

The liberal international project has evolved over the last century and is evolving again today. In the past, shifts in the logic and character of liberal international order came in the aftermath of war and economic upheaval. In contrast, the current troubles that beset American-led liberal internationalism are not manifesting in the breakdown of the old order. The crisis of America's liberal hegemonic order is a crisis of authority. It is a crisis over the way liberal international order is governed. It is a crisis that is generating pressures and incentives for a reorganization in the way sovereignty, rules, institutions, hierarchy, and authority are arrayed in the international system. The American hegemonic organization of liberal order no longer appears to offer a solid foundation for the maintenance of an open and rule-based liberal order. The liberal project itself has partly brought us to this impasse; its success has helped strip away the foundations of the liberal order.

What comes after liberal hegemonic order? In the absence of war or economic calamity, the old liberal order is unlikely to break down or disappear. As in the past, liberal international order will evolve. The character of governance will shift with changes in the way states share and exercise power and authority. Precisely because the crisis of liberal order is a crisis of success, leading and rising states in the system are not seeking to overturn the basic logic of liberal internationalism as a system of open and rule-based order. Rather, the pressures and incentives for change are felt in regard to the way roles and responsibilities are allocated in the system.

The way in which liberal order evolves will hinge in important respects on the United States—and its willingness and ability to make new commitments to rules and institutions while simultaneously reducing its rights and privileges within the order. The United States is deeply ambivalent about making institutional commitments and binding itself to other states—ambivalence and hesitation that have been exacerbated by the end of the Cold War, American unipolarity, and new security threats. But the United States still possesses profound incentives to build and operate within a liberal rule-based order. Just as importantly, that order is now not simply an extension of American power and interests but has taken on a life of its own. American power may rise or fall, and its foreign policy ideology may wax and wane between multilateral and imperial impulses, but the wider and deeper liberal global order is now a reality to which America itself must accommodate.

Eight
Conclusion: The Durability of Liberal International Order

≡

For half a century, the United States held the keys to global order—and in many ways it still does today. No country has ever been as powerful as the United States or had as many opportunities to put its mark on the organization of world politics. After the world wars, after the Cold War, and again today, the United States has been in a unique position to lead in the creation of rules and institutions that guide the global system. At key turning points, it stepped forward with liberal ideas about world order and struggled to reconcile them with the geopolitical realities of the day. The United States has been a liberal order builder. It has sought to create an open and loosely rule-based international order, anchored among the advanced democracies. This vision of order was in part driven by America's national interests as a large and advanced state seeking access to world markets. But it also reflected a set of calculations about the virtues of a legitimate and durable international order that would provide a long-term flow of economic and security benefits not just to the United States but to the wider world.

The pivotal moment in liberal order building occurred in the years after World War II. It was then that America's desire for a congenial world order—open, stable, friendly—turned into an agenda for the construction of a liberal hegemonic order. But this shift was not entirely deliberate. The United States took charge of the liberal project and then found itself creating and running an international order. America and liberal order became fused.

It was a distinctive type of order—organized around American hegemonic authority, open markets, cooperative security, multilateral institutions, social bargains, and democratic community. It was also built on core hegemonic bargains. These bargains determined how power and authority would be apportioned. So although the United States ran the liberal order and projected power, it did so within a system of rules and institutions—of commitments and restraints. It underwrote order in various regions of the world. It provided public goods related to stability and openness, and it engaged in bargaining and reciprocity with its allies and partners. The center of gravity of this order was the West—and as it moved outward to Asia, Latin America, and the developing world, the liberal logic gave way to more traditional imperial and great-power domination. Globally, the order was hierarchical—dominated by the United States—but infused with liberal characteristics.

This American-led liberal hegemonic order is now in crisis. The underlying foundations that support this order have shifted. Pressures for change—and for the reorganization of order—are growing. But amidst this great transformation, it is important to untangle what precisely is in crisis and what is not. My claim is that it is a crisis of authority—a struggle over how liberal order should be governed, not a crisis over the underlying principles of liberal international order, defined as an open and loosely rule-based system. That is, what is in dispute is how aspects of liberal order—sovereignty, institutions, participation, roles, and responsibilities—are to be allocated, but all within the order rather than in its wake.

If the old postwar hegemonic order were a business enterprise, it would have been called American Inc. It was an order that, in important respects, was owned and operated by the United States. The crisis today is really over ownership of that company. In effect, it is a transition from a semiprivate company to one that is publicly owned and operated—with an expanding array of shareholders and new members on the board of directors. This is true even as non-Western states—most importantly, China—continue to rise up and struggle to define their relationship to liberal international order.

To arrive at this argument, the preceding chapters have explored the theory and history of international order. We have examined both the organizational logic of different types of orders and ways in which these orders rise and decline. This exploration has allowed us to identify and situate liberal international order in the context of wider types of international orders—orders defined in terms of their mechanisms of stability and control (balance, command, and consent). This exploration has also allowed us to situate American-led liberal hegemonic order within the wider types of liberal international order. From these theoretical considerations, we could trace the great historical shifts and evolution in the liberal international project. The liberal internationalism of Woodrow Wilson gave way to an updated vision by Franklin Roosevelt, and after this to a Western-oriented hegemonic project built during the Cold War. We have seen that the underlying foundation on which this American liberal hegemonic project rested has been transformed. The Westphalian underpinnings of liberal order—not fully appreciated by some liberal internationalists—have eroded. Unipolarity, eroded sovereignty, the shifting scale and scope of economic and security interdependence—all have intensified the dilemmas and tensions within the liberal vision.

This leads us to the question: what comes next? I argue that there are several possibilities, including a future in which the United States renegotiates for an ongoing leadership role in the management of the system. Even if the global system transitions away from America Inc. to a publicly owned and operated company, the United States will inevitably be a major shareholder, even in an era of slowly declining unipolarity.

The movement away from the American-led order will raise a number of dilemmas and tensions inherent in the liberal project. There is pressure for the reallocation of authority and leadership, but how will a post-hegemonic system provide public goods relating to open markets and the stability of rules and institutions? There is pressure for more extensive forms of international cooperation—and global institutional capacity—to deal with economic and security interdependence, but how can this be reconciled with democratic accountability? There is pressure for new rights and capacities for the international community to intervene in the domestic affairs of troubled states, but how does liberal order develop governance mechanisms to generate the necessary collective action and also safeguard itself against liberal imperialism? These dilemmas will run through the struggles over reform of liberal international order, even as rising states and new global issues shape and constrain what comes next. What does seem certain is that the demand for more and increasingly sophisticated forms of cooperation will not abate in the decades ahead. Indeed, countries large and small will face a crush of new demands for more extensive cooperation. In other words, if the current organizational logic of liberal international order is in crisis, the solution to this crisis is more—not less—liberal international order.

We can look more closely at the forces for change and continuity in the current international system, the rise of China and its relationship to the evolving liberal international order, and the American agenda for liberal order building. In each of these cases, I argue that the future is actually quite bright for a one-world system organized around open and loosely rule-based principles and institutions—and in which the United States remains centrally positioned.

Crisis and Continuity in Liberal International Order

This book argues that the current hegemonic organization of liberal order is in crisis—but it is a crisis of success. The problems that beset the current system are ones that, for the most part, emerged out of the expansion of the American-led postwar system. The postwar liberal order took root inside the bipolar system, but after the Cold War it spread outward and became the outside system. The American order went global. Markets spread, states rose up, and the scale and scope of the liberal capitalist world expanded. Taken together with the emergence and spread of liberal internationalism in the nineteenth century, the world has witnessed a two-hundred-year liberal ascendancy. The main alternatives to liberal order—both domestic and international—have more or less disappeared. The great liberal international era is not ending. Still, if the liberal order is not in crisis, its governance is. Yet, given the fundamental weakness of the past international orders—brought down by world wars and great economic upheavals—the challenges of reforming and renegotiating liberal world order are, if anything, welcome ones.

The authority crisis of the liberal order is not a crisis that fulfills the predictions of past critics of liberal order—that it would be an idealist enterprise that simply could not take hold in the actual world of anarchy and power politics. The crisis of liberal order today is precisely the opposite of this classic charge. It is because the world has become *less* realist than liberals anticipated that its problems ensue. That is, the liberal project has succeeded all too well. The international system under conditions of liberal hegemonic rule has boomed, expanding and integrating on a global scale, creating economic and security interdependencies well beyond the imagination of its postwar architects.

In effect, this is not an "E. H. Carr moment"—that is, a moment when realists can step forward and say that liberal idealists had it all wrong and that the return of anarchy and war reveals the enduring truths of world politics as a struggle for power and advantage.[1] This was E. H. Carr's famous indictment of Woodrow Wilson and the liberal peacemakers of 1919. Carr was right that the conditions were not right for Wilson's liberal-order-building moment. But he was wrong in the sense that Wilson and other liberals did, in fact, offer a coherent vision

[1] E. H. Carr, *The Twenty Years Crisis, 1919–1939: An Introduction to the Study of International Relations* (London: Macmillan, 1951).

of how open markets, collective security, and international rules could operate in a world dominated by war-weary democracies. It was not a project built on dreams; it was built on a theory about the way the world worked and how it could be made to work. In thinking that he was witnessing a worldwide democratic revolution that would provide the foundation for a new system of stable peace, Wilson was simply ahead of his times. Later generations of American and European order builders picked up this liberal agenda.

Regardless of the validity of Carr's claims, today's crisis is not a crisis of the sort he identified. Today's problems cannot be explained or solved by a return to realist thinking and action. Today, the crisis of liberal international order is more of a "Karl Polanyi moment"—that is, the liberal governance system is troubled because of dilemmas and long-term shifts in that order that can only be solved by rethinking, rebuilding, and extending it.[2] Polanyi understood the problems of the nineteenth-century Western order in these terms. Indeed, he saw deeper contradictions and problems in the organization of market society than exist today. What is similar about the two eras, as Polanyi would no doubt argue, is the way in which the geopolitical and institutional foundations that facilitated an open system of markets and societal exchange outgrew and overran those foundations, triggering instabilities and conflict. In other words, liberal order has generated the seeds of its own unmaking, which can be averted only by more liberal order—reformed, updated, and outfitted with a new foundation.

In fact, beyond the navigation of the current crisis, there is reason to think that some type of updated and reorganized liberal international order will persist. The liberal ascendancy is not over. This is true for several reasons.

First, the old and traditional mechanism for overturning international order—great-power war—is no longer likely to occur. Already, the contemporary world has experienced the longest period of great-power

[2] Karl Polanyi, *The Great Transformation: The Political and Economic Origins of Our Time* (Boston: Beacon, 1957).

peace in the long history of the state system.[3] This absence of great-power war is no doubt due to several factors not present in earlier eras, namely nuclear deterrence and the dominance of liberal democracies. Nuclear weapons—and the deterrence they generate—give great powers some confidence that they will not be dominated or invaded by other major states. They make war among major states less rational and therefore less likely. Nuclear weapons have a double-edged effect. They put limits on the power of even the most preeminent state in the system. The United States may be unipolar, but it is not capable of engaging in conquest of other major powers. In this sense, great military powers of the past may have been less dominant than the United States, defined in terms of share of material capabilities and military expenditures, but they were nonetheless more threatening to other major states because the threat of war was real. Nuclear deterrence removes the threat of war and makes American unipolarity less existentially threatening to other great powers. At the same time, the removal of great-power war as a tool of overturning international order tends to reinforce the status quo. The United States was lucky to have emerged as a global power in the nuclear age, because rival great powers are put at a disadvantage if they seek to overturn the American-led system. The cost-benefit calculation of rival would-be hegemonic powers is altered in favor of working for change within the system. But, again, the fact that great-power deterrence also sets limits on the projection of American power presumably makes the existing international order more tolerable. It removes a type of behavior in the system—war, invasion, and conquest between great powers—that historically provided the motive for seeking to overturn order.

The dominance of liberal democracies further reinforces continuity in the system. Chapter 1 provided a depiction of the liberal ascendancy. This is the two-century rise of liberal democracies to global preeminence. The centrality and sheer bulk of these states creates stability. If

[3] Robert Jervis, "Theories of War in an Era of Leading-Power Peace," *American Political Science Review* 96, no. 1 (2002), 1–14; and John Lewis Gaddis, "The Long Peace: Elements of Stability in the Postwar International System," *International Security* 10, no. 4 (Spring 1986), 99–142.

liberal democracies are less likely to go to war against each other, this creates a massive zone of peace. If liberal democracies are more likely to trade and cooperate with each other, this reinforces their dominance. If liberal democracies are more able to make political adjustments among themselves to accommodate the rise and decline in their power, this, too, creates more stability in the existing system than in past international orders. Together, nuclear weapons and the dominance of liberal democracies make war less likely as a dynamic of change. If the violent overturning of international order is removed, the logic of crisis and change takes a new turn and a bias for continuity is introduced into the system.

Second, the character of liberal international order itself—with or without American hegemonic leadership—reinforces continuity. In previous chapters, I have described this postwar liberal international order as "easy to join and hard to overturn." The big reasons it is hard to overturn have just been discussed. But it is also worth observing that the complex interdependence that is unleashed in an open and loosely rule-based order generates expanding realms of exchange and investment that result in a growing array of firms, interest groups, and other sorts of political stakeholders who seek to preserve the stability and openness of the system. In effect, the liberal international order has self-reinforcing features. Beyond this, the liberal order is also relatively easy to join. In the post–Cold War decades, countries in diverse regions of the world have made democratic transitions and connected themselves to various parts of this liberal system. East European countries and states within the old Soviet empire have joined NATO. East Asian countries, including China, have joined the WTO. Through its many multilateral institutions, the liberal international order facilitates integration and offers support for states that are making transitions toward liberal democracy. The liberal order also provides space within for shared leadership. Again, the many multilateral institutions and groupings provide entry for states as they rise up and seek a leadership role. Japan, for example, found these opportunities as it joined the GATT, the WTO, and the G-7 and G-20 leadership grouping. And the liberal order also provides for a relatively wide sharing of wealth and economic gains. Many countries have experienced growth and rising incomes within this order. Comparing international orders is tricky, but the current liberal international order, seen in comparative perspective, does appear to have unique characteristics that encourage integration and discourage opposition and resistance.

Third, the states that are rising today do not constitute a potential united opposition bloc to the existing order. There are so-called rising states in various regions of the world. China, India, Brazil, and South Africa are perhaps most prominent. Russia is also sometimes included in this grouping of rising states. These states are all capitalist and most are democratic. They all gain from trade and integration within the world capitalist system. They all either are members of the WTO or seek membership in it. But they also have very diverse geopolitical and regional interests and agendas. They do not constitute either an economic bloc or a geopolitical one. Their ideologies and histories are distinct. They share an interest in gaining access to the leading institutions that govern the international system. Sometimes this creates competition between them for influence and access. But it also orients their struggles toward the reform and reorganization of governing institutions, not to a united effort to overturn the underlying order.

Fourth, all the great powers have alignments of interests that will continue to bring them together to negotiate and cooperate over the management of the system. All the great powers—old and rising—are status quo powers. This is true if only for reasons related to nuclear weapons and deterrence, but they are also all beneficiaries of an open world economy and the various services that the liberal international order provides for capitalist trading states. All the great powers—the old and the rising—worry about religious radicalism and failed states. Great powers such as Russia and China do have different geopolitical interests in various key trouble spots, such as Iran and South Asia, and so disagreement and noncooperation over sanctions relating to nonproliferation and other security issues will not disappear. But the opportunities for managing differences with frameworks of great-power cooperation exist and will grow.

Overall, the forces for continuity are formidable. The declining benefits of conquest and the collapse of rival great-power ideologies take away an old source of geopolitical conflict. The shared sense among the major states that modernization and advancement essentially follow a liberal pathway is an extraordinary source for stability. The major states all know that fascism, communism, and theocratic dictatorship are dysfunctional as systems of rule if the goal of the state is to grow and modernize. In effect, if a state wants to be a global power, it will need to join the WTO. Of course, there are many forces operating in the world that can generate upheaval and discontinuity.[4] The collapse of the global financial system and an economic depression that triggers massive protectionism are possibilities. Terrorism and other forms of transnational violence can also trigger political panic and turmoil that would lead governments to shut down borders and reimpose restrictions on the movement of goods and people. But in the face of these earthquake-type events in world politics, there are deep forces that keep the system anchored and stable.

The Rise of China and the Future of Liberal Order

What about the challenge of a rising China? The rise of China is one of the great dramas of the twenty-first century. To some observers, we are witnessing the final end of the American era and the gradual transition from a Western-oriented world order to one increasingly dominated by Asia. The historian Niall Ferguson argues that the bloody twentieth century is in fact a story of the "descent of the West," a "reorientation of the world" in which the Atlantic powers cede mastery of the world to the East.[5] The journalist Martin Jacques argues that China is adopting the trappings of Western capitalism but is pioneering a very different

---

[4] See discussion of possible upheavals and discontinuities in Ikenberry, "Conclusion," in Ikenberry, *America Unrivaled*. For historical reflections, see Harold James, *The End of Globalization: Lessons from the Great Depression* (Cambridge, MA: Harvard University Press, 2002).

[5] Niall Ferguson, *The War of the World: Twentieth-Century Conflict and the Descent of the West* (New York: Penguin, 2006), xvii.

form of hegemony—illiberal, hierarchical, and culturally based—that amounts to a sharp movement away from the Western logic of liberal modernization. China will rule the world and will do so on very different terms.[6] Scholars have begun to explore, more generally, the possible character of a post-Western international order.[7] To be sure, China is indeed booming. The extraordinary growth of its economy and its active diplomacy—is already transforming East Asia. Coming decades will almost certainly see further increases in Chinese power and further expansion of its influence on the world stage. But what sort of transition will it be? Will China seek to oppose and overturn the evolving Western-centered liberal international order, or will it integrate into and assert authority within that order?

China is in critical respects the "swing state" in world politics. It is possible that China could emerge as a world power and resist integration into the existing American-led system of rules and institutions. It could seek to construct a rival order—non-Western and nonliberal. In doing so, it could draw in other states that were similarly estranged from the existing system, perhaps including Russia and Iran. But if China resists this move and takes gradual steps toward integration and participation in a reformed and updated liberal international order, it is almost impossible to envisage a rump coalition of states that would be sufficiently large and powerful to create a rival order. As China goes, so goes the international system. The future of a one-world system that is open and loosely rule-based hinges on China. But China's choices also hinge on how the United States and the other liberal democracies act to reform and renew the existing rules and institutions. Indeed, there are reasons

[6] Jacques, *When China Rules the World*. See also Leonard, *What Does China Think*; Eva Paus, Penelope B. Prime, and Jon Western, eds., *Global Giant: Is China Changing the Rules of the Game?* (New York: Palgrave, 2009); and Stefan Halper, *The Beijing Consensus: How China's Authoritarian Model Will Dominate the Twenty-First Century* (New York: Basic, 2010).

[7] See Naazneen Barma, Ely Ratner, and Steven Weber, "A World without the West," *National Interest*, no. 90 (July/August 2007), 23–30; Charles Kupchan and Adam Mount, "The Autonomy Rule," *Democracy: A Journal of Ideas*, no. 12 (Spring 2009), 8–21; and Steven Weber and Bruce W. Jentleson, *The End of Arrogance: America in the Global Competition of Ideas* (Cambridge, MA: Harvard University Press, 2010).

to think that China will continue to actively seek to integrate into an expanded and reorganized liberal international order.[8]

Several features of this Western-oriented system are particularly relevant to how China makes decisions about whether to join or oppose it. One relates to the rules and institutions of the capitalist world economy. More so than the imperial systems of the past, the liberal international order is built around rules and norms of nondiscrimination and market openness—creating conditions for rising states to participate within the order and advance their expanding economic and political goals within it. Across history, international orders have varied widely in terms of whether the material benefits that are generated accrue disproportionately to the leading state or whether the material benefits of participation within the order are more widely shared. In the Western system, the barriers to economic entry are low and the potential benefits are high. China has already discovered the massive economic returns that are possible through operating within this open market system.[9]

A second feature of this order is the coalition-based character of its leadership. It is American led, but it is also an order in which a group of advanced liberal democratic states work together and assert collective leadership. It is not just an American order—and a reformed liberal international order would be even less dominated by the United States. A wider group of states are bound together and govern the system. These leading states do not always agree, but they are engaged in a continuous process of give-and-take over economics, politics, and security. This, too, is distinctive—past orders have tended to be dominated by one state. The stakeholders in the current order include a coalition of *status quo* great powers that are arrayed around the old hegemonic state. This is important. Power transitions are typically seen as playing out in dyadic

[8] See Ikenberry, "The Rise of China and the Future of the West"; and Ikenberry, "The Rise of China: Power, Institutions, and the Western Order," in Robert Ross and Zhu Feng, eds., *China's Ascent: Power, Security, and the Future of International Politics* (Ithaca, NY: Cornell University Press, 2008), 89–114.

[9] See essays on shared American and Chinese visions of economic modernization and global integration in Richard Rosecrance and Gu Guoliang, eds, *Power and Restraint: A Shared Vision for the U.S.-Chinese Relationship* (New York: Public Affairs, 2009).

fashion between two countries: a rising state and a declining hegemon. This larger aggregation of democratic-capitalist states—and the resulting aggregation of geopolitical power—shifts the balance back in favor of the old order.

A final feature of the American-led liberal international order is its unusually dense, encompassing, and agreed-upon rules and institutions. International order can be rigidly hierarchical and governed through coercive domination exercised by the leading state, or it can be relatively open and organized around reciprocal, consensual, and rule-based relations. The postwar Western order has been more open and rule-based than any previous order. State sovereignty and the rule of law are not just norms enshrined in the U.N. Charter. They are part of the deep operating logic of the order. To be sure, as we have seen, these norms are evolving, and America has historically been ambivalent about binding itself to international law and institutions, and at no time more than today. But the overall system is remarkably dense with multilateral rules and institutions—global and regional, economic, political, and security-related. These institutional creations are one of the great breakthroughs of the postwar era, establishing the basis for greater levels of cooperation and shared authority and governance of the global system.

Together, these features of evolving liberal international order give it an unusual capacity to accommodate rising powers. Its sprawling landscape of rules, institutions, and networks provide newer entrants into the system with opportunities for status, authority, and a share in the governance of the order. Access points and mechanisms for political communication and reciprocal influence abound. China has incentives and opportunities to join, while, at the same time, the possibilities of it actually overturning or subverting this order are small or nonexistent. Furthermore, as I argued above, in the past, old international orders were ultimately overturned through hegemonic war. In the age of nuclear weapons and great-power deterrence, this mechanism of historical change—thankfully—is taken away. The United States was able to build an international order because the old order was destroyed in war.

But if that circumstance is not presented to China, its ability to build a new international order from the ground up is essentially impossible. And so, together, these characteristics of the American-led liberal international order have implications for how a rising China makes choices, increasing the incentives to join rather than seek to overturn it.

It is not surprising, therefore, that China has already made moves to embrace the American-led system of international rules and institutions. China's initial use of these rules and institutions has been largely pursued for defensive purposes—protecting its sovereignty and economic interests while seeking to reassure other states of its peaceful intentions by involvement in regional and global groupings.[10] But as the scholar Marc Lanteigne argues: "What separates China from other states, and indeed previous global powers, is that not only is it 'growing up' within a milieu of international institutions far more developed than ever before, but more importantly, it is doing so while making active use of these institutions to promote the country's development of global power status."[11] The result is that China is already increasingly working within rather than outside this liberal international order. It is seeking to increase its status and authority within the existing system rather than laying the foundation for exerting leadership in an alternative world order.[12]

---

[10] China has incentives to try to reassure other states in the international system as it rises. To do this, it will find that an important way to signal restraint and commitment is its willingness to participate in existing institutions. This logic of restraint and reassurance will lead China deeper into the existing order rather than away from it.

[11] Marc Lanteigne, *China and International Institutions: Alternative Paths to Global Power* (New York: Routledge, 2007). For an important account of Chinese participation in regional and global institutions and its impact, see Alastair Iain Johnston, *Social States: China in International Institutions, 1980–2000* (Princeton, NJ: Princeton University Press, 2008).

[12] This is the view of Yong Deng, who argues that Chinese foreign policy is fundamentally oriented toward gaining greater status and recognition in the international system but not seeking a radical reorganization of its underlying organizational principles. The aim is to gain position and respect within the existing system and work with American hegemonic leadership. As Deng suggests, since the late-1990s, the Chinese government has been more concerned "over how the U.S. hegemony is managed than over the power configuration itself." See Yong Deng, *China's Struggle for Status: The Realignment of International Relations* (New York: Cambridge University Press, 2008), 44.

China is, of course, already a permanent member of the U.N. Security Council, which puts it at the center of great-power diplomacy. It has also joined the WTO and has increasingly integrated into the capitalist world economy. Moreover, it is not just that China needs access to world markets; it also should want access to the protections afforded by the rules and institutions. The WTO provides the Chinese with multilateral trade principles and dispute settlement mechanisms that should be a huge attraction to Chinese leaders because they offer tools with which to defend against the threats of discrimination and protectionism that rising economic powers confront. The sequence of Chinese policy fits this logic: as Beijing's commitment to economic liberalization led to expanded foreign investment and trade, its embrace of global trade rules followed. It would be an irony if China came to champion the logic and functions of the WTO while the support of the more mature Western economies waned. It is more likely that both rising and declining market-oriented countries will find value in the quasi-legal mechanisms that allow conflicts to be settled or at least defused.

These considerations suggest that China is not doomed to use its growing power to challenge and seek to overturn the basic organizational logic of liberal international order. It certainly will put liberal rules and institutions to the test. The deep dilemmas of liberal order and the struggles over its basic aspects—authority, sovereignty, binding commitments, rights, and obligations—will be intensified with the entry of China into the mainstream of this system. But a convulsive hegemonic conflict between China and the United States is not inevitable. Indeed, the United States and the other liberal democracies have some leverage over how the rise of China unfolds. The more they cooperate among themselves and reform and renew the basic foundations of liberal international order, the more likely it is that China will find incentives to integrate and participate—and perhaps even to help lead.

China may, in the end, exceed or fall short of the great projections being made today about its rise. But the capitalist democratic world is an existing reality—a massive geopolitical area and, taken together, is a powerful constituency for the preservation and, indeed, extension of the existing international order. If China intends to rise up and challenge the existing order, it has a much more daunting task than simply confronting the United States and grabbing control of the international order. At its best, this larger order is not simply an aggregation of GNP or defense spending. It is a more or less institutionalized political order, an order that with renewed leadership can continue to expand and grow.

Grand Strategy as Liberal Order Building

American dominance of the global system will eventually yield to the rise of other powerful states, including, of course, China. The unipolar moment will pass. The global distribution of power is always shifting. In facing these circumstances, American grand strategy should be informed by answers to this question: what sort of international order would we like to see in place in 2020 or 2030 when America is less powerful? We might call this the great neo-Rawlsian question of our era. It was the distinguished political philosopher John Rawls who suggested that political institutions should be designed behind a veil of ignorance, that is, under conditions where the architects of the institutions did not know precisely where they would be within the resulting socioeconomic system. This thought experiment forced the institution builders to design institutions that would safeguard their interests regardless of where they ended up, weak or strong, rich or poor.[13] The United States needs to engage in a similar thought experiment. What institutions should we try to put in place today that will safeguard our interests in future decades when we will not be a unipolar power, doing so when we are at least a bit uncertain where we will be within the wider and shifting distribution of power?

The answer to this neo-Rawlsian question is clear: we should be planting the roots of a reformed liberal international order as deeply as possible. The idea is to make the liberal order so expansive and

[13] John Rawls, *A Theory of Justice* (Cambridge, MA: Harvard University Press, 1971).

institutionalized that China will have no choice but to join and operate within it. China and greater Asia will inevitably have more power and authority than they do today. America's goal should be to see that Chinese power is exercised as much as possible within rules and institutions that we have crafted with other liberal states over the last century, and in which we ourselves want to operate, given the more crowded world of the future. America's position in the global system may decline but the international order it leads can remain the dominating logic of the twenty-first century.

Where does this leave American grand strategy? Grand strategy is, as Barry Posen argues, "a state's theory about how it can best cause security for itself."[14] As such, it is an exercise in public worrying about the future—and doing something about it. Grand strategy is a set of coordinated and sustained policies designed to address the long-term threats and opportunities that lie beyond the country's shores. Given the great shifts in the global system and the crisis of liberal hegemonic order, how should the United States pursue grand strategy in the coming years? The answer that emerges from this book is that the United States should work with others to rebuild and renew the institutional foundations of the liberal international order and, along the way, reestablish its own authority as a global leader. The United States is going to need to invest in re-creating the basic governance institutions of the system—invest in alliances, partnerships, multilateral institutions, special relationships, great-power concerts, cooperative security pacts, and democratic security communities. That is, the United States will need to return to the great tasks of liberal order building.

It is useful to distinguish between two types of grand strategy: positional and milieu oriented. As noted in chapter five, with a positional grand strategy, a great power seeks to diminish the power or threat embodied in a specific challenger state or group of states. Examples are Nazi Germany, Imperial Japan, the Soviet bloc, and perhaps—in the

<hr/>

[14] Barry Posen, *Sources of Military Doctrine* (Ithaca, NY: Cornell University Press, 1983), 13.

future—Greater China. With a milieu grand strategy, a great power does not target a specific state but seeks to structure its general international environment in ways that are congenial with its long-term security. This might entail building the infrastructure of international cooperation, promoting trade and democracy in various regions of the world, and establishing partnerships that might be useful for various contingencies. My point is that under conditions of unipolarity, in a world of diffuse threats, and with pervasive uncertainty over what the specific security challenges will be in the future, this milieu-based approach to grand strategy is necessary.

Looking into the twentieth-first century, the United States faces a complex array of global challenges. But it does not face the sort of singular geopolitical threat that it did with the fascist and communist powers of the last century. Indeed, compared with the dark days of the 1930s or the Cold War, America lives in an extraordinarily benign security environment, and it possesses an extraordinary opportunity to shape its international environment for the long term. As we have seen, the United States is the dominant global power, unchecked by a coalition of balancing states or by a superpower wielding a rival universalistic ideology. Most of the great powers are democracies and are tied to the United States through alliance partnership. State power is ultimately based on sustained economic growth, and no major state today can modernize without integrating into the globalized capitalist system. What made the fascist and communist threats of the twentieth century so profound was not only the danger of territorial aggression but that these great-power challengers embodied rival political-economic systems that could generate growth, attract global allies, and create counterbalancing geopolitical blocs. America has no such global challengers today.

Rather than a single overriding threat, the United States and other countries face a host of diffuse and evolving threats. Global warming, nuclear proliferation, jihadist terrorism, energy security, health pandemics—these and other dangers loom on the horizon. Any of these threats could endanger Americans' lives and way of life either directly or indirectly by destabilizing the global system upon which American security and prosperity depends. Pandemics and global warming are not threats wielded by human hands, but their consequences could be equally devastating. Highly infectious disease has the potential to kill millions of people. Global warming threatens to trigger waves of environmental migration and food shortages and may further destabilize weak and poor states around the world. The world is also on the cusp of a new round of nuclear proliferation, putting mankind's deadliest weapons in the hands of unstable and hostile states. Terrorist networks offer a new specter of nonstate transnational violence. Yet none of these threats is, in itself, so singularly preeminent that it deserves to be the centerpiece of American grand strategy in the way that antifascism and anticommunism did in an earlier era.[15]

What is more, these various threats are interconnected—and it is their interactive effects that represent the most acute danger. This point is stressed by Thomas Homer-Dixon: "It's the convergence of stresses that's especially treacherous and makes synchronous failure a possibility as never before. In coming years, our societies won't face one or two major challenges at once, as usually happened in the past. Instead, they'll face an alarming variety of problems—likely including oil shortages, climate change, economic instability, and mega-terrorism—all at the same time." The danger is that several of these threats will materialize at the same time and interact to generate greater violence and instability. "What happens, for example, if together or in quick succession the world has to deal with a sudden shift in climate that sharply cuts food production in Europe and Asia, a severe oil price increase that sends economies tumbling around the world, and a string of major terrorist attacks on several Western capital cities?"[16] The global order itself would be put at risk, as well as the foundations of American national security.

What unites these threats and challenges, as I noted in chapter 7, is that they are all manifestations of rising security interdependence.

[15] This is our judgment in the final report of the Princeton Project on National Security. See Ikenberry and Slaughter, *Forging a World of Liberty under Law*.

[16] Thomas Homer-Dixon, *The Upside of Down: Catastrophe, Creativity, and the Renewal of Civilization* (Washington, DC: Island, 2006), 16–17.

More and more of what goes on in other countries matters for the health and safety of the United States and the rest of the world. Many of the new dangers—such as health pandemics and transnational terrorist violence—stem from the weakness of states rather than their strength. At the same time, technologies of violence are evolving, providing opportunities for weak states or nonstate groups to threaten others at a greater distance. When states are in a situation of security interdependence, they cannot go it alone. They must negotiate and cooperate with other states and seek mutual restraints and protections. The United States cannot hide or protect itself from threats under conditions of rising security interdependence. It must get out in the world and work with other states to build frameworks of cooperation and leverage capacities for action.

If the world of the twenty-first century were a town, the security threats faced by its leading citizens would not be organized crime or a violent assault by a radical mob on city hall. It would be a breakdown of law enforcement and social services in the face of constantly changing and ultimately uncertain vagaries of criminality, nature, and circumstance. The neighborhoods where the leading citizens live can only be made safe if the security and well-being of the beaten-down and troubled neighborhoods were also improved. No neighborhood can be left behind. At the same time, the town will need to build new capacities for social and economic protection. People and groups will need to cooperate in new and far-reaching ways.

But the larger point is that today the United States confronts an unusually diverse and diffuse array of threats and challenges. When we try to imagine what the premier threat to the United States will be in 2020 or 2025, it is impossible to say with any confidence that it will be X, Y, or Z. Moreover, even if we could identify X, Y, or Z as the premier threat around which all others turn, it is likely to be complex and interlinked with lots of other international moving parts. Global pandemics are connected to failed states, homeland security, international public health capacities, et cetera. Terrorism is related to the Middle East peace process, economic and political development, nonproliferation, intelligence cooperation, European social and immigration policy, et cetera.

The rise of China is related to alliance cooperation, energy security, democracy promotion, the WTO, management of the world economy, et cetera. So again, we are back to renewing and rebuilding the architecture of global governance and frameworks of cooperation to allow the United States to marshal resources and tackle problems along a wide and shifting spectrum of possibilities.

In a world of multiple threats and uncertainty about their relative significance in the decades to come, it is useful to think of grand strategy as an investment problem. Where do you invest your resources, build capacities, and take actions so as to maximize your ability to be positioned to confront tomorrow's unknown unknowns? Grand strategy is about setting priorities, but it is also about diversifying risks and avoiding surprises.

This is why a milieu-based grand strategy is attractive. The objective is to shape the international environment to maximize your capacities to protect the nation from uncertain, diffuse, and shifting threats. Engaging in liberal order building is investment in international cooperative frameworks—that is, rules, institutions, partnerships, networks, standby capacities, social knowledge, et cetera—in which the United States operates. To build international order is to increase the global stock of "social capital" which is the term Pierre Bourdieu, Robert Putnam, and others have used to define the actual and potential resources and capacities within a political community, manifest in and through its networks of social relations, that are available for solving collective problems. Taken together, liberal order building involves the investment in the enhancement of global social capital so as to create capacities to solve problems that left unattended will threaten national security.

If American grand strategy is to be organized around liberal order building, what are the specific objectives and what is the policy agenda? First, the United States needs to lead in the building of an enhanced protective infrastructure that helps prevent the emergence of threats and limits the damage if they do materialize.[17] Many of the threats mentioned

[17] See Ikenberry and Slaughter, *Forging a World of Liberty under Law*, 10.

above are manifest as socioeconomic backwardness and failure that generate regional and international instability and conflict. These are the sorts of threats that are likely to arise with the coming of global warming and epidemic disease. What is needed here is institutional cooperation to strengthen the capacity of governments and the international community to prevent epidemics or food shortages or mass migrations that create global upheaval—and mitigate the effects of these upheavals if they in fact occur.

It is useful to think of strengthening the protective infrastructure as an investment in global social services—much as cities and states invest in such services. It typically is money well spent. Education, health programs, shelters, social services—these are vital components of stable and well-functioning communities. The international system already has a great deal of this infrastructure—institutions and networks that promote cooperation over public health, refugees, and emergency aid. But as the scale and scope of potential problems grow in the twentieth-first century, investments in these preventive and management capacities will also need to grow. Early warning systems, protocols for emergency operations, standby capacities, et cetera—these are the stuff of a protective global infrastructure.

Second, the United States should recommit to and rebuild its security alliances. The idea is to update the old bargains that lie behind these security pacts. In NATO, but also in the East Asia bilateral partnerships, the United States agrees to provide security protection to the other states and bring its partners into the process of decision making over the use of force. In return, these partners agree to work with the United States—providing manpower, logistics, and other types of support—in wider theaters of action. The United States gives up some autonomy in strategic decision making, although it is more an informal restraint than a legally binding one, and in exchange it gets cooperation and political support. The United States also remains "first among equals" within these organizations, and it retains leadership of the unified military command. The updating of these alliance bargains would involve widening the regional or global missions in which the alliance operates and making new compromises over the distribution of formal rights and responsibilities.

There are several reasons why the renewal of security partnerships is critical to liberal order building. One is that security alliances involve relatively well defined, specific, and limited commitments—which is attractive for both the leading military power and its partners. States know what they are getting into and what the limits are on their obligations and liabilities. Another is that alliances provide institutional mechanisms that allow accommodations for disparities of power among partners within the alliance. Alliances do not embody universal rules and norms that apply equally to all parties. NATO, at least, is a multilateral body with formal and informal rules and norms of operation that both accommodate the most powerful state and provide roles and rights for others. Another virtue of renewing the alliances is that they have been useful as "political architecture" across the advanced democratic world. The alliances provide channels of communication and joint decision making that spill over into the wider realms of international relations. They are also institutions with grand histories and records of accomplishment. The United States is a unipolar military power, but it still has incentives to share the costs of security protection and find ways to legitimate the use of its power. The postwar alliances—renewed and reorganized—are an attractive tool for these purposes.

Third, the United States should reform and create encompassing global institutions that foster and legitimate collective action. The first move here should be to reform the United Nations, starting with the expansion of the permanent membership on the Security Council. Several plans have been proposed. All of them entail adding new members—such as Germany, Japan, India, Brazil, South Africa, and others—and reforming the voting procedures. Almost all of the candidates for permanent membership are mature or rising democracies. The goal, of course, is to make them stakeholders in the United Nations and thereby strengthen the primacy of the United Nations as a vehicle for global collective action. There really is no substitute for the legitimacy that the United Nations can offer to emergency actions—humanitarian interventions, economic sanctions, uses of force against terrorists, and so forth. Public support in advanced democracies grows rapidly when their governments can stand behind a United Nations–sanctioned action.

Fourth, the United States should accommodate and institutionally engage China. China will most likely be a dominant state, and the United States will need to yield to it in various ways. As I argued in the previous section, the United States should respond to the rise of China by strengthening the rules and institutions of the liberal international order—deepening their roots, integrating rising capitalist democracies, sharing authority and functional roles. The United States should intensify cooperation with Europe and renew joint commitments to alliances and multilateral global governance. The more that China faces not just the United States but the entire OECD world of capitalist democracies, the better. This is not to argue that China must face a grand counterbalancing alliance against it. Rather, it should face a complex and highly integrated global system—one that is so encompassing and deeply entrenched that it essentially has no choice but to join it and seek to prosper within it.[18]

The United States should also be seeking to construct a regional security order in East Asia that can provide a framework for managing the coming shifts. The idea is not to block China's entry into the regional order but to help shape its terms, looking for opportunities to strike strategic bargains at various moments along the shifting power trajectories and encroaching geopolitical spheres. The big bargain that the United States will want to strike is this: to accommodate a rising China by offering it status and position within the regional order in return for Beijing's acceptance and accommodation of Washington's core strategic interests, which include remaining a dominant security provider within East Asia. In striking this strategic bargain, the United States will also want to try to build multilateral institutional arrangements in East Asia that will tie

[18] In a similar way, Timothy Garten Ash argues that the United States and Europe have about twenty years more to control the levers of global governance before they will need to cede power to China and other rising states. Timothy Garten Ash, *Free World: America, Europe, and the Surprising Future of the West* (New York: Random House, 2004).

China to the wider region. China has already grasped the utility of this strategy in recent years—and it is now actively seeking to reassure and co-opt its neighbors by offering to embed itself in regional institutions such at the ASEAN Plus 3 and Asian Summit. This is, of course, precisely what the United States did in the decades after World War II, building and operating within layers of regional and global economic, political, and security institutions—thereby making itself more predictable and approachable and reducing the incentives that other states would otherwise have to resist or undermine the United States by building countervailing coalitions.[19]

Finally, the United States should reclaim a liberal internationalist public philosophy. When American officials after World War II championed the building of a rule-based postwar order, they articulated a distinctive internationalist vision of order that has faded in recent decades. It was a vision that entailed a synthesis of liberal and realist ideas about economic, national security, and the sources of stable and peaceful order. These ideas—drawn from the 1940s experiences with the New Deal and the previous decades of war and depression—led American leaders to associate the national interest with the building of a managed and institutionalized global system. What is needed today is a renewed public philosophy of liberal internationalism—a shift away from neoliberalism—that can inform American elites as they make trade-offs between sovereignty and institutional cooperation.

What American elites need to do today is recover this public philosophy of internationalism. The restraint and the commitment of American power went hand in hand. Global rules and institutions advanced America's national interest rather than threatened it. The alternative public philosophies that have circulated in recent years—philosophies that champion American unilateralism and disentanglement from global rules and institutions—did not meet with great success. So an

[19] See G. John Ikenberry, "Asian Regionalism and the Future of U.S. Strategic Engagement with China," in Abraham Denmark and Nirav Patel, eds., *China's Arrival: A Strategic Framework for a Global Relationship* (Washington, DC: Center for a New American Security, 2009), 95–108.

opening exists for America's postwar vision of internationalism to be updated and rearticulated today.

To be sure, recently, massive budget deficits and public debt have placed new constraints on leaders and foreign policy agendas. Intense partisan and ideological conflicts pervade American politics, exacerbated by high levels of unemployment and sluggish economic growth. While the United States struggles, other countries—particularly in Asia—seem to be prospering. The old optimistic view that the United States is at the forefront of global progress and destined to lead the world has fewer adherents—both at home and abroad. As one journalist observes, "Both as individuals and as a nation, Americans have begun to question whether the 'new world order' that emerged after the cold war still favors the US."[20] These are not ideal conditions for American leaders to affirm the virtues of American-style liberal internationalism. Yet, in another sense, it is precisely in an era of growing economic constraints and interdependence that liberal internationalism should have a practical appeal. At the heart of liberal internationalism is a vision of multilateral partnership, cooperative security, and collective action. If the United States cannot defend its interests by turning inward and hiding from the world, then it will need to find ways to work with other states, sharing the costs and responsibilities of leadership with allies and partners.

The leading ideas of this liberal public philosophy are ones that the United States should embrace today:

- Lead with rules rather than dominate with power. The United States is best able to garner support for its central position in the world political order by championing and working within a system of loosely agreed-upon rules and institutions. As I have argued, this draws other states into the order while also establishing frameworks of cooperation that can last beyond America's era of preeminence and safeguard its interests in the coming era when it cannot simply relay on its commanding power position.

[20] Gideon Rachman, "End of the World as We Know It," *Financial Times*, 23–24 October 2010, Life and Arts section, p. 19.

Ironically, strategic restraint is a vital aspect of power, particularly in a global democratic age.

- Provide public goods and connect their provision to cooperative and accommodative policies of others. With the end of the Cold War, the task of providing—and getting credit for providing—services for the global system has been harder, but it is also more essential than ever. Security, economic openness, stability—these are the aspects of global order that the United States can still uniquely influence. And it should wrap its foreign policy in its hegemonic responsibility and engage other states in sharing burdens with and giving support to it as it renews this liberal hegemonic role.

- Build and renew international rules and institutions that work to reinforce the capacities of states—that is, national governments—to govern and achieve security and economic success. The liberal international order emerged in the 1940s as a successful system as it provided services and supports for their expanding socio-economic and security agendas. The Bretton Woods institutions were central to the establishment of a working international order. States agreed to make commitments and obligations with the anticipation that a flow of benefits and capacities would come their way in return. A liberal international order is not just a commitment to open markets; it is a political pact aimed at providing stability and security in the midst of openness. This logic should be rediscovered and made the heart of liberal order building.

- Keep the other liberal democracies close. Close affiliation with other democracies has multiple benefits. Working with other high-capacity like-minded states leverages capacities to get things accomplished. It is easier to work with these states and engage in sustained and complex forms of cooperation. In domestic political circles, it is often easier to make the case for internationalism when it is directed toward cooperation with other liberal democracies. And beyond these considerations, seeking the counsel of other liberal democracies serves as a potential check on imprudent foreign policy.

■ Let the global system itself do the deep work of liberal modernization. History may not have ended, but liberal internationalists believe that history is on their side. Countries will make small moves over many decades to integrate into an open, rule-based system. Capitalism and internationally oriented economic development reinforces the commitments that states make to an open, rule-based system. If the world is moving in a congenial direction, it is less necessary to engage in risky interventions or brute exercises of force that end up, directly or indirectly, making the liberal order less legitimate. Keep the system open, tolerate diversity, and let the complex global machinery of modernization push and pull the world on a pathway that the United States, too, is traveling.

Looking into this brave new world, the United States will find itself needing to share power and rely in part on others to ensure its security. It will not be able to depend on unipolar power or airtight borders. To operate in this coming world, the United States will need, above all else, authority and respect as a global leader. It has lost some of that authority and respect in recent years. In committing itself to a grand strategy of liberal order building, it can begin the process of gaining it back.

Index

Abbott, Kenneth, 94n25
Acheson, Dean, 172, 192, 203, 210
Adams, Henry, 187, 187n48
Albright, Madeline, 235, 243
Allen, Danielle, 74n59
anarchy, 48, 66, 147, 255; and power balancing, 36–37, 54
Annan, Kofi, 247–48; on state sovereignty, 248
anti-Americanism, 3
Ash, Timothy Garton, 358
Asia, 89, 134, 166, 168–69, 173, 210–11, 298. *See also* East Asia
Asia-Pacific Economic Cooperation (APEC), 223, 233, 234
Atlantic Charter, 159, 165, 187, 190, 194–95, 201
"Atlantic community," the, 185–90, 185nn46–47, 187n48

Baker, James, 233
balance of power. *See* international order, liberal, and balance of power

balancing; absence of, 154–55; security binding as an alternative to balancing strategies, 183–84. *See also* power balancing
Bass, Gary, 16–17n17
Bevin, Ernst, 188
bilateralism, 150, 199–200; bilateral agreements, 101–2, 114, 115–16, 170, 215–16; bilateral partnerships, 150
bipolarity, 9, 17, 38, 122, 152n49; Cold War bipolarity, 66, 137, 138, 141, 144, 148, 151, 153, 222, 243, 244–46, 279
Bolton, John, 266, 267
Boot, Max, 266n83
Bosnia, 291
Brazil, 302, 341, 357
Bretton Woods agreements and institutions, 159, 167, 177, 194, 195, 196, 198, 200, 218, 247, 286, 305
Brezhnev Doctrine, 226
Brilmayer, Lea, 299n22
Brooks, Stephen G., 41, 43, 46
Bryce, James (Lord Bryce), 187
Brzezinski, Zbigniew, 319